Black Shamrocks

Accommodation Available – No Blacks, No Dogs, No Irish

GUS MICHAEL NWANOKWU

ISBN-13: 9781523490912
ISBN-10: 1523490918

Dedicated to my beloved parents Michael and Margaret Nwanokwu
I think about you every day

Foreword

It's important for me to set the tone for the reader before you commence.

I've tried to encapsulate and share my feelings, reactions, thoughts and ideas on those experiences that impacted on me (and my family), and to some degree still do, whilst I was growing up as a young man of mixed-race heritage.

Inevitably, it would appear, the intensity of these experiences led me to develop what might be considered to be intense and, on the surface, radical and non-negotiable views about certain elements of life and relationships, and the dynamics that exist among and between groups of people.

My intention is not to offend, exclude or isolate *any* person or group in this attempt to provide an account of my experiences, all of which are true.

My hope is that the reader is able to understand and identify with the many aspects of joy and pain, serenity and anger, love and hate that life often brings to us all. Such experiences vary and are perceived and experienced based on a plethora of personal, social, emotional, psychological, historical, economic and political attributes and factors that most often lay beyond our control as individuals.

I've also learnt that perceptions, understanding, feelings and ideas change as we mature and progress through life. This has certainly been the case for me, and at this point in my life I'm not sure whether

I'll become even more mellow than I am at the moment. Only time will tell I guess!

As an incorrigible optimist I also hope that my account of life's very many negatives are counterbalanced with life's very many positives.

Lastly, I hope you enjoy what you read!!!!!

Gus Nwanokwu

One

"Black bastard!"
    "Wog!"
"Coon!"
"Nigger!"
"Half breed!"
"Chief!"
"Half caste!"
"Jungle bunny!"
"Spade!"
"Sambo!"
"Nig nog!"
"African!"
"Coloured!"
"Onyeocha!"
"Oyibo!"
"Baturi!"

We've been called them all, by blacks and whites alike, ugly, gargoyle-like faces either contorted with rage as they vent their troubled spleens, or calm and serene in the belief that their invectives, delivered cold, will hurt the most; and they do, regardless of the colour of the messenger.

But I wouldn't have it any other way. I have never wished that I'd been born black, white, brown or yellow, or any other colour that we may describe members of the human race. I understand that we have no control over how, and to whom, we're born, so our colour is not

1

prescriptive of us as humans, though in life society often treats us as if that is the case.

Thankfully, and luckily, I was born to a couple who were incredibly liberated for their generation, who met in the early 1950s in London, fell in love, and stayed together forever; a black Nigerian father, from a relatively "comfortable" background, and a white Irish mother, from a distinctly destitute, poverty-stricken background. They were worlds apart in virtually every way. What are the odds of such a meeting of minds and souls?!

Though vastly different, they shared certain similarities. Dad, Michael Aduonye Nwanokwu, was born the only child of his mother Sarah, and grew up in the previously-known country of Biafra, now part of the south east region of the Federal State of Nigeria, an ex-colony of the British Empire and still members of the British Commonwealth of Nations.

Dad: Michael Aduonye Nwanokwu – Early 1950s

Related to the Hogan, Hickey and Flynn families (Hollywood film superstar Errol Flynn was mum's second cousin), mum Margaret Mary Hevey was born and grew up in the small rural village of Lackabeg,

Cappamore, in County Limerick, Eire (southern Ireland), which, again, was an ex-colony of the British empire. In fact, Ireland was one of, if not the very first-ever plantation colonies, dating back to the 12th century.

Mum: Margaret Mary Hevey – early 1950s

England rampaged rapaciously over Ireland during this time to steal and settle, just as they were to do four hundred years later all around the world, including "Nigeria", a name it's alleged was either conveniently (though lazily) formulated by the British settlers for the land they'd stolen around the river Niger; or proffered by Flora Shaw, the wife of Lord Frederick Lugard, who in 1912 returned to Nigeria as Governor (it's also documented that he 'loathed the educated and sophisticated Africans of the coastal [Biafran] regions'). Apparently, this eminent woman was referring to this land mass as being inhabited by "niggers", from whence the name Nigeria derived. Another example of such lazy and disrespectful nomenclature is the origins of the West African country name Liberia, which derived from the merged term "Liberated Area", after freed slaves had been returned from the United Slave States of America. However, European maps of the 15th century West African region clearly identify the Kingdom of Biafra, the Atlantic coastline being named the Bight of Biafra, and both of which existed prior to European invasion.

The origin of the Hevey surname derives from France as the altered spelling of French Hévé, a variant of the Normandy name Dévé, a nickname from desvé, translated as 'mad'; 'insane'. No surprises there then when it comes to my family I suppose!

Just as the English were prominent forerunners in the unseemly, though inestimably profitable, "scramble for Africa" in the 16th century, competing with other European nations including France, Belgium, Holland, Portugal, Germany and Spain to rape, plunder, pillage, enslave and settle the "dark" continent, this proved to be a practice they were very well versed in, having done the same in and to Ireland 400 years earlier. Both Ireland and Africa, including 'Nigeria', were carved up by the invading hordes in order to capitalise upon the abundant human and natural resources of the two countries.

It is beyond any doubt that the advanced capitalist economic system we enjoy in contemporary 'Great' Britain was only made possible on the resources stolen from its 'colonies' dating back to the 12th century and beyond. Without building on the proceeds of slavery and colonialism, the industrial revolution in the 'United' Kingdom and Europe would never have taken place, and the world would have been a very different place to the one we know today.

It seems King James VI of Scotland inherited the English throne on 24th March 1603, becoming king of England, Wales, Scotland and Ireland; one hundred and four years later, on 1st May 1707, the parliaments of Scotland and England (which by this time included Wales), formally united, with the act of union, creating a state known as the Kingdom of Great Britain. The Kingdom became 'United' in 1801 when the parliaments of Ireland and Great Britain united, and the realm remains the United Kingdom today, even though southern Ireland (Eire) seceded from the union in 1921.

Probably similar and consistent with most political systems that operate for the benefit and privilege of society's elite echelons, it's questionable whether the slaves, serfs and peasants, mere minions and subjects of the state, felt as 'United' as those who have held power for the past millennia.

I'm proud, inspired and uplifted that Eire fought for their independence and seceded from the union in 1921.

I'm equally crestfallen that, given the opportunity to salvage national independence, pride and dignity through a referendum in September 2014, Scotland chose to remain in servitude to the English. Oh how the 13th century Scottish warrior 'Braveheart' William Wallace must be spinning in his grave! Shame on you Scotland!

Both Mum and Dad were religious. They shared a belief in God. They were certainly both raised to believe in God and practice their faiths as a devout Anglican, in my dad's case, and a devout Catholic (no surprises there either!), in my mum's case, though she began to lose her faith later in life, probably due to the culmination of a life of perceived and actual injustice, bigotry, prejudice and discrimination.

Interestingly (for me anyway), it was actually my white mum who politicised me and my brother and sisters, not my black dad. Dad was more relaxed, laid back and easy going than mum about many things. Mum was far more passionate, reactionary, fiery, and carried that fire burning to her final days. I try to understand this apparent anomaly by imagining their younger lives. Dad never experienced racism as he ran and played barefooted in the hot red dust of the villages and towns where he grew up in Nigeria, whereas mum certainly experienced the 'isms' as she ran, played and toiled barefooted in the harsh, cold, often wet fields of Limerick; the two main isms being the evils of English oppression and the bigotry of Catholicism in rural Ireland.

Yes, dad was a colonial subject of the Crown, but there weren't that many white faces to abuse him, whereas mum grew up on tales of IRA allegiance to fighting against the tyranny of the Black and Tans (in fact, the hay loft where she and her sister used to sleep as children was a hideout for IRA fighters when the Black and Tan British army were active in their immediate vicinity), and saw at first-hand how the English had violated, exploited and oppressed Ireland and its people for centuries.

They clearly also shared a love for music, which was a love they passed on to their five children, especially so in one case. They met at the Hammersmith Palais in early 1950s London. Mum was with a friend, and neither of them had been asked for a dance all night (which I find really unbelievable because mum was a stunner!). Fed up with being overlooked by potential suitors, mum and her friend decided to leave. As they were about to retrieve their coats from the cloakroom assistant, she was intercepted by a handsome and dashing zoot-suited young black man who asked her why she was leaving so early? She explained that she hadn't been asked for a dance all night and that she was going home. Thankfully, dad managed to dissuade her, escorting her back to the dance floor where they spent the remainder of the night in each other's arms. They obviously clicked on many levels, because they had a real synchronicity when they danced together! I remember always feeling really proud when watching them dance with each other, because they were so good! Unlike many parents who cause their children untold levels of embarrassment, mine were on-point when it came to throwing shapes together on the dance floor! Thankfully I was never forced to endure or suffer the embarrassment and pain of 'dad-dancing' at family and social events!

Mum and Dad – mid 1950s

Little did they know that their chance meeting was to lead them to spend the rest of their lives together! They arranged to meet again after the Palais and the rest, as they say, is history.

In this case, our family history.

TWO

D ad was sent to London by his moderately wealthy (in Nigerian terms at the time), single mother Sarah, to study medicine. He nearly died in the famous 'pea-souper' "Great Smog" that killed 4,000 people over a four day period in London, and 8,000 in total over the following weeks and months. However, when the money she was sending to sustain him dried up, and he wasn't being supported by wider family, Dad had a fit of pique (a bit of a tantrum really), and changed his surname to Egwuonwu (pronounced Egwong) in order to spite those he felt had abandoned him. Forced to discontinue his studies in medicine, he went on to train as a general nurse and then, eventually, a psychiatric nurse.

Dad (zoot-suited and seated) – with mates in Nigeria (late 1940s)

When they met mum had already achieved secretarial qualifications and was working as an administrator. She'd liberated herself from the crushing oppression of bigoted catholic Ireland at the time, vowing never to return. This commitment was intensified when, after mum and dad had 'become an item', news got back to her family of her blossoming relationship with a black African Methodist, upon which her father stated that she was disowned by the family, and that she should "never darken his doorstep" again.

Mum was particularly strong-minded. She always had the courage of her convictions, and never (during the remainder of her father's lifetime), as ordered, 'darkened his doorstep' again. However, she lightened and enlightened many others for the remainder of her own life!

Mum – early 1950s on
holiday in Switzerland

Another thing they shared (unfortunately for us children in some ways), was a very authoritarian approach to child-rearing. Not quite in the Victorian mode of "children should be seen and not heard", but verging very closely on it. Dad was a traditional Nigerian, head of the household, the sayer of the last word on all matters, and mum invariably supported him in his decisions and, when we were the active, boisterous children that we grew to be, she readily (much to our despair and all too regularly!) uttered the most dreaded caution:

"Wait til your father gets home!"

Whilst both shared a fierce temper, mum was good, VERY good, at the psychological punishment, with the ability to ignore you for days if you'd misbehaved, (as well as the physical), whereas dad didn't bother with the psychological, he just went straight for the nearest object at hand to beat us with: belts, rulers, tree branches, bits of broken furniture, anything that would deliver pain. I preferred dad's punishments, to take the beating, wounds healed quickly on young bodies, and move on. I couldn't stand being ignored for what seemed like (and often was), days on-end by mum. It got to a point where I'd feel like begging her to beat the hell out of me, just so we'd be talking again and I'd be wrapped in the warmth of her totally unconditional love.

Don't get me wrong, our parents loved us all totally. They always had our best interests at heart, always wanted the best for us, always inspired us to achieve, always believed in us, always trusted in us, always supported us, and always beat the shit out of us when we screwed up! It seemed really harsh at the time, but in all honesty I think we deserved (most of) the beatings, especially me! As a parent myself I can now fully understand and identify with their frustrations with us. No doubt the discrimination and poverty we experienced as a family contributed to their frustrations, and was also part of the cause of the increased tension in their relationship.

I've referred to my brother and sisters, so I'll introduce them here, in order of arrival:

"Chi-chi", is my older sister and first child and daughter of the family, born 17th June 1956 in Parsons Green Maternity Hospital, southwest London.

Chi-chi – bath time (1957)

Her full Igbo name is Chinyere, meaning God's Gift, and a truly gifted person she is too! Chi-chi reminded me that when mum was getting ready to leave the clinic with her, one of the midwives cheerily said to her:

"See you next year!"

Mum gave her an admonishingly withering look as if to say "How dare you?!" She could barely look the midwife in the eye when she was back there eleven and a half months later, to give birth to me.

"Gus". Me. Born 1st June 1957 at the same place as my sister Chi-chi in Parsons Green.

My full Igbo name is Ngozi, which means "Blessing". I've never been sure if I was blessed with any stand-out personal attributes or talents, but I've definitely been blessed with a lot in life as far as family, wife and children are concerned. 'Gus' is a derivative from Ngozi. Dad used to call me Goz, mum, brother and sisters called me either Gos or Gossie, and the overwhelming majority of others I've met and worked with throughout my life have settled for the more Anglicised version of Gus.

Then the arrived twins: my younger brother and sister "Ijem" and "Obi".

Me – 6 months old
with dad in Aba,
Imo State (now Abia
State) Nigeria

"Ij" was born 9 minutes before brother Obi on 13th February 1959 at Westminster hospital in London. They were born after heavily-pregnant mum was rushed off an aeroplane at Heathrow airport when she returned from Nigeria with me as she'd gone into early labour. I was rushed off to a Dr Barnados Children's Home where I'd be left to fend for myself on my own for 6 months until the twins, and mum, were discharged from hospital. Their full Igbo names are Ijeoma, which means "safe journey", and Obinna, "father's heart".

Ijeoma and Obi – the twins (1959)

Incidentally, Nigerians have the highest twin-birth rate in the world. Luckily for Ijem and Obi, the Igbo tradition of killing twins had ceased in the 1930s!

According to Nancy French:

"In West Africa's pre-colonial period, the Igbo people believed twins were a bad omen. Single births were considered "human," but multiple births belonged to the realm of animals. When a mother delivered two healthy babies instead of one, the parents would leave one newborn to die in the *ojoo ofia* ("bad bush") outside the town, or simply suffocate one.

During the late 19th and early 20th centuries, Christian Europeans so lamented these barbaric twin killings that it became one of the great mission causes of the time. Every Christian denomination sent missionaries there until the late 1930s, including the famous Mary Slessor of Calabar. Eventually, the twin killings stopped".

Last but definitely not least our youngest sister "Kele" arrived, born at home in the village of Blean, in Kent, on 30th June 1964. Her full Igbo name is Kelechi, which means "Thank God". I think it was Obi who told the midwife, when asked by her what he was wishing for, another brother or sister, he replied a donkey!

Kele Chartham,
Kent (1966)

Mum was almost constantly pregnant throughout our early child-hoods; true to her Catholic roots, but lost four other children during early pregnancies, including another set of twins and another single child. She lost one in the public baths where we used to go to wash because mum wouldn't let us use the shared and filthy bath in our Ascham Street (Kentish Town), tenement. Apparently, mum was bath-ing in one of the cubicles when the centrally-controlled water heating system went on the blink. The hot water suddenly shot up in tempera-ture and mum was scalded. Luckily, she wasn't scarred and she soon recovered from the pain, but lost the twins she was carrying at the time.

So, there should have been ten of us, and today my mind boggles at the thought! Considering how we were to grow up and the experi-ences that lay ahead for 'only' the five of us, the idea of there being four others is almost inconceivable. I don't know how we would have survived! As a family of seven around the table at meal times, mum's favourite comment before we ploughed into the fare on offer, deliv-ered as a joke but which had true meaning, was:

"SOS – Stretch or Starve!"

Essentially she was advising us, or any guests who happened to be eat-ing with us, not to be shy and get stuck in quickly, before it's gone! We very quickly learnt to get to the table very quickly when called, and eat quickly when food was served!

Dad, me, Chi-chi and Mum – Trafalgar Square 1959

Three

I'm so glad we were all given traditional Igbo names and, almost just as traditionally, given middle names that were either English or meaningful (or both), in some way. Chi-Chi's middle name is Adah which, again in Igbo, means first daughter. Mine is Michael, after dad. Ijeoma's is Shirley and Obi's are Roger Peter, after the nurses who helped deliver and care for them after their premature births. And Kele's are Christina Sarah Paulina, Sarah being our paternal grandmother's name.

Four weeks after I was born mum and dad decided to go to live in Nigeria. I know mum managed a book store in Aba, the capital city of Imo State at the time, in the heartland of the Igbo nation. I think dad was either teaching or working in the health services in some capacity. It must have been some experience for mum, with her cold, grey and rainy Irish and London background, to arrive in the bright, colourful and intense tropical heat of Nigeria. And the tables were definitely turned; *she* was now in the minority living in the most highly populated of black African nations, and she loved it! She never really learnt to speak Igbo, but understood it quite well, and knew when she was being called or referred to:

"Beke!" – white person.

In fact mum made more of an effort to teach us the Igbo language than dad:

Otu, abwo, ato, anno, isse, issi, assa, assato, itolu, iri – predictably, 1-10.

"Kedu?" "Odinma!" - again, predictably, "How are you?" "I'm fine!"

Mum only ever spoke of her time in Nigeria in positive tones. She clearly had fun, enjoyed her status and work, cherished the friendships she developed, and relished raising her two children. When she fell pregnant with the twins she made the reluctant decision to return to London for their birth. She was the original 'earth mother', and I can imagine her worrying about the relatively poor maternity and postnatal facilities in Nigeria, so much so that she returned to London with 20-month-old me to ensure safe delivery, leaving dad and Chi-chi at home in Nigeria, to return to London 6 months later. However, her waters broke on the plane on our descent to Heathrow where, thankfully, there was an ambulance waiting for her to whisk her off to hospital, and I got whisked off to Dr Barnados!

Strangely enough, I do remember some experiences at the children's home. I remember missing my mum, that's for sure! I also remember climbing the dome-shaped climbing frame on the concrete play area at the back of the home and, for some reason, I thought I could fly, so I dived off the top of the climbing frame and very quickly learnt that I actually didn't have the ability to soar through the air! Unsurprisingly I came crashing to the ground, face first, hitting the concrete and nearly severing my bottom lip clean off my face as my teeth sliced through it with sinew-slicing ease. I remember lots of blood and it being *my* turn to be whisked off to hospital where my lip was sewn back in place from the inside of my mouth. I remember mum visiting me while I was there, and a nurse telling me what a brave little boy I'd been, for which I was given a garish red and green sword and scabbard that I insisted on wearing as I made a triumphal return to Dr Barnados. I remember showing off with this sword in front of the other orphans as I strode valiantly into the main day area with it securely fastened around my waste. It's only now I realise what a complete and absolute dickhead I must have looked like. *SO* embarrassing!

I also remember the nickname I was given at Barnados: "Oliver", because I was always asking for more food!

Dad and Chi-chi arrived in London either shortly before or after mum and the twins were discharged from hospital, I was released after 6 months and good behaviour from Dr B's, and we were soon looking for accommodation for our rapidly expanding family. I know we lived for a while on Shorrolds Road in Fulham, south west London, where we shared with other recently-arrived black friends of my parents from Africa and the Caribbean. This was pretty typical of the time among newly-arrived immigrants from the Commonwealth who, when confronted with ignorant racist landlords, strived to help each other out with accommodation, often meaning entire families living in one room in tenements and two-up-two-downs. What else could they do?

I remember the signs as we trudged the streets of London looking for accommodation:

"Accommodation available - no Blacks, no Dogs, no Irish."

Usually in that order, but variations upon the theme were down to each landlord's discretion and priority. According to Historical Geographies Blog Spot:

'In the 1950s and 1960s English homes were frequently seen displaying the signs: "No Blacks, No Irish, No Dogs". Because of the chequered historical relationships these two groups of humans (Blacks and Irish people), were linked with dogs as undesirable residents across the land.

Irish identity – relating especially to English identity – has been at the root of centuries of continuing divisions and antagonisms between the two nations. In 1652 King James 1 ordered that all Irish political prisoners were to be transported to the West Indies and sold as slave labour to the planters. In 1637 a census showed that 69% of Montserrat inhabitants were Irish slaves.

Oliver Cromwell (who ruled the Commonwealth from 1649-1659) continued the process of ethnic cleansing sanctioned by previous English monarchs when he demanded, in 1652, that all Irish inhabitants settle west of Shannon, in the province of Connaught, or be transported to the West Indies after being charged with high treason. The area around the province of Connaught and County Clare was, at the time, dry arid land that was difficult to cultivate. The Irish were given effectively the choice of hardship in their country of origin or hardship in the West Indies.

The captured Irish people were often sent to Barbados and this gave rise to a popular term of the time that described this process: 'Barbadosed'. These Irish people were sold as slaves or indentured servants without any influence over the length of their stay in forced servitude.

Soon every minor breach of the law carried the sentence of transportation and Irish people were regularly being sold as slaves. Despite this, there were not enough people being supplied to the West Indian planters and a similar process to the one on the African continent was employed in Ireland: slaver groups began to travel the countryside kidnapping people to meet the requirements of free West Indian labour.

As Eddie McFields annotates in his 2015 blog:

'They came as slaves; vast human cargo transported on tall British ships bound for the Americas. They were shipped by the hundreds of thousands and included men, women and even the youngest of children.

Whenever they rebelled or even disobeyed an order, they were punished in the harshest ways. Slave owners would hang their human property by their hands and set their hands or feet on fire as one form of punishment. They were burned alive and had their heads placed on pikes in the market place as a warning to other captives.'

According to McFields, 'the Irish slave trade began when James11 sold 30,000 Irish prisoners as slaves to the New World. His Proclamation of 1625 required Irish political prisoners be sent overseas and sold to English settlers in the West Indies. By the mid-1600s, the Irish were the main slaves sold to Antigua and Montserrat. At that time, 70% of the total population of Montserrat were Irish slaves.

Ireland quickly became the biggest source of human livestock for English merchants. The majority of the early slaves to the New World were actually white.

From 1641 to 1652, over 500,000 Irish were killed by the English and another 300,000 were sold as slaves. Ireland's population fell from about 1,500,000 to 600,000 in one single decade. Families were ripped apart as the British did not allow Irish dads to take their wives and children with them across the Atlantic. This led to a helpless population of homeless women and children. Britain's solution was to auction them off as well.

During the 1650s, over 100,000 Irish children between the ages of 10 and 14 were taken from their parents and sold as slaves in the West Indies, Virginia and New England. In this decade, 52,000 Irish (mostly women and children) were sold to Barbados and Virginia. Another 30,000 Irish men and women were also transported and sold to the highest bidder. In 1656, Cromwell ordered that 2,000 Irish children be taken to Jamaica and sold as slaves to English settlers.'

McFields makes the interesting point that 'many people today will avoid calling the Irish slaves what they truly were: Slaves. They'll come up with terms like "Indentured Servants" to describe what occurred to the Irish. However, in most cases from the 17th and 18th centuries, Irish slaves were nothing more than human cattle'.

He goes on to state that, 'As an example, the African slave trade was just beginning during this same period. It is well recorded that African slaves, not tainted with the stain of the hated Catholic theology and more expensive to purchase, were often treated far better than their Irish counterparts.

African slaves were very expensive during the late 1600s (£50 sterling). Irish slaves came cheap (no more than £5 sterling). If a planter whipped or branded or beat an Irish slave to death, it was never a crime. A death was a monetary setback, but far cheaper than killing a more expensive African. The English masters quickly began breeding the Irish women for both their own personal pleasure and for greater profit. Children of slaves were themselves slaves, which increased the size of the master's free workforce. Even if an Irish woman somehow obtained her freedom, her kids would remain slaves of her master. Thus, Irish moms, even with this new found emancipation, would seldom abandon their kids and would remain in servitude.

In time, the English thought of a better way to use these women (in many cases, girls as young as 12) to increase their market share: the settlers began to breed Irish women and girls with African men to produce slaves with a distinct complexion. These new "mulatto" slaves brought a higher price than Irish livestock and, likewise, enabled the settlers to save money rather than purchase new African slaves. This practice of interbreeding Irish females with African men went on for several decades and was so widespread that, in 1681, legislation was passed "forbidding the practice of mating Irish slave women to African slave men for the purpose of producing slaves for sale." In short, it was stopped only because it interfered with the profits of a large slave transport company.

England continued to ship tens of thousands of Irish slaves for more than a century. Records state that, after the 1798 Irish rebellion, thousands of Irish slaves were sold to both America and Australia. There were horrible abuses of both African and Irish captives. One British ship even dumped 1,302 slaves into the Atlantic Ocean so that the crew would have plenty of food to eat.

There is little doubt that the Irish experienced the horrors of slavery as much (if not more in the 17th century) as the Africans did.'

Irish people who lived in the West Indies were not only sold as slaves, there were many Irish slave owners there as well. In 1670 10% of property owners in Jamaica were Irish, and by 1729 20% of all colonial assembly men had Irish names. When slavery was abolished and compensation was paid to the planters for the loss of their 'stock' of African slaves, the largest amount received by any slave holder in the British Empire went to the Blair brothers from Newry who ran a slave agency and received over £83,580.00 (21st century value = £3,685,897.00).

Slavery affected many nations and people, all to different degrees. The United Nations (UN) now holds a day of Remembrance of the Slave Trade and its Abolition on the 23rd August every year: it was first commemorated in 1998. Britain, who was at the forefront of the transatlantic slave trade as the British Empire expanded inexorably on slave labour, has no national memorial or remembrance day recognising the effects of slavery within Britain.

In 2001 France passed a law recognising slavery as a crime against humanity. The French now hold a national remembrance day on the 10th May for the victims of slavery. The French President, Jacques Chirac, said, in 2005, "Slavery fed racism, when people tried to justify the unjustifiable, that was when the first racist theories were elaborated... Racism is a crime of the heart and the spirit... which is why the memory of slavery remains a living wound."

21st century ideas about national identity perpetuate based on uneducated and often inherited beliefs that are founded on racist perceptions. In Britain today, people declare that only 'white' Anglo Saxon people can be English and that all other people are foreigners and, therefore, are undesirable interlopers. The English relationship with the Irish and the African has altered to include people from Eastern Europe and Asia as equally unwanted citizens of the country'.

Needless to say, things were quite difficult for us as a family consisting of a black African man, a (white) Irish woman, and four children under four years of age; at least we didn't have any dogs I suppose!

But my first real memories of house and home were of Ascham Street in Kentish Town, a north London Borough of Camden. The six of us lived in one room on the second floor of a three-floor tenement, sharing the toilet and kitchen with all the other families in the house. I remember often being cold, and hungry, and the real sense of community that is common among the less privileged poor, competing for scarce resources but ready to help each other when things got particularly tough.

There was a particular family that stood out in my mind. The mum was called Gay and she was a hugely fat white woman married to a white guy who we rarely saw, because of his frequent holidays at 'Her Majesty's Pleasure' (HMP) and, judging by the constant stream of men 'friends' who visited her on a regular basis, I'm fairly certain Gay was a brass (prostitute, ashawo). A member of the lumpen proletariat, she was definitely lumpen!

Gay had a son who we played with occasionally, but she was very concerned at the thought of her son playing with these "half-caste" kids. A typical feature of the British obsession with social class, the working class also distinguished amongst themselves between their "acceptable" and "unacceptable" members. I think being a black and Irish family put us pretty firmly at the bottom of the social hierarchy in the minds of our working class "brothers and sisters". But what did we care? We were here and here to stay, so our attitude was "get used to it!"

I started primary school at the local one up the hill and round the corner, Burghley School, now known as Acland Burghley School. I don't remember anything from there other than two experiences, the first one being learning how to gamble with the Greek kids in the playground, throwing pennies to cover each other's. If you covered your opponent's penny with yours, you took your own and his penny back. The other thing was Chi chi going missing, resulting in me being kept at school as the police and members of the community looked for her. She turned up safe and sound eventually and we all went home happy.

More prominent among my memories of our time in Kentish Town are of other more adventurous and risqué outings. Like the time me and my brother and sisters burnt down a warehouse. The police were alerted and tipped off that it was us. Mum quickly learnt of the impending house visit by the police, so she hid us in any available nook and cranny in the room, giving us strict orders not to make a sound. I was crammed into a cupboard near the front door to our room when the officers arrived. I heard them asking if four black kids live here, and remember her saying in her thickest Irish accent that no, that wasn't the case. She stood toe-to-toe with them at the door, slipping deeper and deeper into her bog-Oirish brogue to emphasise her false claim that she didn't know any black kids. Mum was a fighter and always defended her children in the face of any adversity, especially in confrontations with racist police and English people.

Another was when I had my first "driving lesson", at the ripe old age of five. For some reason the police were at the top of our road, something had happened and a crowd had gathered. Ascham Street has a slight incline, but in my childish memory it was a long steep hill. Chi-chi and I joined the inquisitive crowd of onlookers, trying to find out what had happened. Then I noticed that the parked police car that was pointing down the hill was unmanned and unlocked. I couldn't resist the temptation and climbed into the driver's seat, playing with everything I could get my hands on, one of those things being the handbrake. The car obviously didn't have a steering lock because, within seconds, I remember really enjoying trying to navigate the car down the hill that was Lady Margaret Road, with Chi-chi running along beside the car (probably screaming at me in fear for me, or reckless excitement at yet another caper), until I smashed it into a wall (or house), at the bottom. I think I managed to hit virtually every parked car on my descent which ended unceremoniously in a heap of crushed glass, metal and brick, and I just knew I'd done something wrong, so I legged it from the police who'd chased me on foot in Chi-chi's slipstream all the way down the hill.

Shamefully in retrospect, I and my siblings, for some reason still unknown to us, took great pleasure in terrorising a recluse old man who lived in a basement flat at the top of our road. High on our list of entertainment priorities was to break into his flat when he was out and at times eat his food, and at other times piss from the road into his little patch of garden. Don't ask me why! We'd broken into his flat one day and he returned unexpectedly. We hid where we could. I was under his small dining table near to the rear patch-garden exit, the furthest away from the front door exit and safety. Chi-chi, Ijem and Obi rushed for the door at the most opportune time, making their safe exits hammering up the stairs to street level. I panicked at this point and decided on stealth, heart pounding, trying to time my bolt for safety and freedom just right. And I fucked it up! He always walked with a walking stick and, to my horror and imminent pain, he hadn't put it down. I nearly timed it right, but nearly wasn't good enough in my desperate head-long charge for the door. His adrenalin and reflexes were still hyped from his short dash for the others, so when I made my sprint he was still wired and, with cane in hand, lashed at me, catching the back of my legs with a hot lash of the cane. And I screamed like the baby I was!

Of course on our return home we gave mum a severely doctored version of events and she, true to form, stormed up the road to batter him with her mouth, warning him NEVER to touch her kids again. I must admit, I was ashamed by our behaviour, I knew we were in the wrong, and seeing mum tear into him, totally unfairly, triggered a deep sense of shame and guilt that I think in some ways has stayed with me throughout my life. That's not to say I went on to live a 'holier than thou' life thereafter by any stretch of the imagination, but recognising the difference between right and wrong, and the attendant guilty conscience every time I'd break the deeply internalised code, has never left me.

I think the combination of mum's almost genetically inherited Catholic guilt syndrome, along with dad's almost innocent, naïve and pure sense of right and wrong contributed to my developing a conscience and an acute sense of right and wrong, good and bad, fair and unfair, just and unjust, justice and injustice. Not that I allowed this mixture to determine my actions for many years to come!

For much of the time in Ascham Street, dad worked away at a psychiatric hospital in Kent, which meant mum often struggled to keep the four of us in order. In all honesty, we were fast becoming uncontrollable tearaways in our crumbling Kentish Town manor, though we had learnt not to misbehave at home or push mum too far, the punishment for which would be the inevitable beatings. We also learnt not to bring trouble home for fear of being in double-trouble with mum. Hence I was relieved when an old woman unwittingly saved me from a certain top-10 beating that would have registered on the Richter scale.

I was walking along the road with my little brother Obi after having been to a local shop to steal sweets, happily chomping on our ill-gotten gains. I was 6 and Obi was 4 or 5 years old. We heard the caterwauling wail of a distant siren that emanated from an ambulance on an emergency call. This became evident when the vehicle screeched around the corner, heading up the road towards us on the other side. I don't know what possessed me but, inexplicably, I picked up a stone and threw it straight through the front window of the approaching ambulance. The window shattered and the driver was forced into a glass-shard-showered blind emergency stop.

Understandably, he came charging out of the cab, raced over to us and started to hit me. Just then an old Angel of a lady who was doddering along the road steamed into him, hitting him with her umbrella, shouting at him to "leave the little boy alone!" I'm certain she hadn't witnessed my earlier indiscretion, and I wasn't of a mind to hang around for it to be explained to her. Me and Obi ripped up the road, round the corner, little arms, hearts and legs pumping like crazy until we made it, panting and gasping, to the sanctuary of our one-room haven-of-a-hovel that was home. Of course we didn't mention anything to mum, about stealing sweets or de-commissioning the ambulance. We weren't going to jeopardise our punishment-free misdemeanour by telling her, because she would have battered me senseless, and quite likely Obi would have got a good beating just for being with me on the caper!

Chi-chi, Obi, Ijem, Me - Ascham Street,
Kentish Town, London (1961)

Four

Dad was eventually offered a staff house with his job in Kent so, before the start of my second year in primary school, we shipped out of Kentish Town and moved to Blean, which was a village located a few miles outside of Canterbury. We moved into a house, a *real* house, with large front and rear gardens, and hedges and fences that demarcated our new mansion from those neighbouring us. And it WAS a mansion. A three-up-one-down with separate kitchen-diner mansion! Compared to the one-room hovel that was home in Kentish town, this was luxury! We even had our own bedrooms, Chi-chi and Ijem in the bigger one, me and Obi in the smallest and mum and dad in the main one at the front of the house. Total bliss!

But it was really cold in Kent at winter times, our house didn't have central heating, and this must have coincided with one of the hardest, and harshest, times of our lives. If, that is, any meaningful distinctions could be made between the hard times as we grew up throughout our childhood!

I and Chi-chi started to attend Blean County Primary School, which was probably a mile and a half or two miles away from our house. Ijem and Obi joined us there for their first year. It was a red brick building with concrete playgrounds to front and rear, and a huge grass sports field. The school uniform was foul, a brown jumper with yellow ribbing and grey trousers for the boys, and a yellow and brown blouse and skirt combination for the girls. It was here that I first made and threw snowballs, or 'stone balls' as they were soon to be more accurately described. Winters in Kent were really long, cold and snowy, with thick drifting snow making picture-postcard scenery all around us. To gain an unfair advantage, and to inflict as much pain on our targets, we used to pack our snowballs around one or two stones or pebbles before pelting them at our friends and classmates in the playground. This practice had to stop when one target, friend, classmate, victim, was hit and cut above the eye, covering his face with blood. We never *really* thought things through before acting them out, often to our own detriment!

I really enjoyed our time at the school though. Thankfully, I was reasonably intelligent, sporty and popular. I did well in the classroom where I found most lessons quite easy to understand and pick up. I wasn't shy, I was vocal, and at times a bit of a clown, always ready to have a laugh and wind the teachers up where possible, without directly confronting them or being openly disrespectful. I think I inherited a bit of my dad's charm and was always able to win people over, well, most people!

Children are notoriously cruel to each other and, in the jungles that were our playgrounds, I quickly adapted to the cut and thrust of self-preservation and survival in them. Like my brother and sisters I was a very fast runner (Chi-chi was exceptionally fast!). However, one of my favourite games was "Kiss-Chase", where girls and boys would take it in turns to run after each other and, when a kiss was planted, the recipient was out of the game. I hardly ever got kissed because I was always able to out-run the ever-growing chasing pack of squealy-giggly girls. Invariably, when I did get kissed, it was because I quite fancied the girl chasing me, so I *allowed* her to catch and kiss me!

"British Bulldog" was another favourite of ours, where one person stood in the middle of the playground while everybody else had to run from one side to the other without being 'tagged' by whoever was 'it' in the middle. Again, we were very adept at avoiding being tagged until late into the game when it seemed like the whole school was waiting for you in the middle!

Athletics, football, and sports in general were to become significant features of our lives. Though a giant to me at the time, dad merely scraped five foot in height. This became very evident at our first school sports day at Blean primary. After all four of us had trashed all-comers in our respective sprint races, dad got up to run in the dads' race. As he lined up it soon became clear that he was the shortest by far of all the dads. I was terrified. Apart from saving our family honour and reputation, I desperately wanted him to win, and desperately wanted to avoid the shame and embarrassment of him losing. He took off his shoes and socks to run barefoot and took his place for the standing start.

"On your marks, get set, go!"

Dad fired out of the starting line-up to totally waste the opposition, his short legs hammering like pistons to easily forge an ever-increasing gaping gap between him and, what were soon to become, his unsuccessful pursuers, in his fu-fu fuelled dash to the tape. I was SO proud of him when he crossed the line way ahead of them all, I couldn't stop shouting and cheering. I wanted everyone to know that he was my dad. I shouldn't really have bothered. It hadn't occurred to me that his being my father was abundantly obvious. We were the only black family in the school!

Like he did with most things in life, dad took his champion status with humility, grace and a smile. He was a genuinely good, intrinsically nice person who was fun and loved life. He wasn't cowed by his behemoth-like opposition, was completely confident in his ability and, if he didn't win, he would have clapped the victor on the back like the true sportsman he was, and poked fun at himself and his failure to win (though probably privately he would have berated himself, because he was VERY competitive, which was a trait we all inherited from him!).

Both I and Obi turned out to be decent footballers as children. Like Obi I was the best in my year. We both grew to love and become totally besotted with football, taking every opportunity to kick something, anything, about. Our parents couldn't afford toys, so we never got footballs to play with, but tin cans and the occasional stolen tennis ball were more than suitable substitutes. Other than the most atrocious hair cut that I've ever been subjected to (by a local white barber who'd obviously never cut 'curly' hair before), this and a football incident were my two most embarrassing moments at Blean primary school.

Just as an aside at this juncture though, what is it about white people that makes them so love to put their hand in black peoples' hair? It's *so* annoying!

Anyway, the day after the barber had butchered my hair I went into class and hoped I'd be able to keep my school cap on all day. Alas, no chance! My teacher wasn't having it and insisted I remove my cap in class. I was mortified at what I knew was to come and, post-partum, my 'classmates' didn't disappoint as they howled with laughter, tears streaming down their faces as they pointed at my head that now resembled a nuclear fall-out area. Though totally gutted and miserable, I learnt the value of being able to laugh at yourself and to not show that you're upset. The derision soon died down and we got on with the day.

The other moment of utter embarrassment came with football. Firstly, dad had promised to buy me a (new/my first) pair of football boots. I couldn't wait and, after having waited for what seemed like decades, I accompanied dad into Canterbury to buy them. I went into the sports shop, heart pounding with excitement as I cast my eyes over the display of new style football boots. Dad was casting his eye over their prices, and soon asked the shop assistant if there was another sports shop in town. Devastatingly for me, we were directed to what was, in my mind, a cast-off bric-a-brac shop that sold a wide variety of odds and ends, probably a forerunner of the Oxfam charity shops of today! Dad spotted what he was looking for, a cheap pair of boots! They were disgusting. BROWN leather with huge toe-caps and leather studs that had to be nailed into the soles with a hammer! They looked like a dual purpose combination of Stanley Matthews-signed boots designed for coal miners who enjoyed a kick-about on a Sunday morning after having worn them 'downt pit' all week! I hated them, Dad bought them.

Now, considering the fact that I'd been boasting to my schoolmates about my new boots before they'd been purchased, the idea of putting these monstrosities on my feet in the changing room was an apparition from hell. What could I do? I'd been selected to play (in goal!) this day, so I had to put them on. The boys waited expectantly as I delved into my "kit" bag, which was in fact a well-used, scuffed and fading plastic carrier bag. I slowly withdrew the offending articles and, even worse than the howls of laughter at my butchered hair, the boys actually empathised with me and *didn't* laugh at my boots, they actually *felt* my pain! This was even harder for me to take than the derision I'd anticipated, but was quickly relieved from the situation when we were ushered out to play the match.

I can't remember the score, but I do remember scoring an own goal from just inside the edge of my goalkeeping area. I had the ball in my hands and went to dropkick it up the pitch. The bulbous toecaps of the boots were so big that I inadvertently kicked the ball over my own head back into the unguarded goal. I felt utterly ashamed as the watching school crowd groaned at conceding such a ludicrous own goal! I never wore those fucking things again, preferring to wear my worn out, no-grip plimsolls than suffer the humiliation of being seen alive in those hobnail boots again!

To be honest, we were so poor that our footwear started life as plimsolls, and very soon became 'plims', we wore them so often the soles eroded and wore out, leaving plims without the solls, the continued wearing of which was only made possible by the ever-decreasing pock-marked and pitted web of rubber that kept the uppers attached to the soles. But at least they weren't signed by Stanley Matthews!

Less embarrassing, but more frightening, was a lunch time episode that was linked to mum's SOS joke, which, had I been able to, I would have screamed out a personal SOS in the school dining hall. We were one of the few families that qualified for free school dinners, a stigma we soon grew to ignore as satiating our hunger was more important than preserving our pride. Empty stomachs willingly sacrifice pride. But it was cruel how we were forced to endure the daily humiliation as the queue for dinners developed in the hall. We'd have to hang back because the 'paying' pupils always went first, not that it was a private school, it very definitely wasn't, more yet another legacy of the English obsession with social class and privilege, ensuring that the lowest and least privileged demonstrated due deference to their more affluent social superiors.

When all the paying pupils had collected their lunches the dinner staff would then call out "Free dinners!" That was our cue to surge to the serving area to get our lunches. Without fail, when the announcer called out "Seconds!" (which denoted an unrestricted free-for-all for those who wanted more), we'd be first back up to get it, after ravenously scoffing our first helpings. It was whilst I was scoffing a chunk of meat, lamb I think, without chewing it properly in a desperate attempt to be among the first back up to get seconds that the meat got lodged in my throat. And I couldn't get it down or back up. With a steadily decreasing supply of oxygen, beads of sweat broke out on my forehead as my eyes started to bulge out of my head, tears started to stream down my face, and I was just about to shit myself in fear of losing my life. I thought I was going to die with this piece of meat stuck in my throat and, had I been able to, I would have screamed out a personal SOS for someone to come and help me!

I started to heave in shuddering spasms, like a cat bringing up a fur-ball, and almost miraculously, this cleared my throat (I must have unwittingly performed a Heimlich manoeuvre to save myself!). I managed to gather myself and my full senses, quickly chewed the meat sufficiently well for it to be swallowed, gulped it down effortlessly and raced up to the serving area for the much-sought-after seconds!

Despite the fact we were always happy, poverty really is a bad thing!

Five

I loved the sights, sounds and smells of the Kent countryside though! In my view there's nowhere better for children to grow up than the countryside. Often in summer I'd walk home on my own up "the back-way" through farm fields, along dirt tracks, and over a stream, down and up the "hilly bit" between school and the village church. I used to see wild rabbits as well as the farm animals, up close. It was sometimes eerily spooky and quiet, with the occasional birdsong the only sound to break the silence. Every now and again I'd be accompanied by a classmate or one of my siblings, but I preferred to be on my own.

I like nature and wildlife. I respect wild animals as they spend every day battling to survive in their often challenging and hostile natural habitats. I don't have the same sort of respect or liking for domesticated animals, especially house pets, which I would never consider keeping. The first job I ever did was on a farm milking cows and cleaning out the sheds they were milked in. I was eight years old and enjoyed the independence and sense of responsibility I got when working ankle-deep in cow shit on the farm, and every now and then the farmer would give me a shilling or two, which I'd always give to mum on my return home, filthy and stinking of cow dung, but I felt I'd made a much-needed contribution to the family income.

The farm was just near a village called Harbledown, which was on the road between Blean and Canterbury. Mum used to work as a cleaner at a huge private school for boys, St Edmund's, which is now part of the Kent at Canterbury University campus. I hated mum having to go to work there. I hated the thought of her cleaning up after those snobby rich kids, but we needed the money, we were REALLY poor in Blean!

I much preferred it when mum got a second job in a bakery in Canterbury, selling bread and cakes. When I could, and usually after working on the farm, I'd walk the mile and a bit down St Stephens Hill into Canterbury to meet mum at the bakers in the hope that I'd get a cake treat, and she never let me down! She'd also occasionally bring bread and cakes home from work, which was always a fantastic surprise treat and addition to our pretty meagre diet of staples, potatoes, bread, cabbages etc. Mum made the best bubble-and-squeak ever!

In retrospect though, and considering the current and ever-increasing obesity epidemic afflicting children and young people in the UK and much of the western world, I don't have any complaints about our diet! As children we were never overweight, and always fit, always the quickest, strongest and most athletic. We were healthy. However, it's not the case that mum and dad were able to buy all we ate, which for me meant digging up the front and back gardens in Blean to grow our own vegetables. I had green fingers with the potatoes and cabbages, but for some reason my carrots always let me down. When our provisions were bought, invariably it would be me (as the oldest son and also physically the biggest), who had to walk the half mile or so to the local store. Mum would always ask for a volunteer and, met with the stony silence that usually follows this type of request in families, she'd either ask me directly or I'd volunteer. I worshipped my mum as a child and throughout her life, so getting the groceries was a chore that I was more than happy to do for her. I saw how hard she worked and scraped, trying her best to look after us. Going to the store was easy, I'd generally either run or jog. Coming back from the shop was a totally different proposition though. The shopping was heavy! I always remember the weight of those bags as they cut into my small, wiry hands, and the aches and pains in my arms, shoulders and back as I trudged home. I sometimes wonder if this actually contributed to my having the relatively long arm-span that I have now which, it has to be said, left me in good stead for the unknown but fast-approaching fights, brawls and punch-ups that became a regular feature of my later childhood and youth.

We were never over-indulged with food, treats and gifts, but we became very adept at making our own entertainment. Living in the country had many benefits. We'd often go out scrumping apples during the summer months, and getting temporary paid jobs apple- and potato-picking, which also added a bit more to the family income. Mum always made sure as far as possible that we were well turned-out, even if that meant knitting much of our clothes! She even knitted a pair of swimming trunks for my brother Obi which, on his first use, looked great before he got in the pool. But after he dived in he soon discovered that wool absorbs water at a phenomenal rate and, as he rose to the surface, his saturated knitted trunks were down by his ankles. Thankfully, he didn't allow the shame and embarrassment of this experience to haunt him forever, and we still laugh about it now.

I do remember being excruciatingly hungry at times, and I guess mum went without to try to feed us as best she could. She was under immense pressure and, as the original 'earth mother', this must have been terrible for her, but she always put us first. Throughout our childhoods she'd often quip:

"God, my stomach's hitting my backbone I'm so hungry!"

Even today, this thought makes me well up, I hate the thought of mum having gone hungry in order for us to be fed, especially when you consider the current obesity problem among young people that suggests one third of children leaving primary school at eleven years of age in the UK are overweight or obese. Interestingly, the statistics are highest among working class black African-Caribbean children in inner-city London boroughs, the lowest among middle class white children of the same age in St Albans, Hertfordshire; Winchester in Hampshire; and Wavereley in Surrey. Today, it seems, eating a healthy diet is expensive if you can't get it for free. Being surrounded by an abundance of fresh fruit and vegetables in the countryside, having a healthy diet was never a problem for us!

Christmas time was always good though. My memories confirm that excitement and happiness really are relative concepts. In addition to the extra food that mum made available, there'd also be presents. Our own individual presents! Though only one or two at most, they always seemed special. Dad would go through the ritual of handing them out to us in turn (a tradition I've continued with my own children), and we'd almost explode with anticipation. We were such boisterous children that our toys never lasted for very long, and we'd soon be back to making our own entertainment, including the things we used to play with.

One Christmas in Blean was sensational though. I remember it because there was what seemed to me to be a massive pile of presents on the living room floor on the night before Christmas, all wrapped in real festive paper as opposed to newspapers, our usual choice of wrap. It was much later that I learned that the parents of friends and neighbours in the village had made the effort to make this Christmas a special one for us. In other words, they'd taken pity on us and clubbed together before delivering the presents to my parents. Ignorance, at times, truly is bliss!

The same can't be said for some of the children at Blean primary school at Christmas time though. The school had a tradition of each child bringing in gift-wrapped toys that were put in a huge sack and, en masse in the dining hall, each child in the school would be called up to receive a surprise present. A bit similar to the 'Secret Santa' ritual that's played out on a yearly basis in work places today. This was a guarantee for my brother, sisters and I to get brand new toys, and we couldn't wait. It was also a guarantee for four other unfortunate pupils to be totally and utterly crest-fallen and devastated. We could always tell the unlucky ones who'd received our secret presents as, after opening the presents we'd donated to the sack, they'd instantly go into meltdown, wailing and crying with disappointment as it dawned upon them that they'd never be able to use or play with the wreckage of an old and battered toy that was well past its use-by date!

Totally unashamed, we quickly developed the art of maintaining a poker face so as to avoid being identified as the guilty 'Santa's Little Helpers', before going off to have great fun with our brand spanking new toys.

We weren't only boisterous out of school; we were boisterous *in* school also. So much so that we were regular tenants on the Headmaster's mat which was strategically placed outside the door of his office for all to see the miscreants to whom he was about to deliver punishment. Invariably, this punishment was corporal, in the form of the cane, the traditional 'six of the best'. I got caned so much it didn't bother me, and I got quite good at feigning pain to reduce the number of lashes I was to receive. I think 'three of the best' was my all-time low!

The funniest was when I'd got in trouble with three other class-mates and, after waiting 'on the mat' sufficiently long enough to be observed and tutted at by passing onlookers, we were summoned into the inner sanctum that was the headmaster's office. I knew from experience that we were going to get the cane and, as soon as I realised this fat and lazy headmaster was going to line us up in a tightly packed row with our hands out together in order for him to cane us simultaneously, I successfully managed to manoeuvre myself into the middle of the row. With our hands placed together, out, and palms up, the flogging began. I got the timing just right. After the metre-long cane whistled through its arc of descent, and a split second before it made contact with all four supplicant palms, I dipped mine slightly so my three mates took the full brunt of the first lash. The big mistake I made was not to react with the appropriate howl of pain that the others made. My rouse was immediately obvious and earned me an additional lash for my troubles!

Over forty years later my older sister Chi-chi visited Blean County Primary School in 2011 as part of a television documentary that was being made about her life and career. During the visit she got the opportunity to check one of the headmaster's discipline and punishment record books, which provided ample evidence of my many misdemeanours as a pupil at the school, which remains one of my few claims to fame!

On the other hand, it was at this time that Chi-chi started to demonstrate and develop an amazing array of musical and athletic ability. As previously mentioned, we were all particularly talented athletically, always crushing our opponents when it came to sprinting and football. I think being the only children in the village to walk the one and a half miles to and from school every day regardless of the weather, watching our friends take the tuppenny bus ride, served as our fitness and conditioning programme!

However, Chi-chi (and eventually Obi), was exceptionally quick when it came to running, but whilst we lived in Blean a special musical ability started to flourish.

Despite being dirt poor, mum and dad were always highly aspirational for and with us. They always told us that we could achieve whatever we wanted to achieve in life, and reassured us that we were just as good as any other child. It was only later that they explained we'd also have to work four times harder than our white friends to get the same as they did! Mum took seven-year-old Chi-chi into Canterbury for private piano lessons, and it seemed she had a natural musical talent and ear, because she very quickly began to master the instrument and 'read' music (I don't know how *anyone* can '*read*' music!). But probably more importantly, she developed a deep love and passion for it.

It just so happened that one set of neighbours in Chestnut Avenue, the Brice family, had an old piano that the husband used to play but was on the verge of throwing out. 'Mrs B' and mum were good friends and, in view of Chi-chi's interest and passion, the piano was saved from meeting its maker and ascending to that great music hall in the sky, and wheeled up the road to take pride of place in our front room.

Unbeknown to us, hell had descended upon us in the form of this fucking piano! The front room now became, for all intents and purposes, off-limits to the rest of us and, in effect, Chi-chi's room. She'd practice on it for hours! 'I am C, Middle C, left hand, right hand, Middle C', as well as Chopsticks and boogey-woogey riffs. She was good! However, her sanctuary meant our exclusion, out on the street playing which, if the truth be told, wasn't too bad a deal.

It was in Chi-chi's sanctuary that I first remember being beaten by dad. I don't mean a little clip round the ear or whack on the legs or backside, we'd received them regularly. I mean a proper beating that leaves you injured and aching. I'd actually been in the room with dad, behaving myself impeccably, when my little brother Obi came running in, crying and screaming, bitterly complaining that Owen Scamp (a son of another set of 'ruffian' neighbours), had just beaten him up. Dad switched on me in an instant, beating me good and proper, before ordering me out to beat up Owen Scamp in order to restore our family honour. I ran out, tears streaming down my face, and battered him. I made him pay for the unfair beating I'd just received from dad. Owen had older brothers, but they never sought revenge on me, so I must have done a pretty good job on him to dissuade any thoughts of reprisals! It's strange how the first beating I remember, and the first fight I remember, took place on the same day.

Dad was working at St Augustine's hospital in Chartham, a village about four miles the other side of Canterbury from Blean, so he often slept in staff accommodation while he was on duty, and came home for his off-duty days. I began to resent the days when he was home, because, whilst he was a fun guy and loved us deeply, he was also very quick and harsh with the belt, slipper, cane, ruler, electric flex, tree branch, whatever was close at hand to beat us with. He was also very musical and took great joy, pride and satisfaction from Chi-chi's developing prowess on the piano. This resulted in an almost toxic and very dangerous dilemma for us. Chi-chi's previously unquestioned and unrivalled status and influence over her younger siblings was now indelibly written in stone. There would be hell to pay if any one of us disturbed her whilst she was practising. I must admit she rarely abused her position to deliberately set us up for beatings, but she certainly didn't cover for us if we'd distracted her and we received the due beatings as a result. We were just children, who were boisterous and loved to play, so it was a bit harsh to lose one of our potential hiding-places in the front room, but we soon adjusted to playing outside in safety and away from the wrath of our parents!

Chi-chi was also academically quite gifted and did well enough for my mum to warn me that I had to do at least as well as her in school. So Chi-chi, as first child, definitely set us a good example to follow. However, the first real experience of race and racism hit home when she did her 11+ exam at Blean primary school. She was one of the brightest no doubt, and certainly as bright as most of her classmates and closest friends, one of whom was the daughter of a very famous children's TV producer. As families we'd become quite close, and often played at their house, which had the set of one of his programmes in their barn. We later learnt that Chi-chi passed her 11+ exam, but the fat slob of a headmaster was only allowed to recommend a certain quota of pupils to progress on to the prestigious Simon Langton Grammar School for Girls in Canterbury. Predictably Chi-chi didn't make the cut and was subjected to attending the local secondary modern school.

With the benefit of experience and hindsight of the tripartite education system in the UK at the time, 'failing' the 11+ plus exam in the last year of primary school meant being sentenced to secondary education at a secondary modern school, which was tantamount to being written off for the rest of your life!

It wasn't coincidental that, by the 1960s and 70s, about 75% of the UK population were working class and 25% middle class, and, hey presto, about 75% of state schools were secondary moderns and 25% technical high schools and grammar schools. Even more astounding (not!), was that the secondary modern schools were overwhelmingly built in working class areas, and were populated with the children of working class parents. The technical high schools and grammar schools were invariably built in middle class areas, and virtually totally populated by the children of middle class parents. Needless to say, the level, standard and quality of education in the technical high and grammar schools was light years ahead of, and greatly superior to, that provided and delivered in secondary modern schools.

Essentially, as a result of their performance in these culturally-biased 11+ exams, working class children were being prepared for low paid, low status, mundane working class jobs, and middle class children for high paid, high status, managerial and professional middle class jobs. This meant bestowing comparatively privileged and enhanced life chances, lifestyles, security, self-actualisation, power, status and satisfaction for the 'successful' middle class kids, and the exact opposite for the 'failing' working class kids, who experienced infinitely higher levels and rates of social and economic deprivation, unemployment, ill health, mental breakdown, divorce, frustration, poor housing, crime, imprisonment, exploitation and powerlessness.

It seems unequivocal that the British state education system was (and still is in some counties that have retained the 'selective' school system, one of which is Kent), inherently corrupt, benefiting middle class children and handicapping working class children. The UK is obsessed with social class and maintaining the power and privilege status quo, resistant to change and begrudging of the successful 'lower' classes. Strangely, the working class still (metaphorically at least), doff their caps in unwavering deference to their (supposed) middle class social superiors.

Thankfully, mum and dad never made us feel that we were inferior to anybody, regardless of any characteristic or trait, including gender, race, or social class, that may have distinguished others from us. They both encouraged, advised and supported us in their own way. Mum was mainly hurt and angry. How dare anybody treat her children unfavourably?! Dad was more naive and idealistic, unsullied by any personal experiences of racism, he sincerely felt all we needed to do was work hard, "*study your books!*", and we'd succeed. Clearly, mum had a more realistic appraisal of what we were up against, having experienced the ravages of racism in Ireland at first-hand.

However, I think the combination of the two resulted in children with fairly balanced approaches to these matters. None of us have ever discriminated against others because of their race, colour, gender, culture or religious beliefs, and have always welcomed people, regardless of their backgrounds, into the warmth of our family. None, that is, except our youngest sister Kele. For some (inexplicable?) reason, in her mid- to late- 20s, she developed and freely expressed bigoted views against people from the Indian sub-continent generally, especially Pakistanis who she mockingly referred to as 'Ricky Ranis'; and 'West Indians' generally, Jamaicans especially, all of whom she referred to dismissively as useless, dirty, worthless 'reject' slaves. Which, if the truth be spoken, is an attitude I think she developed after living in Nigeria for several years, and it is shared by Nigerians in much the same way that 'Ja-my-cans' refer to Africans in the pejorative (divide and rule!).

If further truth be known, other than the above which is my attempt to explain the inexplicable in isolation, I really don't know what 'happened' to make her develop and harbour these views, but I hope she discards them eventually, if she hasn't done so already.

Six

Mum was under intense pressure throughout our time in Blean, to provide and care for her growing family, much of the time on her own while dad worked away in Chartham. We saw more of him when, one day, he bought a scooter which he drove to work on a daily basis rather than continue being an 'off-duty' dad. It was a Lambretta scooter, the type that 'Mods' became synonymous with in their 1970s heyday as they engaged in prolonged punch-ups with their hated 'Rockers' adversaries. Dad was THE worst driver on the face of this earth! He didn't seem to have any road-sense, and it was totally amazing how he wasn't involved in more accidents than were to eventually befall him.

Apparently dad was reassured by an obia (witchcraft) woman before leaving Nigeria that he would never die as a result of a car crash. I think this may have, in his own mind at least, absolved him from accepting any sense of responsibility on the road, safe in the knowledge that he wouldn't be killed on it!

The DVLA system was nowhere near as tight as it is today, because dad took his driving test 21 times and never passed it. But he always drove, badly! It also didn't help that the cars he bought were usually crap and forever breaking down. After having sent off for a renewal of his provisional driving licence, almost like manna from heaven (or divine pity!), the DVLA mistakenly sent him a full driving licence in return. He never declared the error and happily used this licence forever.

Many were the times he'd call us to give him a push-start and, come rain, sleet or snow, we'd always oblige. His scooter failed to start (yet again), in Blean and he summoned us all to get pushing. We dutifully obliged and, when the engine spluttered and kick-started, he gave it full throttle and he was away, careening down Chestnut Avenue to wend his way to work. The only problem on this occasion was that Obi had, for some reason best known to himself, held onto the rear parcel assembly above the wheel, and all we could see was him being dragged down the road, eating exhaust fumes, at ever-increasing speed as dad was clearly intent on making up on lost time. Fearful for him being killed or badly injured, we screamed at dad to stop, but he couldn't hear us. Luckily, Obi managed to let go and roll away when they reached the T-junction at the bottom of the road where dad *had* to slow down. An uninjured, totally embarrassed Obi came jogging back up the road, his cheeky grin splitting his face from ear to ear, to re-join us before we embarked on another journey through another day.

Another driving incident that involved Obi was when we'd been out on a family visit to friends. Dad had bought some old jalopy-looking thing that resembled a 1930s American depression-era Bugsy Malone mafia gangster type car. Hurtling (bone-shaking?) our way back home, all of a sudden, with the four of us crammed in the back seat and mum and dad up front, the rear door next to Obi flew open as we were swinging around a corner. Obi must have an instant and very effective survival instinct because, rather than allow momentum to drag him out of the car to almost certain death, he somehow managed to dive away from the gaping door and cling onto us as we simultaneously raised the alarm (synchronised screaming!), and dad stopped the car. Judging by the majority of taxis I've had the misfortune to be transported by in Lagos, it wouldn't surprise me if dad just sellotaped the door back in place and continued to run the car into the ground, before running it to its eventual and inevitable demise!

I also remember the front door of our house in Blean for two main reasons. The first was when I shat in my pants after walking home from school. I'd been dying to have a dump and, when I realised my bowels were close to taking the decision out of my hands, I left my mum, brother and sisters to run the remaining mile or so in a desperate attempt to beat the call of nature. Nature won! It was so cruel. I'd made it to my front door step only to lose the fight. I stood at the front door feeling totally and utterly ashamed and worthless as nature had its way with me. I stood there, motionless, until my brother and sisters got home to see my school regulation shorts sagging low behind me to the back of my knees (pretty much like the so-called gang-affiliated 'road-boys' of today wear theirs), stinking. Totally humiliating!

The 'back door' (which was actually to the side of our house) reminded me of one thing only. It was situated next to the toilet where I remember mum pulling what felt like yards and yards of tapeworm out of my arse one day!

The second reason I remember the front door is because that was where I stood pleading for my mum to stop doing what she was doing. As we rounded the path into our front garden after trekking home from school one afternoon, we saw mum leaning out of one of the front bedroom windows, throwing dad's clothes into a disorderly heap on the front door step and garden. We didn't know what had happened and why she was doing this, but it was painfully obvious mum was upset, distressed (deranged?), and certainly not the mum we knew. It was almost as if she didn't recognise us, her beloved children, as she gazed almost wildly at us and through us, with almost feral insanity. She didn't respond to our pleas, and continued ranting and raving, shouting and screaming as she continued to jettison dad's clothes outside.

We were all in tears, and stayed outside until dad got home. I think he'd received a call to get home as a matter of urgency, which he did. Mum was taken off to hospital, ironically, the same hospital that dad worked in, St Augustine's. She'd had a nervous breakdown under the relentless, grinding, and ultimately soul-destroying pressure of trying to survive, almost single-handedly at times, on and below the poverty line. There was also talk of dad having had a string of affairs with some Swedish women which had tipped mum over the edge, but my child's mind didn't really understand what 'affairs' meant and the impact on couples if either one had been caught, but I remember the distinct feeling that affairs are not supposed to happen.

Anyway, the 'talk' was never confirmed and, looking back, I never saw or sensed any evidence that he might ever have strayed. In fact, the complete opposite was the case. Dad adored mum, he was proud of her, he listened to her. He never, ever, hit her and never gave me the impression that these thoughts ever crossed his mind. To be fair, mum always appreciated this, and told me regularly that she'd been lucky with dad for these reasons:

"He's a good father to ye, he tries his best, he loves us all and he's never hit me."

Such sentiments and appreciative recognition may well have been more a statement and reflection of the norms of marriage and conjugal relationships at the time, especially amongst the working classes where women traditionally held lower status in the family hierarchy. Post Second World War working class families tended to be 'status-' or 'position-orientated', with the father being the main breadwinner and final decision-maker on all things and matters of importance. Certainly never to be challenged or questioned. Whilst this was generally true in our household, mum was no shrinking violet, and dad was able to share responsibilities with her without damaging his ego or any macho ideas he may have had about himself.

Mum was hospitalised for 6 to 8 weeks, which was a disaster for us. Not only did we miss her warmth and love intensely, we also missed her cooking! To be honest, dad wasn't a bad cook, but nowhere near as good as mum when it came to the food we were used to, and he seemed to fry everything! But he was fantastic when it came to cooking Nigerian dishes. Fu-fu, jeloff rice, plantain, chicken, egusi soup, pounded yam, semolina, fish. It was truly glorious!

There was a stage where mum didn't appear to be responding to treatment, and someone felt it would be a good idea for her to receive a visit from her two oldest children, in the hope that this would trigger and recharge her maternal instinct. Chi-chi was 7 or 8, I was 6 or 7. Fearfully trailing behind dad, we walked into what felt like a massively long, huge, smelly and cavernous ward, each side furnished with beds along the walls that were occupied by strange and disturbed-looking occupants. Mum was in a bed adjacent to a window, it was horrible, I hated seeing her here with these odd people who clearly weren't normal and had 'something wrong' with them.

What on earth was my mum doing in such company?!

We nervously sidled up to her bedside, fully conscious of the role we were expected to play and, on the face of it, the immediate outcome was that we failed. Mum seemed to look straight through us and showed no sign of recognising us as her children. This was THE most painful experience of my life. Mum didn't know me! She seemed to be glazed over and, to use one of her favourite terms, "away with the fairies." In their efforts to bring the mum that we knew back, both dad and the doctor gently urged and cajoled her, reminding and telling her that we were her children, but didn't appear to get much of a response.

We left under a very dark cloud. I've never felt so low and confused in my life, before or since. I didn't know why mum was the way she'd been during our visit, nor why she'd effectively denied and rejected us. It was all too much to bear for one so young.

It recently dawned on me that it probably wasn't coincidental that Chi-chi and I are possibly the most emotional among the five of us. We are an open and emotional family in general, and we are able to express our feelings as and when appropriate. But where things get intense, especially if it's concerning family-related matters, Ijem, Obi (especially), and Kele are far more able to keep their emotions in check, whereas Chi-chi and I are the ones most likely to go into meltdown and cry.

Interestingly, this would coincide with one of Sigmund Freud's many developmental theories in psychology. According to the eminent professor, both my sister and I would have been in the 'phallic' stage of psycho-sexual development where boys are fixated on their mothers (Oedipus complex), and girls their fathers (Electra complex). Freud argued that any trauma experienced by the child during this stage, if left unresolved, would result in future adult personalities and behaviours that would indicate such trauma. 'Regression' is one of these personality traits and, without doubt, both Chi-chi and I cry (regress), at the drop of a hat when emotive issues threaten or impact on our family.

Eventually, we started to receive the news that mum was improving, dad started to find a spring in his step again, and the mood at home began to lift. We went to visit her again and she was much better, and I knew it would be only a matter of time before mum would be back with us. The mum we knew and loved. Our mum. Not the strange person with the vacant (sedative-induced?) expression we'd seen in the mental hospital.

We were SO excited and happy when mum came home. She had that same sparkle in her blue-grey eyes and the same warmth in her heart on being reunited with her brood. Her homecoming was totally joyous!

That's not to say things got any easier for us financially, or that mum had lost any of her passion, quite the opposite in fact. She returned full of vigour, resolve and purpose, and so did the hidings she dished out. Whereas I always preferred the physical beatings as opposed to the mental anguish of her ignoring me completely for days on end, I remember mum screaming at me for something I'd done wrong (yet again!), and ordering me to get up to my bedroom and ready for bed. So early in the afternoon? I knew what was coming. Mum always had the knack of perfect timing and, on this occasion, she burst into my room when I was stark naked and started to beat the doo-doo out of me with a piece of wood (I can't remember exactly what it was, but it felt like a Yule log!). Now I *knew* the mum we loved was back!

To this day I never fail to be intrigued by the apparent cultural differences between groups of people when, in discussion with friends, family and colleagues, reminiscences consistently indicate clear disparities between reasons for, quantity, and severity of childhood beatings. I've noticed, almost without exception, that white people my age appear to have rarely been beaten by their parents when they were young and, when beatings are reported, they seem exceptionally mild in comparison to my own experience.

On the other hand, when having the same type of 'back in the day' reminiscing sessions with black African/Caribbean friends, family and colleagues, routine, daily beatings with anything close at hand ranging from a belt, ruler or tree trunk seems to have been the common, shared experience.

The question for me is: just how true are these stories? And, if indeed they are true, what is it that has happened in the black African/Caribbean experience that has resulted in having parents who are quick to resort to corporal punishment in order to resolve all and, sometimes, any domestic situations?

In my mind, there is a similarity between this phenomenon and the propensity for the self same status/position-orientated family structures of the traditional white working classes. Here, family dynamics tend to be dictated by the breadwinning husband-father, who comes home from mind-numbingly boring, tedious and repetitive work, where he has no sense of self-worth, status, or meaningful responsibility. So, who does he take out his frustrations on? Answer: his family.

It wasn't that long ago that queues of wife-mothers could be seen forming at the doors and windows outside pubs every Friday night, waiting to get the timing just right as to when to dash in, request the house-keeping money from her husband before he drank it all, and then flee with the money safely in-hand!

White working class children, much like black African/Caribbean children, when they had the temerity to ask for an explanation as to the decisions of their dads, were often told:

"Because I'm your Father!"

or

"Because I tell you!"

Thus reaffirming his status as head of the household, and more importantly, never to be questioned.

It probably made these fathers feel satisfied that they were 'kings of their own castles', after all, "an Englishman's home is his castle", but it certainly didn't encourage logical reasoning, speaking, listening and thinking skills among their children. And often out of frustration they'd resort to 'the belt' to resolve issues, thus teaching the child that, if an issue can't be resolved through discussion and negotiation, then brutality is the next legitimate step.

Historically, 'traditional' white working class family culture, it can be argued, set down its roots very firmly during the industrial era when the overwhelming majority of working class families, men, women and children, worked on production lines, up chimneys and on machinery, where very little, if any, skill was needed to complete the job task. Certainly, little status or prestige was given to the industrial manual worker, who was always at the behest of the supervisor, foreman or factory owner.

Certainly, direct comparisons can be made with the colonial 'subjects' of the 'Great' British empire of the day, and their relationship with the District Governors of the colony; and even more so with the slaves in the Caribbean and Americas, who had zero status on the plantations where they were worked to death by their plantation overseers and their slave-owning masters.

It seems Igbos, "the Jews of Africa", were considered to be industrious and bright, so Nigeria's colonial Governors regularly appointed Igbo men (not only were the Imperialist Governors racist, they were patronisingly sexist also!), to relatively important administrative positions to act as their eyes and ears, translate, scribe, and generally help run their local districts.

Interestingly, though highly-prized and sought-after, Igbos were also well known for "not making good slaves", and were the ones most likely to commit suicide (often by throwing themselves overboard from the slave ships at any and every opportunity), rather than suffer the indignity of the 'middle passage' and the ignominy of slavery. Apparently, Igbo culture supports and promotes individual success, the "I" where, in comparison, Yoruba culture supports and promotes collective success, the "We". So, where Yorubas were more likely to attempt to arrive at survival as a group, Igbos couldn't bear the personal shame and disgrace, so were far more likely to attempt and actually commit suicide.

The famous story of Eboe Landing in St Simons, Georgia, provides ample testimony of this daunting feature of the slave trade:

47

"It is said that the chanting of Igbo people can still be heard at the mouth of Dunbar Creek. The creek is near Sea Island on the southeast coast of St Simon Island. In the 1850s a group of chained enslaved Igbo people were being held on the beach. They had just arrived in America on board the slave ship, The Wanderer, which crashed when the vessel ran ashore. While being held on the beach, the slaves made a suicide pact. Instead of living the rest of their lives in chains, they ran, chained to each other, into the water and drowned. The site is supposedly haunted by their ghosts, with people having reported hearing irons chattering as the slaves ran from the beach into the water.

This saga influenced the slave tale of 'The Flying Negro'. This tale inspired the slave population of America and still exists in storytelling today. The story's emphasis on the Igbo emphasises the magical and mystical aura creole slaves saw African-born people in, with the story ending with a group of Igbo people flying back to Africa with a slave ship. Igbos, through the assurances of Oba, an Igbo leader, believed:

"The water took you, and the water will bring you home."

That's not to say Igbos didn't become slaves. Hundreds of thousands, indeed millions, were forcibly transported across the Atlantic as chattels of the British Empire and other European slaver nations. Embarking from two major sea ports in the Bight of Biafra, Bonny and Calabar, once enslaved, they were highly sought after by the slave masters for exactly the same reason as their popularity among the settler Governors, namely their industriousness and intelligence. Also, Igbos tend to be far more lighter skinned than Yorubas and Hausas (the other two main ethnic groups that make up the majority of Nigeria's conservatively-estimated 150 million population), and were often, as a result of their lighter skinned complexion, more sought after as the unwilling bed-partners of rapist overseers and slave masters.

Female Igbo slaves were worth approximately three-quarters the value of Igbo male slaves, which was unusual in that male slaves tended to sell for much more money than females. The reason for this among female Igbo slaves (similar to those from the Congo), was their high fertility rate and maternal instincts, they actually cared for their children and attempted to organise a semblance of 'family life' even under the inhumane plantation existence of the slave states.

In Jamaica, especially in the parish of St Elizabeth, people with lighter complexions are, to this day, often referred to as "Red Ibos!"

If there's one thing that traditional Nigerian families, especially Igbos, are obsessed with, outside of status, pride, prestige and money, that thing is education. Gaining a 'good' education, especially to degree level, is very important in Nigerian society and culture, indeed, the Nigerian psyche. Nigerians, possibly as a result of colonialisation and the recognition that actually being bright, intelligent, and able to read and write, is advantageous, are driven to achieve academic excellence (not that there are the sufficient number of professional jobs actually in Nigeria to enable its burgeoning number of graduates to obtain gainful employment!). So much so that parents will ignore virtually every other detail of their children's lives, but will always, without fail, every day, remind their children to:

"*Study your books!*"

Often in conversation, discussion, debate and argument in Nigeria and among Nigerians living abroad, where one protagonist wishes to deliver the ultimate put-down to his or her adversary, the following one-liner is usually sufficient to shame and embarrass:

"You noh go school?!"

I knew every day when I got home from school that, without fail and with unwavering consistency, the first words dad would utter would be, in ascending order of importance:

"How was school?"
"What did you study today?"
"Do you have homework?"
"Go and study your books!"

If I ever mentioned anything unrelated to books and studying, he wasn't in the least bit interested and totally ignored me, not wishing to engage in any other topic of conversation like sports or leisure pursuits, teenage stuff, whatever. He just didn't want to know! And where we made the mistake of failing, or getting in trouble at school, thus adding to dad's frustrations, we'd be in even more trouble at home, which usually meant a variety of only one outcome. Beatings!

Seven

Black people, the descendants of slaves, in the Caribbean and the Americas tend to, significantly, share another feature of the huge legacy of colonialism and slavery with Nigeria and Africa in general. And that is an obsession with skin colour:

"Colourism".

To be more specific, whether a person is light-skinned or dark-skinned, and whichever other description lies in between.

To be light-skinned, it seems, is the preference.

On both sides of the Atlantic, lighter skinned black people tend to experience and enjoy higher social, economic and political status, prestige, power and privilege. So much so that, even today, thousands (if not millions), continue to bleach their skins with creams and oils, and ingest tablets in order to lighten their skin colour! Michael Jackson wasn't the first, and he definitely won't be the last!

In the so-called enlightened west, Europe, the UK, England, London, it's still common place to hear young black men referring to "lighties" in their descriptions of the girls they prize most highly and in whom they invest most time and effort to pursue.

It's also still commonplace to hear young black girls and women articulating their dream to:

"Marry a light-skinned guy so my babies will be light-skinned and have 'good' hair."

It was very evident in my youth and early adulthood that lighter skinned mixed-race children were the 'trophy' partners of both blacks *and* whites. So it's probably quite accurate and honest to say that I 'benefited' from this situation! I always had stacks of girls chasing me. My younger sister Kelechi regularly complained that she'd been reduced to secretarial and telephonist duties at home, screening my calls and providing strings of girls with excuses as to why I wasn't available. More often than not there was usually only ever one explanation, I was with (yet) another girl!

Clearly, once the invading imperialists' physical battles had been won by virtue of the power of the gun, the settlers and slavers also won the battle for the minds of their (African) subjects and (Caribbean) slaves, through the imposition of the Bible. Lamentably, the results of such conditioning still live with us today! As black people, many of us are still in psychological chains. We still want to be (white) like massuh!

So, Nigerians gained, and continue to gain, their status through education, which they value most highly. In the UK educational success statistics support this view. First and second generation black children of African descent tend to do far better academically than those of black Caribbean descent, especially boys, who tend to underachieve academically when compared with virtually every other group, and tend to (disproportionately) make up the majority of school exclusions and PRU (off-site Pupil Referral Unit) populations.

Undeniably, the legacy of racism includes the destruction of the black (African) family. Today in the UK, Black African-Caribbean families are almost all (and for all intents and purposes) single-parent units, overwhelmingly headed by women. It seems the impact of slavery, where marriage amongst slaves was impossible in most cases, with 'couples' languishing under the threat of being sold away to another plantation owner, has resulted in black fathers abdicating their responsibilities to their partners and children, and black mothers accepting the probability that she'd be raising her children single-handedly.

Has single-parenthood among black African-Caribbeans become almost a tradition that has been passed down from the plantation? Certain things seem synonymous with the Caribbean, such as artistic creativity, as well as athletic and musical ability, especially (but by no means exclusively), in Jamaica.

Jamaica, an ex-slave plantation island in the Caribbean, apart from music, Rasta, ganja and lightning-bolt sprinters, is also synonymous with violence, both domestic and public. Where the public variety is often put down to warring political factions, the domestic variety may well be the result of frustrated, disempowered and emasculated men, men who have never enjoyed responsibility and a realistic sense of self-determination and purpose, a mind-set that may possibly (probably?) have developed under the enforced dehumanisation and degradation of the black slave on the plantation, and the black male slave in particular.

Another interesting facet that Nigerians and Jamaicans share is that, when white English people talk about Africans and West Indians, invariably they are referring to Nigerians and Jamaicans! It's almost as if Africa was in Nigeria, and the Caribbean was in Jamaica! It's even more interesting that in predominantly white western societies where 'the black problem' exists, invariably it is Nigerians (probably Igbos!), and Jamaicans (probably descendants of Igbos!), who aren't taking shit from anybody and aren't afraid to let it be known!

My first experience of this group resistance, other than the protest marches I attended as a 10-year old with my dad in London in support of Biafra during the Nigeria-Biafra civil war, was later in my mid-teens when 'Paki-bashing' was the Friday night sport of choice for the thick, pea-brained, nicotine-stained, knuckle-dragging, tattooed, aggressive, beer-swilling, drink-fuelled white working class thugs. We've all seen them, the little Englanders who indignantly whinge:

"Fucking blacks and pakis, taking our jobs and houses, shouldn't be allowed!"
"Aint no black in the Union Jack!"
And so on.

It wouldn't be that long before those same blacks and pakis would be taking their women as well, the same women these Neanderthals would be going home to beat and abuse after, and to cap off, a "good night out on the beer with the lads!"

It astonished me and my black friends how Asian youths would take such severe beatings by these guys and not retaliate! It became so sickening and intolerable that we'd steam in on behalf of the 'Pakis' being bashed, to turn things around. First generation African-Caribbean youngsters, increasingly born and bred in the UK, weren't prepared to take those beatings or stand by to watch them being meted out to other children of immigrants. We soon developed a reputation not to be messed with and, if you do, be prepared to slug it out!

However, much like the lesson we were being indirectly taught that violence is a legitimate means to solve problems indoors, it seemed the same applied out on the streets as well. Black youngsters, by virtue of our refusal to accept racially-aggravated beatings and to fight back, soon became feared by the thugs, but also prioritised by the police and demonised in the press and wider media.

Getting back to the subject and vagaries of skin colour, of the five of us, Chi-chi, Obi and Kelechi are relatively light-skinned, and all three have green eyes. Obi's twin sister Ijem and I, in comparison, are relatively darker skinned with brown eyes. When pushing the twins in their ramshackle pram as babies, my white mum was often stopped in the streets around Kentish Town in north London by white passers-by who'd want to peek in to see and 'coo' at the babies. This 'cooing' was often accompanied by the statement:

"Ahhhhhh, isn't he cute!" (referring to Obi, with his light skin, green eyes and blonde curly hair).

This was almost instantly followed up by the question:

"Are you looking after *that* one?" (referring to Ijem, with her darker skin, brown eyes and black curly hair).

Obviously, mum would react with exaggerated indignance to such comments, proudly proclaiming that both children were hers, and making it quite clear to the ignorant white English that she didn't appreciate such comments about her children. Mum was such a proud fighter from day one!

Whilst genetics intrigues me, I suppose it doesn't or shouldn't really amount to much. That is if we weren't so damned obsessed with magnifying the arbitrary differences that exist between us. After all, as I've stated previously, none of us chose to be born the way we were, none of us determined our gender, skin colour, class or caste, citizenship status or nationality, before making our grand entrances onto the world stage.

As the venerated English scribe William Shakespeare observed in his 'As You Like It' monologue:

"All the world's a stage:
And all the men and women merely players"

We are merely players, so I suppose we really ought to judge our achievements in life by HOW we play the game of life, before we make our exits!

So what is it that lurks among us (in our DNA?), that drives us to segregate and discriminate, with birds of a feather flocking together for the dual purpose of defensive safety as well as predatory action? Some might label this as the classic behavioural characteristics of the racist. Firstly, like-looking and like-minded (ignorant and insecure) people clubbing together to cement and exalt their shared characteristics, then secondly, to exaggerate the differences between themselves and non-group members who, by definition, must be inferior and therefore legitimate targets for disdain and discrimination.

But what happens with the hybrids, the 'half-castes', the mixed-race kids who are neither black nor white, who don't 'belong' on either side?

My experience, being born and bred in post-war 1950s England as a first generation child of immigrants to the UK, is that white people don't, or can't, make the distinction between mixed-race and/or lighter-skinned people and darker-skinned black people. So long as you're not white, you're black.

"They're all the bleedin' same!"

And thus, by convenient automatic default, worthy of their instant derision and rancour.

In retrospect, it's quite possible much of the reactions we received from neighbours and strangers were racially-motivated but, at the time, we put them down to OUR fault for being noisy and boisterous when out playing. As a child, your local environment and neighbourhood is your world, to be explored and conquered. So to be screamed at by angry others:

"Clear off back to your own end!"

And on occasions:

"Clear off back to your own country!"
came as quite a shock, because we didn't understand.

Without question, black people, in my experience, are far more accepting and open, and far less likely to discriminate against others. Very rarely has it been the case that, as a mixed-race person, I've felt unwanted or that I don't belong in the company of other black people. Black people tend to be more inclusive and welcoming, and more interested to learn about you as an individual, than white people.

However, that's definitely NOT to say that ALL black people are like this. Many have been quite open in their resentment and rejection of me *because* I'm mixed-race (and accepted by the black group), and for no other reason. After being accepted by the (black) group, it's easy (only natural?) to slip into the black mindset and assume there are no issues. Wrong!

I've been told by ignorant black people that:

"You're not black though!"

The implication being that, by virtue of being half white, I don't fully qualify or belong to their exclusive 'black only' club and, as such, shouldn't be enjoying full status and membership rights which, I think in their warped manner of thinking, they probably feel they've fought hard for as 'full' black people, so why should a half-caste benefit? On the occasions this has been said or intimated in company, it's often been accompanied by the abject embarrassment of the other black members of the audience.

Initially such rejection is painful. It hurts!

Imagine the situation:

Born and bred in England, constantly discriminated against and racially abused by white people, taunted with foul, racist bile and invective. It's inevitable (even as an identifiably mixed-race person), to develop a black identity, and to experience, see and relate to the world through the eyes of a black person. Constantly being referred to as a 'black this' and a 'black that' eventually leads to you adopting the mindset and characteristics of the label. That's definitely what happened in my case.

And then to be rejected by that black group, your reference group that you grew to feel safe in, to stand up for, to represent, and to fight for. It's painful. As social human animals, the need to 'belong' is a very powerful survival instinct and mechanism that, once threatened, triggers the 'fight or flight' mechanism in many of us. With the strong parents we had, we chose to fight!

Life has a way of making us more resilient.

"What doesn't kill you will only make you stronger!" (and, as in my case, fatter!).

I grew to actually enjoy the odd occasion when 'black' ignorant people voiced their feelings, thoughts and, what was essentially, evidence of their own self-doubt, insecurities, lack of knowledge and fear. Despite their claims to some sort of black racial superiority, none of them were aware of their own racial or cultural history. I enjoyed educating them about themselves, and letting them know their ignorance was a "disgrace to the race".

Revenge truly is a dish best served cold, and I enjoyed watching these unconscious arseholes eat humble pie, especially when rounded upon, shouted down and laughed out of sight by their own 'black' brothers and sisters.

I understand the process though. Being observably closer to massuh, even if only by virtue of being lighter-skinned or with straighter hair, was used by white settlers and slavers to generate and sustain essential 'divide and rule' policies and practices.

"If you're white, you're alright."

"If you're brown, stick around."

"If you're black, stay back!"

Engendering such practices was essential because, whether in colonial Africa or the Caribbean and American slave plantations, whites were always in the precarious and overwhelming minority. So, such a divisionist approach was pivotal to maintaining authority over the (previously) 'pagan', 'mumbo-jumbo-believing' black majority. Despite the fact that this perceived legitimate authority was tenuous at best, it became so ingrained it actually worked to the point where black African/Caribbean/American people continue to exacerbate differences between ourselves today!

Colourism, as currency, has retained its value over hundreds of years. Whites still remain in power and are the assumed and often perceived 'betters'; brown people are probably far more likely to continue to enjoy social, political and economic advantage in comparison to their black brothers and sisters; blacks, invariably, remain at the bottom of the socio-racial hierarchy, and are tasked to continue to serve, survive and endure the ravages of the historically and socially-constructed ill-effects of colour-coding.

A similar syndrome also exists in Nigeria, but it's never been my experience that it's delivered to cause pain or to mark you out as different. In fact, the opposite generally tends to be the case. Nigerians in Nigeria tend to be excessively welcoming and inclusive. However, again very much like Jamaicans, Nigerians are far more likely to address you in the form of a literal description based on how they see you. So, though totally gutting at first, as I make my way around certain (usually rural) areas in Nigeria I've now grown used to being hailed:

"Onyeocha!"
"Beke!"
"White man!" - (I suppose compared to many in Nigeria, I am virtually white!).

I understand the greetings are made sincerely and not in the pejorative or with malice.

Whilst living and working in Jamaica for a year, Jamaicans called me "Big Man!" and "Brown Man!" as they asked me to "queeze up and mek room" for more passengers to enter the minibus. I always wondered why people didn't take offence, and I learnt it was because no offence was intended, so women being hailed in the streets as they sashayed past often took the descriptions about them as compliments:

"Hey! Red gyal inna de red dress!"
"Hey! Fat gyal!"
"Hey! Brown gyal!"

In a society where being lighter-skinned ('red' or 'brown'), or of bigger, rounder proportions, then it's more likely that being referred to in such a manner is very definitely a positive description and, as such, willingly and appreciatively accepted.

In the UK, publicly announcing such literal descriptions would be severely frowned upon, with the caller being rejected by the receiver as one not worthy of their attention at the very best, and at worst writing him off as a racist, misogynistic, chauvinist pig, with every chance of a physical fight leading to police intervention, arrests, charges and convictions of some public order offence or another!

Eight

I referred to William Shakespeare earlier. Apparently he was a fantastic story writer and teller. But he was nowhere near as good as my mum!

Mum missed a great calling in life as she fought against all odds to drag and bring us up, and that calling was the ability to tell wonderful stories. I don't think she'd ever kissed the Blarney Stone in Ireland, so she must have been *born* with the gift of the gab, the ability to tell a story and totally captivate and enthral her willing and appreciative audience, us!

Worryingly though, the stories she always told us were without fail always of the horror variety. I mean Hammer House of Horror! With main characters who were, by coincidence, young children "about your age". I don't remember mum ever telling us a story about toys and teddy bears, pixies and elves, and sweet little children skipping around the place with gay abandon. Mum's characters were always naughty kids who, invariably, were up to no good and got caught bang-to-rights, usually on a cold, dark night, deep in the woods, alone (or never any more than two in number!), who were desperately trying to escape a giant one-eyed dog that was loping after them, its main aim to devour them for the dastardly deeds they'd committed. These deeds generally ranged from being noisy, fighting with their brother or sister, not tidying up their bedroom, any manner of 'being naughty', and "woe betide" the child who dared to speak back to their parents!

The panic-stricken children always made it to the little log cabin situated in a clearing in the woods. But the bloody door was always locked with a rusty latch that couldn't be prised open! The children would scream and wail in terror as the light in the eye of the giant one-eyed dog got bigger and brighter as it bounded towards them, lips and jowls covered with dripping and foaming saliva as it snarled and growled in its descent upon the frantically screaming and cowering children. The children would start to claw at the door, blood streaming down its structure as their finger nails ripped out of place in their panic-driven battle for safety just beyond the obdurate door!

The endings always depended on how good or bad we'd been that day, and ranged from the children (miraculously somehow), making it to safety inside the cabin with the door giving way just in time to allow them entry, or the light in the giant one-eyed-dog's eye turning out to be a lantern being held by their 'saviour' mum or dad who'd been relentlessly and heroically searching for them through the forest, or they'd simply get ripped to shreds and eaten by the giant one-eyed dog.

Whichever ending was served up, we loved these stories! We'd beg to be told them and would gather around mum, settle down, and wait to be whisked away to a wonderland of terror! No doubt we all realised that we were the characters, and the morals of the stories always seemed to be directly related to the misdemeanours we'd committed during the day, and inextricably linked to the miscreant(s) gathered rapt and adoringly at mum's feet!

Mum was born in the Land of the Little People, the enchanted 'Emerald Isle' of Ireland, where Leprechauns would appear as if by magic, with a sagacious look on their faces and a mischievous twinkle in their eyes, to tell spell-binding lyrical yarns of days, events and people gone by, as they sat on top of the inevitably ever-present rustic rickety rural fence. She clearly inherited the ability to tell a great yarn!

She also completely inherited the Irish inclination to believe in fate and superstition. Black cats, walking under ladders, salt over the shoulder, dropped cutlery, lucky numbers, star signs, the list of things to avoid or to be mindful of seemed endless! I must admit though that I adopted her lucky numbers 1 and 5 for some reason, and I guess to some extent I've been pretty lucky in life though, if you ask me, I think I worked hard to earn the luck that came my way!

It was whilst still living in Blean that we first started to meet some of dad's friends from Nigeria, the first real time I remember meeting other black people, and dad would really enjoy the opportunity to speak Igbo with them. We all found it really frustrating because it was obvious dad loved speaking Igbo, but he never spoke to us in Igbo! We could, and should, have been raised to speak both Igbo and English!

My inability to speak Igbo remains one of my few main regrets in life. Being able to speak Igbo would have been a real blessing. There weren't that many opportunities for us to speak it during our childhood and youth, but on our now very many visits home to Nigeria, it would have been liberating to be able to speak it.

However, strangely enough, I did develop the ability to follow conversations in Igbo which, when spoken, is often spattered with English words anyway. It seems on my return from Nigeria and upon my incarceration at the Dr Barnados children's home I was very adept at speaking pidgin English, the 'brokin' English that is commonly spoken throughout West Africa, but particularly sweet-sounding and easy-on-the-ear from Nigeria. Not that I'm biased at all! I think it's possible my apparent easy ability to learn and speak 'foreign' languages later in life may be linked to the listening skills I developed in the company of dad and his friends. I'm very proficient in French and German, which I learnt formally at school, as well as Portuguese and Spanish which I learnt 'off the bat' on my travels in Europe and south America.

Incredibly, I actually joined the Cub Scouts while we lived in Blean. Please don't ask me why! I think a couple of my classmates were members of a Cub Scout 'pack', the headquarters for which was situated just off St Stephens Hill in Canterbury. I think I must have had some urge to get out of the house, and this seemed quite a legitimate pursuit for that purpose. I remember being a member for a few months, and waiting ages for the arrival of my cub uniform, so I had to attend in civvies until it arrived (a euphemism for when mum could afford to buy or knit it!), not that I really cared! I was the only black boy in the pack, so it didn't make any difference that I had no uniform, I already stuck out!

We went on a really enjoyable week-long camp out in the country-side, for which mum gave me the princely sum of a thruppenny bit, thruppence, three old pence for pocket money. I spent all of it on a present for her and, upon receiving it, she scolded me for not having spent it on myself. Though deep-down I think she was totally chuffed and made up at the idea I'd thought of her before myself. So, when the other cubs were spending their pocket-money (which seemed like absolute fortunes to me!) on treats and sweets for themselves, I went without. Which didn't bother me; I was used to going without, and I got my kicks from adventure!

I really wanted to join the pack, and remember practising and rehearsing the UK Cub Scout Promise, Law and Motto:

"I promise that I will do my best, to do my duty to God and the Queen,
to help other people, and to keep the Cub Scout Law"
"Cub Scouts always do their best, think of others before themselves, and
do a good turn every day"
"Be prepared"

If truth be known, I've probably flopped miserably on the Promise, I'd like to think I've done pretty well on the Law and, at 58 years of age, I think I'm pretty much prepared for most things that life might send my way!

I don't think I've always 'done my best'. If I had I would have been far more successful than I have been. But how do we measure and quantify 'doing your best', and 'success' for that matter? Both of these things are constantly evolving and relative concepts. I could have worked a lot harder, been more focused and serious, less profligate, but unhappy and morose in life. Sod that!

As for 'doing my duty to God and the Queen'. No chance!

Whilst still in Blean I was a choirboy in the village church (where Chi-chi began playing the organ), would you believe? I even sang solo at a Christmas mass! It brought tears to everybody's eyes (I didn't think I was *that* bad!). I attended my first funeral, as a choirboy, at this church, which was in a very rural setting set far back off a country lane. The spooky type of place mum would tell us stories about in fact! Chi-chi and I would have to perform three times a day every Sunday. I couldn't stand it, getting dressed up like a tart or Christmas turkey in the black and white liturgical vestments of habit and surplice. But dad was *so* proud; he loved the church, God, singing and solemnity. This wasn't the way I wanted to spend my free time! The seeds of my disdain and rejection of God and religion were irreconcilably sown.

It would be inaccurate for me to say I haven't 'done my duty to the Queen'. I have done, and continue to do so every month, in the form of the taxes I've paid to her and her free-loading offspring and entourage, to keep them in a manner to which they have become accustomed. What hurts even more is that I have no choice in this arrangement. It's taken out of my wages before it hits my bank account. With regard to allegiance, I would abjectly fail the (Norman) 'Tebbit Test', and would probably also fail the current Citizenship and Nationality tests in which contemporary immigrants to the UK endeavour to succeed, in the hope of gaining British citizenship status.

I'll be honest. I can't stand hearing the English National Anthem. Every time it's played on the television before international football matches and other events, I turn the volume off, as opposed to standing up with hand on heart. Every time I see the Queen and representatives of the monarchy in their pomp and splendour, I see evidence and remnants of the spoils of local exploitation and oppression, and of global slavery and colonialism.

And as for that dirge (in my eyes and ears) "Rule Britannia"! How foul and obscene?

Here we have a so-called civilised and developed first-world country, revelling in their nautical history of pillaging and looting around the world, boasting about their raping and murdering conquests in far-flung regions, disgusting and despicable:

"Rule Britannia, Britannia rules the waves!
Britons never, never, never shall be slaves."

This from a nation that purports to be civilised, but continues to sing and gloat about its foul, thieving history and legacy, heading a 'Commonwealth of Nations' made up of the self-same previous subjects and slaves whose previously imposed status they swear never to be bestowed upon themselves.

My feelings and views are nothing personal. The English monarchy, Queen Elizabeth, Prince Phillip and their heirs, like everybody else, lords, serfs and peasants, industrialists and proletarians, upper, middle and working classes alike all had no choice as to the family and status into which they were born. I just can't stand what they represent. What I don't understand is the slavish idolatry the English monarchy continues to be afforded by its deferential minions. Incredible!

I've definitely 'helped people' throughout my life, and the Cub Scout Law became irrelevant and redundant in my life many years ago.

As a 7 year old boy the Cub Scouts, to me anyway, meant adventure and 'doing boys' stuff'. As a 58 year old man, and in light of the current headlining revelations concerning Jimmy Savile's alleged kiddie-fiddling paedophile indiscretions with underage girls *and* boys, I wonder about the motives of 'Lord' Baden Powell, the founder of the Boy Scout Movement. By definition underage *and* wearing uniforms. Hmmmmm. Anyway, I wasn't a member for very long before we moved house again, and my "dyb-dyb dob-dobbing (Do Your Best – Do Our Best) days of cub scouting ended prematurely!

After living in Blean for three or four years, dad was offered another hospital house in Chartham. St Augustine's hospital was in the same village, and the house on The Downs was only a 10 or 15 minute walk to work for him, though he still insisted on (attempting) to drive a range of clapped out cartons to and from work! So it made sense for us to pick up sticks and leave Blean. The house was a three-up-one-down, separate kitchen and bathroom arrangement with external brick-built shit-house converted into a coal shed.

Nine

The house on The Downs was scary, spooky even. Though semi-detached (this sounds very grand; it wasn't; more end-of-terrace!), and like the house in Blean, in the absence of central heating, freezing cold in winter. It was surrounded by woods and a spinney at the end of the garden, with massive fir trees. The side garden in front of the spinney became our 'Wembley' as our passion for football took hold. We'd have matches that would last all afternoon and often went late into the evening until mum called us in. First team to 20 was the winner, and the score always ended in hotly and bitterly disputed 20-19 cliff-hangers! The games were two-a-side, unless friends were around, in which case the numbers on each side would increase in accordance with the attendant number. Obi and I were always team captains, Chi-chi and Ijem made up the rest of the team, but were always second- and third-draft choices if we had mates around.

Chi-chi started her secondary school career at Chartham Secondary Modern School, while Ijem, Obi and I attended the local Chartham Primary School, where the twins started their schooling. Much like Blean, it was a red-brick building with concrete playgrounds at both sides, one of which bordered on an orchard. Amazingly, we weren't the only black family in the village! There was a mixed-race boy, Kevin Pace, who was adopted by a white family, and a black family called the 'Edwards' who lived on the same road as Kevin.

Another interesting factor regarding immigration to the UK is that the overwhelming majority of it is made up of economic migrants, involving people leaving their countries of origin for improved occupational opportunities. However, it's important to appreciate that this didn't happen in a random, haphazard manner.

It's not coincidental that, in towns and cities where there are large numbers of immigrant groups, they tend, generally, to have come from the same area of the world. This was a direct result of British government departments actively recruiting for specific types of workers for specific types of jobs in the UK. So, for example, the vast majority of black people in Reading, Berkshire, originate from Barbados and came in response to recruitment campaigns in their island; the same for the high number of people from St Vincent in High Wycombe, Buckinghamshire; Jamaicans in Brixton, south London; Trinidadians in Shepherds Bush, west London, and so on. If there was a shortage of bus conductors, road sweepers, postal workers, or nurses in any given area, the UK government would deputise the appropriate department to recruit from a certain Island region in the realm of its Empire.

This certainly explained the high number of black Africans and Caribbeans working in the health services and on London transport, and quite probably explained how Kevin and the Edwards family ended up in rural Kent. St Augustine's hospital recruited from members of the commonwealth just like most other hospitals and public transport organisations up and down the country.

Even more interesting was that the first really vicious fight I had with a relative stranger, was with the oldest son of the Edwards family, George. For a reason unbeknown to us, the Edwards family seemed to have a problem with our presence in the village community, there always appeared to be a simmering, undeclared enmity between us. I can't remember which school they attended, they didn't attend ours so maybe they were all at the local secondary modern school. Our walk to school meant we had to pass their road every morning en-route. Kevin had been the bearer of the news that 'big George' was planning to smash my head in, and would be waiting to intercept us on our way either to or from school.

The confrontation took place on our way to school one morning. Both George and I had our brothers and sisters as 'seconds' in our respective 'corners' (no gloves, gum-shields, towels, bottled water or dolly-birds were made available!), the 'ring' was a grassy patch on the roadside and Kevin acted as referee. It was a tough fight, he was very strong, quick and slippery, but I think surprised and unnerved by my strength and lack of fear at the prospect of fighting an older and bigger boy. I steamed in and went wild on him, throwing hay-makers like a threshing machine as if my life depended on it. It seemed to go on for ages, we both hurt each other with stinging and painful blows, but I wouldn't back off or capitulate. With both of us bruised and bloodied, the fight was ended by the arrival of the school bus that the Edwards took to school. Kevin announced me the winner, and the Edwards didn't argue but, more importantly, they never messed with me or my family again!

Mum started to train as a nurse at St Augustine's and, much to her credit, pride and pleasure, she qualified first as a State Registered Nurse (SRN), before going on to qualify as a Registered Mental Nurse (RMN), the same status dad had obtained. We were all really proud and pleased with mum's achievements, because her natural self-deprecatory disposition was to under-estimate her own ability through lack of confidence.

Dad suffered his first experience of racism, to my knowledge, whilst working at St Augustine's. Apparently he'd gone to use the toilet and, whilst sitting down in the cubicle evacuating his bowels, he sensed he was being watched. He looked up to see two white men peering over the tops of the adjacent cubicles. He flew into a rage and, after completing his ablutions, chased down his audience with a view to knocking the shit out of them. Both pleaded with him not to exact retribution on them, and thankfully he relented. But when he asked them what the hell they were doing watching him have a crap, they both said they wanted to check if it was true that black people had tails like monkeys!

Sometimes I wondered how mum and dad managed to understand and reconcile the ignorance of, and differences between, their racial backgrounds and cultures. How would dad have relayed this story to mum, and how would she have replied?

It was in Chartham that I also first became aware of the colour of my skin, and the fact that we were 'different' from all the others. Even more bizarrely, it was the 'fully' black Edwards children who were the first to refer to our skin colour in a derogatory manner. They actually taunted *us* as black so-and-sos! However, I was becoming increasingly aware from the comments and innuendos of teachers and classmates of my being 'coloured'. This troubled me because, whilst I knew I wasn't white, it didn't bother me, and I didn't care that virtually everybody else in my world was white. Why should it? After all, my mum was white!

It seemed our blackness clearly bothered them though.

I used to take stock of what it might have been that I'd done to offend, and couldn't come up with anything. Surely it wasn't the fact that Janet Brown (the prettiest girl in my class), had focused her attentions on me since my arrival in the school, and away from Bobby Mills, the blonde-haired blue-eyed ex-most-sought-after pin-up boy in the games of playground kiss-chase and behind 'the bicycle sheds'? I was aware of my popularity in my class, and being a faster runner and better than him at football, taking the school captaincy away from him shortly after my arrival. But being captain didn't matter to me, so long as I was playing, I was happy, and I didn't fancy Janet Brown anyway!

The school held annual, week-long 5-a-side football tournaments that were played on the concrete playground surfaces, with the whole school population of pupils and teachers watching every round of the knock-out tournament. England had won the World Cup at Wembley in 1966 for the first (and only) time in its history, and the whole country was obsessed with football. This playground tournament was our World Cup. It meant EVERYTHING to win it, and complete and utter devastation to get knocked out in the qualifying rounds or to lose it in the final.

Woefully for the boys, each team had to have one girl playing for it (which was an immensely laudable gesture at early Equal Opportunities Policy and Practice for the time!), and team members were randomly selected from the oldest three years in the school. Unbelievably, as captain of my team, Ijem and Obi were (randomly?) selected in my team, along with some fat kid who loved football but struggled to shift his bouncing bulk around without teetering over the verge of collapse, and another boy who was totally indifferent to football. He was totally laid-back and didn't really mind if he played or not. If he did, great, he was passable and made the effort, and if he didn't, he really didn't give a toss.

I was ecstatic that Ijem and Obi were in my team, confident in their ability, determination and drive to succeed, and devastated at the selection of the other two who, for different reasons, were, undeniably, total liabilities! Throughout the early rounds of the tournament, in which Kevin's team was eliminated, fat boy puffed and panted his way through in a committed, enthusiastic and eager-to-please way. 'Laid-back' did OK, but didn't overly exert himself.

Bobby Mills' team was, in comparison, sensational on paper, and the clear favourites to win the tournament outright, and I thought they probably would! But I wouldn't, I *couldn't* accept losing without going down fighting. Ijem, Obi and I played as if our family honour, if not our lives, depended on winning this tournament, and we made our way through to the final after a closely-fought extra-time semi-final. Bobby's team crushed all opposition as they made their imperious way to the final, with captain Bobby being compared with Bobby Moore as he captained England to winning the World Cup final against West Germany at the old Wembley stadium. We had no chance!

On the day of the final I tapped into the fever-pitched atmosphere and mood that engulfed the school in my pre-match team-talk. Ijem and Obi were safe, but Fat-boy and Laid-back needed serious motivating, inspiration and confidence-building. I felt like a warrior as I lead my team onto the pitch, *our* Wembley, which was surrounded with the entire school population either standing or sitting on those long school gymnasium benches, cheering and screaming wildly. I actually think we had the neutral and sympathy supporters on our side, whilst sweet-boy and bully with nose-out-of-joint Bobby received the *very* vocal support of his acolytes and friends.

Five minutes each way, we went 1-0 down early on. Fat-boy, panting and heaving with sweat pouring down his face looked deep into my eyes. I think he was ready to roll over like a jelly ring-doughnut and give up. Laid-back was actually up for it and tried his best which, in all honesty, was half decent. Late into the second half and playing out of our skins, I scored the equaliser that took the game into two minutes each way extra-time. Obi scored the winner, and all hell let loose among the hundreds of supporters at the final whistle, with Bobby Mills, his acolytes and bullies cowed into losers' despair. I *really* enjoyed being presented with the winners' trophy in front of the whole school and, cup in-hand, I deliberately sought eye contact with him, just to ensure he was in pain as he watched. We made deep yet fleeting eye contact, and it was confirmed, he was in pain!

St Augustine's hospital had extensive grounds that included a football pitch and tennis courts which, of course, we made regular use of, especially me and Obi. He was exceptionally competitive and athletic, and had natural flair and ability in most sporting pursuits. We also made full use of their indoor facilities, including table tennis and snooker, which I think was the only pastime I actually managed to beat Obi in on a regular basis, largely due to my longer reach advantage! Dad was brilliant at table tennis, and lawn tennis. Lawn tennis especially which, to my eternal shame, he thrashed me at when I was in my youthful and athletic peak and prowess at 19! He wasn't so good at cricket though. I've rarely felt such acute embarrassment as when he trotted on to the cricket green as last (ditch/hope/chance?) batsman. As he jogged on brimming with confidence, I wondered why he didn't appear to be running as smoothly as I would have expected him to. Then the reason became immediately apparent. He'd put his oversized pads on upside down, so his movement was severely impaired and restricted. After his mistake had been pointed out to him, and the howls of laughter had died down, including him laughing at himself, dad was out for a duck after being clean-bowled by the second ball.

Dad was a top sport, if not all-round sportsman.

We saw our first 'real' ghost at St Augustine's too, well, me and Obi did. We'd been playing football virtually all day with some mates on the hospital football pitch, which was only separated from the hospital mortuary by a cabbage filed. A dark night had begun to fall, and a mist had started to settle over the ground. All of a sudden our attention was attracted to this misty human-sized shape that appeared to be gliding at ground level through the cabbage field towards the mortuary. An instant, deadly silence fell among us, before we erupted into a silent panic-driven stampede home. Every man (well, boy) for himself! Needless to say, me and Obi were the first to make the 10 minute dash home!

Financially, things started to improve for us in Chartham, especially with mum now working full time as a nurse. Mum and dad would work alternate shifts, including the night shift, to make sure that either of them was always at home for us, especially to care for Kele, our youngest sister.

The world to be explored and conquered by us in Chartham was infinitely bigger than in Blean. Our house stood on the ridge of the South Downs that rolled its way towards Chilham and other distant destinations. The countryside in Kent is truly stunning, and the White Horse county is totally deserving of its title as the 'Garden of England', and it was our back garden!

Surrounded by green fields and golden meadows in the summer, these soon turned to cold, rutted, barren expanses during the bitter winter. The field down the road to our right that led in the direction of our school and the main part of the village was where we did potato picking towards the end of the summer. We got paid by the farmers per sack. We also nicked and sold sack loads privately in and around the village.

The cornfield immediately opposite our house became the venue for my next fight.

We'd got wind that Bobby Mills and his gang were out to get us, and I also think it may well have been Kevin that tipped us off. Kevin was fast becoming a bit of a match-maker of Don King proportions, and his hairstyle wasn't too far dissimilar either! Rather than hang around waiting to be picked off by any surprise attack, me and Obi decided to go on the offensive and take the fight to them, one at a time. We decided to take on the two leaders first, in the belief that, once having beaten them, their entourage wouldn't dare bring it on to us. So, Bobby Mills and his wing-man Michael Mulligan were our prime targets.

Michael Mulligan was dispensed with quite viciously and maliciously, tied to the trunk of a tree in a spinney to the rear of our house, slapped, punched and kicked, before we applied a tourniquet to the ropes that bound his wrists. He was soon crying, screaming, and begging to be released. We granted his request, on the condition that he never, ever, even thought about ganging up on us again in the future. He agreed, so we left him, still tied to the tree. To do this day we don't know who released him, but he kept his promise, until one day a year or two later when he had no choice.

Next, and most important on our two-boy hit-list, was Bobby Mills. I hid in the deep cornfield as Obi enticed him to come and fight. He was quite disdainful at the thought of beating Obi up but wanted to get the inevitable victory out of the way in the most expeditious manner. He confidently strode into the cornfield where he started to fight with Obi. Obi gave as good as he got before I intervened to deliver the killer, knockout blows that left him bloodied, bruised and beaten amid the trampled stems of somebody's future morning breakfast cereal. He was in a mess when we walked away, after having delivered the same warning as to his future conduct.

"Don't even think about ganging up on our family in the future!"

Another ginger-haired boy, Stephen Price, was a fully paid-up member of their gang, but wavered in his allegiances. On hearing about the beatings his gang leaders had suffered at our hands, he very soon switched his allegiances to us to become one of our 'friends'. I think his family were quite destitute also, because he was forever coming round our house to play, *and* eat! Mum cottoned on to his tactics and, after school one day, knowing he was walking in behind me, she shouted her hello to me, at the same cautioning me that:

"I hope that bloody Stephen Price isn't with you!"

I nearly died with shame and embarrassment for him. His face went bright red, even brighter and redder than his carrot-top, before he slunk back out of the door, never to return to our house. Mum was clinical like that. She didn't put on any airs or graces for anybody, refused to suffer fools gladly, and always spoke her mind directly, regardless of the consequences. If she thought something was so, it was so; there were no grey areas or ambiguities. We learnt never to bring any old Tom, Dick or Harry home for fear of them receiving instant (and what were later to become legendary), disapproving tongue-lashings from mum! I think, to some extent, I've taken much of this trait from mum, but I like to think I'm a bit more diplomatic and subtle with delivering the verbal hammer-blows than she ever was.

I had a 'special' friend in my class. She had straight, stringy blonde hair and, what was good about her, was that she was a real tomboy. So, absolutely nothing romantic between us, not even undisclosed mutual or one-way attraction, but Ann Holmes was great fun, as was her dim-witted little brother who we regularly encouraged to eat earthworms, which he did without protest, laughing like an idiotic, inbred, redneck hillbilly. Ann and I would sometimes buck up with each other on the walk to school and we'd chat, laugh and joke all the way.

One day during a half term break we were playing together around the remains of a disused quarry, along the side of which was a short-cut to school, the infamous 'slippery slip'. For some reason we decided to climb the 60 to 70 foot face of the quarry from bottom to top. Going up, though tricky, was doable, though Ann negotiated it with the ease of a mountain goat. Going down, on the other hand, was terrifying for me. I completely lost my nerve and unashamedly pleaded with her to help me down, which she did, without taking the piss or ridiculing me. I respected her for that.

The other side of the quarry was a long, steeply sloping hill field which, in snowy winters, was perfect for sledging down. Virtually every-body would be there, wrapped up against the cold, to hurtle down the snow-covered hill on a variety of home-made sledges, dustbin lids, flat bits of furniture, metal serving trays, basically anything that would slide. It was fantastic, exhilarating, exciting fun, shooting down the hill at ever-increasing speed with the bitter wind and cold biting your face until you levelled out and slowed down to a graceful snowflake-shrouded stop at the bottom. An essential part of the descent was to successfully aim and steer your sledge so as to avoid hitting a huge concrete-based, metal cattle trough at the bottom. We were all involved in near-misses, which added to the sense of danger and excitement on every death-defying descent.

Our senses were brought back to reality when a group of spoilt show-offs turned up at the top of the hill with a huge, 6-seater *real* toboggan that actually had steering reins and metal runners. The proud 'big boy' owners of this machine spent a bit of time loudly bringing attention to themselves and their brand new, super fast sledge which was, obvious to say, way above and beyond comparison with any other contraption on the slope. After a few dummy runs on the small, minor dips at the top of the slope, they eventually lined up once they were satisfied all eyes were on them. Everything and everybody fell silent as the envious crowd watched all six take a huge run-up to dive onto the sledge and shoot their way down at never-before seen, totally uncontrollable and breakneck speed to the bottom and, on this their maiden voyage, straight into the immovable ice-filled cattle trough!

Partway through their hurtling descent it became evident to the jealous observing masses at the top that these guys really do need, at some stage very soon, to alter the direction of their record-breaking debut run in order to successfully complete the ride. Having overloaded the sledge with six, the machine was totally unresponsive to the futile attempts of the front-rider to steer to avoid the inevitable. He failed miserably in his valiant attempt to correct the course of their descent, which ended in a wood-smashing, metal-bending, bone-crushing confrontation between sledge and cattle trough. The cattle trough won!

The sledge disintegrated into a totally unrecognisable mass of wood chip, sawdust and twisted metal. Even the riders were mangled to a pulp of bumps, bruises and broken limbs. To add humiliating insult to massive injury, the two rear-riders could see what was coming and rolled off before impact, the front four took the brunt of the impact as they smashed into the rusty, cold metal cattle trough, only for the other two who'd jettisoned to slide, almost surreally, into their severely injured mates to further compound their injuries. It was hilarious! We couldn't stop laughing on our way down to get a closer look and, when we got to within feet of the disaster area, we were shocked by the scene. The injured joy-riders lay moaning in excruciating pain, and, watching them roll around in the blood-covered snow, soon sobered us all up!

I really enjoyed attending Chartham Primary school. I think I was popular, I was a bit of a clown in the classroom, but nothing malicious, and much of it was to do with camouflaging my weakness in Maths. I was crap at Maths, always have been, always will be. I can add, subtract, multiply, divide and calculate percentages very well, so my practical, everyday, functional, working Maths is not a problem. But decimals, fractions, equations, logarithms, geometry, ratios and proportions, algebra, mensuration, Pythagoras and Trigonometry. What's all that about? No chance!

So it's fair to say I got distracted during maths lessons. I was really good at English though, and I developed a very keen interest in Personal, Social and Religious Education type subjects, human subjects, and I was always interested in trying to understand how and why people behaved the way they did, this always intrigued me. I'd love nothing better than to discuss ideas and issues, usually in the simplistic form of 'boys versus girls' debates in the classroom. I was confident, reasonably eloquent and quite articulate, certainly not shy, and always had an opinion on something!

Essentially, I was intellectually and academically bright.

To my amazement, this view didn't appear to be shared by my teachers! After having shown mum around the school one Parents Evening, proudly showing her my poster work on the walls and written work in my books (though not, clearly, the error-strewn red-corrected contents of my Maths exercise book!), we left the school to walk home. Holding my hand as we negotiated our way up the slippery slip, mum turned to me and said:

"Well Gos, it seems like you won't be passing your 11+ at the end of the year!"

I was stunned speechless for a while. I couldn't believe that my teachers had given my mum this message. I *knew* I was one of the brightest in the class, so how dare they say I won't pass the 11+! When I recovered from the shock, I simply said:

"Don't worry mum, I will pass it."
That was the end of the discussion.

The very next day saw the beginning of my increased effort in Maths, which I knew I had to conquer, even if only to pass this damn test! I told mum I'd be back late from school on certain days because I'd be doing extra Maths lessons with others in my class.

I was one of only four pupils to pass the 11+ that year in my school year. I was *so* happy and proud for myself and my parents, and flipped the figurative middle-finger at the school who'd so dismissively labelled me as a failure.

Working on Maths wasn't the only work I did at the time. Always conscious of money, or the lack of it, being an issue at home, I did my best to get as much paid work as possible. So I did a lot of potato and strawberry picking to help 'make ends meet' for my parents. I got a weekly paper round when I was 10, and was paid the princely sum of a 'bob' (one shilling) a week. Twelve pennies made a shilling, and twenty shillings made one pound in the pre-decimal currency of the land, which was introduced by King Henry II in his reign that lasted until 1175.

My one shilling per week wages was the equivalent of 5 pence in today's currency!

Interestingly, the guinea coin, currency at the time of King Henry's rule, was made of gold, and named after the Guinea coast in West Africa, which was fabled for its gold, Ghana (previously known as 'The Gold Coast') especially. As gold became more precious, the guinea coin went out of circulation as the increasing value of gold meant they were more valuable as collectors' items. It goes without saying that such coins were rarely, if ever, in the hands of the poor, to be either spent or collected!

Ten

This period of time also coincided with the catastrophe that was the Nigeria-Biafra civil war, which started on 6th July 1967 and finished on 15th January 1970. There were rumblings of war before we moved from Blean to Chartham. In fact, it was in Blean when I first saw my dad cry. Apparently, as hostilities between Biafra and Nigeria steadily worsened, with political gaps widening, Biafra was desperate to be 'recognised' as an independent nation. Most western European countries, especially Britain, were openly supporting Nigeria in their insistence on retaining Biafra and not allowing it to secede. Then, one day, the ex-French colony of Haiti in the Caribbean, 'recognised' Biafra, and rarely have I seen my dad so happy and joyful, tears of joy streaming down his face, shouting, singing and dancing around our front room. I didn't really understand what war and talk of independence was all about, but I did understand it meant everything to my dad.

Unknown to me until very recently, it was the Igbo slaves of Haiti that orchestrated the many slave uprisings in this troubled island. The Igbos refused to accept their sub/non-human slave status, and were responsible for the most violent and history-changing revolts in the annals of this sordid era. It seems Igbos were mainly transported to Jamaica, Cuba, Trinidad and Tobago, Belize, Hispaniola (to become Haiti after the rebellion), Guyana, Brazil, Maryland and Virginia in the USSA. Igbo slaves, along with Congolese and Angolans, were the slaves far more likely to commit suicide or to flee captivity. There is no coincidence in the fact that Igbos populated the Congo and Angola in very high numbers throughout earlier historical periods, and that the slaves from these two nations were just as likely to commit suicide or orchestrate rebellions as the Igbos.

I also understood that Britain was supporting Nigeria against Biafra, which pained dad, and by default, me also. My understanding at the time was that Britain didn't want to risk losing the extremely profitable proceeds of the oil trade which was starting to boom. The majority of Nigerian oil is concentrated in the south east region of Nigeria, Biafra, therefore Britain wanted Nigeria to keep Biafra under its wing, under its control, to keep the trade and profits from the oil industry coming Britain's way. It seems Britain has now established a track record of being very selective and adept at becoming involved in the political concerns of other countries around the world, especially when those countries are oil-producing nations!

Dad wrote to Colonel Ojukwu, applying to get involved in any future war effort, and received an appreciative written reply from the Biafran leader advising dad to stay in the UK to look after his family. Dad had already served Britain in the medical corps in South Africa, India and Burma during the Second World War, but desperately wanted to serve his homeland Biafra in their bid for independence. Dad became very actively involved in the Biafra Movement in London, often taking me and Chi-chi up to London to listen to speeches at Hyde Park Corner and then to participate in the ensuing demonstrations. I remember wondering where all these black people came from who looked and spoke like dad!?

I'd just turned 11 years of age when the war was declared. It was almost as if there was an immovable dark cloud hovering over our house and everything we did as news reports of losses and gains on both sides were broadcast. Like most people of my generation and older, I'm fairly certain if asked today about the war, most would probably only remember the television images of starving Biafran children with distended stomachs, suffering from extreme malnutrition and kwashiorkor as Britain very effectively helped Nigeria to annex and blockade Biafra into agonising submission.

This reminds me that we did, actually, have a television in Blean, which we brought with us to Chartham when we moved. It was *the* crappiest and cheapest available on the market monochrome mess that ever fell off a production line. It was so rubbish that it seemed it had taken the idea of black and white too literally, as all it really ever showed was programmes in differing shades of grey! Our friends used to talk excitedly and boast about their colour TVs, while we'd be at home 'imagining' colour on our telly, sometimes to the point of convincing ourselves that colour was, actually, seeping onto the screen!

This probably goes some way to explaining why we were forever playing outside, because, unlike the children and young people of today, our telly certainly didn't keep us sufficiently entertained indoors. Watching Miss World competitions was always hilarious with dad though. He'd sit in front of the telly and criticise, without exception, every contestant, without fail, and he'd find something unique about every one of them to justify his critiques.

He'd employ any combination of the following (and more!), to describe the contestants who still hadn't had the opportunity to explain how she'd "try to save the children of the world" if she won the contest:

"Ah ah! Diz one......"
..... get nose like tunnel
..... is too fat/thin
..... lips are too fat/thin
..... mouth is too big/small
..... eyes are too close together/wide apart/crossed-eyed
..... make-up is useless, she resemble clown foh circus
..... nyash (bottom) is too big/small
..... teeth are detty (dirty)/too wide apart/resemble a basket
..... legs are too big/skinny
..... get k-leg (knock-knees)/is bow-leg like she get rickets
..... is too tall/short
..... look like she get belleh (is pregnant)
..... too black/white/yellow into her mouth (to emphasise the contestant's depth of colour!)

..... get breasts like calabash

..... get head/face/nose/legs/ breast weh dey resemble goat/ namma (cow)

..... is a bush woman! (*the* ultimate of all put-downs!)

..... and so on. It was hilarious watching the show with him, and he'd always get the (wildly exaggerated but perfectly apt) description for each contestant spot-on!

Eleven

Another summer job I enjoyed was strawberry picking, and along with being able to eat as many as you liked, it paid quite well too! I met lots of different people from different backgrounds while strawberry picking, youngsters and middle-aged people mainly, and travelling itinerant workers, often referred to in the strawberry fields as 'pikeys'. Mum admonished me when I innocently used the term at home, and she explained that it was a 'horrible' word often used by the English to describe Irish people. Knowing mum was Irish, I never used it again. She did, however, say gypsy is a more acceptable term to use, because gypsies are travellers so, of course, we adopted the term 'gyppos'. We didn't realise that this term was also considered to be derogatory until much later in life.

Travellers arrived annually across the Kent countryside to earn summer wages during the harvest period. We worked with many whilst hop- and apple-picking. Quite often the older women of their travelling communities would turn up at our doorstep, selling bits and pieces, and especially lucky charms. Mum would take these women dead seriously, and never disrespected them! She always gave them the time of day, and never failed to buy some little trinket or another, so as to avoid any hex or bad luck being bestowed upon us by them. I still have a 'lucky' horseshoe in my house today. Superstition and the Irish!

It's interesting how repetitively cyclical life can be. England is made up of migrant workers, and has been so historically for millennia. Just as the 'gyppos' caused alarm and concern among the host population amid ludicrous fears and moral panics of jobs being 'stolen', houses being 'taken' and crime 'soaring' in the 1960s, fast forward 50 years and the same is being said about the eastern Europeans who are 'swamping' the UK. Replace 1960's Enoch Powell with 2014's Nigel Farage and the theme and rhetoric remain the same. Whilst shrouding their positive contributions to British society under a veil of political secrecy, scapegoat the immigrants in a hysterical wave of public doubts and fears, add grist to the mill of England's suspicion of 'Johnny Foreigner' so as to maintain the deep-rooted and now undeniably endemic xenophobia that most aptly characterises the British psyche. This, in conjunction with the hypocrisy that presents Britain as a kind, caring, tolerant nation of charity-donating do-gooders to the world, will ensure that the inequality status quo remains firmly in place for the political and financial elite to maintain their position and to continue to thrive, living off the fat of the land.

It was also whilst we were living in Chartham that, totally out of the blue, we were paid a visit by mum's sister Joan, our *white* Irish auntie, and her two children, our *white* cousins. Mum didn't make a big issue of it (and I understand the reasons for this now), so I only have very vague memories of the occasion.

Having since seen photos of their mother, our grandmother, mum was the spitting image of her! Mum had become hardened to life and had accepted the fact that she'd been disowned by her whole family so, with unwavering resolve, she was cool about the meeting and didn't make any effort to maintain contact with 'auntie' Joan when they left after spending the week with us. Mum didn't want her children to be affected by her past, and tried as far as possible to protect us from any potential emotional distress.

Apparently, we'd been visited by our Irish grandmother when Chi-chi was a few months old. She stayed a week with mum, dad and Chi-chi in Shorrolds Road, Fulham, and got on like a 'house on fire' with dad. As it turned out they both shared a passion for talking politics! This was also the last time mum ever saw her mum. There is no question this must have been an emotional week for mum, but her new brood took precedence and I think a semblance of relief and endorsement must have occurred as mum simply got on with her life and new family! She was never to be seen by any of us again. Again, mum didn't make arrangements to facilitate keeping in touch with her, mum really was as tough as old boots!

It was great having mum and dad working locally, and we often went into the hospital grounds to play and, probably more accurately, cause a nuisance of ourselves. Like building rope-swings to swing forty or fifty feet over the long tree-covered hospital drive as the bus to Canterbury was approaching! Great (insane?) fun and feats of daring for us, but I sometimes wonder what the drivers thought when confronted with what must have been a totally surreal sight of these feral black kids suddenly bursting out from the foliage on rope swings?! Probably thought they'd been transported to the deepest darkest jungles in Africa with Tarzan swinging majestically through the trees. Well, maybe not. The great hero Tarzan, Lord and Saviour of the Jungle and black Africans was, after all, white. Ahem!

The hospital used to put on social events and film nights for their employees, the latter being very popular among its patrons who couldn't afford to go to the cinema, or who had crap televisions like ours at home! The first 'major' film I saw in technicolour on one of these nights was the epic 'Zulu', starring Michael Caine.

Watching it made me feel *very* uncomfortable for a couple of reasons. Whilst we'd got used to seeing the white cowboys *always* slaughtering the savage, uncivilised, wicked, duplicitous, never-to-be-trusted 'Red Indians' in western movies made popular by the likes of John Wayne, Audie Murphy, Charles Bronson and co, Zulu wasn't set on the plains and prairies of America, but in the sub-Saharan jungles of Africa. The Red Indians were replaced with black Africans.

The covert sub-plot remained the same across the genres though, with the heroic and outnumbered white cowboys and soldiers triumphing over their Red Indian and black African adversaries. Even in the case of Zulu, where the white English army was pulverised by Zulu spears and sjamboks in the January 1879 battle for Rorke's Drift during the Anglo-Zulu war in South Africa. Not only did the English survive and 'win' the physical battle, they were also portrayed as winning the 'moral' battle. I was aware of the tension building among the audience as the 150 'brave' machine-gun-toting English soldiers battled it out with the 4,000-strong Zulu army. The audience *so* wanted the soldiers to win in the battle of good over evil, white over black. I saw it as, effectively, a hopeless battle of armed white soldiers against (comparably) unarmed black warriors. I couldn't and didn't share the will for the white soldiers to win, and neither could I share the communal relief and celebrations on their victory. In fact, to be honest, I was devastated.

Barring a few notable exceptions (such as Sidney Poitier, Denzel Washington, Morgan Freeman, Will Smith, Forest Whittaker, Jamie Foxx), very rarely do any black leading characters in films make it to the end. It was only until relatively recently that they 'made it to the last reel', as opposed to being killed off in the first five minutes or so. Prior to the current regime, black people were mainly portrayed as bug-eye-rolling maids and servants shuffling to gratefully fulfil their masters' requests, or as incompetent non-entities that were quickly disposed of.

Television and media play a powerful role in our psychology, but I just couldn't be persuaded to buy into the underlying messages. These messages made me feel uncomfortable, because they didn't even begin to portray how I saw myself, which was in a very positive, intelligent, competitive, competent, bold and adventurous light. I've watched Zulu on a few occasions since, and my feelings still haven't changed, other than to say I dislike the film and its message even more today!

I pretty much sailed through my time at Chartham Primary School and, after having passed my 11+ selection exam, had the choice of attending Canterbury Technical High School for boys, or Simon Langton Grammar School for Boys in Canterbury, as opposed to being condemned to attend Chartham Secondary Modern School, where Chi-chi had attended for the previous academic year.

Technical High Schools provided 'technical' subjects for boys who had an interest in or were good at things like woodwork, metal work, technical drawing and design, in combination with a sound GCE O Level academic curriculum. Simon Langton provided a sound academic curriculum only. I chose the Technical High School for neither of these reasons (because I was crap with my hands!). I chose it because they played football, whereas the grammar school played rugby which, to my mind, was total anathema. The thought of not playing football was unbearable for me. I think my dad was disappointed, but I went to great lengths to remind him that I'd passed my 11+ exam and had the choice, and that the only difference between the choices was the sports they played! He wasn't to know or fully understand the difference in academic provision and reputation, and I wasn't about to explain it to him!

I was made house and team football captain in my first year, playing mainly in central defence, centre midfield or centre forward when we needed to score a few goals. I was even selected (once) for the school cricket team! I think they thought I may have hailed from the West Indies and therefore assumed, as such, that I must be brilliant at cricket. Wrong. I was no better than my dad, and he was absolutely crap! Out for a duck on the first ball, I was never invited back to play.

I was the only black boy in the whole school but, psychologically I think I was prepared for this, and ready to face anything that might come my way. Three things stand out in my mind that came my way:

First, our Geography teacher explaining in front of the class that I wouldn't have survived a sheep cull and the inevitable trip to the abattoir and butchers because I would have been the 'the black sheep' in the herd. This statement shocked me but, even more so, I was shocked that the teacher, who I actually liked and respected, had come out with it. I went into my shell a bit from that moment on, and never assumed that I wouldn't be made the butt of jokes in any more classes based on my skin colour.

Second, a fight I had on the school playing field when I was attacked by a third-year boy who'd constantly bullied me with never-ending name-calling and taunting. I tried my best to ignore him, but there's only so much a kid can be expected to take without reply. So one day he started with the name-calling, in the school corridors, and I, for the first time, gave him some verbals back. He objected to my having the temerity to dare speak to him in such a manner, and challenged me to 'sort it out' on the school sports field at lunch time. Of course I had to accept, for to decline would have meant me consigning myself to a dog's life every day that I stepped into school from that point on.

As always in the realm of school, word got around and, come lunch time, hundreds of excited and eager boys from the first-year right through to the upper-sixth forms assembled on the playing field to watch the arranged punch-up (I was half expecting Kevin to have been involved somewhere in the promotion of the event, but this wasn't the case this time!), and all bar none expected me, as a first-year, to get beaten up by this third-year bully and, to be honest, so did I.

I was shitting myself! We were about the same height and, I don't know why, but he kept charging in at me with his head lowered, and I kept swinging left and right upper cuts to his face, but he just wouldn't stop coming at me! I think he couldn't take the shame and embarrassment of being beaten up by a first-year, and a black one at that, the only one in the whole school! Knuckles hurting and heart pounding, I didn't stop punching the boy. He never laid a finger of any effect or consequence on me, and I was *enjoying* myself, battering him.

The fight got split up by the Tuck-Shop manager who, whilst not a teacher, was very influential on the pastoral side of the school provision. He dragged us both apart, blaming me for the fight and for the injuries my assailant had sustained. I looked at the boy as he was crying, bleeding profusely from his eyes, nose, mouth and ears, with one eye swollen half shut and accusing me of having attacked him!

This led directly to the third 'thing' to come my way: overt institutionalised racism.

The Tuck-Shop manager roughed me up, stopping just short of actually hitting me! He called me a 'black thug' and wrote a report claiming to have witnessed the fight from start to finish, blaming me for starting it. His written report even went so far as to describe me in writing as a 'black thug'. The thing that saved me was the testimonies of the many pupil witnesses who confirmed that the boy had been picking on me, calling me names, and had challenged me to a fight which he started, and, as mum had always insisted, I finished!

Sadly for me, I couldn't enjoy my victory and bask in the adulation of my first-year friends because, not being allowed to return to my afternoon classes, it dawned upon me that the school would be contacting my parents. Dad was the typical authoritarian parent type who believed if his child got in trouble at school, he *must* have been in the wrong. This meant the child would need to be beaten for his wrong-doing.

Dad, like most African-Caribbean immigrants of the 1950s, had total faith, trust and belief in the teachers and educational system with whom they'd entrusted the custody of their children. The almost inevitable caning I was going to receive from the housemaster would pale into insignificance compared to the flogging I'd receive from dad!

After completing the investigation of the incident, including listening to pupil accounts, I was spared the cane, but received a warning as to my future conduct. Worse, a letter was hastily typed up which I was to take home to show my parents. Travelling home on the bus with this letter in my satchel felt almost like I was couriering my own written death sentence to the executioner – dad! Mercifully, dad was on a late shift at work and mum was at home when I arrived. I explained the situation to her to get her on my side, before presenting her with the letter. She supported me 100% and reiterated the instructions she'd given us all on occasions throughout our early school days:

"I don't want ye coming home telling me ye got into trouble at school for bullying or starting fights, but if someone hits ye first, I don't want ye coming home telling me ye didn't fight back. If they hit ye first, make sure ye finish it!"

This applied to anybody who may have seen fit to attack us, regardless of age, size or race!

Dad arrived home after a long shift at work, and mum started to attempt to explain the events of the day. In an instant dad had removed the belt from his trousers, it literally whistled its way into his hands like a snake leaping to catch a rat. He'd heard the words:

"Gos, school, trouble, fight".

That was enough for him to fly into a rage. Mum shouted at him to *listen* and not to beat me. He listened, and put his belt back on.

Mum would have gone through hell for her children (and often did!). She made it clear to us though that, as long as we told her the truth, she'd support us.

This was at or around the time when, significantly, dad actually started to listen to mum. There was almost a slight and subtle change in the power relationship between them. I think mum was quick to realise that her children would be facing hell in school from teachers and pupils, white (and eventually), black alike. Dad was still under the impression that the school and teachers, like all authority figures, were always in the right and never to be questioned.

Dad's Biafran friends would meet at our house to discuss developments in the civil war and would, to mum's ear at least, intellectualise about it far too much. She'd butt in, and offer her own (simplistic but true?) passionate analysis:

" Ye should never have let the English into your country in the first place! Now Biafra's become a part of Nigeria, it's lost to Nigeria, because the English won't let ye walk away with your oil, that's all they care about, they don't care about Nigeria!"

She made her point vehemently and without any doubt. How right she was! Again, with reference to the cyclical nature of human existence and history, we've seen the same or similar occur in places around the world where the UK and the USA deem worthy of intervening. Sierra Leone is a prime example. Had Sierra Leone not been so diamond-wealthy, under no circumstances would the UK have sent troops under the guise of beneficent 'aid'.

Then she'd go on to relay stories about the IRA and how they'd mounted resistance against the English and their Black and Tan army. She'd retell nightmarish stories of suffering and losses, and heroic tales of triumphs and gains. The IRA was still active and engaged in ongoing guerrilla warfare with the English in Ireland, Northern Ireland (which was and still is effectively England), and the English mainland. Mum despised the Northern Irish Protestants for not only continuing to be ruled by England, but for relishing and revelling in the fact. She saw their relationship with the English as one that was based totally on historical tyranny, exploitation and oppression. How could anybody meekly accept that as their fate?

Very little sickened mum more than the sight of the Union Jack flag-waving processions of the Protestant Orange Order and the Apprentice Boys as they made their tub-thumping, whistle-blowing, fife-playing, umbrella-swirling, bowler-hat-wearing way through the meandering streets of Belfast in remembrance of, and commemoration to, the 1690 Battle of the Boyne in which the Protestant William of Orange vanquished and deposed the Catholic King James V11, culminating in the eventual demise of a united Ireland, Eire.

However, true to form, the kiddie-fiddling paedophile Catholic priests always topped her vomit list!

Twelve

Obi and I developed a keen interest in watching motorcycle speedway racing. Don't ask me why, and we'd regularly make our way (walk the four miles) into Canterbury to watch the daring Canterbury Crusaders Speedway Team take on all-comers. We loved the action, noise, excitement and petrol-soaked smell of the competition, and especially enjoyed the crashes that took place every week.

I soon started to make my way into Canterbury under my own steam for other reasons. When we lived in Blean mum thought, due to Chichi's success and proficiency on the piano, that I also should take up lessons with the same teacher. This meant me going into Canterbury every Saturday morning, which when I started my secondary education at the Technical High School, clashed with playing football for the school. I instantly gave up piano lessons for two reasons. Firstly, so that I could play football for the school team and, secondly, I was crap on the piano. I never even mastered 'I am C, middle C, left hand, right hand, Middle C'!

When it appeared I may need to fight my way through school as the only black boy in it, I started boxing training at a boxing club in Canterbury, and I'd make my way into town twice a week, and three times when I eventually started having competitive bouts. Training for boxing is the hardest I've ever done in my life! As an 11 year old I started the gym's fitness regime, running, skipping, push-ups, stomach crunches, medicine ball, light dumbbell weights, punch bags, pad work and then sparring. It was truly tough! My trainer, a big, fat, grizzly white guy with a flat, broken nose that appeared splattered all over his face, was the boxing club owner, trainer and president and, very quickly, identified me as a prospect.

After about 6 weeks training and getting my punching technique right during endless and painful shadow-boxing and pad sessions with him, he said I was strong, great on my feet, and that he was in the process of arranging fights for me. The truth is I couldn't wait to have a 'proper' fight but, after having watched so many other hopefuls and fully-fledged boxers sparring in training sessions, the thought of actually getting into the ring to fight against an opponent who I didn't know, and who didn't know me, was also very daunting!

I think he had great expectations and high hopes for me, he even started driving me home, which was way out of his way, after training, something he'd never been known to do before. He was old-school, hard as nails, expected and received the utmost loyalty and respect from the boxers in his 'stable'.

My first official fight arrived, and I made my way into Canterbury without telling anybody at home, wanting everything to appear 'normal'. The truth was I was shitting myself and didn't want my family to see me lose! I did the pre-match warm-up, got a good sweat on, and my trainer reminded me of his preferred approach:

"Keep your guard up, chin down, lead with the left jab and follow up with the right cross in combinations, keep moving and keep throwing combinations and you'll be alright my son!"

He looked me in the eyes telling me not to be afraid. I think, secretly, he was looking me in the eyes to see if he saw fear. He didn't. I was excited. I couldn't wait to smash someone's head in and be congratulated for doing so! Anyway, the experience I'd already had facing down imminent combatants had enabled me to develop the ability to convincingly hide fear and appear confident.

I climbed through the ropes, the bell rang, I met my opponent (a tall, fit-looking white boy), in the centre of the ring where we went through the gladiatorial pre-match ritual of touching gloves before receiving the referee's instruction to:

"Box!"

No chin down, no effective guard up, no leading with the left jab. I just smashed him with one punch, a right-cross to the temple, and he crumbled to the floor like a pack of cards. He didn't (or couldn't) even attempt to beat the mandatory 10-second count.

I'd won my first competitive bout with a one-punch knock-out that stunned everybody watching, especially my hapless opponent who, whilst watching, didn't actually see the punch coming. When he was hauled off the floor on spaghetti legs that were no longer able to sustain his weight, I actually felt *really* sorry for him, and I felt bad, guilty, about what I'd done.

My trainer, on the other hand, was ecstatic. He even bought me a Wimpy burger on the way home that I scoffed in the back of his van! He dropped me off, congratulated me again, and told me he'd have to start lining up better opponents for me. I walked indoors to be greeted by mum:

"You're home early tonight!"

I gave her a dead excuse about training finishing early that night, and she was left none the wiser.

Late afternoon about four weeks later I left home just as surreptitiously for, what unbeknown to me, were to be my second and third bouts. My trainer had arranged a 'fight' for me, not a 'bout', but a 'fight'. I wasn't aware of the difference between the two at the time, but I was aware that there were far more people at the club, the atmosphere was a lot louder and tension seemed to be higher. I could also tell that the majority of the expectant faces were men of the travelling communities, 'pikeys', or 'gyppos' as we ignorantly and disrespectfully called them.

To my horror, I instantly recognised my first opponent. I'd been strawberry-picking with him and his mate a couple of months earlier, they were both two years older than me, and we'd chatted quite a lot and become 'work mates'. This confused me. How could I hit a mate? After the pre-match instructions of my trainer, and the obligatory ring-rituals were dispensed with, I quickly learnt it's very easy to hit a mate, especially when that 'mate' is hitting you!

He was taller and heavier than me, and it quickly became evident that the spectators were his relatives and friends. So, not wishing to disappoint his band of very vocal supporters, he took the fight to me, and I wasn't having that! He landed a few punches that didn't trouble me, and I actually learnt that 'keeping your guard up' is a very useful bit of advice! I jabbed him with the left as instructed, which opened him up. I could see his face and head clearly, so I delivered the trusty right-hand in the form of an upper-cut to his jaw. He was asleep standing up before he crashed to the canvas, and I pitied him. I felt really bad, guilty again as he regained consciousness, stared forlornly at his dad, and started crying, lip cut and eye swollen.

My night wasn't over yet though! I'd hardly broken a sweat in the first fight, and my trainer said he thought this might be the case, so he'd arranged another fight for me. No prizes for guessing that it was with my first opponent's mate who I'd also met strawberry picking. The crowd of spectators were even louder on our entrance to the ring, and stunned into similar levels of silence 30 second after the bell when he, too, was reduced to a blubbering wreck on the ring floor after a flurry of combination punches and the (what was now becoming my trademark) right hand finish. Though I felt desperately sorry for the first boy, I was still hyped and pumped up for the second, so he had to get it as well!

I'm fairly certain quite a bit of money was won and lost on that night amongst the 'gyppos' and the boxing club members. I still didn't mention anything when I got home. Though I still felt bad for the boys, I'd enjoyed the night, felt good about myself, and didn't want to jeopardise being allowed to continue with my boxing.

So, going into my fourth fight 3 and 0, you'd never guess who my opponent was. I never knew that Michael Mulligan, the same boy we'd beaten up, tied to a tree and tortured by tourniquet, had been sent to boxing training by his angry dad to ensure he didn't get beaten up again. They were an Irish family, so I understand the fighting spirit. Though anxious at the prospect of him getting his revenge on me, I couldn't wait for the bell. I wanted this to be settled once and for all! I battered him senseless within a minute, having toyed with him delivering hard but deliberately non-knockout punches. I wanted to hurt him a little bit more, to cut him up and bruise him but, with his guard all over the place and his brain disoriented, head presented on a plate, I couldn't hold back any longer. I delivered one of the sweetest right upper-cuts of my life, swift, powerful, with textbook beauty and ferocious intent. When they'd finished scraping him off the floor and depositing him in the changing room, I never felt worse. Again, I had an attack of guilt and empathy with my battered opponent! I didn't *want* to feel like this, but couldn't help it. I wanted to fully enjoy the successes I had in the ring, but always left fights feeling bad about what I'd just done to my opponents.

According to Sigmund Freud's Theory of Moral Development, I must have developed a very healthy 'internalised parent' of a guilty conscience that kicked in whenever I did something wrong. In this case, it was battering people to a pulp in a boxing ring. Freud argued that our conscience lay in the pre-conscious mind, in our Superego, which makes us feel guilt. It works to try to regulate the more violent and aggressive urges and instincts that continually struggle to express themselves in our deep, unconscious mind, otherwise known as the Id, which also houses our fight-or-flight reflexes.

Maybe my aggressive fight instincts were competing with an equally strong guilt mechanism! Freud argued that the Id operates on the Pleasure Principle as it seeks to satisfy our aggressive and sexual instincts. This clearly explained why I did actually enjoy punching these boys up! The Superego, operating on the Morality Principle, acting as the internalised parent, was obviously telling me that the bashings I was meting out were wrong!

So, in many ways, I just couldn't win!

However, my fifth and last fight, which was a proper bout, was against the Yorkshire Schoolboy Champion. Stepping into the ring I noticed massive differences between him and the previous four. Apart from being blonde-haired in the classic Teutonic Aryan mould, he was leanly ripped, pouring with sweat already, snorting like a bull out of his nose when he shadow-boxed, hot snot flying everywhere, his shadow-boxing looked awesome. I was crapping myself! The bell sounded to signal three rounds of hell. For me. He savaged me throughout the first round, but I recovered in the second round, and, courtesy of my natural strength, fitness and aggression, won the third round. The fight was given a draw, but I felt I'd lost, because not winning, in my eyes, meant losing. Even worse, he'd played a timpani orchestra all over my body with his punches, I was in pain, and I had bruises on my face. None of which bothered me particularly, but I knew I'd have even more hell to pay when I got home!

As I stepped into the kitchen mum looked at my face and asked me:

"What happened?!"

I had to explain that I'd been having competitive fights for a few months, and that I'd won four by knockout and had drawn tonight with the Yorkshire Schoolboy Champion. Her response was immediate:

"That's your last fight!"

I was distraught! I wanted to continue but I knew by the look on mum's face that no way on earth was she going to allow me to. My crying like a baby didn't help persuade her either. Her decision was final!

Chi-chi's athletics career started to take off when she was around 11 or 12 years of age. She was exceptionally quick over 100 and 200 yards, and always crushed her opponents by embarrassing distances. She ran at school and county level, and was considered a very real prospect at national level. She was contending with Sonia Lannaman at the time, who went on to become Great Britain 100 metre champion, as well as to represent GB at Olympic and Commonwealth Games. Sadly, Chi-chi's sprint demise was partly down to me! In her later teens I encouraged her to join and play for the Reading Ladies Football Club, which she did. Alas, for her, a football-related knee ligament injury put paid to her very promising career in athletics.

Sorry Chich!

However, as mum used to say:

"Everything for a reason!"

Ijem and Obi were getting on well and progressing through primary school and I wasn't made aware of any concerns, and little sister Kele started her primary schooling in Chartham. I remember seeing her sitting alone on the back seat of the bus on her way to school one morning and feeling desperate for her as she started to make her own way in the big wide world. But she grew up to be more than capable of looking after herself!

Disappointingly, neither Ijem nor Obi passed their 11+ exams, so they too were condemned to start their secondary education at Chartham Secondary Modern School, where Chi-chi was now in her fifth and final year. It became apparent that Chi-chi had been regularly bullied at the secondary modern school, without ever fighting back! Unknown in our family! A 'gyppo' girl, her family and bully friends had been making Chi-chi's life a misery. One day the girl spat in Chi-chi's lunch and, when it came to Ijem's attention, it was the last time this girl bullied Chi-chi. Ijem, in her first year (so four years younger than the girl) waylaid her at the school gates at the end of the lunch-spitting day. Ijem was fired up and, after pummelling the girl to sub-mission, threw her off her feet into the air before she landed in a battered, crumpled heap on the ground.

On retelling the story at home later that evening, we adapted the famous song from the Walt Disney classic film 'Dumbo', where the crows were professing never to have seen an elephant fly! Our version of the refrain was:

"I saw a fireside chat, I saw a baseball bat,
And I just laughed till I thought I'd die,
But I'd been done seen about everything,
When I see a *gypsy* fly!"

Ijem was fast on her way to becoming a strong, resilient, no-nonsense protector of the family, much in the same 'earth-mother' mould as mum. It soon became evident that people would be taking their own lives into their hands if they messed with Ij! She had a close scrape though when she was followed home by a weirdo-stalker (paedophile?). With night falling, and his footsteps matching hers, she quickened the pace of her trek home and, as she did so, he quickened his. She had a decision to make. Continue walking along the road to our front door (which probably would have resulted in him grabbing her), or make a run for it through the spinney that adjoined our back garden. She made the right choice by swerving through the bluebell-bedecked spinney. He charged after her as she dodged in and out of the familiar undergrowth, bushes and trees. She ran for her life and dived for the whole in the fence that divided the spinney from our garden. He made a desperate lunging grab for her plim-clad trailing foot but, using every ounce of fear-generated adrenalin, energy and speed, she wriggled through the whole and ripped across the garden to safety through the back door.

Thirteen

True to our parents' wishes, we all attended Sunday school in Chartham. Not only did it require us to pay the usual homage to the blonde-haired blue-eyed God, it also provided us with a type of unofficial youth club where we could express ourselves in the riotous games we'd make up, so it was good. However, one Sunday prior to the Easter Bank Holiday, the Sunday School teacher set all the children with a task to complete, that task being to draw crayon pictures of Jesus Christ rising heavenward on the third day of being entombed after his death on the cross. We happily set about our drawings, only to be interrupted by the teacher as our pictures were developing quite nicely. Chi-chi, Ijem, Obi and I had drawn our pictures with a black Jesus surrounded by trumpet-playing black Angels rejoicing in his ascendancy to sit beside our omnipotent Lord, God and Saviour.

She wasn't having a bar of it! She proceeded to explain to us that we were wrong to draw Jesus and the angels as black, stating that:

"Jesus and the Angels are white!"

My response was:

"But ours are black!"

She steadfastly refused to accept our position that Jesus and the angels were black, and insisted that we rub out and re-draw our pictures. I refused, got up, and told my brother and sisters to leave with me, at which we strode out of Sunday school, never to return.

We explained what had transpired to mum, and she supported us in our stance. Miraculously, even dad agreed that the teacher "was very foolish!" (one of his favourite put-downs which, when delivered in a Nigerian accent, is classic!).

My church attendance, much like today's current national figures, plummeted off the face of the earth. I think I must have been an unwitting founder member of the Secular Society of Great Britain!

To hell with church, religion, and especially Christianity for me! Whilst at the time I couldn't articulate it, I just *felt* uncomfortable, being told by a supposedly educated and respected white woman, that black people, people who looked like me and my family, couldn't be, and weren't, depicted in Christian books and imagery. I was even more aggrieved at the idea that Jesus probably originated from Sweden! In my way of thinking at the time, we were being told in no uncertain terms that Jesus (and God by virtue of being his dad), was white. Definitely not black! This is almost as gut-wrenchingly sickening as the poem written by William Blake in 1804, the lyrics of which were added to music written by Hubert Parry in 1916 – 'Jerusalem'.

I can't bring myself to relate the hymn in its entirety, but will emphasise its covetous and delusionary sentiments with reference to its final two lines:

"Till we have built Jerusalem In England's green and pleasant land."
How preposterous! What a load of tosh! Bollocks! Bullshit!

I can probably quite reasonably be accused of misunderstanding the hymn, but I make no apologies. I'm sick to death of the British equating themselves, and England, with all that is to be admired, revered and venerated.

Jerusalem in England? Behave!

It still astounds me when I go into the houses of black African/ Caribbean people today, to be met with images and personally signed photographs of a blonde-haired blue-eyed Jesus taking pride of place on the walls and lace-covered, doyley- and trinket-laden sideboards in their precious, rarely-if-ever-used front rooms. This is another thing that Nigerians and Jamaicans share in common. The revered and legendary front room!

It seems there was an unwritten law among our pioneering immigrant parents and grandparents that, once a house had been bought or acquired, the front room must become a shrine to Our Lord Jesus and his fearsome and vengeful father, God (in ours you can add St Mary into the equation also!). Paintings and photos of the dynamic duo, either alone or together with Jesus at God's right hand, were strategically placed to ensure they'd be looking down from on-high in positions of absolute power and authority. To add extra-special emphasis and gravitas, the 'Christ on the Cross', the crucifix statue with clear evidence of him having been stabbed and dying to save us from our sins, was also very popular and prominently placed. All of this imagery contributed to commanding our total obedience and deference on entry to the shrine of the front room.

The only furniture and decor permitted in the front room was the obligatory gramophone with accompanying stack of 7" records; the foulest and most garishly colourful carpet covered with see-through protective plastic walkways; a brand new three-piece suite still shrouded with even more protective plastic to keep it clean and free from Gerry-curl gel deposits; a two-hundred foot-long side board packed with the family's 'best' china (for show purposes only, of course, never to be actually used!); every possible surface covered with frilly, lacy doyleys and glass figurines; the most disgusting stripy wall paper covered with a string of (minimum three) ducks in flight (who knows where to or from?!); an invariably chipped-in-transit-earthenware white swan; (small) drinks cabinet comprised of a bottle of sherry and red wine (the blood of Christ, of course!); and, other than the room stinking of moth balls, last but not least, though definitely the most bizarre and incongruous of all things, a bloody snow globe!

Fourteen

Dad got a new and better-paid job that included promotion for him in another psychiatric hospital, Fairmile Hospital in the village of Cholsey, near Wallingford in Oxfordshire, so at the end of my first year at Canterbury Technical High School for boys, just after I'd turned 12 years of age, we were on the move again. We were happy for dad, because he knew his stuff and worked hard for his promotion, and as I said before, Nigerians are all about education, status and recognition, so this was good for him and us! Mum got a job there as well, so things were definitely on the up!

On arrival we first moved into a three-storey hospital-owned property on Papist Way, about a quarter of a mile walk down the road to work for mum and dad. Ijem and Obi continued their primary school education at the local Cholsey primary school. Chi-chi didn't have any choice but to attend Blackstone Secondary Modern School in the old market town of Wallingford, which was about a twenty to thirty minute bus ride away. In effect, I didn't have any choice as to which school I would attend. There was no Technical High School to choose from, so the choice was between Blackstone Secondary or Wallingford Grammar School for boys. No way was I going to attend the sink secondary modern school, so Wallingford Grammar was the only alternative!

Despite having evidence of having passed my 11+ and having attended Canterbury Technical High School, I still had to have an interview at the grammar school before gaining entry. In some parts structurally reminiscent of Harry Potter's Hogwarts School of Witchcraft and Wizardry, I couldn't believe the imposing physical stature, design and layout of the school and its facilities. Surrounded by acres of tree-lined sports fields comprising athletics track, rugby and hockey pitches and cricket green, it even had its own open-air swimming pool! It was very grand in a way I'd never witnessed before, and the masters all swished around the place from class to class, staffroom to office, donning their flowing black robes denoting the university colleges they'd attended and graduated from (either Oxford or Cambridge, nothing less would do!), reminding me of caped crusaders like Batman and Robin!

The oak and mahogany decor stunk of history, wealth and privilege, this was obviously a very serious place of learning, what the hell was I doing here?!

There were academic and athletic rolls of honour on all the main walls, especially around the headmaster's office and reception area, which listed the achievements of staff and students gone by, ornately mounted paintings of current and past teachers dating back (what appeared to me anyway), centuries. It felt like being in a museum where you just had to pay homage and utmost respect to the school and its traditions. Clearly, judging by the rolls and paintings, many of the school's previous teachers and scholars had served actively in British campaigns and war efforts around the world in general, and the Empire in particular. The school was formally built and established in 1877, however, its origins dated back to 1717.

Fortunately, the reports I received from Canterbury Technical High School with regards my ability, attendance, punctuality, conduct and potential were all very positive. They didn't include the 'black thug' report in their bundle, which was very thoughtful of them! The bundle also included a letter of recommendation in support of my application that described me as a decent young man of good potential.

Mum had accompanied me for my interview, and I *know* she was just as, if not more, nervous than me! The subdued gravitas of the place had that effect on us. We sat there in the reception area, quivering in awe, waiting to be escorted to meet the headmaster for my interview, feeling intimidated and solemn, overwhelmed by that status-dissonance feeling of being totally out of your comfort zone in massively unfamiliar surroundings. Mum told me to smile, be pleasant and polite, and to speak clearly. I wished she hadn't. Her anxious, whispered, stuttering voice and advice only served to pile the pressure on me! But I'd made my mind up. I really wanted this.

"The headmaster will see you now."

Another 'walk of the condemned' began at this instruction (similar to that experienced by the losing team on an episode of The Apprentice being summoned by Sir Alan Sugar into his 'boardroom!), and, as we approached the huge and heavy oak door to the headmaster's study, the nerves really started to kick in. The receptionist rapped on the door and, upon his invitation, she opened the door, almost reverently, to usher us inside and introduced us to the headmaster, before exiting like Michael Jackson doing his moonwalk, head bowed in deference, naturally. It almost felt like being in the presence of royalty, God, or, even more importantly, Pele!

Sinking into a very plush and buffed burgundy leather Chesterfield sofa, I smiled (as instructed), and tried to swallow before the anticipated barrage of questions, and I couldn't. My mouth had dried up! I must have looked like a rabbit caught in the glare of car headlights, but I didn't *feel* like that, I actually felt quite confident and comfortable having crossed the threshold of the inner sanctum. He obviously noticed that both mum and I were nervous, so he very graciously made small talk to help us relax. He was very proper, and spoke very 'posh', his vocabulary was extensive and his enunciation precise, clearly a very learned scholar, academic, and gentleman.

After commending me on my reports and questioning mum about our domestic circumstances, he asked her to wait outside whilst he continued the interview with me. I was relieved at this as I hate having to perform like a trained seal, and felt much more comfortable when given the leeway to 'blag' my answers to his questions away from the disbelieving eyes of my mum!

I dredged up all the 'big' words that I'd never used at home but learnt in school in a valiant effort to impress him with my own vocabulary. I was very honest with my answers and very earnest with the manner in which I delivered them, which included my favourite and least favourite subjects, hobbies, sports played etc. I must have impressed him enough because he confirmed my place in the second year, to start the following Monday, which gave us enough time for mum to buy me a new (though oversized in the hope it would last into my early twenties!) school uniform.

I was really pleased because mum was *so* happy and proud at my success. She was *never* deferential to anybody or any institution, but it was obvious to me that my gaining a place in this prestigious seat of learning meant a lot to her. Dad was ecstatically happy at the thought of his first son being educated alongside the sons of the elite. No doubt he had dreams of me progressing onto either Oxford or Cambridge universities in the future, after having sailed through my 'O' and 'A' level exams at the school. He kept repeating in celebration with the cheesiest proud smile on his face:

"Opara!" ("First Son!")

I grew to learn and understand (in theory, *not* in practice or experience!), the importance of 'first son' status in traditional Igbo culture. It seems almost obligatory, compulsory, for Igbo men to ensure that they get at least one male 'issue' among their children. So, not only had dad fulfilled this requirement, but it also seemed his Opara! might well be one that brings pride and success to the household, in the form educational success at the very least. What more could a fully-fledged-dyed-in-the-wool-fu-fu-consuming Igbo man want in life?!

For a man to be followed by a son means his status in Igbo society is confirmed. He has contributed to helping sustain the patrilineal system of inheritance. Related to this is the role Igbo men play in society. They must provide for their families which, before the advent of Christianity, often meant more than one wife and multiple family units. In fact, my patrilineal grandfather had six wives! I've often tried to persuade my wife about the benefits of such a system, but for some reason she just won't accept the idea! Igbo men form the Umunna in their (village) communities and societies. The Umunna are responsible for deliberating over and deciding upon issues of dispute and contention, the highest levels of respect and honour being afforded to the male village elders in this practice. Traditional Igbo society is based on exceptionally democratic principles, and this was the case long before the Spanish (and any other white European), first set foot on Igbo soil. Again, one of the reasons Igbo men (especially) weren't considered to be 'good slaves', was because they had this inherent sense of entitlement, to have a say, to contribute to the direction and governorship of their own lives and communities which, once denied, often leads to manifest discontent and trouble:

"Wahalla foh you oh!" (Nigerian pidgin for "You're in trouble!").

I mentioned previously that Nigerian pidgin is the sweetest on the ear, and I stand by that, even at the risk of being accused of bias, but it is! Whilst it has no official status (English is the official language of Nigeria, followed by the local Igbo, Yoruba, Hausa and Fulani tongues, and thousands of derivatives thereof), it is the second language to tens of millions in Nigeria. It's also very similar, not only to other West African countries (especially Equatorial Guinea, Sierra Leone, Cameroon and, to a lesser extent, Ghana), but to islands in the Caribbean.

Nigerian Pidgin, along with the various pidgin and creole languages of West Africa share similarities to the various dialects of English found in the Caribbean. Some of the returning descendants of slaves taken to the New World of West African origin brought back many words and phrases to West Africa from the Jamaican Creole (also known as Jamaican Patois or simply Patois), and the other creole languages of the West Indies which are components of Nigerian Pidgin. The pronunciation and accents often differ a great deal, mainly due to the extremely heterogeneous mix of African languages present in the West Indies, but if written on paper or spoken slowly, the creole languages of West Africa are for the most part mutually intelligible with the creole languages of the Caribbean.

The presence of repetitious phrases in Jamaican Creole such as "su-su" (gossip), "passa passa" (street party) and "pyaa-pyaa" (sickly) mirror the presence of such phrases in West African languages such as "bam-bam", which means "complete" in the Yoruba language. Repetitious phrases are also present in Nigerian Pidgin, such as, "koro-koro" (clear vision), "yama-yama" (disgusting), and "doti-doti" (garbage).

Furthermore, the use of the words of West African origin in Jamaican Patois, such as "boasie" (meaning proud, a word that comes from the Yoruba word "bosi" also meaning "proud") and "Unu" - Jamaican Patois or "Wuna" - West African Pidgin (meaning "you people", a word that comes from the Igbo word "unu" also meaning "you people"), display some of the interesting similarities between the English pidgins and creoles of West Africa and the English pidgins and creoles of the West Indies, as does the presence of words and phrases that are identical in the languages on both sides of the Atlantic, such as:

"Me a go tell dem" (I'm going to tell them) and
"Make we" (let us).

Use of the word "deh" or "dey" is found in both Jamaican Patois and Nigerian Pidgin English, and is used in place of the English word "is" or "are". The phrase:

"We dey foh London"

would be understood by both a speaker of Patois and a speaker of Nigerian Pidgin to mean:

"We are in London".

Other similarities, such as "pikin" (Nigerian Pidgin for "child") and "pikney" (or "pikiny", Jamaican Patois for "child") and "chook"

(Nigerian Pidgin for "poke" or "stab") which corresponds with the Jamaican Patois word "jook" (stab), further demonstrate the linguistic relationship.

Several theories exist to suggest that "Bim", the word used by the local black African slave descendants in Barbados as their island's name, was a word commonly used by slaves and that it derives from the phrase "bi mu" or either ("bem", "Ndi bem", "Nwanyi ibem" or "Nwoke ibem") from an Igbo phrase meaning "my people". Barbados, like Jamaica, received hundreds of thousands of Igbo slaves from the shores and ports of Biafra, principally Bonny and Calabar. Being derived partly from the present day Edo/Delta area of Nigeria, there are still some leftover words from the Portuguese and Spanish languages in pidgin English (Portuguese and Spanish trade ships traded slaves from the Bight of Benin). For example:

"You sabi do am?" means "Do you know how to do it?"
"Sabi" means "to know" or "to know how to" just as "to know" is "saber" in Portuguese and Spanish.

However, I digress.

Fifteen

Probably unsurprisingly, the highlight of my first week at Wallingford Grammar School for Boys was a fight! Not only was I the only black boy in the school (again!), I was one of only a handful of working class boys who'd successfully managed to gain entrance to its hallowed halls!

I thought I'd worked really hard at fitting in and, despite the obvious racial and social class differences, thought I did a pretty good job. I'd proved myself more than capable in adjusting academically, and though it was a rugby-playing school, I proved myself the best footballer in the playground, where we used tennis balls and jumpers for goal posts. I wasn't too bad at rugby either, though I wasn't keen on getting crunched by the many boy-units on the pitch. I was eventually selected to represent the school as a winger, due to my speed, but I hated being chased down or intercepted by giant, broken-nosed, cauliflower-eared full backs that looked like they'd eaten their parents for breakfast! So I soon ducked out of playing rugby for the school!

People, I think, have problems with other people who encroach into their domain and thrive. Unknown to me at the time, Igbos are well known for assimilating into alien host communities and, before long, rising to the top and taking over. In the realm that was Wallingford Grammar School, I made the mistake of successfully adjusting too quickly and, as a result, becoming popular (kids who are good at sports, especially football, tend to be popular in school!). Towards the end of my first full week I was approached in class before the teacher's arrival by a tall, lanky, skinny white boy, Adrian 'Doc' Drummond who, with a malicious twinkle in his eyes, started to bait me.

He got in my face and, buoyed by the support of his toff cronies, referred to me as a Nigger!

I was below average height throughout my primary and secondary school years (lack of nutrition or genetic factors?), only beginning a significant growth-spurt at around 16 or 17 years of age, when I reached 5' 11" (I never quite made 6 foot, damn!). This guy was already touching six foot in our second year, but he was skinny and he didn't't really scare me! The inevitable pushing and shoving started (the usual 'handbags at ten paces' prelude to either things fizzling out or escalating!), and then he made the mistake of hitting me.

I battered him to a crying, screaming, quivering wreck of a jelly within seconds, his previously jeering supporters instantly stunned into a complete and utter stony silence. Not only at the brutal efficiency I'd demonstrated to dispatch him to la-la land, but also because our teacher had walked in unnoticed and had witnessed everything! To diffuse the situation, I was sent to the headmaster's reception area, whilst the school nurse was summoned to attend to and assist Doc's recovery and return to the land of the conscious living.

Again I was saved by the teacher's testimony, and those of the 'ringside' pupil witnesses. Doc's parents came into the school to complain about their precious, but beaten and bruised, son. Their complaints fell on deaf ears.

Whilst I detest the inherited and never-to-be-questioned status, privilege and power of the middle- and upper-middle classes, there is something to admire about the British sense of 'fair play' in certain situations and circumstances. This was certainly a factor in this situation because Doc's parents assumed I was the aggressor and came in to voice their angry complaints about their son having been attacked and beaten up. But the school, admirably, disabused them of this notion and put the record straight, firmly placing their son in the role of the protagonist bully-aggressor who 'got what he deserved' (a 'damned good thrashing' in toff vernacular!).

My popularity sky-rocketed and I could do virtually nothing wrong which, for me, was great, because I really liked this school. I enjoyed the curriculum (apart from Science and Maths); I started to learn French and German (both of which I picked up instantly and became very proficient in); I opted out of Religious Education (no surprises there!); the teachers were superb and really inspiring (apart from one who reminded me of the Child Catcher in 'Chitty Chitty Bang Bang'. He really freaked me out as he swished effeminately around the school in his skin-tight ankle-swinging trousers, winkle-picker shoes, black gown billowing out behind him with tie draped over either shoulder with gay abandon!); I usually won the weekly cross-country races; I'd successfully negotiated being allowed to play football for Blackstone Secondary Modern School for the dispossessed, disempowered and disaffected working classes that was situated within walking distance on the same road in the middle of a pre-fabricated 1960s built council housing estate where Chi-chi attended; and the food was to die for!

At lunch times the whole school would assemble in year groups at the doors of the main hall. The superhero-like gown-clad masters resembling a swarm of bats returning to their nocturnal cave would enter the hall first and, on instruction, the pupils would follow in year-group order. Long tables seating 30-40 pupils were already set with cutlery, condiments and garnishes, and pupils filed obediently to stand behind their seats. I quickly learnt that timing and positioning were key elements to ensure maximum consumption, because pupils who arrived first and last at the ends of each table had the responsibility of serving for the rest. So, in the event I wasn't first in our year-group queue, I tried as hard as possible to count, assess, and then strategically negotiate my place in the queue that would ensure I was at the top of the table and serving. I was generally successful in this daily quest (my every-day common-sense ability in Maths rarely let me down as it was put to regular use in the dinner queues!), and resentful when I failed. Where individual pupils were at loggerheads with each other in and around the school, being at the head of the table was always an opportunity to serve up meagre helpings to the person you were at loggerheads with! Small portions were also served up, virtually as a matter of ritual, to the wimps, creeps and do-gooding teachers' pets!

The quality of the food was, in my opinion, 5-star hotel standard which, for a hungry free-school-meals pupil, was absolutely superb value for money! Unlike the school meals that 21st century school children are provided with, we received a generous array of freshly cooked vegetables, fish, succulent meats (as a confirmed Igbo man and thus, by default, confirmed carnivore, for me it was culinary heaven!), gravy, fresh fruit desserts, and jugs of juice and water that were regularly refilled by the dinner ladies. In short, excellent!

I think I developed the ability to spot other relatively impoverished working class pupils, of which there were very few, at Wallingford Grammar School. There were certain give-away clues, like dirty, less well-laundered school uniforms, general scruffiness, ill-fitting clothing, worn out shoes, lack of hygiene and the way they smelled. It was no wonder they tended to be less confident! Apart from one, Stephen Harris, who had fantastic artistic and creative ability. He was totally scruffy and stank like the others, but he was very high profile and confident. Predictably, his favourite subject was Art, and his drawings were brilliant. Especially notable were the cartoons he used to draw, either caricatures of teachers or other pupils, and a variety of the most popular boys' comic superheroes of the day, including Batman and Robin, Superman, and one he modelled on himself, 'Harris-Man'. He'd draw, write and serialise the adventures of Harris-Man in cartoon-strip style that kept us all hanging on in suspense until the next episode, while killing ourselves laughing at the capers he'd get up to. He was a *very* talented young man, with no airs or graces, who should have gone on to make millions from his talent. I've never heard of him since!

Ijem and Obi completed their primary school education at Cholsey Primary School, and as I mentioned before neither of them passed their 11+ exam, so both were sentenced to attend Blackstone Secondary Modern with Chi-chi.

Cholsey was quite a large village and, more importantly, it had a boys football club that played in organised competitive Sunday morning league, cup and 5-a-side competitions in and around Oxfordshire. The great Cholsey Bluebirds! As the name suggests, the team played in blue, the light blue of Coventry City FC at the time. Obi and I were in our element being able to play as part of a team every Sunday, though Obi's team were far better than mine. His age group seemed to have fantastically gifted, talented and committed players in virtually every position, and they won everything in sight. My age group, as a team and in comparison, was rubbish. Apart from a couple of players including myself (naturally!), we were useless and got hammered nearly every week.

I was also aware that, once Ijem and Obi had started secondary school with Chi-chi, all three were fighting their own battles against racist pupils, teachers, and the state school system, in their own ways. Kele was making her own steady way through Cholsey primary. I think our family bucked the prevailing trend of assumed working class indifference to school and education. Largely determined by dad, and supported by mum, we actually valued education, but our schools didn't value or recognise our commitment to it. We aspired to do well, but of the four of us that sat the 11+ exam, only one passed and, in so doing, seemed to provide support for the developing stereotypical theory that black children were uneducable in comparison to their white counterparts, and as such, were inevitably destined to fail.

Our parents constantly encouraged and supported us, always attended school parents' evenings, ensured we completed our homework, tried where affordable to provide us with additional textbooks and extra-curricular support, reminded us of the importance of educational success, and generally supported us in every way possible. They did all the things that working class parents, according to the theories, didn't bother to do for their children. Yet still our efforts weren't reflected in the 25% 11+ success rate that we'd achieved as a family. We can cancel genetic inheritance as we all shared the same parents, and we can cancel environmental factors, as we all had it hard! So what other factor could explain our 75% 11+ failure rate? Ingrained systematic institutionalised racism?

Academically I did exceptionally well at the grammar school, and I grew to love learning to speak French and German, especially German.

I loved the teacher of this subject, a pretty cool and younger white guy that didn't always wear his gown (mind you, it didn't take much for a teacher to look cool alongside the majority of the teachers at this school!), Mr Fitzhugh. He noticed my apparent 'gift' for languages and the apparent ease with which I picked them up:

French, the smooth and silky language of love and romance, and German which, in comparison, was harsh and abrasive:

"Je t'adore"
"Ich liebe dich"
"I love you"

Three different ways of expressing the same term and emotion, the French clearly have got it right, even the English expression beats that of German!

I even went on heavily subsidised school trips and pupil exchanges to France and Germany with the school. On the short school day trips we'd bring our own lunches, which for me, like my brother and sisters, was always a source of embarrassment! My classmates would be packed off by their mamas and papas with a wonderful assortment of exquisitely filled, nutritious and tasty sandwiches, fruit, tomatoes, chocolate bars and soft drinks. Ours never varied - dry bread and butter and, on a good day, a thin scraping of jam in between! I'd deliberately slink away to eat my lunch in private, so as to avoid the other boys seeing my sandwiches, and for me to avoid seeing and smelling theirs! I had a great time in Germany on a pupil exchange trip. I stayed with a family who had a son the same age as me, Peter Ronthaler. He stayed with us first and, in all honesty, he was *the* most boring person I'd ever met! He just enjoyed staying indoors and didn't want to come out and muck about with us at all. I couldn't believe it when, at the end of his stay and day of departure, he burst out crying, saying it had been the best week of his life! Incredible! I dread to think what would have constituted a bad week for him!

My trip to Germany and Peter's house was, in contrast, really enjoyable. I made sure to keep in contact with some of my classmates, and we all arranged to meet up to go to watch football matches together, as well as other trips here and there. It was great speaking German actually *in* Germany, and even Peter lightened up a bit and had a good time! However, there were certainly no tears on my departure. I was looking forward to getting home and being back with my family!

Dad had a Nigerian friend who'd been ordained as a Catholic priest and was living and working in Munich, the capital city of Germany's Bavarian (Aryan?), heartlands. I couldn't stand the guy and what he stood for, but it was an opportunity to go to Germany when Chi-chi and I were 13 and 12 respectively. We had a laugh at dad when, whilst waiting for 'uncle' to meet us at Munich train station, a drunken German guy pointed at dad saying:

"Vati? Vati?"

In German, V is pronounced as F, so it sounded like the guy was calling dad "fatty!" We nodded in agreement (because dad was putting on a bit of a paunch!), but either way, we were right. Yes, he was our father, and yes, he was getting fat!

I was struck by how clean, tidy and orderly Germany was in comparison to England.

Even more impressively, everything, trains, buses, and even people, seemed to operate with clockwork efficiency!

As had the Dachau concentration camp that we visited one day, deep in the Bavarian countryside, about 10 miles northwest of Munich...

"Arbeit macht frei". "Work makes you free"

...was the arched wrought-iron proclamation overhead on entry through the daunting gates. We strolled around what remained of the camp, much of which was presented as a museum, with the actual ovens used to burn Jewish people alive or dead; the gas chambers where dispossessed Jewish men, women and children were herded into, having been mislead into believing they'd be having a shower, only to be gassed to death by cyanide; furniture and lampshades made out of the inmates' skin; photos of the Jewish living walking dead being lined up and shot in the back of their heads, falling into conveniently and strategically placed mass graves; huge, vicious, snarling and salivating German Shepherd dogs straining at the leash to get at cowering starved skeletal figures dressed in stripy pyjama-type prison wear; train loads of Jewish people wearing civvies topped off with yellow 'Juden' stars packed into trains ostensibly to be relocated from their homes, but really en-route to hell-on-earth in the camps; and, worst of all, photos of the strutting German SS and Gestapo, resplendent in immaculate uniforms, bedecked with medals and toting their armoury. Totally disgusting!

The Nazis under Adolf Hitler's regime during the Second World War 'disposed' of (murdered) approximately 32,000 Jews. It is estimated that, in total, 6 million Jews throughout Europe died in the many concentration camps constructed for this purpose, the annihilation of the Jews. Why? Germany, like other nations across the world, was suffering a severe economic depression. Adolf Hitler, an opportunist politico, seized upon the chance to gain popularity and power by scape-goating the Jews in Germany, by blaming them for the economic woes of the country. Hitler was charismatic and his message appealed to the German populous. He said what they wanted to hear, and provided someone to blame!

In many ways the German populous were similar to the Neanderthal working class white English thugs of the 1950s, 60s and 70s who went 'Paki-bashing' every Friday night, and who complained about the "fucking foreigners coming here taking our jobs and houses!" They were also very much like the now more sanitised 21st century UKIP-ex-EDL supporters, who still point their fingers at the "fucking foreigners coming here taking our jobs and houses!"

The Jewish Holocaust, quite rightly, has remained a very high profile and shameful aspect of European human history, and claims of (monetary) reparation have been discussed and agreed between nations. According to the March 27th 1953 agreement, Germany was to pay Israel for the slave labour of Jews during the Holocaust, and to compensate for Jewish property stolen by the Nazis.

Without wishing to denigrate the horrific experience of the holocaust, or to appear resentful and trite, what price reparation for the lives of tens of millions of Africans removed forcibly and against their will by Europeans over a 500 year period? What price reparation for hundreds of years of colonial debauchery and theft of Africa's human and natural resources? What price reparation for the slave labour of Africans in the Caribbean and the Americas for 500 years? What price reparation for 900 years of looting and pillaging in Ireland? What price reparation for the 1740-1741 potato famine in Ireland that took one million starving Irish lives whilst being governed by England, and forcing millions more to emigrate?

Answer: we got an "expression of deep sorrow" from Tony Blair, 150 years later!

David Olusoga's 2015 BBC2 documentary provided a fascinating and shamefully revealing insight into the economics of slavery, focusing on the abolition of slavery in Britain, emphasising "the extraordinary choice by the government of the day to compensate slave owners for their loss of 'property'". Olusoga went onto explain how slave-owning had become so endemic in Britain that 'ordinary' people, even housewives and spinsters, owned and traded slaves on the stock market as if they would trade any other commodity! Records demonstrate that this practice wasn't only restricted to the political and power elite, but was also avidly exercised by thousands of 'lesser' British individuals spanning the length and breadth of England and the UK, all of whom would be handsomely recompensed for their losses.

The idea that Igbo pride and sense of self-worth resulted in colonial administrators that commanded and demanded recognition (at the expense of 'trouble' if overlooked or ignored), fits in with the history of slave rebellions and uprisings across the Caribbean and the Americas where Igbos were transported to. A consistent feature of these rebellions in Guyana, Brazil, Haiti, Jamaica, Barbados, Trinidad and Tobago, Virginia, and South Carolina, was that Igbos were at the heart of them all, resisting servitude and slavery. They didn't fear the penalty of death, because death meant they would return to Africa.

It's often posited that the most rebellious of slaves (the vast majority of whom were Igbo), were deposited in Jamaica, where they were subjected to *the* most sadistic and brutal plantation regime, resulting in a projected life span of three years, at best, after arrival for the most rebellious. To survive such brutality, it seems only logical that harsh and hard minds and hearts needed to develop. Again, it's not coincidental that, where 'black trouble' has brewed in England, it's often Nigerians (Igbos) and Jamaicans (probably of Igbo origin), that are being referred to.

Estimates are that, in America, 1 in 6 African-Americans have Igbo origins. These include such notables as Paul Robeson, Ice Cube, Cobe Bryant, Johnny Gill, Whitney Houston, Queen Latifah, Blair Underwood, Forest Whitaker, Edward James Roye, Nnamdi Asomugha, to name but a few. It's also estimated that 1 in 4 white Americans have 'black blood' in them, so it's quite likely that those same white Americans who raped, lynched, beat, murdered and resisted desegregation and the civil rights movement right up to the 1970s, did so to the detriment of their own blood relatives.

Sixteen

With lynching in mind, I survived lynching-by-swimming-pool during my second year at Wallingford Grammar School. During my first summer term I won the 100m, 200m, and 400m races achieving school records in all three events, and the long jump, at school sports day. Come the following academic year and throughout the winter months, cross-country running was a regular event during games lessons. I was good at cross-country, and usually won, but the races were always keenly contested by me and another pupil, Paul Beadle, a blonde-haired boy who was very athletic. Sometimes the races would only be decided in the final straight down the road, with both of us hammering neck-and-neck into the playground before finally crashing through the doors into the sports department changing rooms.

This was the case one day, after we'd ran the course in the freezing autumn weather through the cold, cloying mud in fields of Brussels sprouts, over metal field-dividing turn-styles and huge, ankle-deep icy puddles. After successfully managing to elbow Paul out of the way as we crashed through the doors, I won. However, my 'unsportsmanlike' shove was witnessed by the games teacher and, much to my dismay, he pronounced Paul the winner. Worse though, was that I was to be punished at lunch time, before which I was advised not to bother taking a shower. So, after all the others had trailed in and showered, and at the lunch time bell, I was paraded out onto the playground towards the school open-air swimming pool. My punishment was to swim the length of the pool from deep to shallow end (mercifully, in that order!). Apart from our youngest sister Kele who was a brilliant swimmer, the rest of us were rubbish. I'd only ever managed to swim a width of any pool I'd been in, so the thought of swimming a whole length was at best daunting, and at worst suicidal. But with hundreds of pupils and masters waiting excitedly to witness my humiliation, I just couldn't be seen to fail. I couldn't live with such shame and ignominy.

Dressed only in my swimming trunks (thankfully they weren't of mum's knitted variety!), I walked into the fenced-off swimming pool area alone, feeling like a forlorn Christian walking into a Roman amphitheatre to face a pride of underfed lions. I was already exhausted from the cross-country run, and I was shivering in the freezing cold. The jeering and hooting from the assembled throng of toffs reached a deafening crescendo as I dipped my big toe into the water. It was absolutely freezing! I couldn't wimp out though. I had to do this. The question was how?

I decided to make a running dive into the pool that would propel me a few further yards down the length, rather than getting into the pool and starting from the edge. I stepped back and fearfully hurled myself in. It was the worst belly-flop in aquatic sporting history, which only served to deliver pain from head to toe and totally disorientate me. Then, as I tried to break the surface and breathe, the effects of the freezing cold water hit me! With muscles beginning to cramp and seize up, I was nearly totally debilitated which, combined with my usually pathetically inept swimming ability, rendered me virtually incapable of actually swimming!

Upon breaking the surface (eventually), I was met with roars and howls of laughter. Clearly my struggle to breathe and swim (avoid drowning!), was providing great entertainment and amusement for the hundreds of chortling, braying toffs. The water-blurred image still lives with me today, and will do for the rest of my life, but I had to make it to the shallow end. It seemed like hours before I finally managed to doggy-paddle my way to the shallow end safety, after having swallowed gallons of water in the process and suffered the hoots and jeers of the hooray-henrys throughout the ordeal!

As I clambered out of the pool, the fever-pitched entertainment-feeding-frenzy of the crowd dissipated, to be replaced by a huge round of applause (such gentlemen, spiffing wheeze!). I felt cold outside, and cold in my heart. They weren't aware how close I'd come to dying that day, and my pride wouldn't dare allow me to show it as I made my way, barefoot and shivering with cold and fear to have a warm shower and get dressed.

I began to excel in most of my subject lessons, especially languages, and even started to develop and understand the sciences (though not Maths, of course!). I also developed an ability to play hockey as well, a game I'd never played before but, with the positions and rules basically the same as football, I made a seamless transition to this game with sticks. I particularly enjoyed settling the odd youthful disagreement with other boys by ensuring they got severe accidental-on-purpose raps around the legs with the hard-wood inverted shepherd-like sticks.

Bizarrely, at the start of my third year at the school, another black boy arrived in the first year!

Yay!

Nay!

This boy had tighter curlier hair than me, thicker lips than me, bigger and flatter nose than me and, generally speaking, 'blacker' features than me. The only difference was that his skin was white. Not albino white. But white! At an opportune moment I approached him to have a chat, and to reassure him (as a brother), that I'd look out for him. My expectation was that he'd definitely be faced with much of what I'd experienced regarding racist taunting and discrimination of one sort or another. The conversation was very short. He let me know immediately that he wasn't interested in me, and didn't want to be associated with me. Apparently, one of his great-great-grandparents was black, but his parents, grandparents and great-grandparents were all white. He was a throwback, an atavism, the definition of which is:

"the reappearance in an individual of characteristics of some remote ancestor that have been absent in intervening generations."

No wonder he didn't want to be associated with me, he was looking at me through the eyes of a white boy! In retrospect, I feel *so* sorry for him. He must have been really fucked up!

On skin colour alone he would have passed as white, but exceptionally obvious and overly-accentuated black features unequivocally betrayed an 'anomaly' in his ancestry. Under the US 'One Drop Rule' which was adopted as law in the early part of the 20th century, he would have been classified as black. The principle of 'invisible blackness' is an historical example of 'hypodescent', which effectively meant mixed-race children, even by virtue of only having one drop of 'negro' blood, would automatically be consigned to the lowest level of social status and privilege, so as to maintain the prevailing notions of white 'superiority', power, status and privilege.

Predictably, in (often vain) attempts to be considered white, mixed-race people during the American antebellum era who were exceptionally light-skinned *and* with white features made every effort to "pass" as white. Success in this endeavour would secure higher status and privilege, access to recently-created 'equal opportunities', and the full benefits of freedom.

White apartheid South Africa operated a similar, and equally degrading, race categorising procedure, the 'Pencil Test'. This involved a pencil being inserted into a person's hair. If it fell out (loose hair), they were considered white; and if it stuck (tight curly hair), they were considered black. Obviously, to 'qualify' as white meant the successful participants would go on to enjoy full citizenship status and privilege, whilst those who failed were doomed to black disempowerment and under privilege amongst the nadir of South African society.

I find it very interesting how, when looking at people, especially black people, generally I'm pretty good at making physical and mental distinctions between different groups. I can identify and tell the differences between white English, Irish and Eastern Europeans; Igbos, Yorubas and Hausas; between Nigerians and Ghanaians; between Africans and Caribbeans; with each group generally sharing specific and particular stereotypical physical and personality traits. Obviously, these are (probably) biased and impressionistic and certainly not as the result of extensive research!

In our family the standing jokes tend to revolve around the combinations we've inherited: relatively short stature - Igbo and Irish; big calves - Irish; big heads and obtuse head shapes - Igbo and Irish; stocky 'heavy-set' structure - Igbo and Irish; thin lips - Irish; flat nyash (bottoms) - Irish; sense of humour - Irish; poverty-driven approach to food - Igbo and Irish; attitude to education - Igbo; attitude to hard work - Irish and Igbo; mad personalities - Igbo and Irish; sense of justice and injustice - Irish; compassionate natures - Irish; motivation and aspiration - Igbo.

Despite the genetic and personality similarities we share as humans, there are also significant differences that exist between African and Caribbean mindsets when it comes to identity and unity. The prevailing view is that Africans despise "doze West Indies pipple!", and Caribbeans hate "dem blasted Hafricans!"

This mutual enmity, in my opinion, is yet another legacy of colonialism and slavery, and evidence of the very effective conditioning processes both groups were subjected to by their colonial and slave masters. Not including the more enlightened and educated, there remains a very deep-rooted and distasteful hatred and distrust between Nigerians and Jamaicans (pronounced Ja-my-cans and abbreviated to 'Jammohs' by Nigerians). Whilst irrefutably linked by blood, though separated by the Atlantic Ocean and 500 years of history, among many on both sides there is complete and utter mutual disdain, contempt, ridicule and rejection, a complete refusal to be compared with each other and identified as being, essentially, one and the same.

Many older Jamaicans passionately claim to originate in Jamaica, and not Africa.

"Mi not a bomberclaat Hafrican, mi a Jamaican tru and tru!"

Nigerians, on the other hand and other side of the Atlantic, will claim:

" we sent and sold di ones wey dey uzeless and no get sense!"

Both parties express their claims of rejection and disgust with absolute scorn, contempt and derision for each other, but rarely if ever appear to question in any logical way the reasons as to why they hold these vehement beliefs. If they were to adopt an honest appraisal of their pasts, it might occur to them that not only were they physically manipulated, they were also psychologically manipulated and conditioned.

Slave buyers, slave kidnappers and colonialist thieves would stand to benefit from exaggerating the differences between Nigerians in Africa and Nigerians already shipped into slavery (in this case Jamaica), by propagating the fallacy that the slaves were, indeed, the useless ones (this would also provide a legitimate reason to negotiate purchase prices down at the point of sale, and justify local Africans selling their kindred into slavery!), thereby justifying their disposal.

Plantation owners in the Caribbean and the Americas would propagate the fallacy among plantation-born slaves that newly-arrived Africans were savage, dumb, and they couldn't even speak English!

The net effect of these divide-and-rule tactics on both sides of the Atlantic slave trade was that neither African nor slave, Nigerian nor Jamaican, would identify, empathise or unite with each other. Indeed both sides totally absorbed the lies they were fed, foolishly or unwittingly contributing to their continued colonial oppression, exploitation and enslavement. So effective was the conditioning and indoctrination, that 150 years later, with freedom and independence fought for and won, we don't need the white man any more to put each other down. We are now more than capable, willing and ready to do it to ourselves thank you very much!

Cholsey, much like Blean and Chartham in Kent, was a country village, surrounded by farm fields, greenbelt land essentially and, true to form we'd find our entertainment in the surrounding fields and countryside, and Obi and I started to see a bit of the outside world on our away fixtures with the Cholsey Bluebirds football team. Our biggest and most hated local derby rivals were Crowmarsh Boys Football Club based in Wallingford and, for children's football, such intense rivalry! Not always and only between the boys, but the parents!

"Break the little black bastard's legs! Don't let him do that to you!"

These invectives weren't solely aimed at Obi and I. There were two other black families in Cholsey, 'fully' black families, the Kaipah family from Malawi in East Africa, and the Johnson family from Barbados in the Caribbean. Again, true to form, Peter Kaipah and David Johnson were great footballers, and Obi's age group, therefore in his team. Rabson Kaipah was Peter's older brother and, whilst not bad, he was nowhere near as good as Peter, but in my team. However, it was great having 'brothers' in our teams, sharing the same fight and cause. Both their families lived on Celsea Place, just around the corner off Papist Way.

For some reason the hospital offered our parents the opportunity to move into a house on Celsea Place, which was a fairly new circa 1950s-built three-up-two-down. It was the first house we'd lived in that had central heating! This meant Obi and I never had to sleep in the same bed again during the winter months, taking turns 'spooning' each other to keep warm.

It's also the house where Obi and I had our famous and legendary 'underpants' challenge! The challenge, over the Christmas holiday from school, was to see who could last the longest wearing the same pair of underpants without having them washed. Shamefully (now), I couldn't remember who won, so I had to call and confirm with Obi. Unsurprisingly, he said I won!

For me though, one of the most memorable events that took place in Celsea Place (other than watching mum kill the chickens we'd reared in our back garden to put meat on our plates!), was watching the 1970 World Cup finals beamed live from Mexico City. Specifically, watching Brazil versus England and the incomparable Pele! The Brazil team were total beauty and poetry in motion. I could hardly breathe in suspense for 60 minutes until Jairzinho scored to ensure Brazil won 1-0, and I was in ecstasy, not only had Brazil beaten the holders England, they were a team that had so many black players and the best-ever in the world in Pele (forget Christiano Ronaldo and Lionel Messi!), and they beat the 1966 holders England! Forget Gordon Banks' save from Pele's header, and Bobby Moore's block tackle on the edge of the area, Brazil won, England lost. I literally and unashamedly cried with joy!

I couldn't wait to watch their games, and lauded the achievements of the 'Samba Boys' in their gold shirts, blue shorts, white socks and

Puma boots as they crushed Italy 4-1 in the final after allowing Roberto Boninsegna to equalise Pele's 18th minute opener. When Brazil captain Carlos Alberto crashed home the final nail in the coffin for Brazil to put the result beyond any doubt, I went into complete and absolute ecstatic meltdown again, sobbing with relief and joy. It couldn't get any better, watching a team with so many black and mixed-race players crush all before them to obtain the ultimate prize in world football. Life couldn't get any better for me.

I remember having seen images of the 1968 Olympic Games showing two black African American men standing shoeless (to represent the dispossessed status of their fellow ex-slave black African Americans), on the 200m winners' medal podium with fists, clad in black leather gloves, thrust defiantly in the air as they looked to the floor. I didn't understand the meaning and significance of the gestures, but I remember the indignance of the white world TV commentators, press and media, incensed and outraged at the temerity of Tommie Smith (gold medal) and John Carlos (bronze medal). How dare these uppity negroes make such a stance and spoil 'our' games?

It was bad enough that they'd won, no need to rub salt into white world's wounds!

And then I became increasingly aware of the impact on the world of another African American, the greatest ever boxer called Muhammad Ali.

When I was 13 years old Ali, born Cassius Clay on January 17th 1942 in Louisville, Kentucky, had already won and been stripped of his World Heavyweight Champion Crown. He'd already won Olympic gold, beaten black mafiosa puppet Sonny Liston to win the Heavyweight Championship of the world, joined the Nation of Islam and become a Muslim, and been incarcerated for three years by the American 'political establishment' for refusing the draft to fight in the Vietnam War in 1966, stating:

"Man, I aint got no quarrel with them Viet Cong".

The salient point being, why should a black man, suffering degrading post-slavery racial humiliation and segregation in his 'homeland', travel around the world to kill other people of colour in a war not of his making?

Muhammad Ali, one single black man who looked the world in the eye, standing up against the establishment, he faced down 'the man', the white establishment of the (segregated and disunited) 'United' Slave States of America that presumed to police the world!

It's interesting that the pariah nations of England and America describe themselves as the 'United' Kingdom and the 'United' States of America respectively, in my view oxymora in both cases, unless you are white Protestants then sure, you'll enjoy the benefits and privileges of full citizenship status and equality of a truly united nation. As Tommie Smith stated with regards his raised fist 'Black Power' podium salute:

"This was not a Black Power salute, but a Human Rights Salute".

All very forceful images, sentiments and messages that served to embolden and empower hungry, conscious black minds all around the world; mine, like those of my brother's and sisters', especially Ijem's, was open and receptive to this new powerful and positive message:

"Say it loud, I'm black and I'm proud!"

We'd all been vaguely aware of racial-political developments in the USA, particularly those surrounding the revolutionary Black Panther Movement, which first came to prominence in 1966. The Black Panther Party for Self-Defense started life as a far-left wing African-American revolutionary socialist organisation and, under the leadership of Huey P Newton and Bobby Seale, advocated Black Nationalism in the USA, stipulating a 10-point plan of demands which, if granted (no chance!), would deliver wide-ranging equalities to the ghettoised and (still) downtrodden and oppressed black African-Americans.

Apart from the coolest imagery of black leather gloves, black jackets, shades, bell-bottom trousers, guns and berets worn at the jauntiest of angles they, like Muhammad Ali when he first won the heavyweight championship of the world, 'shook up the world!'

They, working in collaboration with other black (though often lighter-skinned) radical activists such as Angela Davis, put the plight of black African-America on the world map, warts and all! Though the Black Panther Party folded in 1982 without formally achieving the demands in their revolutionary 10-point plan (which were far too extreme for white racist America!), they had, by then, contributed immensely to raising racial-political consciousness and awareness in America and across the world. Often associated with violence and criminality, the Panthers were, in my mind, an essential element of American and world political change.

Certainly perceptions of black people changed, the 'don't fuck with me!' message was indelibly written and irretrievably spoken, loud and clear!

We were far less aware of the 1955-1968 African-American Civil Rights Movement which, unlike the Panther's Black Power Movement, lobbied for social movement aimed at outlawing racial discrimination against black Americans and restoring voting rights to them, through non-violent means only. The adoption of protests and demonstration marches, bus boycotts and sit-ins, civil disobedience falling short of violence in segregated America were key elements of the movement. Most prominent among the many iconic figures of the Civil Rights Movement were, for me, W. E. B. Dubois, Malcolm X, Rosa Parks and, the ultimate world statesman, Dr Martin Luther King, Junior.

Like the world, Black African-America would not be as it is today if not for the selfless commitment and sacrifice of all of the above. However, the contributions of their slave and ex-slave forefathers and foremothers must never go unrecognised in this achievement.

As geographically distant as these 'movements' may have been, the trickle-down factor they had on our lives in England was immeasurable. Whilst as a pre-teen black boy in racist England I hadn't really developed any truly meaningful understanding of the concept of racial pride (other than mum's clear directive not to 'take shit' from anybody!), the movements instilled an irreducible curiosity, sense of identity, self-worth and, probably most importantly, self-determination which, supported by my parents, were to contribute to and help formulate my future development.

Mum and dad appeared to be prospering at work. Mum was a Staff Nurse and dad a Charge Nurse. We were all getting on with school and doing our best. Living on Celsea Place meant we had ready-made mates and play-pals a couple of doors down the road. We grew very close to the Kaipah and Johnson families, though it crossed my mind that 'Kaipah' was an unusual name, but it was an African name so therefore I understood why it seemed unusual. What struck me as strange was the fact that David's family surname was 'Johnson'! How could black people have English surnames?

How can a black man be named Mr White, Smith (pronounced Simmit in Jamaica!), Brown, Gordon, Daniels, Williams, Jones, Anderson, Hunte, Francis, Holder, Wheeler, McAnuff, Roberts, Regis? It didn't make sense to me! It was only several years later when I learned that black African slaves who were taken to the Caribbean and the Americas were stripped of their names and identities and, even worse, had the names of their owner slave masters imposed on them. In many cases, when slaves were bought by new owners, this meant their surnames automatically changed to that of their new owner, so it was often the case that a slave would have more than one surname throughout his or her life, depending on the number of sales they'd been subjected to!

I'd like to be able to say, with utmost outrage and indignity, that this is an abomination in Igboland, but I can't, because it's not. Many Igbos living in the port and coastal areas (as is the case elsewhere in Nigeria), answer absurd English names! Mr John Harry, Henry David, William George, Goodluck James, and a host of ridiculous combinations of English names are common and prevalent in and around the Port Harcourt, Bonny and Calabar regions, adopted by local predecessors who worked alongside and in collusion with the white invaders and slave traders centuries ago!

Seventeen

The five of us kids were growing up and gaining a bit more independence. My early teens were punctuated by what seemed to be and felt like an ongoing battle with my dad. I felt like he hated and resented me. I knew I couldn't stand him, so the feelings between us were probably mutual, though I didn't understand what had happened to bring this about! I couldn't do a thing right by him, and he didn't hesitate to put me down, humiliate and castigate me at any and every opportunity. He never, ever, came to watch me play football and, on the very rare occasion that my team won, he'd say that the opposition must have been "uzeless!" He never congratulated me on any of my achievements and it was almost as if he resented my very being. Interestingly, much later in our adult lives when Obi and I were chatting, he actually stated that he noticed this period between me and dad, and that he felt sorry for me. He felt uncomfortable throughout this particular stage of my rite of passage.

Obi and I enjoyed a great relationship. We were, and have remained, very close brothers. We've never really had a fall-out and, when we've had disagreements, we've always been able to resolve them over a chat that usually ends in us talking about football. The same cannot be said, on the other hand, about our sisters, who seemed to quarrel and argue throughout their teens, especially Chi-chi and Ijem!

When we were younger, 5, 6, 7, 8 years old, we'd all argue and 'take sides'. Significantly, and totally unconsciously, Chi-chi and Obi (the lighter-skinned ones), would side-up against me and Ijem (the darker-skinned ones), and vice versa. When 'sides' were to be chosen, almost without fail, the sides would be lighter versus darker! I'd always 'choose' Ijem, and she'd always 'choose' me, and the same dynamic prevailed with Chi-chi and Obi.

Our horizons started to expand also. Chi-chi was developing her athletic and musical abilities, gaining admirable proficiency and recognition in both disciplines as she worked towards achieving the magical holy grail of the Grade 8 in piano, whilst still destroying all-comers on the athletic track. Ijem and Kele were growing up and were advancing a long way down the road to becoming beautiful young women. Obi and I were still pretty stupid boys but, with the relative freedom traditionally afforded to boys in all sexist societies, we started to spread our wings a bit further afield.

Without a penny in our pockets, on Saturdays we started bunking on the train from Cholsey into London, then bunking the tube from Paddington to Upton Park, then walking down Green Street before bunking into the Boleyn Ground by any means necessary to watch West Ham United Football Club play. This team included the three World Cup winning heroes in Bobby Moore, hat-trick hero Geoff Hurst and Martin Peters, as well as the black man-mountain centre forward Bermudan international Clyde Best and tricky Nigerian attacking midfielder Ade Coker. Absolute bliss!

Other than our obvious insane and passionate obsession for football, I don't know what possessed us to make these regular pilgrimages! Avoiding paying British Rail and London Underground fares was pretty straightforward, non-problematic, and the least of our concerns, as was scaling the walls, squeezing through fences and ducking under turnstiles to gain entry into the ground, where we'd sit and watch the game safely ensconced in the famous 'chicken-run' family enclosure. And we'd sing the famous West Ham supporters' song with excitement and glee:

"I'm forever blowing bubbles,
Pretty bubbles in the air
They fly so high, nearly reach the sky
And like my dreams they fade and die

Fortune's always hiding,
I've looked everywhere
I'm forever blowing bubbles,
Pretty bubbles in the air
United! United! United!
For us, it was game on!

Far more disconcerting and troubling were the chillingly mindless and brutal punch-ups we'd witness on the trains, stations, and on the road to the ground. This was during the early days of the bovver-booted white-boy skinheads, thugs in denim jackets and trousers rolled up around their ankles to expose their menacing Dr Marten air-cushion boots, tightly laced right up to the top. Frenzied fights between opposition 'supporters' would break out anywhere and everywhere en route. As members of the ICF (Inter City Firm), they'd steam into each other, wildly kicking, punching, gouging and slashing, to prove their allegiance to the 'Ammers. No firm was spared, Chelsea, Arsenal, United, City, Leeds, Wednesday, Millwall, whoever, they all got a right good kicking by the hooligan West Ham Inter City Firm of London's fabled East End.

Apparently, according to the Compact Oxford English Dictionary, the word hooligan may have originated from the surname of a fictional rowdy Irish family in a music hall song of the 1890s. Clarence Rook, in his 1899 book, *Hooligan Nights*, also claimed that the word came from Patrick Hoolihan (or Hooligan), an Irish bouncer and thief who lived in London. No surprises on either explanation there then! Obi and I successfully managed to navigate our way through and around these skirmishes, and never became the targets of their attention. However, we were both aware that there weren't many black thugs and hooligans involved in the affrays, or spectators in the crowds for that matter!

I've often thought about these experiences in order to understand the mind and behaviour of the thug. The white working class thug who'd impatiently see out the intervening working week, eagerly living for the weekend so as to kick the shit out of opposition supporters who dared to have the audacity to encroach on their manor!

Classic animalistic territorialism of the disempowered and dispossessed?

Unstinting allegiance and commitment to defend the honour of their clubs?

The expression of latent, repressed and deep-rooted aggression and violence?

Thuggery for thuggery sake?

Whichever, football violence was a dangerously seductive and exciting feature of our regular weekend away-days, and one that we'd never *voluntarily* get involved in!

Like most teenagers, we were becoming increasingly aware of popular fashion, music, and the importance of appearing trendy and current. I'll never forget the first time I saw Chi-chi wearing a pair of burgundy satin hot pants! Unfortunately for me, it would take me ages to save up enough to buy the latest garb out of my paper-round money, 'sta-pressed' straight-legged ankle-swinging trousers, checked button-down collar Ben Sherman shirt, Dr Marten boots, two-tone jacket and trousers and blue Crombie coat. I never had the full set at any one time, but had varying combinations of them all depending on the health (or lack thereof!), of my perpetually ailing and meagre finances!

When I was fourteen and a half and part way through my penultimate year of secondary school at the grammar, we were on the move yet again! Probably for the first time ever I was devastated at the thought of leaving good friends behind, especially the Kaipah and Johnson families. Believe it or not my nemesis Doc Drummond and I grew to become great friends at Wallingford Grammar School, despite the fact that he'd called me a nigger and I'd been forced to pulp him, and I knew I'd miss the weekly Harris-Man cartoon strip! Apart from my German teacher, I wouldn't miss any of the others (especially the Child Catcher!), though that's not to say they weren't great teachers, they were. It's just that Mr Fitzhugh had gone the extra mile for me; he'd filled me with confidence and believed in me. I'll remember and appreciate that forever.

Eighteen

We moved to Caversham in Reading, in the royal county of Berkshire, Newport Road to be precise. Mum and dad had got better-paying jobs at Borocourt ('Mental') Hospital, situated seven or eight miles outside of the town on the back road towards Oxford.

They'd bought a cramped mid-terrace three-up-two-down which required serious damp-proofing, redecorating and rodent removal. On arrival and exploration of the rear square patch of space that masqueraded as a back garden, I found the rusted head of a discarded oil drum which, when hit, made beguilingly haunting sounds, the remains of a West Indian steel drum. It sounded beautiful to me. I associated it with much of the music we'd listened and danced to when we went to parties as children with mum and dad in London, especially at Auntie Margaret's and Uncle Ben's house!

Auntie Margaret was the stereotypical paper-white, severely short-sighted and blind-without-spectacles, red-haired Irish woman, and mum's best friend; Uncle Ben was the stereotypically jovial and care-free Igbo 'back-in-the-day' mate of dad's. Both loved a house-party and held them regularly, and we were always willing guests. They played old soul, ska, calypso, high-life and what is now (very) rare groove! Though childless they were great fun and treated us as if we were their children, at times spoiling us rotten with treats! I think the five of us developed a love and appreciation of popular music and dance over the years of attending parties at Auntie Margaret's and Uncle Ben's.

Most importantly though, Reading was packed with black people, the majority of whom originated mainly from Barbados and Jamaica.

We were surrounded by them, even down our road. We even had Indian and Pakistani neighbours. We'd moved into a melting pot of nations. It was brilliant!

Again, I was faced with the dilemma of choosing which school to attend. Reading still had secondary modern schools, as well as grammar schools for boys and girls. The town also had a modern, new comprehensive school which catered for all academic abilities, played football as opposed to rugby, and was co-ed. GIRLS attended Highdown Comprehensive School so, in my mind, there was no choice. Highdown Comprehensive it was!

I was prepared to defend my choice in the face of dad's inevitable disappointment by arguing the comprehensive was organised into ability streams, and that I'd go straight into the top stream for all my subjects, thus maintaining my elite education. Plus, I was tired of going to school on my own. I wanted to go to school with my brother and sisters. Dad bought my pleas on the proviso that I wouldn't let my studies slip and that I'd remain focused, which was a promise I swore blindly to keep, and one that I was destined to under-perform on! And spectacularly so!

Somehow Chi-chi managed to blag her way into gaining admission to the prestigious Kendrick Grammar School for Girls near Reading town centre. Mum and dad had accompanied her to her interview, but like mine at Wallingford, she had to speak up and represent herself, which she clearly did with flying colours! Her successful application was due mainly to her interview performance, along with the positive and glowing references and recommendations she'd received on her athletic and music ability, and the fact that she'd actually passed her 11+ in the first place! Great news for Chi-chi and the family, she deserved it and wouldn't waste the opportunity.

Ijem, Obi and I started at Highdown Comprehensive which had retained its old red-brick sixth-form centre, but built a brand new school around it that included several sports and athletics fields, a few football pitches, an expansive and well-equipped indoor gymnasium, and an indoor heated swimming pool. Sports were high on the curriculum at Highdown, and the three of us continued to excel. I particularly remember the (what seemed like) very many children of the Anderson family during our first days at the school, Ivy, Hyacinth, Susie (who was to become Ijem's life-long friend), Derrick and Mikey.

Though still only in my fourth year, after watching me play football, the Head of Games Mr Berry arrived at the door during one of my lessons and, after speaking very conspiratorially with me outside in the corridor, told me I was selected to play for the school first XI. I was proud and excited at the prospect as it was proof positive of my above-average ability. It was great playing for the school, with the players gaining almost hero-status in home matches where classes were suspended in order for the whole school to come out and support the boys. I loved it!

Whilst still at Wallingford Grammar I'd suffered from quite serious osteochondritis in both knees, at one stage having both legs in hip-to-ankle plaster casts for four weeks. I walked round the place like Lon Chaney's Frankenstein monster! I was totally devastated and demoralised at not being able to play football, and now at Highdown I was playing in front of hundreds of screaming supporters, I'd gone from one extreme to another in the space of a few months. Total bliss!

Highdown Comprehensive served as a huge learning curve for me on several fronts.

I hadn't been in a school with so many black and Asian students before. This meant that I'd need to start expanding my repertoire of social-skills to be sensitive to different and new cultures, perceptions, expectations, and, essentially, to do whatever was 'cool' in order to assimilate myself into my new friendship and reference groups. I didn't want to look like a country bumpkin, I wanted to fit in in every way. It really helped being good at sports, especially football, and athletics.

It also helped being reasonably good-looking, especially bearing in mind the fact there were girls in the school! It just so happened to be the case that, at the time during the early 1970s, thanks to the prevailing images of the Black Power Movement from the USA, the afro hairstyle was 'in'. Like Ijem, I had a huge afro and, almost by virtue of said afro, gained automatic status at the top of the 'most wanted' pecking order in school. I wasn't used to receiving so much female attention and adulation and, at times, I found it quite embarrassing and often felt uncomfortable having to deal with such attention from so many girls. However, suffice is to say that, once I'd developed my confidence and lyrics, things very quickly settled down to a manageable (and enjoyable!), procession of black, white, mixed-race and Asian girls that I 'spent time with'!

Not that I would ever claim to be remotely attractive, modesty wouldn't allow me! But interesting current theory suggests mixed-race people are consistently considered and voted to be the most talented, attractive and desirable by their black *and* white peers. Similar theory also suggests that mixed-race people are physically fitter and tend to suffer less from common ailments than non-nixed-race people and, further, the more disparate the genetics of the parents, the more likely this is to be the case. So, it's probably reasonable to argue, on this basis, that there are no more disparate racial groups than black and white in terms of genetic characteristics, so a simplistic conclusion may well be that mixed-race people benefit fully from the best of both worlds, genetically!

That's not to say that I necessarily agree with these propositions. I remain exceptionally sceptical and concerned about any 'theory' that borders on the eugenics of the 1920s and 30s which depicted black people as genetically sub-human. These theories also propagate and maintain racial stereotyping that invariably results in one race, or races, either suffering or benefitting depending on the persuasions of those people writing the theories. At risk of sidelining the environmentalist 'nurture' side of the debate, we don't really want to encourage the fallacy that white people are genetically more intelligent than black people, or that black people are better at sports than white people. Do we?

Initially I didn't consciously discriminate along the lines of colour with regards friends. If people were decent and fun, I'd spend time with them, no problem. However, I became increasingly aware of concern among my black friends if and when I was spending time with groups of white or Asian kids. I noticed there was hardly any integration and crossing of racial groups when it came to friendships. Birds of a feather really did flock together in this school! So, it was normal for groups of white, Asian and black pupils to spend time together in classes but then, at break times, veer off to form very distinct friendships groups that were determined by skin colour. Whites would stick together, blacks would stick together, and (the comparably small number of) Asians would stick with any group who'd allow them access and temporary membership!

This didn't bother me in the slightest at first. Whoever I felt like spending time with, that's where you'd find me, irrespective of their colour. Then, slowly, my perceptions, along with other things, started to change. I noticed that pupils weren't treated equally and, quite regularly, were discriminated against in a number of ways.

I understood the principle and philosophy of 1970s comprehensive education was to educate pupils from a wide variety of backgrounds and abilities in the same school. This would entail boys and girls, blacks, whites and Asians, working class and middle class, high ability and lower ability, all being taught the same subjects in the same schools, with the only distinction being made between ability levels. I noticed that the top streams in all the subjects were uniformly populated mainly by white pupils who appeared to be middle class. The overwhelming majority of black students were in the lower streams.

I noticed that teachers would punish pupils differently for the same, or very similar, misdemeanours.

The pastoral side of the school was arranged in houses, North, South, East and West. I was put into South House which appeared to have a lot of the academically 'brighter' pupils, as was Obi. Ijem, for some reason, was put into North House which, in view of the make-up of the majority of its pupil constituents, ought to have been more accurately named 'North Ghetto'! It seemed like North House was constantly blighted by riots!

Bullying and fights were common and regular occurrences in the school, and not all perpetrated by black pupils, in fact, far from it. There was a very high profile white working class bullying culture in the school, mainly directed at younger pupils of any racial background. I'm talking about really nasty thug-types, the ones that always finished their education at the earliest possible opportunity and left without any, or very few, qualifications, the ones who identifiably developed a counter-school culture, resistance towards teachers and education in general, rejecting school values and belittling all those who aspired to achieve. You know the type I'm talking about, the ones who started drinking alcohol at an early age, got their girlfriends pregnant in their teens, went into low- or unskilled jobs or permanent unemployment, got wound up in petty crime and drug-taking, benefits-seekers, 'scroungers' and survivors who, fully cognisant of their rights, but fully ignorant or dismissive of their responsibilities to society, felt the world owed them something!

I thought I had it tough at school in Canterbury and Wallingford being the only black boy in the school! What explanation was there for the regularity of punch-ups in this melting-pot? When fights between a white pupil and a black pupil broke out, it was amazing how all the pupils would gather around to cheer on and support the scrapper of their own colour.

Mr Berry, a straight talking northerner from Bolton in Lancashire, was Head of South House and, after observing such a scrap from the second floor window, called me to his office. Despite the fact that I wasn't fighting, I was, by this time, supporting the black boy. He noticed that the support for the antagonists was racially divided and determined, and questioned me on this after having called me into his office. I told him that I thought it was only natural these types of allegiances had developed in the school, especially considering the discriminatory treatment that was meted out by the teachers. He wasn't happy with my response and, regardless of the fact that I was his star footballer, he accused *me* of having started a 'Black Power Movement' in the school, and warned me that he was going to 'keep a very close eye on me' from that point on!

'Incredulous' doesn't do justice to how I felt. How did he arrive at that conclusion? Was it my huge afro, or the fact that he was aware of my growing popularity? Who knows? He actually said at one stage that he thought I should have intervened to stop the fight! No chance! EVERY school kid loves a fight, so long as they're watching it and not fighting in it! But to be honest, deep down, I actually liked the idea of my being considered to be a leader, especially if comparisons were being made between me and the likes of Huey P Newton and Bobby Seale! So, whilst secretly I took the accusation as a compliment, externally I was indignant about the slur on my character and forthrightly denied the accusation.

Everything started to go wrong for me in the classroom though. When I first arrived I brought with me a zest, joy and love for learning. I was positive, interested and committed to education. I had an insatiable thirst for knowledge, I wanted to learn, but didn't hesitate to question things if they didn't feel or seem right. I had remained very vocal and always featured highly in classroom discussions and debates. In short, I loved everything about school and education!

I'd been put into the upper streams for all my lessons, but I wasn't being stretched in the slightest. I was being taught alongside the so-called crème-de-le-crème of the new progressive comprehensive education system, yet, at the risk of sounding dismissive and arrogant, all my 'elite' peers appeared thick to me. I'd covered everything, years ago and at a much higher level, at Canterbury and especially Wallingford. At first I'd be zapping my hand up in response to the teachers' questions, to the point where it got embarrassing, so I stopped. I didn't want to be labelled the class creep, swot or know-all, I just wanted to be like the others.

I got bored, distracted, and became increasingly lethargic. I couldn't be bothered to work in class or at home for that matter, and thought I'd sail through all my GCE exams (which I never even bothered to study or revise for!). Wrong! I spent much of my final fifth year at school bunking off lessons, either on or off school premises, either thieving from local shops or generally mucking about. I also developed certain (disreputable?) entrepreneurial skills during this period. In view of my popularity in the school and the presumed clout and influence I had over my year group, I became empowered by the teachers.

Though falling short of declared and officially-nominated prefect or monitor status (a position I would have rejected outright), I was 'entrusted' by the teachers to assist with certain aspects of the school. For example, I was given wads of dinner tickets which I was supposed to sell on to students, which I did, whilst only returning half the face value of the tickets, claiming the wads had been stolen from my locker. My claims were never disbelieved or investigated, I'd just be given even more tickets to sell!

Also, whenever there was an event on at school, I'd be given event tickets to sell. I applied the same procedure with these also! I also ran a protection racket for younger pupils. I never threatened or extorted money from them, but they understood they'd be safe from the bullies if they weighed me in on a regular basis, which they were only too happy to do. Lastly, I also organised poker games in which I earned and lost a lot from, but it was great fun and I'd become addicted to the rush, the highs and lows, the bluff and counter-bluff!

As a direct result of my 'business' activities in the school I was, for the very first time in my life, relatively well-off and financially independent, though much of my earnings, in combination with my paper round money, was spent either on clothes, football boots, or helping mum out every now and again.

The only problem with being a 'top-boy' is that you get called out every once in a while and, to save face and maintain your unassailable reputation, you have to stand up to your responsibilities. This was the case when two of the biggest white thug-bullies in my year, though inmates of North House, had been beating up on little third year kids in Ijem and Obi's year. We hatched a plan for the first thug.

Obi and one of his best mates, Andrew Holder, would shout abuse at Thug 1, making their escape from his inevitable pursuit through the doors at the rear of the school library that adjoined with the rear entrance to North House, where I'd be lying in wait for him. Predictably, he rose to the bait and came charging after Obi and Andrew and, after slamming through the North House doors in hot pursuit of his fleeing prospective victims, he was met by me, unhinged and displaced wooden locker door in hand, that I smashed into his shocked face. This only served to stun him, but that was all I wanted or needed, as I followed up with a few more slab-of-oak-to-face smashes. The guy was big, thick, but big, and started to wobble. The blood pouring from his battered nose provided me with the perfect target upon which to rain blows, and I did, four or five right-handers to the face saw him crumple to the floor. For me, that was it, all over, job done, especially considering there was a crowd of fifty or sixty North House ghetto-dwellers watching. He'd never bully anybody in school again. As he grovelled at my feet, pawing at the blood-spattered floor in his semi-conscious efforts to get back to his feet, I saw a brown Doctor Marten bovver-boot penetrate my peripheral vision in its unerring journey to connect with Thug 1's supine face. Blood, snot and teeth exploded everywhere as he crashed fully prostrate and unconscious to the floor. Unbeknown to me but a black friend of mine, fourth year AG, had been constantly bullied by Thug 1 since he started at the school, and this was his opportunity to exact revenge, and boy did he take it?! Thug 1 never returned to school after that day.

A few days later we were on a school trip that included a convoy of buses transporting us to and from the venue. Thug 2, unaccompanied by his wing-man Thug 1, inexplicably went on the trip. True to form, he bullied a little first-year black boy which, when reported to me, left me in no position other than to sort it out, and I made my intentions known. Knowledge of the planned retribution spread like wild fire around the eagerly expectant throng and, on our return to school, a huge mob of kids of all ages followed me in tracking down Thug 2. When I caught up with him by the side of South House, the baying crowd was at fever pitch, much like a hue and cry dating back to the middle ages! I barely managed to attract his attention:

"Oi B!", at which he turned round and tried to give me some lip. I wasn't having it, I wasn't getting involved in a slanging match, and I wanted this over quickly, so I stuck one on him, right hand, bang! That ended my involvement because, as soon as he started to totter, the by now feral mob descended upon him, battering him senseless. I couldn't (and didn't need to) get near him again as he got savaged by those kids!

Like Thug 1, he never returned to school after that day. Neither of them sat their GCSE exams at the end of the year which, in my mind, was anathema, but proof of the fact that I still valued education.

Mr Berry had heard about Thug 1's beating prior to the school trip and, again unknown to me at the time, observed Thug 2's exile from his office window on the second floor of South House. He DIDN'T punish me for either incident, so I was only left to assume I'd done the school a favour by running these two thugs out, never to return. Interesting!

I used to walk the two miles to school from Caversham to Emmer Green with a small group of black friends who lived on my road, or those immediately surrounding us. All the houses were terraced, built during the heyday of the industrial revolution to house the exploited, powerless and dispossessed unskilled production-line workers of the long-vanished factories that once provided wage labour for the working class masses in Reading.

Mum would always recount the story of the knock on the door in the morning, when big Win, who lived round the corner from us, would call so we could walk to school together. Big Win was BIG! His family must have been THE most effective and productive cane-cutters in the history of Barbados! In my fifth year at school I was still only about 5' 5" or 5' 6" in height. Big Win was a unit, 6' 2", ripped and built! He'd never wear a jacket or coat to school, even during the winter months, favouring the tightest of tight T-shirts to show off his formidable muscular frame. He had muscles on muscles, the perfect V-frame, with huge chest, rippling torso, and tiny waste. Mum would stand at the door as we sauntered off to school, quietly laughing at her puny, diminutive son walking along beside this onyx colossus!

Big Win was famous for brutality when he was in the mood, but rarely bothered to get into confrontations when he didn't feel like it, he just couldn't be bothered, because nobody would dare to confront him and, those he picked on when he was in a mood, were battered and reduced to pulp almost instantly. It got to the point where, for Big Win, beating people up wasn't fun anymore! I thought we were good friends until, one day, during break time in South House, I saw 'that' look in his eye, he was in the mood, only his gaze this time was directed at me!!!!!

After shitting myself instantly at the certain knowledge that my life would soon be over, either through death or disability at the hands of Big Win who, for some reason, obviously thought it might be fun to smash me up. What could I do? I'd witnessed Big Win in action! Most people, the sensible ones, just took the beating, which probably explains why Big Win got bored picking on people. But, on the rare occasions that his victims attempted to mount any form of defence, as futile as it would most definitely be, he'd get 'that' look in his eyes, a small grin on his face, and then wreck them!

Thinking quickly as he started playing with and pawing at me, I knew I'd have zero chance if I tried to defend myself physically (and, if it got to a fight, this is what I would have to have done!), he'd rip me apart limb from limb, so I had to use my brain. Igbo sense!

He started squaring up in front of me, oozing menace and painful intent as the other kids went quiet, expecting to be unwilling witnesses to the inevitable and imminent demise of my popular self.

I went cold.

I stared him straight in the eyes and, voice firm, slow and steady, said:

> "Win, *do not* fuck with me, because if you do, you'll have to kill me, because you know I won't stop coming back for you!"

I learnt the powerful effect of maintaining eye contact with a bully aggressor. When they're going through the pre-fight rigmarole, never move your eyes away from theirs, look deep into them, look deep into their souls. It freaks them out, unnerves them, because it's not supposed to happen! Victims are supposed to timidly whinge and beg for mercy and, when this doesn't happen, the aggressor invariably reconsiders their position, spooked at the prospect that they might just be picking on a lunatic who will stop at nothing to exact revenge. That was my tactic with Big Win, and it worked, thank fuck for that!

Nineteen

Mum and dad continued to work opposite shifts at Borocourt Hospital, usually mum on nights and dad the day shift. Chi-chi started to flourish at Kendrick Girls Grammar School, I think for the first time since primary school she felt she was in more comfortable, suitable and civilised surroundings. The twins were progressing well through Highdown, and Kele was doing well at primary school. The sisterly squabbles between Chi-chi and Ijem about clothes and personal space were developing healthily, with Chi-chi, as the senior 'apple of the family's eye', usually gaining support and credibility over Ijem, though she wouldn't have been interested in taking Ijem on in a fight!

As with all teenagers, we started to seek entertainment more outside of the home. Reading had a massive nightclub situated above the town's bus station, the Top Rank. It was *the* place to go on a Saturday night, bedecked with lush red carpets, chrome and glass fixtures and fittings, a huge dance floor, disco lights, several bars on both levels and a stage upon which the DJs would play the music for the thousands of their loyal Saturday night revellers. Chi-chi, me, Ijem and Obi were regulars, Ijem and me (as the increasingly more wayward of the children!), more so than Chi-chi and Obi. We'd aim to arrive at around 10.00-10.30pm, giving us enough time to take our positions in the queue (and push in if necessary!), to ensure entry, get warmed up and in the mood, before the second floor annexe opened at 12.00pm midnight, the Night Owl.

The Night Owl was a far smaller venue than the Top Rank, with a maximum capacity probably of 500 or so. Entry was through a double swing-door off the Top Rank mezzanine level. There were distinct differences between the Top Rank and Night Owl. Firstly, the Top Rank played more top-40 pop-type disco music, whereas the Night Owl played more soul and funk, with a little bit of reggae thrown in; secondly, the Night Owl was populated mainly by black party-goers who'd desert the Top Rank at 11.59pm on the dot; thirdly, the best dancers (male and female) were in the Night Owl; fourthly, the coolest people were in the Night Owl; fifthly, and last but not least, the majority of major fights were in the overwhelmingly white Top Rank!

There's something about the English, the white 'British', and booze! They love it, but just can't handle it! Listening to groups recapping their previous night's out, they always seem to assess their enjoyment of it in terms of quantity of alcohol consumed (usually pints of lager), and their consequent drink-induced antisocial behaviour thereafter!

"I must have had about ten pints last night, and puked up in some old dear's garden!"

"I had fifteen pints last night and pissed meself in the back of me mate's car!"

"I had twenty pints last night and couldn't get a stiffy when I got back to the missus!"

"I had twenty five pints last night and kicked some cunt's head in, can't remember why though!"

"I had two thousand pints last night and woke up this morning in my front porch face-down in my own puke, *and* I'd pissed and shat meself!"

All of these confessions would be received with guffawing, back-slapping approval and mirth.

It was quite funny spending a bit of people-watching time in 'the Rank' before the Night Owl started though, especially watching white people dance! It was hilarious! Much of the time it was impossible to match the movements they were making with the sound and rhythm of the music being played. Some of the girls weren't too bad (but not great, or particularly good even), when it came to dancing. The boys, though, were rubbish, totally off-beat and lacking any sense of co-ordination, to the point that, at times, their efforts were embarrassingly pitiful and cringe-worthy! Even with the slow dance tunes, after plucking up the (alcohol-fuelled Dutch?) courage to ask a girl to dance, if she accepted, they'd proceed to engage in the twirl-around-in-a-circle-body-knocking-while-clinging-on-and-groping-each-other-out-of-tune-and-coordination dance. Oh so romantic. Not! But I suppose it didn't really matter if they were having a good time!

With a few beers on-board drunken fights broke out, without fail, every Saturday night in the uncivilised Top Rank. These were also fun to watch! It was always the case that some white boy with a skin-full had taken umbrage to some unintended slight by another of the same ilk who, after slurring an apology or telling the slighted one to "fuck off", would then steam into each other, slogging wildly in the general direction of their alcohol-blurred opponent. It was then that you'd witness the might of the Top Rank bouncers swing into action. Clad in tight black suits and cold-defying black or navy blue Crombie coats, the team would bear down on the brawlers, separating the antagonists with ultimate ease, before ejecting them from the premises.

Big Win's older brother 'Russian' was the universally dreaded head-bouncer who had a fearful reputation, that's Fear with a capital F! He was about the same height as Big Win, but much broader across the chest and even more muscle-bound, if that was possible! Observably k-legged and top-heavy, he posed a far more daunting threat than any silverback alpha male gorilla I've ever seen on any of David Attenborough's TV nature programmes! Russian didn't take prisoners, and didn't discriminate, black white, drunk or sober, if you were in a fight he'd be throwing you out. His 'throwing out' usually meant he and his team of employed and paid thugs would give you a good kicking before physically picking you up off the floor and throwing you through the chrome and glass entrance swing-doors, without bothering to open them first! Brutal summary justice was instantly, and entertainingly, meted out to all those who ended their "great night out" by making their 'assisted exits' through the swing doors!

As mixed-race kids we were very quickly assimilating lots of new information about others. For example, white people definitely saw us as black, which wasn't a problem, because that's how we saw ourselves! We were developing the ability to distinguish between light-skinned black people, and other mixed-race people, some of whom (strangely!), *didn't* see themselves as black. Some of these actually (inexplicably!) fully identified with white people and never associated with black people! We began to absorb the differences between Bajans and Jamaicans, who made up the majority of the black African-Caribbean population of Reading. We started to develop even further a very well-informed black identity, awareness and consciousness of racial issues, which didn't seem anywhere near as imposing and influential in our previous rural-based lives. This element was pretty difficult to ignore.

In smaller more intimate rural communities everybody seems to know everybody else, and their business, so it's pretty difficult to 'do things' without others in the community eventually (or very quickly) finding out. In the larger and more impersonal towns and cities, we become faceless, or just another black, white, brown or yellow face that we'd never recognise again for any particular reason. In such circumstances we're less willing, or able, to self-police. It's certainly the case in local communities and villages in Nigeria that young people need to behave themselves appropriately when out and about because, in the event you misbehave, any older member of the community who witnesses one's indiscretions is entitled to beat you!

This is never done with a malicious or perverse motive. It's done because the child or young person's behaviour is unacceptable, disrespectful or inappropriate in the community, bringing shame upon the family and kindred.

Imagine if we attempted to adopt the same approach in the UK! The courts would be full of angry, stressed-out, angst-ridden adults facing charges of child cruelty, molestation, assault and battery! So we entrust such duties to our wonderful professional police force, which prefers to be referred to as the police 'service', yet dispenses its duties in a very forceful way!

We were forever being stopped by the police in Reading, walking to and from school, to and from the town centre on a Saturday afternoon, to and from the Top Rank and Night Owl on a Saturday night! It almost became normal practice for us to expect to be stopped, questioned and searched by the police, especially after we'd moved house from Newport Road in Caversham, to Emmer Green, which was a predominantly white 'sought-after' area, much closer to our school, and considered to be a far more salubrious suburb of Reading. Next stop Caversham Heights! Our new house was perched at the top of a long, sweepingly steep hill. Even our black friends started to refer to us as 'the Africans on the hill'!

We actually got our first home telephone installed in the new house, irrefutable evidence of our upward social mobility! I was so proud and excited, I couldn't wait to phone home! I made the 2p call from a red public phone box in town at the first opportunity, and it was answered by a woman with a strange and totally unrecognisable voice. It was mum, and she sounded Irish! This was the first time I ever noticed my mum's Irish accent, which seemed to be massively accentuated over the phone!

Anyway, the police harassment got to the point where mum was no longer prepared to take it, so she stormed into Reading police station one afternoon to confront and challenge the Chief Constable. She battered him with her tongue and threats of exposing his force as being inherently racist against her children. An almost palpable decline in the embarrassing and degrading police stop-and-searches immediately ensued her haranguing of the Chief Constable who, in response (and probably fear of mum's tongue-lashing!), must have ordered his officers to lay off 'the Africans on the hill'.

This is not to say we were totally immune from their attention though and, in my case especially, I brought it on myself every now and again. I went through the typical rebellious stage at 15 and 16, constantly getting up to no good and getting in silly little wrangles with the police, none of which led to anything serious. For example, Obi and I used to play 'Chicken!' in the back garden where we'd stand facing each other and take turns to throw a knife into the ground next to each other's feet. If the knife stuck in, you'd have to move your feet further apart to touch the knife, then take your turn throwing it until either person cried 'Chicken!' indicating they wanted to stop, or they couldn't reach the knife with their foot. Either of the two scenarios would bring the game to its conclusion.

We'd been playing 'Chicken!' one Saturday afternoon and, later that night, I had a first date with a beautiful, sexy and highly-prized and sought-after (at the time!), black girl, Delores Lee. We'd arranged to meet at the funfair near Reading Bridge and, in eager anticipation of impressing her, I wore the latest fashions that were bound to impress, brown stack-heeled shoes, beige flares, butterfly-collared shirt and the obligatory tight-fitting sleeveless tank-top jumper. We met, and all was going well, until she persuaded me to go on the Waltzer. I was really reluctant to step foot on it because, on the odd occasions I'd done so in the past, it always made me feel nauseous. However, not wanting to wimp-out or disappoint her, I got on it. Big mistake! When it reached its maximum speed, shooting round and round and up and down, I began to feel disgustingly queasy.

The operator clearly recognised the signs and symptoms of my distress, hanging on to the bar of the car for dear life while going blue then green in the face whilst shouting, pleading, begging for the ride to stop. This fag-in-mouth grease-covered scruffy bastard never left the side of our car, constantly spinning it, harder and faster every time I squealed for mercy. I could barely keep my head up as it began to whip-loll side to side as determined by the relentless ride. I started to lose focus, all I could see was a blur of funfair lights dashing past my peripheral vision, and the masochistic smirk on the face of this psychotic and clearly deranged Waltzer attendant.

Then the inevitable happened, slowly, surely, and agonisingly for me, irretrievably. I tasted that foul, acrid pre-vomit bile in my mouth and just knew I was going to heave my guts up in deference to the centrifugal force of the Waltzer (it's much like trying to sit on the blade of an egg-whisk at full throttle!), which I did, as the ride was still going, and we were still being spun at breakneck speed by psycho, and I lost my battle to keep it down, and I projectile-vomited what felt like a never-ending stream of my stomach's contents, all over the beautiful and perfectly presented Delores Lee!

My dream-girl date was covered, plastered from head to foot in my hot, fetid, stinking and steaming vomit. I can still see the putrid, rancid steam rising off her in my mind's eye today, poor girl! My sincere apologies Delores, and I hope you haven't lived the rest of your life since in trauma as a result.

When the ride eventually slowed down to a halt, psycho cheerily loosened the safety bar permitting our release from the car. I teetered dizzily and almost punch-drunk away from the offending nightmare ride, clean as a whistle, not one speck of vomit on me (apart from a bit of dribble at the side of my mouth), result! Then I turned to see Delores clamber down the steps of the ride, splattered and sticky with glutinous bile, her clothes totally ruined and reduced to an unequivocal never-to-be-worn-again state.

Needless to say, that was my first and last date with Delores Lee! On the odd occasions I saw her again afterwards, I never knew where to put my face, I was *so* ashamed and embarrassed! But to heap even further insult to injury on the 'Night of the Waltzer', after having gathered my senses and offered my crest-fallen apologies to the soaking and steaming Delores, I was approached by two policemen who wanted to search me for some spurious reason, in the funfair.

Being very familiar with this experience, I allowed them to proceed, trying to affect as much boredom and disdain for them whilst they carried out their 'duty' on behalf of the public they 'served'. I'd forgotten that, after finishing the game of 'Chicken' with Obi in the back garden that afternoon, I'd absent-mindedly stashed the pen-knife in my trouser pocket. My relatively mild embarrassment and irritation at being searched in public instantly changed to abject shame and regret as one of the officers produced the knife from my pocket. A triumphant smile spread across his face as he raised the knife in the air for all to see. He looked *so* happy, almost as if he'd won the pools, as he handcuffed me, loudly reading me my 'rights' for all to hear.

Not that there was any future for me with Delores after I'd redesigned her clothes, make-up and hairdo, but any remote lingering chance was completely obliterated as I was arrested in front of her, the smirking psycho, and the hundreds of funfair revellers, then marched off to an awaiting squad car. I was only released from the cells when mum came to collect me. It wasn't the first time she'd done this for me, nor would it be the last time either! She was getting tired of the regular visits she'd made on my behalf to extricate me from the cells in Reading police station, but she stood by her word and, on listening to my explanation that I'd innocently forgotten I had the knife with me, she pleaded on my behalf.

Luckily, the blade of the knife was just under the length permitted for those considered illegal to be carried in public, so the DPP (Department for Public Prosecutions), didn't pursue their offensive weapons charge against me! Clearly, the 'Luck of the Irish' was still with me!

That same claim could not be reiterated a few months later when I was back in the cells again!

Me, Obi and five of our schoolmates had been to watch Reading play against Arsenal in an evening pre-season friendly match. Six of us were black and one, Kevin Cross, was white. We were making our way home on the opposite side of the road from Reading train station when we were confronted by a baying crowd of Arsenal supporters, shouting and screaming threats at us. In view of our relative youth compared to the mob (I was the oldest at 15, as was my good friend George Spence, Obi was the youngest at 13), and the sheer number in their crowd, we decided honour was the better part of valour (in truth, life was better than death!), so we attempted to make our life-saving getaway down the subway underpass that exited by the Reading Bus Terminal underneath the Top Rank.

Hearts pounding and fear soaring, we pounded down the steps of the underpass with the mob after us, only to be confronted by another mob coming the other way along the underpass. We were hemmed in as they'd caught us in a classic pincer formation. There was no escape, no way out of this but to lie down and take a kicking, or fight.

We fought.

Back to back, and totally outnumbered, we faced down these huge grown men who were snarling (almost salivating at the mouth in anticipation), their intentions to kick the shit out of us. I've rarely been in fights or witnessed fights that didn't adhere to these pre-fight rituals of threat and counter-threat, bluff and counter-bluff. We didn't actually respond verbally, I don't think any of us, frozen by fear, could actually summon enough spit in our mouths to speak, let alone trade macho insults of savage intent. We'd witnessed the carnage of football hooliganism at many matches that we'd been to, both in London and Reading, but we'd never before been the intended victims!

The seething circle of hate surrounding us got smaller and smaller as they inched in towards us, selecting their targets as they encroached. Then, almost as if in response to a silent starter's pistol at the beginning of a 100m race, they surged at us, madly shouting and screaming as the boots and punches started to fly. Three of the biggest louts descended on me, two from in front and one from behind. I was punching and kicking for all that my life was worth, until my jacket was pulled over my head from behind, almost totally disabling me.

'*Don't* go down, *don't* go down!' was all that was going through my head as I was getting battered by wildly flailing fists and DMs (the Doctor Marten boots that were much favoured by all and any self-respecting football hooligan at the time).

I managed to wriggle out my jacket and, on full adrenalin, started to lash out frenziedly in desperate death-defying self-defence. Having managed to stay on my feet, I decked two, three, four of them. I looked around to see Obi and our mates heroically doing the same. One started on Obi and I went over and smashed him, pummelled him, destroyed him.

Don't fuck with my family!

Unbelievably, we'd turned the tables on them! They were taking a monumental hiding from seven little kids!

They started to run away, back up the underpass steps to street level and safety. Charged and pumped with adrenalin, we gave chase, catching the biggest, fattest and slowest as he tried to make his bid for freedom. Consumed by a raging blood-lust, we battered him, punching and kicking him relentlessly. It was only when we received the legal papers from the DPP detailing the charges against *us* prior to our Crown Court appearances that we learnt we'd broken three vertebrae in this guy's back!

We didn't stop battering him until we were surrounded by police. The guy's mates had run screaming to them like pussies, accusing us of attacking THEM!

Interestingly, the police allowed white Kevin Cross to go home and, funnily, 'Loofus' (one of our mates who was a sandwich short of a picnic), didn't appear to realise what was happening and somehow managed to wander off in a world of his own without being arrested! So, only the five of us were arrested, including Obi, and we were taken to Reading police station (my second home from home!), in the back of a Black Maria, handcuffed, panting, puffing and wheezing, but still alive!

I knew I was in deep doo-doo though, and not necessarily because of the police and the unavoidable charges and court case, but also because of mum! Strangely, I still had a trust and belief in the British system of justice, and felt that when this went to court we'd be completely exonerated. However, as the (now fully wayward?) older son and big brother, Obi was in my care, I was totally responsible for his welfare and well-being. I knew mum would put two and two together and find me guilty of getting innocent Obi in trouble. I wasn't wrong.

After separating us in cells and taking statements from us, and upon mum's arrival in the custody suite, she walked over to me without saying a word. She had a face like thunder and I knew what was coming.

The open-handed slap she delivered to my face taxied down the runway and took off in Camdonagh, on the northern coast of the Republic of Eire. It quickly gained altitude over Donegal, to achieve normal cruising height and speed over Galway, breaking the sound barrier, making the attendant sonic boom over Limerick, and crashlanded in Cork, my face, with record-breaking speed and ferocity!

Everything stopped and fell quiet in the custody suite when mum 'took her hand off' my face. The shocked and stunned (though not as badly as me!) arresting officer dealing with me intervened, asking mum to calm down so he could explain the night's events as had been reported to him and as he understood them.

I didn't react, I couldn't. I stood there feeling totally indignant and betrayed by the system and mum's reaction. I didn't blame her. I understood her. She'd been at work on the night-shift, only to receive a call from the police informing her that BOTH her sons (this time), had been arrested and charged with offences ranging from affray, ABH (Actual Bodily Harm) and GBH (Grievous Bodily Harm) with intent. I was further mortified by the fact that dad had accompanied her to the police station for the first time ever. He'd never, to my knowledge, seen the inside of a police station before. He was totally out of his comfort zone and stood speechless and confused at the activity unfolding around him.

It was the hottest, dettiest (dirtiest) slap I've ever received in my life and, under normal circumstances, would have reduced me to tears of indignant humility and pain instantly. But I couldn't cry. I wouldn't cry in the face of this disgusting injustice. The majority of these hooligans were all grown white men, adults, married with children, and working. There were only seven of us, all 15 and under, still at school and vastly outnumbered. Surely common sense would prevail?

No chance, at least not ahead of race and racism! The police were happy and more than keen to accept their accounts, and to charge the five of us.

Such was the low depravity of racists at the time. Even when circumstances dictated that we'd *have* to have a shared and ludicrous death-wish among the seven of us to even think about attacking these yobs, they *still* arrested and charged us! The yobs were the lowest of the low, so-called 'hard-men' who'd attacked 'easy meat', got their arses kicked as a result and, rather than take it like men, ran screaming to their white police brothers.

The police though, in my opinion, as officers of Her Majesty's law enforcement constabulary, were even lower. I still struggle to imagine how they can sleep at night, and wonder if they get flashbacks to that night that riddle them with shame. Sadly, I honestly doubt it!

Twenty

Mum and dad were also accompanied to the station by our Uncle Sammy.

Uncle Sammy, aka 'Biafran Soldier', became an absolute legend in our family. He was dad's younger 'brother' who survived the Nigeria-Biafra war. I accentuate *brother* because he wasn't dad's brother in the English manner of speaking, but more likely a first cousin from dad's village, Egbelubi, in Eziama, Ngor-Okpala, Imo State. Igbos, once related, tend not to make distinctions between level or proximity of relationship. English people speak specifically about first and second cousins, Igbos speak of brothers and sisters, terms used to express the fact that the children are all, ostensibly, of the same extended family.

The differences between the two traditions probably reflect differences in inheritance and succession rights. In response to the increasing levels of private, individual wealth, estates and property through the profits of industrial capitalism, the English entrepreneur needed to ensure his lawful sons and heirs would inherit his estate. So the English tradition of marriage and producing identifiable legitimate heirs became a very serious legal, economic and fiscal matter in the nineteenth century (so forget the fraudulent and idealised concepts of English 'love' marriages!). In Igboland, where property and status is automatically inherited by the eldest or remaining son(s), and cannot be contended by wives and daughters, the matter is more straightforward.

Uncle Sammy – Nigeria (1960s)

We'd been receiving sporadic news from Uncle Sammy throughout the duration of the war. Dad often slipped into bouts of depression when the news wasn't good, but didn't really ever go into too much detail, for fear of distressing us. We were already being bombarded with TV images of despicable English-sponsored suffering in Biafra, and I'm certain dad didn't want to add to these concerns by relaying first hand reports to us.

It seems Uncle Sammy was a bit of a local war hero in the Ngor-Okpala district, where he sustained a bullet wound to the leg. He assumed responsibility for the mobilisation of Biafran resistance soldiers and civilians against the advancing professionally well-equipped Nigerian armed forces. He established a very effective intelligence network which supplied him with information on the location and numbers of Nigerian troops in the area, for whom his boys would lay in wait to ambush. He lost many friends, 'age-mates' and some members of our family also, but this didn't deter him. In fact, our Uncle Joshua, dad's half-brother, was among the first Igbos to be slaughtered at the start of the controversy. He was working in Jos, in the Muslim north of Nigeria, when war was declared. He, like thousands of other Christian Igbos, was easily identifiable for their physical characteristics, the areas in which they lived, and the higher-status jobs they were doing. His decapitated body, like many hundreds of others, was despatched back down south on a train specially commissioned for this purpose!

Uncle Sammy wasn't only responsible for ambushing and fighting against the Nigerians, he also hid whole communities of people deep in the surrounding bush and farm lands in order to protect them from rape and slaughter at the hands of the Nigerian soldiers. Though stereotypically 'yellow-skinned' and obviously Igbo, he could speak Yuroba and often disguised himself to infiltrate Nigerian encampments where he'd steal, negotiate, barter and beg for food to feed his people. He was the ultimate Igbo version of Del Boy Trotter of 'Only Fools and Horses' fame, the main difference being Uncle Sammy wasn't wheeling and dealing to become a millionaire, he was wheeling and dealing to save lives, thousands of Igbo lives.

His wheeling and dealing didn't end with the cessation of hostilities between Nigeria and Biafra though. Post-war, he developed his 'people-skills' to gain a fairly high-status and influential role in the Lagos store of the Leventis franchise. On the surface he was an excellent manager, organiser and motivator of his staff. He also successfully managed to 'motivate' a significant amount of Leventis profits over an extended period of time in order to fund his own growing business empire, which included a transport and bus company!

His high profile success didn't go unnoticed however and, when the heat was on, he ducked out and went missing. He was now a wanted man who wasn't prepared to attend court (official or otherwise!), to face charges of fraud, deception and embezzlement (statute 419), regardless of whether the charges were trumped-up or legitimate. After deciding to make his way to his brother in London, he spent many months in hiding and on the run, often sleeping in the wild Nigerian bush.

He eventually made his successful exit from Nigeria via the northern regions, bribing border guards to allow him passage. He made an arduous trek across the Sahara desert, then somehow blagged his way onto a Mediterranean ferry that deposited him in southern France.

Dad started to update us on Uncle Sammy's progress out of Nigeria and through Europe. We could sense his increasing fear, concern and agitation at Uncle Sammy's plight over the months he made good his escape. Then one day we received a call from him in Paris requesting dad to send him some money to finance the final leg of his journey. I've never seen dad spend money so quickly! Uncle Sammy booked his ferry crossing to Dover, and dad and Chi-chi went to meet and pick him up. The rest of us stayed at home, waiting impatiently to lay eyes on our hero 'Biafran Soldier' Uncle Sammy, the man we'd heard *so* much about from dad, for the first time.

They arrived back at our house in Emmer Green in the early evening. Accompanied by dad and Chi-chi, Uncle Sammy entered the front room and I could see he was taking everything in instantly. But his first duty, and action, was to pay homage to mum, his sister-in-law who he'd last seen prior to our departure from Nigeria in 1959.

He burst into tears of joy, exhaustion, relief and celebration, wrapping mum in a bear-hug that nearly squeezed the life out of her! She was ecstatic to see him also and, for us as children, it was reassuringly heart-warming to see confirmation and evidence of such close family loyalty, love and emotion.

He then proceeded to inspect each one of us in turn, shouting and screaming at how big we were, and how well we'd grown up. At just over five foot tall Uncle Sammy was pretty similar to dad in diminutive stature, but he was muscular and powerfully built, with slightly bandy legs and, typically, he was a yellow-skinned Igbo. Just to demonstrate his strength he challenged me and Obi to hang off his biceps as he lifted our body weight clear off the floor – a feat he accomplished with consummate ease!

We were all in awe of this diminutive-though-larger-than-life uncle, who swept into our home and lives with indelible impact. He was fun, passionate, caring and loving, as well as a bit of a rascal, obviously. I instantly identified with him, he was a more fun, laid-back version of dad and I immediately added him to my all-time 'Real-Life Heroes List' which, up to that point, only consisted of two people, my mum and dad.

It wasn't long before dad turned the conversation to the Nigeria-Biafra war. He was clearly itching to hear a first-hand account from somebody who'd actually been there throughout its entirety. Who'd been there, seen it, done it, and got the T-shirt. Mum didn't think it was the right time and suggested Uncle Sammy relax, eat, put his feet up and generally take things easy for a while, but Sammy was more than happy to regale us with his stories of war.

He shouted, laughed, screamed and cried as he relayed some of his experiences and, depending on the nature of the story he was telling, he'd act them out in front of us.

Rolling around on our front room floor firing an imaginary gun at the Nigerian soldiers he could still see in his mind's eye, he told us of the fierce and savage gun fights he'd been in; of sneaking through the bush on reconnaissance and sniping missions; of strategically mobilising and hiding whole communities of people in the bush in order to avoid their being raped and slaughtered by the marauding Nigerian soldiers on manoeuvres; of how he chopped off the head of an unsuspecting Hausa soldier whilst hidden in a tree as the soldier crept past below; of how he was shot in the leg whilst defending Okpala during a fire fight; of how Biafrans were reduced to making their own guns and ammunition in the bush; of losing friends, age-mates and family to the ravages of war; of how they ate anything that remotely resembled food in order to sustain life, including rats and any undergrowth vegetation; of undernourished mothers giving birth in the bush to Biafran babies who, obiah-assisted, made their entries to the world in full Biafran army uniform; of the enigmatic, fearsome and fabled home-made Ogbunigwe bomb, that killed many hundreds of Nigerian soldiers; of how he begged for strength and forgiveness in equal measure; of celebrations at gains, and despair at losses. His stories of atrocities seemed endless and poignant, especially that of Uncle Joshua.

But, like mum and dad, he could tell a story, he had the gift of the oral tradition, passed down from generation to generation, and to captivate his audience. Nigerians, especially Igbos, and Irish share this ability to narrate and enthral. I often wonder if there's the equivalent of the Blarney Stone in Igboland, because I've always been so impressed with their ability to speak in public. This ability applies not only to the elderly or adult members of the community, but also to the children and young people who, unlike the reticent, shy, stuttering and mumbled performances of their UK counterparts, seem equally able to express and articulate themselves eloquently and articulately, with assured aplomb and confidence. This may well owe a lot to the hours sitting under the obiris of the village as the young and old of the Umunna discussed and debated matters to be resolved to the community's satisfaction.

An obiri is a palm-leaf-, corrugated iron- or slate-covered meeting place with no walls, very similar (in design and construction at least!) to the PVC and canvas gazebos we see sprouting up everywhere in the UK when the sun eventually deigns to shine during the 'summer' months.

The famous Ogbunigwe bomb is probably comparable to the present-day IED (Improvised Explosive Device) that was deployed in Afghanistan and the Middle East to devastating effect against British and Allied Forces and, in view of the English-backed Nigerian blockade of Igboland, it wasn't only food and medicine that was denied entry, but guns and ammunition also. So the Ogbunigwe bomb, by necessity, was totally home-made.

Almost to confirm and give substance to the meaning of the term "Necessity is the mother of invention", the Ogbunigwe bomb was much feared by Nigerian soldiers who, when mounting incursions into Igboland, eventually resorted to herding namma (cattle) ahead of them so that the cows would trigger the red-soil-hidden Ogbunigwe, rather than their boots and bodies.

In what was regarded as Colonel Ojukwu's last official war time speech, he said:

"... in three years of war, necessity gave birth to invention... we built bombs, rockets, and designed our own refinery, and our delivery systems and guided them far. For three years, blockaded without hope of import, we maintained all our vehicles...

... the state extracted and refined petrol, and individuals refined petrol in their back gardens. We built and maintained our airports, we maintained them under heavy bombardment... we spoke to the world through a telecommunications system engineered by local ingenuity...

... in three years, we had broken the technological barrier, became the most advanced black people on earth..."

Facing genocidal levels of military onslaught and starvation, Biafra was forced to capitulate, no longer in a position to fight to re-establish the Kingdom of Biafra that history books identify, which pre-dated the more well-known 'Bight of Biafra' that has now disappeared from atlases of the world.

Significantly, when war ceased, the first people to be forcibly removed from Igboland were the Irish Catholic priests who built churches and schools in every community into which they had assimilated. Mum was very aware of the presence of the Catholic church in Igboland and, whilst she praised their educational and developmental efforts and commitments, there appeared to be other deep-lying issues that she wasn't fully expressing. It transpired (eventually), that mum had harboured a deep-seated resentment for many years against the established Catholic Church which, in her mind and experience, wasn't as righteous as it professed to be.

Twenty-One

Mum's mother, and family in general, were dirt-poor and pretty much in disarray, to the extent that she and her brothers and sisters spent much of their early years in Catholic-run orphanages, schools and institutions. Mum relayed many tales of the harsh regimes that existed among the 'brotherhood' and 'sisterhood' that she and her siblings survived, like many thousands of others. Clearly, they were routinely and severely beaten, psychologically, emotionally and physically abused by the so-called and self-styled 'brothers and sisters of mercy'. We'll never know if they were subjected to the systematic and obscene sexual abuse that has been exposed in the media over recent years, and for which the Catholic Church continues to pay compensation to its victims.

Apparently, the fact that their parents were still alive, and that they were able to go home at weekends, made it less likely that they would have been sexually abused, but that didn't mean mum could spare them her ill-feelings for, no doubt, she witnessed and was aware of the abuse that did take place. Though mum was warm and loving and full of compassion, she had a hard, cold streak to her. She saw things in black and white, and was quick to assess and where appropriate (in her mind), condemn! You always knew where you stood with mum, and I appreciated that.

Mum reassured us that, in her own words: "don't worry, justice will prevail, the truth always comes out in the end."

I *so* wanted to believe this!

Our date with destiny and fate soon arrived at Newbury Crown Court. After appointing a fantastic solicitor, Mr Harazi, I felt comfortable and sure that we'd not be found guilty of the charges. The case went for committal at the Reading Courts of Justice, where we confirmed our identities, entered our Not Guilty pleas, and made applications for bail and legal aid support, all of which were granted. The case was then referred to the Crown Courts in Newbury for trial. I felt less confident when Mr Harazi explained that, as a solicitor, he couldn't represent us at Crown Court, however, he reassured us that he'd be appointing a fantastic team of more than competent and capable Barristers to pick up the baton, and he did, they were excellent!

Each of us was appointed our own barrister, we'd seen transcripts of the thugs' statements and police reports, none of which remotely corroborated with the others', prior to the commencement of the case. Now I'd been up in front of the beak in magistrates courts for petty cases that weren't pursued or where I'd been found not guilty, but Crown Court was a completely different kettle of fish. The smell of tradition and oak-panelled court rooms permeated my senses with almost reverential gravitas as we were shepherded into the box where we were to spend the next five days fighting for our liberty and good name.

It must have been a pathetic, but funny, incredible sight. Five little black boys, clad in a variety of ill-fitting school uniforms, fidgeting and sitting in the dock, accused of attacking and injuring a mob of adult football hooligans! The absurdity of the charges and accusations became increasingly ludicrous when the 'victim' statements were read out to the court, as the earnest all-white jury (so much for being judged by our peers!), sat in silent and baleful observation.

The gallows sense of humour, irony and comedy escalated exponentially at the arrival to court of the 'victims'. Huge, thick, ugly men who tried and failed to appear weak and vulnerable as they mumbled and bumbled through their false and poorly fabricated under-oath witness testimonies; the comedic proceedings would have been TV gold, of the comedy classic variety, if not for the fact that so much was at stake, for us!

Our barristers were brilliant! They played with these moronic imbeciles during cross-examination to the point of hilarious embarrassment. These white English thugs could hardly put an idea together, let alone a plausible explanation and case to justify the DPP's decision to spend from the public purse to prosecute us.

Perversely, I *really* enjoyed the entertainment from the box. We had a front-row seat at a comedy show that we'd got into for free!

Three days into the case and I didn't feel so at ease when it was my turn to enter the witness stand to be cross-examined! So much was riding on the veracity of my responses to questions, but mum's advice bolstered me as it rang in my ears:

"Just tell the truth about what happened, don't lie, and ye'll be OK"

For some unknown reason, dad thought it would be a good idea to buy me a new suit for my appearance in the dock. I thought the school uniform would make us appear younger and more innocent, but he bought the suit and, true to form, it was THE cheapest and worst suit ever... *and* BROWN! I started having flashbacks to the Stanley Matthews football boots he'd bought me when I was in primary school, and how they'd let me down on the big occasion (Irish superstition kicking in!). Surely this suit wouldn't have the same or similar impact on my performance at yet another crucial point in my life!

No chance.

Though nervous, I tried my utmost best not to show no fear, and spoke honestly and as clearly as I could. I sailed through the questions from both the prosecutor and my own barrister, and felt angry, indignant, but good as I returned to my perch in the dock. Obi and the others gave me fairly comforting silent glances in support and appreciation.

The judge adjourned the case for him to consider proceedings, and we went out to grab some lunch. At some stage on our way back to court I vaulted over a pedestrian barrier on a roundabout, without noticing a juggernaut-sized lorry that was bearing down on me. It was so close that it actually clipped my arm, ripping a gaping hole in the foul brown suit that I was wearing but, thankfully, only grazed my arm. My problem now was that I'd be returning to court looking as if I'd been in a fight over the lunchtime adjournment. I didn't want to look like a thug *now* of all times!

We returned to the dock and resumed our age-graded positions on the hardwood bench seat. The judge, upon announcement, made his pompous way into court to sit on his elevated throne, from which he would order proceedings.

He announced that, due to the inconsistency in the victim and police accounts, he was not prepared to proceed any further with the case, and charged the foreman of the jury to return a verdict of Not Guilty on all five of us!

We squirmed excitedly on the bench and punched the air in delight and relief. Mum was right, the truth had prevailed!

The judge, before authorising our release from the dock, made his final comment.

"... though I'm duty-bound to inform and caution you that had you today been found guilty of the charges, you wouldn't have been going home, but you'd have gone straight from the court to Oxford Detention Centre to serve between three and six months incarceration."

His parting comments didn't diminish our jubilation, but the report in the local papers in Reading did!

Regardless of our innocence and the outcomes of school and judicial accusations, investigations and reports, we were still made to *feel* like little thugs and criminals in a wide variety of aspects of our lives. The famous symbolic-interactionist sociologist Howard Becker wrote at length about 'Labelling Theory'. This theory doesn't necessarily attempt to explain why people behave in the way they do but, once a person has behaved in a particular way, he or she becomes 'labelled' by society in a way that reflects that behaviour. The theory then goes on to assess the impact of the label on the life of the person.

Essentially, labelling theory argues that people can be rightly or wrongly labelled and then treated in a way that reflects that label.

For example, the education system may describe and label white working class boys as academically less able than white middle class boys. With this label and expectation in mind, middle class teachers would have lower expectations of white working class boys and, as a result, would be more inclined to place them in the lower streams at school. The boys would internalise and accept these lower expectations and, in combination with being taught at a lower level and entered for less prestigious exams, would be more likely to achieve less well academically than their middle class counterparts.

On their way to achieving the 'self-fulfilling prophecy' of academic failure, the boys would also be likely to develop an anti-school culture that included antipathy towards and rejection of school and educational values. Now caught in a spiral of predicted under-achievement, the boys would be more likely to become engaged in higher levels of truancy, vandalism, petty crime and other anti-social activities, eventually leading to more serious and life-defining criminal activities.

Labelling can be positive or negative. Where individuals or groups are positively labelled, then expectations of them are, subsequently, positive. The self-fulfilling prophecy in this case would be more likely to end in success, as predicted and determined by the positive label.

There was massive evidence of negative labelling taking place throughout the 1960s and 1970s with regards immigrant children being assessed (labelled) as Educationally Subnormal (ESN). The Grenadian sociologist Bernard Coard noticed that government statistics revealed 34% of children in ESN schools were of immigrant origin, and four out of five of those were black West Indians. Irrefutably, the message here is that black children, especially boys, are less educable than white children and, as a result, need to be 'educated' outside of mainstream education mainly in off-site PRUs. The resultant lack of motivation and disaffection from school and education ensued, with the boys totally underachieving, and ultimately failing.

Interestingly enough though this same cohort tended to gain positive labels from Sports and PE teachers. So athletics and football teams were over-represented by black boys, but those same boys, when not representing the school, district or county in athletics or football, were left languishing in the bottom streams in school.

Did Mr Berry have the same expectations of me?

Whether he did or not I think, to some degree, I'd already internalised these expectations as I headed into my final fifth year to do my GCE exams, by which time I'd become a 'switched-off' pupil at the very least. I didn't do anywhere near as well as I should, passing only six O Levels (grades A-C), and four CSEs (grades 1-4). Obviously, my worst grade (4) was in Maths!

At 16 I started in the sixth form at Highdown to start my A Levels. I really wanted to go to university to get a degree, and a good set of A Levels was the only way to achieve this goal. However, I hadn't shaken off my irreverent, carefree, ducking and diving 'wide boy' reputation or tendencies, which didn't fit in with the school's regime or expectations. Part of my problem was that, apart from Maths and Sciences in which I had no interest whatsoever, I found education easy. I understood concepts on first explanation, and could analyse, assess and evaluate them with consistently high levels of accuracy and proficiency. So I didn't have to work too hard at education. I rarely, if ever, needed to revise before class tests or end-of-year examinations. I just did a quick refresher scan of texts and exercise books, and went in and smashed the exams.

However, if truth be told, my arrogant, lackadaisical and complacent attitude was inexcusable. I rationalise it by arguing that school failed to stimulate or challenge me sufficiently, so I switched off.

Again I think about my brother and sisters who hadn't enjoyed a Technical High or Grammar school post-primary education at any stage! Given the fact our comprehensive school was supposedly a step *up* from the secondary modern education they'd received at Blackstone, my blood goes cold at the prospect of what they must have endured masquerading under the guise of 'education'.

Though, in all honesty, I really didn't help myself. I started to bunk off school on a regular basis, failed to do or submit work on time, and generally crashed-and-burned my school career. I had part-time jobs all the way through school, doing paper rounds, working in clothes and shoe shops, on building sites and in hospitals and factories, as well as maintaining my very healthy school-based capitalist entrepreneurial enterprises. So I was very well off financially (relatively speaking), but a certain corruption of my very essence had taken hold of me. I was no longer the positive, interested, keen, enthusiastic, diligent, responsible, pleasant young man I'd been growing up to be, but rather a more surly, angry, vain and politicised creature that had lost its way.

My school career ended very abruptly during my first sixth-form year when I was called in by the Head of Sixth Form to discuss my alleged involvement in a 'racial' fight in school.

He asked me whether I 'enjoyed' school.

There could be only one answer.

'Yes.'

He asked me if I wanted to stay on at school.

Again, there was only one answer.

'Yes.'

At which point he informed me that under no circumstances was this going to be the case.

He then proceeded to read a lengthy charge-sheet of the offences and misdemeanours that had littered my school history for the past three years. I wasn't even aware the teachers had any knowledge of most of them! The rackets, the dinner tickets, protection money, event tickets, fights, card schools, increasing truancy rates and, most importantly as far as the school was concerned, my association with black activism! This was absolutely intolerable, and the fights between black and white kids at the school were predominantly down to *my* 'political' agitating.

Had there been any real, substantial truth in the allegations, I would have been happy, because I quite like the idea of being expelled from school for such righteous reasons. But the truth is, I wasn't, so therefore in my mind I was being expelled on totally fictitious and 'trumped-up' charges!

The realisation dawned on me as I walked out of his office that "today would be my very last day in school!"

Indignant, but ashamed and embarrassed, I slunk away from school, never to return, until many years later.

Throughout the long, lonely walk home (all of five minutes, tops!), I was mortified. How could I explain to mum and dad that I'd been expelled from school?

Especially dad!

After reacting to my shocking revelatory announcement with a typically short, concise and to the point statement:

"You're finished!"

Mum calmed down and was, eventually, very supportive.

"So what are you going to tell your father?"

I explained my intention to be one hundred percent honest with dad. I'd let him know just how racist the school was, and how they'd conspired to unfairly discriminate against me, and that I'd be applying to British Telecom (BT) to commence an apprenticeship as an electrician with immediate effect!

Dad, my soon-to-be executioner, arrived later that afternoon from work after completing an early shift. I envisaged him wearing a black cap as he made his weary way up our garden path to the front door. The last thing dad wanted to be met with was having to deal with 'school problems'. Even mum was nervous!

Dad went from zero altitude to outer stratosphere within seconds of hearing the words "expelled from school".

He exploded!

I couldn't look him in the eye, and mum struggled in her efforts to get through to him. When he eventually stopped seething and his heart rate had returned to something close to normal, and after having called me all the names under the sun:

"Ijot!" "Idiot!"
"Ewu!" "Goat!"
"Fool!"
"Uzelez!"
"Bushman!"
"Illiterate!"

He began to calm down.

He didn't even lunge at me to mount the expected physical assault.

He heard me out and, to me, it was clear he still really did not understand the concept of racism in school, and how it might affect the prospects of children succeeding. He was still of the view that 'the teachers *must* be right', therefore any report they make *must* be true.

It also became clear that mum didn't really have much of an idea about education, period! She fully understood how racism worked, but couldn't quite work out how it would be operationalised in the school and educational setting.

So, effectively, I was on my own on this. I tried to explain, in an obviously naive and crude way, the dynamics of racism in education, but it wasn't really working. So I opted to soothe both their concerns by mentioning my plans to start an electrician's apprenticeship with BT.

Dad's response to this idea, face looking like thunder, consisted of a very short question:

"Where are you going to live when you start this apprenticeship?"

I totally respected dad, what he did and said, and everything that he stood for. By now I was well aware of the fact that many of my friends in Reading didn't 'have' dads. Genetically, they all *had* dads, obviously, but where were they? Very few of them were around or played an everyday active role in the lives of their children, they were dads mainly in name only! The idea of this, whilst totally alien to me, was somehow appealing though.

The thought of things being as they were at home but without dad seemed like absolute utopia to me! This would have meant I wouldn't have had to live my life in a constant state of fear, frustration, and rebellion.

Fear because I dreaded dad's being at home. Me and mum were tight, always had been, always would be, forever, but dad?! We were still going through the mutual-hatred stage in my development and our relationship, but he was still my dad so I couldn't outright challenge, confront or disrespect him because, if I did, it would have been beatings for me!

Frustration because dad, as sincere and well-meaning as he was, never, ever really understood or came to grips with the concept and practical impact of racial discrimination on our lives. In many ways his naivety was endearing, but I would have appreciated him being able to identify and associate with the issues his children were facing in their lives, especially me as his "opara!"

Rebellion because I had a brain, and a will, and didn't want every aspect of my life being controlled or determined by dad who, in my eyes, didn't have a clue of the 'real world', my world, the world I survived in, and quite well thank you despite the discrimination! The appeal of this world, my world, was far too tempting for me to ignore. It represented the antithesis of much of what I despised about dad. It was free, fun, vibrant, irreverent, non-deferential, malevolent, risky, sexy, edgy and dangerous, a world in which you lived and died by the sword of your own design and making.

The fact is we weren't the ideal traditional Igbo children that I think dad expected us to be. We couldn't even speak Igbo, let alone *be* Igbo!

We couldn't take a 'clip round the ear' from some stranger in our community, because the overwhelming likelihood is this stranger would have had malice in their heart when delivering that 'clip'! We understood our world, and we weren't taking any shit from it! Especially me and Ijem.

I was aware that me and Ij were probably neck-and-neck in the family all-time beatings league table, though I think I won by a short neck, intensity and overall severity! I became a 'rebel without a cause', though 'rebel without a clue' was probably a more apt moniker!

Ijem, the consistent-with-all-the-theories 'middle child', the one who was always there but in the background, often unseen and unheard, but taken for granted. The 'earth-mother-in-waiting' who'd eventually take over from mum in terms of her caring role in the family, she was a true rock. She often picked up where I left off. Growing vegetables for the family, doing the ironing for the whole family, fighting the family's fights, making life easier and 'liveable' for Chi-chi, Obi and Kele outside of the home, at school and 'on the road', literally.

Twenty-Two

My early days of rebellion included me (and Ijem) not only fully taking on a black identity, but also living it. The self-fulfilling prophecy?

Before being expelled from school I'd become a major, high-profile feature of the club and street life in Reading. I was 'current', 'hip', 'cool', 'rampant', 'on it', I had to be seen wherever 'it' was happening. Ijem was never far behind me. At 16 and 14 respectively, we were making our escapes from home (either individually or together), out of the upstairs back window, onto the shed roof, over the fence, down the alley and away into the darkness to whatever entertainment that was out there, in the land of the free, and the home of the brave, our home from home!

Me and Ijem had maintained our 'special relationship' since we'd taken each other's 'sides' as kids. This is not to say we didn't have close, loving and mutually protective relationships with Chi-chi, Obi and Kele, it was just that our relationship was 'different'.

Chi-chi, by virtue of her classical musical ability, almost lived in a parallel universe to the rest of us. She'd maintained her big-sister role in terms of disciplinary and, more latterly, 'snitching' duties. She always commanded our fear and respect, and still does to this day. However, she seemed never to notice issues of race or racism, both of which were concepts that would never enter her perception or understanding of day-to-day events or experiences, even if they were blatantly obvious to us.

Obi, though Ijem's twin brother, matured two or three years after Ijem. He seemed very happy staying at home making his own entertainment, especially out in the back garden with a football! Ijem 'hit the road' two or three years before him, entering my new world in my slipstream.

Kele was seven years younger than me, so she and I didn't spend much time together throughout my teens, but I know she and Obi spent a lot of time entertaining each other at home and having fun pillow-fights! Me and Kele became closer when I was in my mid to late 20s and she in her early 20s.

Ijem took on many of the domestic duties and responsibilities at home, particularly when mum was at work, including cooking and cleaning for the whole family. Like Obi, she'd take her turn to 'baby-sit' and 'look after' Kele, though the nature of the care both gave her was very different. When it was Obi's turn he'd pillow-fight with her, and when it was Ijem's turn, she'd be dolling Kele up and taking her out to the Top Rank!

Chi-chi spent most of her pre-university home-life in the cotton-wool comfort of the predominantly white upper middle class world of classical music, within which she was slowly but very surely developing a very impressive career as a double-bassist (the instrument she'd started to learn at Kendrick Grammar School for Girls). Almost exempted of all and any domestic duties or responsibilities, her world, compared to ours, was one of indulged privilege, and she'd earned it! After succeeding at Kendrick School, she went on to study at what is now known as Anglia Ruskin University Cambridge, the Royal Academy of Music, and under the tutelage of a variety of classical masters of her industry, including the world famous Franco Petracchi in Italy.

Crudely speaking, she'd entered into, what was for us, an alien white world, and against all odds (if our home background and starting place were to be taken into consideration), she'd succeeded and flourished. We were all beginning to get excited for her and immensely proud of her achievements.

Mine and Ijem's world was completely different, at a diametrically opposed extreme to that of Chi-chi's.

Of the five of us, we'd taken on the 'black' identity more overtly than Chi-chi, Obi and Kele, we were 'blacker' than them, not only in skin colour but also in mind, soul, spirit and 'moves'. I sometimes wonder if this 'troubled' dad. I didn't have much time to wonder when, one day when Ijem was 15 or 16, she'd done something to anger him and he went for her. His intention was to:

"Bit ha well well!" – give her a good hiding.

And I wasn't having it.

With mum screaming in the background, I jumped in between dad and Ijem and grabbed him, pushing him away from her and up against the wall as she cowered, and I told him:

"Leave her alone, she's too big for that now!"

Thankfully, it was the last time he ever tried to beat her.

I'd started a belated growth spurt by the time I hit 17 or 18 and effectively 'towered over' dad, well, I was 6 or 7 inches taller than him! I still feared and respected him and deep down, I suppose I loved him, I just didn't get many, if any, opportunities to show that love. He still hadn't exited the dark, long and oppressive tunnel of hate that was his antipathy towards me. We very rarely, if ever, talked like father and son. It was more often an omnipotent master and obedient servant dynamic that existed between us. He didn't really see, hear, consider or respect me.

Despite the fact that I was making money at school, and I was 'pretty well off', these things are relative. I definitely wasn't making enough to pay rent, clothe and feed myself, so it looked like I'd have to stay at home and do what was 'expected of me'. I committed myself to finding a job until the start of the next academic year, at which point I'd apply to Reading Technical College to continue my A Levels. I explained my plans to dad, and he was happy and at peace, my plans had appeased him, to the extent that he actually arranged an interim job for me at his current work place.

After setting up Uncle Sammy with a Nursing Assistant job at Borocourt hospital, dad left there for another promotion at a hospital in Horley, Surrey, near Gatwick airport. He also set me up with a Nursing Assistant job in this hospital. Farmfield Hospital. The fact that I'd done some school 'work experience' helped me get the job. Dad had been given a three-up-two-down house in a row of hospital houses that were situated at the end of the entrance drive to the hospital, so I could have stayed there on a semi-permanent basis, which I did, but I always went back to Reading on my off-shift days and weekends, because I had a crew of friends that had become my life blood, they were all black boys and, like me, first generation UK-born, whose parents originated from across the Caribbean islands, but mainly Barbados and Jamaica. None of them lived with their biological fathers, though some had 'uncles' and stepfathers. Smiffy, Oggy, Pres and Barry were the nucleus of our 'gang'. We'd go everywhere together, and get up to all sorts!

None of them attended Highdown Comprehensive School with us; they all attended secondary modern schools elsewhere in Reading, mostly single-sex but some co-ed. None of them were academically aspirational; they all looked forward to apprenticeships in one trade or another, or life on the dole whilst sponging off girlfriends. None of them had, or could remember, a teacher who inspired them, or trusted them, or believed in their academic ability; they'd become evidence of Becker's Labelling Theory and candidates for Coard's ESN theory.

We'd often meet in the evenings, especially Fridays, at our local youth club in Emmer Green which, for my 'boys', meant them having to travel across town from various more industrialised and distant parts of Reading. We enjoyed playing bar football and table tennis, and generally hanging out together. We certainly developed a reputation as roguish, street-smart urchins, and became very popular with the girls, though chasing girls wasn't high on our list of priorities.

Fashion, music and dancing went uncontested!

We were the ultimate 'soulheads'! Tight-fitting cap-sleeved t-shirts, even tighter-fitting (if it was at all possible!), straight-leg drain-pipe blue jeans rolled up at the ankles to reveal converse baseball boots. Hot to trot!

So we were very high profile at the Night Owl and every other club and disco that was remotely accessible, including trips to Maidenhead,

Slough, Windsor, Farnborough, Guildford, Newbury, Brands Hatch. We all learnt to drive, during our heyday, in 'borrowed' cars. In the lead-up year to my GCE A Level exams I was out virtually every night of the week except Tuesdays. It was strange but, for some reason, there didn't seem to be any clubs open on Tuesday nights. Damn sure though that wherever we went we took over on the dance floor, and loved the attention!

At 15 turning 16 I was a regular Night-Owler. Like Ijem, every Saturday night it was my Mecca. It was blatantly obvious that the 'hottest' girls would be in the Night Owl. These were the girls who preferred black guys to white guys; and who were more accomplished dancers than their Top Rank brothers and sisters; and the ones who'd tired of the bruise-dances that were most popular among their drunken white male suitors! Ijem would 'move' with her best friend Susie Anderson, a 'brownin' Jammoh who was to become Ijem's loyal 'friend for life', as well as that of the family.

Sadly, this was at or around the same time I started smoking which, in all honesty, is one of the very few major regrets I have in life. I suppose it was all down to wanting to look and be cool, the 'rebel without a clue' syndrome! Not that it's any excuse, but cigarette advertising was still rife on the TV and general media, and smoking was always associated with being attractive, cool, popular, in control, composed, basically all those things teenagers desperately want to be seen to be. I've now developed the predictable addiction to tobacco and, despite several attempts to give it up, I enjoy it too much! Also, I figure life is too short, so enjoy it while you can is my mantra!

I was always regularly exposed to harder drugs during this phase, including heroin, speed, barbiturates, uppers and downers of all sorts and, thankfully, they scared me. I think I have an addictive personality which demands that, if I like something, I do it. I was afraid of liking the heavier drugs, so never, ever touched them. I've smoked weed a few times and it does very little for me, other than to make me giggle stupidly and get the munchies, but I can't say it ever made me 'feel good', so haven't really bothered with it!

Chi-chi and Obi would come out to the Top Rank and Night Owl with us every now and again, Obi more so than Chi-chi. She'd started seeing an out-of-town mixed-race guy with the hugest afro ever, Tony. Little did we know he'd prove to be an obsessive, stalking control freak that would soon begin to make her life a misery! Obi was in the Top Rank with his mates, while me, Ijem and Chi-chi (with Tony in habitual close attendance!), were funking and grooving the night away in the Night Owl to the latest soul dance music.

I was aware that Big Win's older brother Russian, the silverback-gorilla-like head bouncer at the Top Rank, had a bit of a crush on Chi-chi, who'd always rejected his Neanderthal-like advances and date requests. It was clearly far too challenging for this pea-brained primate to see his object of love and desire smooching with Tony to the slowies, so he interrupted them, intending to throw Tony out of the premises for no other reason than the raging jealousy and envy that unrequited love and attraction so readily generates.

Tony attempted to beg and resist Russian's approach, which only served to intensify his anger and resolution to jettison Tony out of the club even more. Russian grabbed him by the afro as part of the to-ing-and-fro-ing that usually preceded the victim's unavoidable humiliation at the hands of the authorised thug and bully that Russian was. Chi-chi tried to intercede to help Tony, but I knew this was a mistake and pulled her away. She wasn't familiar with this world, and I didn't want to see her getting hurt in any way. I also didn't like seeing her being upset by Russian manhandling Tony so, foolishly, I stepped in to prise Russian's hands out of Tony's hair, before he was rushed out of the club by the other bouncers.

As far as I was concerned, Chi-chi was safe and unharmed, job done!

Oh how *wrong* was I? How *wrong* could I be?

I was standing chatting with a girl on the carpeted area next to the dance floor when I felt a whooshing scuff to the top of my head which, it must be noted, displaced my perfectly symmetrical afro that I'd taken ages combing and patting into place to get just right! I turned to see what had happened, only to see Russian ranting at me for having intervened on behalf of Chi-chi. He was swinging at me. ME!

Despite the crowd, noise, dim lights and music, I focused totally on the ape. Russian, the ex-heavyweight professional boxer who'd fought in America, was swinging at ME! He'd *kill* me! I'd seen what he'd done to others he'd unceremoniously and humiliatingly ejected from the club, and instantly imagined me being hurled through the sheet-glass doors to inevitable and never-to-be-lived-down oblivion.

The trusted fight-or-flight instinct kicked in, but I couldn't possibly fight THE Russian and actually *live* to tell the tale! He swung again at me, and this snapped me out of my torpor. I ducked the bombshell he threw at me and, even as I threw my right cross in reflexive self-defence, I was regretting that I'd dared to even think about laying a hand on him, let alone a fist. But I smacked him clean in the face, for which I wanted to instantly apologise! This enraged him to even greater heights of intense embarrassment and indignity. How dare this little runt have the temerity to resist, let alone hit him!

He swung a series of potential haymakers which, had they hit me, would have sent me back to meet my ancestors in Ireland and Biafra, but with adrenalin surging through my body, I ducked and weaved, answering all of his off-target scuffs with rights and lefts that hit him flush in the face. I was petrified, but I wasn't going to take a beating from anybody without fighting back. Mum would kill me!

I became aware that the Noel Edmunds-like DJ had stopped playing the music, and could hear girls screaming amid Russian's grunts of anger and hay-making effort. The crowd had surrounded us to make a fluid and mobile boxing ring that moved in every direction in which the fight flowed. I actually started to enjoy myself. It was surreal.

Heavyweight boxer?

Pah. Take that!

Head bouncer?

Pah. Take that!

He never put a fist on me other than to scuff the back of my head as memories came flooding back:

"Keep your guard up, chin down, lead with the left jab and follow up with the right cross in combinations, keep moving and keep throwing combinations and you'll be alright my son!"

And I *was* alright until his entourage of underling bouncers managed to force their way through the crowd to jump all over me, grabbing me and rushing me down the stairs and through the rear entrance of the Night Owl. I could still see Russian, blood dripping from a cut over his left eye and face all puffed up and lumpy, snarling his rage at me, but I didn't care. I'd survived. I'd lived to see another day.

This other day was in school on Monday morning, and I heard that Big Win had been 'looking for' me. This frightened me even more than the memories of fighting his big brother! Big Win would have dismantled me limb from limb with 'that look' on his face as he did so, and I knew I wouldn't get away with staring him deep in the eyes and using 'Igbo sense' on him again (he'd be battering me to regain family honour!). He'd knock me senseless!

He tracked me down, on my own, in a corridor in South House:

"Gus, you know my brother was only mucking about with you on Saturday don't you?"

"Yes Win, of course he was only mucking about"

"So what's this I hear about you going around saying you beat him up?"

"I don't know Win, I DO know it wasn't me who said that, and I DO know there were hundreds of people watching, so maybe it's other people who were saying it, but it definitely wasn't me!"

"OK, well just watch it!"

At which he walked away, looking confused, he didn't get the answer he expected. That would have led to him justifiably maiming me for life, so what else could he do but shuffle away, never to get in my face again!

Contrary to my expectations and wildest hopes, 'Igbo sense' had worked again!

Being 'banned for life' from the Top Rank and Night Owl meant I, along with Smiffy and the crew, needed to get more imaginative and creative in terms of our weekend entertainment. This lead to us looking and travelling further afield in the pursuit of night clubs, music, dancing and excitement, and we didn't hold back. It became evident wherever we went on our travels that white girls appeared generally unimpressed with their white boyfriends, and tended to make a beeline for us on our arrival. We weren't necessarily 'capitalising' on the attention by looking to get romantically or sexually involved with them at all. Music and dance still remained of paramount importance to us.

Meanwhile, somehow, I was still managing to stay focused on my A Levels at Reading Technical College, studying English, Sociology, and British Government and Politics. I still had this idea that I'd be going to university, despite the shenanigans we were getting up to during the week and at weekends.

My relative schoolboy skill and proficiency in English hadn't deserted me, and I'd retained an intrinsic value and respect for education (all thanks go to mum and dad, especially dad, for instilling this in me during the early days when it mattered!). I understood Sociology to mean something to do with the 'study of society', and I had a fairly good idea what Government and Politics was all about, and both subjects intrigued me. I'd become a very angry young man, angry at society, the police, injustice, discrimination, inequality, poverty, corruption, working class apathy, and the apparent lazy ignorance and lack of awareness among most black people (which I found equally if not even more frustrating than working class apathy!).

So in addition to developing my 'natural' abilities in English, I also started to develop an understanding as to how 'systems' operate and impact on communities, societies, and sections thereof, particularly the differences in social stratification, race, gender, religion, education, health, politics and power, work and leisure, crime and deviance, welfare and poverty – classic Sociology. Although in some ways the discovery of these theories, for me, was revelatory, in many ways I felt like "tell me something I didn't know already!" I *felt* like I'd actually lived the life of those people described in the academic theories as being disempowered, exploited, oppressed and dispossessed! It was very useful though, to be in a position to make practical sense of the theories, and to understand how they impact on our life chances.

Going by the theories though, and especially with our family's origins and starting-point in life, we should have been 'write-offs' with little chance of achieving success of any manner, shape or form! Such insight made me even angrier, and more determined to 'do' something in life and not become a statistic. But things were difficult and this stance required discipline. A discipline that I was fast running out of and, given the choice, in the process of rejecting outright in favour of crime, anarchy, and overthrowing the powers that be.

In many ways, this route was the easy way out. But FAR more exciting and laden with instant gratification!

Twenty-Three

It's only natural for teenagers, youngsters, to rebel against anything and everything, and to be surly and recalcitrant towards authority figures, including our parents. For me, mum was always on-side and didn't represent a potential recipient of my stubbornness. Dad, on the other hand, was far more the embodiment of all I despised about authority – inflexible, inconsiderate, closed, old-fashioned, and cloyingly oppressive.

The 'thing' between us came to a violent head when I was 18. We'd been sitting in the front room one afternoon, dad in 'his' armchair, watching the news on TV (dad was the most avid news watcher!), followed by a political programme that was related to one of the prominent news items. We discussed the contentious aspects of the programme in what I thought was a very amicable and sensible manner, though we 'agreed to disagree' on each other's divergent views on the matter. Dad went up to use the toilet and came back downstairs to the front room to find me sitting in 'his' chair. I'd totally absent-mindedly parked my arse there and wasn't thinking anything of it. On his entrance to the front room he stopped dead in his tracks:

"Ah Ah! So you think you're a big man now?!"

I didn't know what the hell he was talking about. I thought we'd had a good, positive, healthy discussion about the political programme and there was no reason for either one of us to take umbrage at anything the other had said.

"What are you talking about dad?" I honestly didn't have a clue.
"You're sitting in *my* chair!"
I couldn't believe it, and I don't know what possessed me to say:

"Oh leave it out dad!"
"Ah! So you want to use street language on *me* eh?!"

At which he stormed over and punched me repeatedly in the face. I
didn't react. I just sat there being punched. He punched me so hard
and so often that I fell out of the chair onto the floor. He squatted
over me and continued reining blows on my head and face, and I had
no option but to just keep taking them. When he ran out of puff he
stood up, panting and wheezing, glaring furiously down at my prostrate body, and started kicking the shit out of me, because kicking me
in his quickly-exhausting-punch-wielding state was easier.

I took as much as I could but, when I wasn't prepared to take any
more, I stood up and looked him squarely in the face:

"You finished yet?"

Still panting and wheezing, fully spent by his panel-beating exertions,
he said nothing, he just stared at me.

I was disgusted by him, and I'm certain my stoical look of contemptuous disgust was etched all over my face. I silently walked past him,
out of the room and out of the house. I think I must have won some
battle of the minds, if only the one to establish the moral high ground
between us, in this one-way exchange of hatred and violence.

It was the last time he ever hit me.

During my lonely and tearful trek into town to meet up with the
boys, face swollen and body hurting, I began to wonder.

'What did I say or do to deserve this?'

"What have I ever said or done (that he was aware of!), to deserve
all the beatings, other than be a normal kid?"

No answers came to my mind.

On seeing my lumpy face and sensing my downbeat mood, Smiffy and the boys asked me what had happened, wondering if I'd been way-laid by a gang of some sort or another. On assuaging their concerns I had no option but to discuss and explain what had happened. To a man (well, boy), they were incredulous. They couldn't believe dad had beaten me up for sitting in 'his' chair, and struggled even more to comprehend the fact that I hadn't 'stuck one on him' in self defence. It then transpired that, when they'd been in similar situations with their fathers or 'father-figures', they'd beaten the fuck out of them. Smiffy went on to say that he and his older brother Ronald had beaten their dad up when he was in the process of attacking their mum.

I was shocked at the idea that they'd dared raise a finger to their dad. I knew I could never have done that, out of respect, love, fear, whatever, I just *couldn't* have hit my dad. That's not to say I didn't *feel* like it! The macho 'streetboy' in me was furious that I'd been beaten up by a little guy who I towered over. I could and should have beaten the shit out of him, but I couldn't, because this little guy was my dad.

Dad had lit the fuse to a deep and bewildered sense of anger and injustice in me. His 'Opara!'". It was a fuse that would take me years to recover from.

I refused to allow the outward signs of depression to linger on in the public domain of the street, but deep inside I was hurting. I was the life and soul of the party, and so it would remain. I was the first to come up with most of our 'ideas' to keep me, Smiffy and the boys entertained, legally and illegally, and more often this involved fights of increasing regularity, daring and intensity as a virtually permanent fea-ture of our addiction to the street and club lifestyle. I was spiralling into a deep and dark abyss of my own making, and loving every second of it!

Strangely enough we'd adopted a 'cool' white boy into our fold. Just before my epic 'Rumble in the Night Owl Jungle' with the 'Gorilla from Manila' Russian, Andy managed to link up and ingratiate himself with us, almost seamlessly. He really, really, really *wanted* to be black. He had the talk, he'd affected the walk, he had the look (clothes, not skin colour or perma-tan!), and he *at least* tried to dance and strut his funky stuff on the dance floor! We all gave him his dues and ratings though. He *tried*. Oh how he tried! But he was sorely lacking in the rhythm department! He *so* wanted to be one of us though, he even only *tried* to date black girls, all of whom to our knowledge rejected him out of hand. But he was a 'good' guy, great fun, and he'd get stuck in with us, always had money and he owned his own car!

Bingo!

With a gleaming white, jacked- and souped-up Mark 2 Cortina with wide WolfRace wheels there'd be no more 'borrowing' cars and risking further arrests, detentions, court cases and sentences (every single one of my mates had done at least one stretch either in borstal or at Her Majesty's Pleasure!). Andy provided us with our 'staff car' that chauffeured us to our favourite nocturnal hot-spots, and his admission and status at all venues was guaranteed by his association with us (believe it or not, there were many places that allowed us free entry on the grounds of our dancing and 'getting parties started'!).

On the issue of crime and criminality, I don't wish to paint an inaccurate picture of myself. I was *bad*! But, and I always admit this, I was lucky! We got away with a lot of things which, under less fortunate circumstances, would have landed us in BIG trouble. The closest I came to trouble of this magnitude was one night out with the boys in the leafy, all-white, mainly upper middle class environs of Henley (-on-Thames), in Oxfordshire. Without going into too much detail on this particular 'nocturnal escapade', me and four of the boys were arrested, taken into custody, split up into individual cells, and questioned by the interrogating officers. They soon established that I had a bit too much to say for myself, and not all of our statements were corroborating, so they took me up to the desk sergeant for him to question me.

Whilst still handcuffed and seated, hands behind my back, across the desk from the sergeant, I was searched in front of him. This search revealed a plastic black-fist metal-pronged afro comb in my back pocket. When proffered to the desk sergeant he asked me:

"What, is this a wog comb?"

My instant response was:

"Yeah, if that's what you want to call it."

He got up, leaned across the desk, and punched me straight in the mouth.

I rocked back on the chair, pain shooting through my bottom lip as it split and bled.

He asked me again:

"I said is this a wog comb?"

He got *exactly* the same answer again:

"Yeah, if that's what you want to call it!"

I got *exactly* the same response, another fist smashed to my face!

He asked the same question twice more, he got the same response twice more, and I got the same punch in the face twice more!

The fourth punch sent me crashing to the floor, blood and spittle spraying over everything, including the arresting officer's neatly laundered uniform trousers and pristine beautifully buffed big black boots. I staggered to my feet to tell him:

"I'm fairly certain what you've done constitutes police brutality, so I'll be getting photographs taken first thing in the morning. See you in court!"

Needless to say, they didn't pursue any charges, but released us into the night on the mutually agreed terms that we'd never to return to Henley again, and we didn't.

That night I 'took one for the team', but my slate was still clean and I resolved to exact my revenge at some later date. No worries!

Twenty-Four

Emmer Green Youth Club got a bit lively at times, but it was a great place for us to kick back and relax, and show off a bit. I used to 'have goes' on other boys' motorbikes and learnt the theory and practice of changing gears, a skill I was later to develop and use in driving cars, way before I'd passed my test! We'd also do a bit of weightlifting, to appear 'macho' in front of the girls, and we represented the club in bar football, 5-a-side football and table-tennis at Berkshire County Youth Club tournaments.

I had another 'knife incident' at the club. It was a typical Friday night, with me and Smiffy hogging the bar football table. 'Winners stay on!' We were good, so we stayed on most of the night, much to the chagrin of our rivals. Chi-chi's ex-boyfriend cum-stalker Tony, and his black friend Errol, both of whom were a few years older than us, weren't overly happy at being made to wait for long periods in between turns to get beaten by us, and an altercation between Smiffy and Tony's mate Errol erupted. Tony was a nasty piece of work and, within a split second, he'd passed a knife to Errol, which I spotted. As the confrontation rumbled through the door out onto the grass at the front of the club, I could see Errol was preparing to use the knife on Smiffy so I jumped in to cool things down, and to warn Tony we weren't into the knife business.

Me, Smiffy and the boys loved a punch-up, but we were very naive, and retained a sense of honour among ourselves. We'd never have used knives in a fight. This, as far as we were concerned, was for cowards. Tony manifestly didn't share our philosophy however. He was not of the same persuasion, preferring to maximise the probability of finishing fights quickly without actually being threatened or hurt himself.

With Tony agitating for the fight to continue, I managed to cool things down, and the youth club kids seemed to appreciate this. They didn't want to see any bloodshed, especially Smiffy's! Tony and Errol sloped away in the face of the obvious support me and Smiffy were receiving from the crowd of assembled youths, but they did so spitting threats of future hostilities, namely in the Peacock pub tomorrow (Saturday) lunchtime.

The Peacock Pub on Broad Street in Reading town centre was another cool place to see and be seen, so anybody who was anybody, including wannabes and has-beens, would turn up to chill out and listen to music whilst sipping and socialising. Many were the times when I'd seen Big Win saunter into the cellar-level Peacock, survey his realm with 'that look' in his eye, then grab any boy who was sitting with a girl, pick him up, throw him through the air, then sit down and start (play-) chatting the girl up. I never saw a boy dare to challenge Big Win when they were thus humiliated!

I'd played in a football match on the morning after the night before, and was at home when I received a call:

"Get down the Peacock, Ijem and Smiffy are in trouble!"

Knackered, and without having showered or eaten anything, I flew out of the house to catch the next bus into town. It took me right onto Broad Street where I shot down the stairs into the bar, where funk music soothed over a crackling atmosphere. I was met by many strange and unfamiliar faces.

Tony had been busy since the previous night, calling friends from all over the place, London, Slough High Wycombe and Maidenhead mainly. They were amassed on one side of the galley-style bar, glaring at Ijem and Smiffy, who I went and sat with. I noticed Tony indicating to a 'face' that I was 'one of them', and the intensity of the animosity being directed our way ratcheted up a few notches. The stand-off couldn't last all afternoon, and in the end it was broken by Tony urging Errol to continue where they'd left off the night before. I intervened to say we weren't prepared to fight inside the bar (far too many potential weapons to be used against us by far too many faces!), so let's take it outside.

Me, Ijem and Smiffy started to make our way out of the bar, up the stairs to street level, and around the corner down the cleaner section of "Smelly Alley" into the Reading Central Church graveyard, closely followed and surrounded by at least forty 'enemies', unfamiliar strangers with angry, intimidating black faces. Only three of our mates followed us, on the periphery of the crowd, not wishing to publicly declare their connection or any affiliation with us, for fear of being battered as well.

Now I knew we'd had it! We were walking to our deaths and, quite conveniently and most appropriately, our demise was to transpire in a graveyard setting. The three of us were trembling with fear, numbed in the certain knowledge that we were soon to be departing this earth! I felt terrible for Ijem. I didn't want my little sister mixed up in this and hurt in any way, but I knew there was no way she'd leave me and Smiffy to face this on our own. Ij was a *real* fighter! So was Smiffy. Over six foot tall, muscular and strong, with nerves of steel, he loved a scrap as much as I did, but the odds were so highly stacked against us it was ridiculous. It was a good thing my body was still caked with mud from playing football that morning, because the mud would have disguised the detritus of my quickly loosening sphincter muscles.

I was shitting myself!

True to form, on our arrival in the graveyard Tony offered Errol the same knife from the previous night, and again I objected to knives being used. He instantly swung at me with the knife, trying to stab me. I sidestepped him and, forgetting the crowd of would-be killers, let go with a barrage of punches to Tony's head. He kept swinging wildly with the knife, and I kept dodging and punching until the knife flew out of his hand. I grabbed him in a headlock and smashed him repeatedly, while expecting Tony's mates to descend on me in defence of their guy. It didn't happen. Emboldened by the fact it appeared they were going to 'let the best man win', I intensified the ferocity of my self-defence. As we both toppled over to the ground at the foot of a huge centuries-old tree, I grabbed Tony's huge afro. Hair and head in-hand, I proceeded to smash his face against the viciously gnarled trunk of the tree until we both virtually collapsed with exhaustion. But I'd won.

The crowd didn't converge on us. In fact the complete opposite was the case. Almost like the Red Sea, they parted to allow me, Ijem and Smiffy to make good our exit from the scene! It seemed they also shared a sense of honour and fair play that Tony had no intention of demonstrating. He'd managed to rake my face with his long finger nails, and at one stage he actually had them inside my eyelids. I thought he was going to blind me! But all he managed to do was scratch me, 'like a girl'! I saw him later on in the following week. He looked like a Panda, two black eyes and a face swollen to double its normal size! That was good enough for me.

Never having travelled *on holiday* with my family, I actually went on a two-week summer trip to Torquay on the south coast with Andy, the coolest white dude ever! I was nineteen, slim, trim, and with afro in full flow! It was the early summer of 1976, school was out, and I'd just sat my A Levels at college. I later found I got three C grades which, though I was capable of far better, was pretty good considering I didn't really study for them, in favour of my nocturnal distractions. But I felt I'd *earned* a holiday, a bit of time away to basically fuck about and do what young people do.

The feeling of freedom and throwing off the shackles of parental control was so invigorating. It was great to be young and free, without a care in the world as we cruised down the M3 motorway, funk and soul music from the likes of The Commodores, Candi Staton, James Brown, The JBs, Roy Ayres, Brass Construction, pumping out of the 8-track car stereo. Andy loved drawing attention to himself, at times embarrassingly so for me, but I was happy to suffer the odd uncomfortable squirm as he either over-revved the engine at red traffic lights; or hot-rodded other disinterested drivers away from the lights when they turned amber then green; or insisted on winding the windows all the way down when girls were passing; or unnecessarily stopping to ask directions from pretty girls only as a means to get talking to them. It was all good. I even overlooked his constant rear-view-mirror preening checks and upturned (Starsky and Hutch style) shirt and cardigan collars!

I'd actually been to Andy's house on a few occasions prior to our holiday, and even slept over on one and, off the back of these visits, understood Andy even less! They lived in the outskirt suburbs of Reading, not in town. Their detached house was immaculate in presentation, decor and location, set in acres of farmland. They even had dogs, farm animals, chickens, ducks and geese, and horses in paddocks! Inside, the house was pristine and laden with all the most contemporary mod-cons, and the walls were bedecked with photographs of Andy and his older sister competing in equestrian show-jumping events.

Andy was a secretly spoilt and obscenely over-indulged rich-kid!

I tried to get my head around it. What the *hell* was he doing rolling with us, when he comes from this sort of background, the type we all aspired to achieve in our dreams? On the surface he didn't *need* to even associate with us, let alone roll with us! I met his parents and sister, and it very quickly became abundantly clear that he and his sister had been totally indulged throughout their lives. I couldn't believe the way they both spoke to their parents! I knew if I ever spoke to mine in the way they did, I'd no longer be here! To be honest, I wouldn't have even got close to completing a disrespectful sentence to either of my parents. They'd have punched my words straight back down my throat!

I really disliked his sister because, whilst she was pleasant towards me, I think (possibly like his parents), she saw me as Andy's latest plaything. Both parents were also exceptionally (overly?) pleasant and accommodating towards me, and (genuinely?) went out of their way to make me feel welcome. However, even in view of the outward signs of 'normality', I never felt totally relaxed and at home in their company.

It was all very strange because, whilst Andy obviously didn't want for anything in life, he equally obviously desperately needed to feel he 'belonged' somewhere, and to be appreciated by someone. That 'someone' was us. Not only did he feel he 'belonged' with us, but being with us represented to him and, more importantly, to his parents and sister, a complete rejection of the privileged but cold and unloved white world he'd grown up in. His parents appeared to lack passion and compassion, they were remote, disconnected, detached from their son who, in many ways, was crying out for love, nothing else. His dad was a very successful businessman, and it appeared the family dynamics were based upon some cold but rational business model or plan!

In my mind, it was no wonder he rolled with us!

Jamaicans have a most appropriate saying for these types of 'have and have-not' situations:

"Want it, want it, nah get it!
Get it, get it, nah want it!"

There we were, me, Smiffy and the boys not really daring to dream about the lifestyle Andy had at his fingertips, yet he was rejecting it to follow us! We wanted it, but couldn't get it; he had it, but didn't want it!

Me and Andy rolled into the outskirts of Torquay in the early afternoon of our first Saturday on holiday. We were to be staying in a bed and breakfast farmhouse arranged by his parents. After unpacking and offloading the contents of our suitcases, we headed into the centre of the seaside resort to see what was on offer in terms of nightlife and entertainment. There were quite a few pubs, bars, restaurants, clubs and discos, so it seemed Torquay had been a pretty good choice to spend two weeks! The 'feeling' was things would liven up by the time we returned in our glad-rags later that evening.

We weren't wrong. Torquay town centre and beach front was heaving with people, including young 'clubbers' out for the night, families with children, dating couples, elderly people, and hordes of single- and mixed-sexed groups of teenagers and twenty-somethings out 'on the lash'. By the time we arrived it was blatantly obvious that many were already under the influence of copious amounts of alcohol. We strode into a bar and had a couple of halves of shandy (none of us really drank that much alcohol as a rule), and got chatting to a barman to seek his advice on the best clubs to check out. The bar suddenly filled up with a minivan-load of guys from 'up-north', Newcastle, 'Geordie lads' who, at first, seemed quite fun, but who were already steaming drunk (or "stocious" as mum would say!), they were loud but having a laugh and generally enjoying themselves.

We eventually got up to leave with the name and directions of the club we'd soon be visiting, and so did the Geordies, en masse, but in a far less jovial and gregarious mood than they'd demonstrated earlier. As soon as we were out on the street they surrounded us, and their intention was clear. Me and Andy would provide their early evening entertainment in the form of a punch-up before they'd go onto a club or disco. They went through the usual 'hand-bags-at-ten-paces' ritual as they pumped each other up before drunkenly steaming into us, fists and boots flying. Me and Andy instinctively stood back-to-back, ready for the imminent onslaught which was soon to unfold.

And it did. And as they waded into us it was 'easy pickings' really, for us, because they were drunk. I knocked three of the twelve of them out with single right-handers. I was up on my toes and, though fearful, enjoying it. Then, suddenly, I heard a strange noise coming from behind me. It sounded like the elongated death-defying strains of a chicken clucking its final death throes. I didn't want to take my eyes off 'the lads' still in front of me, but I was curious to know what the hell was making that weird noise! The guys who had me in their sights suddenly stopped to attend to their stricken mates who were still rolling around in a semi-comatose state in the gutter, so I took the opportunity to take a quick glimpse over my shoulder to identify the source of this noise.

It was Andy! He hadn't made ANY contact with his attackers because he'd adopted this ridiculous Kung Fu stance, splayed-fingered hands in front of him, and mimicking Bruce Lee with the noise he was making. The Geordies looked confused. They were obviously trying to work out if Andy was for real or not. They erred on the side of caution and chose not to mount their attack on him. I couldn't believe it.

I wanted to piss myself laughing but couldn't because I was still faced with a few more, and didn't want to give the game away (although I didn't know if Andy was a Kung Fu expert or not!). Only one more lad tried it on with me, and he went down to join his mates in the gutter in exactly the same way they'd hit the tarmac.

Just as a Black Maria was arriving!

All fourteen of us were arrested and, amazingly, Andy and I were the first to be released on public witness verbal statements, and the Geordies' own confessions! The four who'd attacked me were detained and taken off in the Black Maria. Was this evidence of my luck changing? I was expecting to be detained and charged, but I was released. Was it because I was with *white* Andy? Would it have been the same outcome if I'd been with Smiffy and the boys? I'll never know for sure, but my money would be on "No!"

We went onto the club and were enjoying ourselves when in came the Geordie boys. This time they were very conciliatory and apologetic, *they* even bought *us* drinks and referred to me as "Big-hitter!" Andy told them that he was really pleased he hadn't had to engage with any of them, because he was a black-belt in Kung Fu and didn't want to jeopardise his licence! They were very thankful to him for being so considerate, given the circumstances, and a certain camaraderie developed between us all from that point.

I thought Andy was a terrible dancer but always gave him points for effort. The Geordies were by far worse than Andy though, *so* uncoordinated and, in a way, that helped to make Andy feel good about himself. We went on to have a really enjoyable night, pulled a couple of girls to dance with, and spent the remaining two weeks of our holiday in much the same vein.

On returning to our B & B at the end of the night, girls in tow, I asked Andy where and when he did his Kung Fu training. He laughed. He'd never seen the inside of a martial arts dojo, but he had recently watched Bruce Lee's classic 'Enter the Dragon', and bullshitted everything!

Top Man!

We made our (surprisingly emotional) farewells to our B & B hosts and their daughter on the final Friday before taking the long cruise back to Reading, and reality.

The car broke down on the M4 motorway just a few miles outside of Reading. The police stopped upon spotting us and, again surprisingly, allowed us to walk off the motorway to a junction where we'd be able to catch a bus into town. We got off the bus next to the Butts Shopping Centre in central Reading, where I saw Barry, one of 'the boys'. He shouted across the road at me:

"Gus, how's your brother?!"

I didn't have a clue why he was asking me this apparently random question with such concern etched across his face:

"What do you mean how's my brother?"
"He got stabbed last Saturday."

I didn't hear any more of what he said. I went berserk. I ran to the nearest red telephone kiosk and, with my last two pence that I'd intended to spend on my bus fare home, I used it to ring home instead.
Ijem answered.
I started screaming at her:

"Where's Obi?"
"He's at home."
"So he's OK then?"
"Yes"
"Did the police arrest who did it?"
"Yes"
"I'm going to the police station to kill them NOW!"
" Gossie, mum's at work, and she said that when you call you *mustn't* go to the police station but to come straight home!"

"What do you mean?! My brother gets stabbed and I don't kill who did it?"

"Yep. Mum said to come straight home!"

Ijem remained unbelievably calm, rational, sensible, and logical considering the pressure I put her under!

Tears of anger and frustration streamed down my face as I abandoned Andy and ran the three miles home from Reading town centre. Everyone except mum was at home, including Uncle Sammy. I couldn't bear the sight of Obi's sutured and bandaged wounds. He'd been stabbed in the back (which was nearly fatal), his ear had been sliced in two, his arm had been butchered by a broken bottle, and he was clearly still in pain.

Apparently, he and a small group of his mates had been the victims of an unprovoked attack by a huge mob of Charlton 'supporters' approximately fifty yards from the spot where the Arsenal supporters had attacked us a few years previous. Before attacking Obi and his friends, the mob had been chanting:

"Zigger, zigger, zigger – Reading's got a Nigger!"

Thankfully, he'd managed to fight his way out, but not without sustaining these horrific injuries.

I was incensed. How *dare* anybody fuck with my family!? I tried to persuade Uncle Sammy to accompany me to the police station. My idea was to try to 'meet with' the guys who'd been arrested. I'd only need a couple of seconds to do what I wanted to do, but I wouldn't have come home that night if this had happened, not for a long time! I wasn't thinking logically, I couldn't, and everybody, including Obi, pleaded with me to stay at home. Eventually I relented and saw sense, happy to be home with my family, and to know that Obi would be alright.

The very next day I went to the spot where Obi ran to seek safety, just outside the Butts shopping centre, and saw a huge, caked and brown blood stain on the pavement where he'd stood bleeding until the ambulance arrived to take him to hospital.

Unashamedly, I cried in public.

Unbeknown to me initially, I became aware of the fact that news of the attack on Obi had spread through the black community in Reading like wildfire on the day. The spontaneous reaction of all was to mobilise to the town centre and the Oxford Road (in the direction of Reading's old Elm Park football stadium), to exact immediate and bloody revenge on anyone resembling a Charlton supporter. Over the following few weeks I heard many stories of these revenge attacks, each one appearing more gruesome and barbaric. Good!

Apart from the fact that so many of my friends were arrested, charged and sent to borstal and prison for the parts they played in the spontaneous revenge attacks (even Smiffy did six months for battering loads of Charlton supporters and the police who needed back-up support to arrest him!), I was happy and proud at this reaction.

Simple.

But given the choice, I'd have preferred to have been in Reading at the time!

My family, on the other hand, were glad I wasn't. They knew I'd have lost control and ended up in prison also, probably for multiple murder!

Twenty-Five

In dutiful deference to dad's wishes I applied to go to university to study combinations of Sociology and Psychology. I got offers from Salford in Manchester; Brunel in Uxbridge, west London; Essex in Colchester; and a couple of others. I visited them all and chose Brunel, not only because it was close to Reading, home and the boys, but also because Essex just felt too remote and desolate, and it always rains in Manchester! I wanted to keep my options open with regards the choice of subject and, luckily, Brunel offered a BSc Joint Honours degree in Sociology and Psychology, which meant I'd get full degree recognition in both subjects. Also, Brunel was essentially a science and engineering university (named after the heralded Isambard Kingdom Brunel, eminent nineteenth century mechanical and civil engineer), with a relatively small school of social sciences. This suited me as all the girls would be more likely to be in our department, plus there ought to be a wide pool of good quality footballers to play for the university, which meant I'd be challenged to get into the first team.

Probably the best thing about Brunel was that the courses were 'sandwich-based', over four years, which meant we'd be at university for six months and on work experience placements for the other six months in the year. My subjects had the option to train as a student nurse in psychiatric health care, studying for the RMN (Register Mental Nurse) qualification at the Maudsley Hospital on Denmark Hill, southeast London. I jumped at this opportunity because, in addition to gaining a professional qualification, it also meant I'd be earning money as a student nurse, and would be provided with accommodation during the work experience periods. That was me sorted!

Course structure dictated that we'd start the nurse training stint first, then the degree, so I'd be starting in March 1977, meaning I had seven months or so to earn some money and have a good time before going off to uni. Also, these were the days of fully paid tuition fees and means-assessed mandatory student grants. Mum and dad's joint incomes against expenditure meant that I was entitled to a full grant, bar a parental contribution of approximately £40 per academic year. Obviously, I didn't ask for a penny from mum and, even when she offered it, I declined the offer. I would NEVER have taken money from my parents to support me pursuing my choices in life. I just couldn't! They'd done enough for me already, I remembered their suffering and the sacrifices they'd made for all of us, and I'd appreciated their efforts in a way I can't fully explain. It goes deeper and way beyond statutory entitlements and requirements!

I continued working at Farmfield hospital in Surrey with dad, and I think our relationship started to improve. I think he started to see me as an independent young man who had started to gain some academic success, was aspirational and getting on with things, plus I was going to university next year!

"Opara!"

The long hot summer of 1976 inched towards two major events in our world, Reading Pop Festival and the August Bank Holiday which, for hundreds of thousands of black people, means only one thing. Notting Hill Carnival!

The venue for Reading Pop Festival was down the bottom of our old road in Caversham, on Richfield Avenue. Me and Obi bunked in each year to watch the artists perform, though he wasn't with us on this occasion. The mighty reggae artist U-Roy, as well as the Mighty Diamonds, was appearing in 1976 so we made sure we bunked in to this one! Pop festivals rarely featured black artists, so we were extra keen. Their appearance on the Friday first day of the festival also drew a wider range of young black people from Reading than usually attended so, as a group, we stayed together among the mass of hippies who'd attended to watch their favourite heavy metal rock artists.

U-Roy was second on to do his skanking, toasting pieces, followed by The Mighty Diamonds to enthral us with their hauntingly melodic Afro-centric roots-reggae pieces. We really enjoyed them, but the hippies didn't! So much so that, fortified with drugs and booze, they started pelting the stage with stones and cans to demonstrate their displeasure. They wanted the black reggae artists off-stage. This, inevitably, led to scuffles breaking out both amongst themselves, and also between some of the black boys and the hippies. We'd occupied a central position in the crowd, so it was a bit dangerous to remain there for too long under the rain of missiles being thrown on stage, so we scarpered to the periphery of the crowd.

Quite a few of us got into scuffles as we made our jostling retreat to the relative safety of the periphery. A hippie guy got in my face trying to obstruct my passage, and I think he was surprised that I resisted his attempts to impede my passage. He swung a wayward punch at me and, as soon as he realised my intention to retaliate, he said:

"You wouldn't hit somebody wearing glasses would you?"

To which I replied:

"No, I wouldn't".

So I whipped his glasses off his face, smashed him in the face with a pummelling right-hand, then replaced his glasses on his now bloodied, displaced and snot-splashed broken nose as he rolled moaning in agony on the litter-strewn grass.

One of our (black) festival-goers, Joe, in a panic had left his pushbike where we'd been stationed. Slightly bigger and one year older than myself, Joe had issues, he was slightly deranged, but whenever our paths had crossed he'd always been civil towards me, and I reciprocated in exactly the same manner. I think he must have been on a medication-free possibly drug-and-booze-fuelled 'bender' that weekend, because, totally irrationally, he ordered a younger member of our number, Junior H, to retrieve his bicycle from amid the maddening hippie crowd.

Junior was, quite rightly, non-plussed and totally bemused by Joe's demand, so he refused to endanger his safety to retrieve the bike. Joe drew out a knife and threatened sixteen-year old Junior that he'd cut him up if he continued to refuse. I wasn't prepared to stand by and watch this, so I, along with a mate called George, stood in between Joe and Junior, and I told him as assertively as possible:

"Joe, leave him alone, he's a little kid man!"

Thankfully, Joe backed off and, once the melee had settled, retrieved his bike under his own steam!

We, Smiffy and the boys, were all preparing for Notting Hill Carnival on the Sunday. Joe went to another event on the intervening Saturday where he stabbed and murdered a woman, for which he received, and served, four years in prison. On his release he went on to kidnap a young girl who he held hostage for two weeks. On being apprehended he was admitted to Broadmoor Prison Hospital, where he died whilst 'being restrained' by warders. Dad was actually working at Broadmoor at the time (on a temporary-in-between-jobs basis), and mentioned the incident, but made it clear he didn't intend to go into too much detail.

It's dawned on me since that "There for the grace of Destiny go I".

No doubt Junior has felt exactly the same. It could have been either of us that Joe murdered that weekend. We just got lucky!

I'd never attended a carnival before. I thought it was a completely Caribbean/West Indian thing. I later learnt it has very strong roots in West Africa, as evidenced by the Jonkonnu street parades and parties, music and festivals, steel bands and competitions, and general celebrations from Brazil, across the entire Caribbean and North America including, most famously, New Orleans; essentially, those islands and countries where slavery had previously existed. Consistent carnival themes are masquerade dancers (a *very* high profile feature of West

African celebrations!), rhythmic drum music as part of the processions, and excessive consumption of alcohol and other mind-altering substances! The tradition is also closely linked with Catholicism in which the post-Christmas celebration of Lent is central. It seems, yet another link between the imposed conversion to Catholicism among slaves across the 'New World'.

Generally, carnival is celebrated between Christmas and Easter. Slaves were allowed 'time off' to vanquish (if only temporarily), the oppressive plantation regimes, and were even permitted to 'meet with their families' as part of the celebrations. Invariably, carnival celebrations occur shortly after or in association with harvest seasons, for example, 'Crop Over' in Barbados, and would appear to be a direct 'carry-over' from the traditional "Yam Festivals" in Igboland. Typical of this in Igboland, are the Mmanwu masquerades that take place between the end of the harvest season, and before the beginning of planting season, during which much fun, music, dancing and celebrating is had by all over a period of weeks.

Africans at home in the Motherland and abroad in the Diaspora, we are undeniably and inextricably linked!

Smiffy's older sister Marcia had a flat near Latimer Road tube station, right in the heart of Ladbroke Grove carnival territory, which we commandeered for the carnival weekend, with the six of us sleeping on her front room floor, this was our base!

I couldn't believe the sights, sounds and smells of my first carnival, it was glorious! Glorious to see so many tens of thousands of black people all in one place, enjoying themselves, laughing, dancing, eating, and generally relaxing in the final throes of the summer-of-'76 heat. Huge sound systems with speakers stacked twenty and thirty feet high outside on the pavements on Portobello Road and Acklam Way, pounding out soul, reggae and calypso music, all genres heavy on the bass and tops; gigantic flatbed lorry floats with steel bands and scantily dressed nubile dancers shimmying their way along as part of the procession; small side stalls selling fried and cooked meals and box-drinks; fried fish, chicken, cow foot, cow tail, souse, rice and peas, bammy, festivals, okra soup, ackee and saltfish; and the hustlers selling their little pre-packed bags of weed. Totally glorious!

And I'd never seen so many rastamen congregated in one place before! They looked so noble and majestic, serious, sagacious guys with serious, regal dreadlocks of all shapes, sizes and lengths, rocking to the heavy bass and conscious lyrics of reggae music thumping through the speakers on Acklam Road, as supplied by sound systems including the likes of Soferno B, Jah Shaka, King Tubby, Stone Love Movement, and Tippatone. It was edgy, exciting, and I loved it!

Me, Smiffy and the boys were under the A40 flyover on Acklam Road, opposite a regeneration building site where the old factory houses had been reduced to rubble in preparation for the new-builds to start. The soul and funk music was pounding away, doubly amplified by the natural acoustics under the flyover. We bumped into Ijem and Susie under the flyover, and we were all chilling, dancing and having a good time. It was intriguing to watch the moves of other revellers, many of which were old, but some were new and we'd be adopting the best of these on future trips to far-flung dance floors!

There were thousands of carnival-goers under the flyover soaking up the funk and soul, and along Acklam Road absorbing the heavy dub reggae. Glorious!

Late in the afternoon of the final day, around 4.30pm, we noticed some scuffling among the crowd under the flyover where we were standing and dancing. We spotted two young police officers harassing a black boy, who knows what for, this was carnival after all, so surely they'd ease up on the 'pressure'?!

Black youths were sick to death of the 'pressure'. That pressure being remorselessly and relentlessly exerted on them every day of the week via the 'sus' laws, the pressure had gotten too much!

The 'sus' law was the informal name for the stop and search law that permitted police officers to stop, search and potentially arrest and detain people on suspicion of them being in breach of section 4 of the Vagrancy Act of 1824, which stipulated that:

...... "every *su*spected person or reputed thief, frequenting any river, canal, or navigable stream, dock, or basin or any quay, wharf, or warehouse near or adjoining thereto, or any street, highway, or avenue leading thereto, or any place of public resort, or any avenue leading thereto, or any street, or any high-way or any place adjacent to a street or highway, with intent to commit an arrestable offence......

..... shall be deemed a rogue and vagabond......."

And would be guilty of an offence, and be liable to be imprisoned for up to three months. This effectively permitted the police to stop and search, and even arrest, anyone found in a public place on the grounds that they *suspected* that they might intend to commit an offence.

In order to bring a prosecution under the Act, the police had to prove that the defendant had committed two acts:

- The first, that established as a "suspected person" (by acting suspiciously), and
- The second, that provided intent to commit an arrestable offence

Two witnesses were required to substantiate the charge, which was usually two police officers patrolling together.

Needless to say, the law caused much discontent among black and ethnic minority communities (as well as traditional white working class communities, though to a lesser degree), against whom the police use of the law was particularly targeted, essentially as a result of their 'racial profiling' expectations, the idea being that black and ethnic minority groups are more likely to commit arrestable offences.

Well, it would appear that the two young police officers and, by definition, 'witnesses', were carrying out the letter of the 1824 law in their attempts to search and subsequently arrest this young black 1976 modern-day 'rogue and vagabond'. Though it was wholly unclear as to which arrestable offence he was about to commit, considering he was surrounded by thousands of people of the same kind, all intent on having a good time, and nothing else. But it didn't really matter, because he wasn't having it.

The boy (supposedly, according to police reports, was a 'known' pickpocket, a sticksman, a tief!), stared contemptuously into their eyes, his body language seemed to be screaming out saying "not this time!"

The atmosphere under the flyover became eerily surreal because, although the music was still pounding, nobody was now dancing or making merry. Everybody stood and watched in silent disbelief that these two officers, probably arrogantly-emboldened by their customary every-day use (and likely complacent harassment-orientated abuse?) of the sus law, would even *dare* attempt to apply it in these circumstances: at carnival, a time for celebration and merry-making; surrounded by thousands of black youth, all of whom 'fitted the profile'; the boy's blatant resolute resistance and refusal to comply; his increasing agitation at their insistent, grabbing, mauling attempts to detain him.

The crowd, as one and to a man, started to slowly encircle the boy and his two blue-uniformed harassers, shutting down any avenue to escape, and any hope to be seen from outside the ever-decreasing circle. It felt as if every one of us under the flyover identified with the youth, as if the officers defiling him were also defiling us, as if their stripping him of his dignity was also stripping us of ours. The police boys seemed to gradually become aware of their situation, paying less attention to the boy and more attention to the crowd now encroaching into their operational space. They adopted very sheepish and cowed expressions as the potential and imminent horror of their predicament slowly unfolded.

That potential horror became very real for them, very quickly. The youth, having shaken himself free of their clutches, made good his escape, zigzagging through the gaps that the crowd made for him, like a wide-receiver attempting to evade the crunching tackles and clutches of a line-backer or defensive back. The gaps closed the instant the youth wriggled through, leaving the two police boys looking at a sea of hostile, hurt, angry black faces.

Then something so spontaneous and surreal happened that I'll remember it for the rest of my life.

A tall, slim, handsome mixed-race boy in his mid-20s broke the silent encroachment.

With his right fist held aloft he screamed one word:

"Soweto!"

Instantly galvanised by the hyper-emotive connotations of that one word, the crowd instantly descended upon the two police boys, ripping them to shreds as they desperately attempted to radio for back-up. Something must have got through between the kicks and punches raining down on them, because within seconds the back-up arrived in the form of 20-30 additional officers, who came racing into the melee. They got battered also, every one of them, as sheer, unadulterated revenge-filled mayhem erupted among the "nah tek no more" youth.

'Soweto', an abbreviation for South Western Townships, is situated in the south western outskirts of Johannesburg, South Africa. For us, recent events there had become synonymous with consistent and systematic racist oppression, brutality and murder against disenfranchised black South Africans. Only three months earlier, on the 16th of June 1976 and with Nelson Mandela still imprisoned, mass protests erupted and demonstrations rose up against the apartheid government's attempts to force education to be delivered in Afrikaans as opposed to English. 200 people, mostly students, were slaughtered on the first day of protest, the very first to be murdered by the police was 12 year old Hector Pieterson. With the vividly stark images of defenceless children, young people and students being murdered by the state in daylight scenes of horror still fresh in our minds, no organised discussion, strategic planning or agreement was necessary.

Me and the boys couldn't believe it! Today was the day to lance the blue boil of our oppression, to lance the canker that had become an ever-present feature of our daily lives, and very few passed up the opportunity. We all responded, instantly, as one, because we all assumed the shared experience of having suffered discrimination, brutality and oppression by the police at some stage in our lives.

Even more back-up-in-blue arrived within minutes, only to be met with showers of bricks and all manner of building equipment and rubble from the regeneration building site. It looked and felt like Michael Caine's "Zulu" with the boys in blue, apart from their batons and dustbin lids, totally unprepared, unprotected and unarmed, and being remorselessly slaughtered in running street battles that lasted well into the dark of night. The frenzied chaos spread like wildfire. Wherever the police were situated in the surrounding streets, they became targets, suffering the wrath of the thousands of 'under pressure' boys.

Over 300 police were injured, with many being detained in hospital overnight. 35 police vehicles were severely damaged, with many torched. Several shops were looted and approximately 60 people were arrested. The 1976 'riots' were the fiercest and most protracted street battles on mainland Britain since the 1936 Cable Street riots. Here, the police mobilised to protect and safeguard the passage of Oswald Mosley and his fascist right-wing Black Shirts on demonstration through London's east end, and the Jewish inhabitants said "No!"

Notting Hill Carnival 1976 ended in a spontaneous, reactionary, non-predetermined anti-police uprising, in which the frustrated, abused and repressed black youth said "No!"

"No more!"

We saw hundreds of police get battered, especially those who became separated from their colleagues, they were brutalised, they all 'took one for the team', that team of corrupt racist police who'd spent years discriminating against black youth; years fitting black boys up on trumped-up charges; years planting illegal substances in the pockets of innocent black boys as they made their way home from school, college and, if they were fortunate enough, work; years brutalising young black boys in cells "down the nick"; years lying under oath as they gave false testimony in the courts; years covering-up their own malpractices; years generating the 'pressure' that finally exploded on the final day of Carnival 1976.

I was advised by a black photographer to 'make myself scarce' because the police were organising a 'snatch-squad' to arrest me! I don't know why me, I was just an excited observer! To stay on the safe side though, I was spirited off to a friend of Smiffy's sister who plaited my afro into long loose braids that cascaded down my face and the back of my neck, changing my appearance pretty effectively. We made our way to Marcia's that night where we jubilantly recounted the sights we'd seen in exaggerated gory detail.

We decided to leave 'The Grove' early the next morning to make our way home to Reading. We left Paddington at about 6.30am, arriving in Reading at around 7.15am. We jumped out of the carriage and onto the platform, where we noticed piles of newspapers stacked ready for delivery to newsagents and homes across our home town. We checked the papers because we could see there were graphic pictures of the Carnival uprising on the front and back pages, and I was featured in virtually all of them, even in the centre-page spreads!

I quickly checked the Mirror, dad's favourite, and there I was. NO!!!!!!! This would soon be delivered to our house and, more importantly, into dad's clutches prior to settling into 'his' chair to catch up with the news.

I'd be dead if I didn't get home before it was delivered so, taking hasty leave from Smiffy and the boys, I ran the miles home to successfully intercept the newspaper boy before he delivered. That paper got shredded! I knew dad would be too lazy to bother going out to buy one himself, so I was eventually able to catch up on some sorely missed sleep!

Twenty-Six

The next six months slipped by in a haze of work, girls, capers with the boys and partying, then before I knew it, I was getting ready to leave Reading to start my sandwich degree course. I was shocked at the response of the boys when it dawned on them that I wasn't actually going to be around as much as usual. We got into quite heated arguments about the merits of pursuing a university degree and professional qualifications, as opposed to apprenticeships and the dole. Unbeknown to me at the time, we were discussing the popular socio-psychological theoretical debate between instant and deferred gratification. Yes it was true that the boys would be earning money earlier than most university undergraduates, but in the long-run it's more likely that the graduate professionals would be in more secure jobs that paid higher salaries. The argument got quite bitter and resentful, and I felt like I was letting them down, going off to poncy university with a bunch of toff snobs!

What could I do? Apart from fighting, I was useless with my hands, so pursuing an apprenticeship in the trades was never going to be an option for me. I'd played football for Berkshire County and was lined up with a trial at Fulham Football Club until I broke my ankle the week before going up to Craven Cottage, so football was out the window! I had very good 'people skills', and was always able to 'get on with', manage and motivate others. Despite my wayward tendencies, I came from a very united, loving and caring family background, with supportive parents who both worked in the caring profession. So I *had* to stick by my guns and start my degree course, but I promised I'd be back on a regular basis because, after all, I'd only be in London!

Also, I'd passed my driving test so nothing would stop me getting up and down between London and Reading. By the way, it took me three attempts before I passed my test which, compared to dad's 20-odd, I thought was pretty good going. Dad had allowed me to drive his car when we were working at the hospital in Horley, near Gatwick airport, which gave me lots of road practice. I also nicked his car on a regular basis when the boys were going out and Andy wasn't available with his. Without any formal, 'paid for' lessons, I took my first two tests in dad's clapped-out Mark 2 Cortina estate, with its spongy clutch and no hand-brake. I thought I did pretty well trying to blag it, but couldn't disguise the hill-start without a hand-brake convincingly enough! I decided to take a couple of lessons before my third attempt, and I only remember one piece of advice from the driving instructor:

"30 miles per hour is a speed limit, NOT a target!"

I think I'd developed quite a few bad driving habits during my wayward activities, which often involved driving 'borrowed' cars at haste!

I desperately wanted, and needed, to pass my test though. Being able to drive would have relieved so much pressure from me! I had the money to buy a car (and insure it even!), but needed to pass the test first. Thankfully, despite the pre-test nerves, I managed to pass it and the prospect of 'being legal' was very inspiring. No more looking in the rear view mirror checking for blue lights behind me from now on!

My first car was a Mark 2 Ford Escort. It was quite racy and I even got Smiffy to employ his newly-acquired electrician skills to customise the dashboard with red, gold and green lights. What a dickhead! Me, not Smiffy. Anyway, I quite fancied myself as an accomplished driver, and at times would 'race' other road users. I made the mistake of doing this one rainy night in Horley on my way back to the hospital house I shared with dad. I'd been 'out and about', but not drinking and, like many foolish young male drivers, I got into 'boy-racer' mode when stuck behind a middle-aged couple on a dark winding country lane. I kept flashing them impatiently to get out of the way and, when the opportunity arose, I roared past them with my best 'angry face' on, glaring at the occupants with *the* utmost contempt.

The speed got to me, and I was enjoying recklessly bombing around on the empty rain-slicked roads. I was approaching Horley train station which was built on the long curve of a humpback bridge, at too high speed as it transpired! Fifty yards before the entrance door to the station I realised I was going too fast and applied the brakes, too hard and too late, the car started to tail-end drift, and it felt like I was skating or gliding in slow motion on ice as the car started to slide. I lost control of it, smashing straight into an eighteen foot cast iron lamppost. Bits of the lamppost crashed to the ground around my car, with the majority of the post underneath the chassis.

I jumped out in a state of shock to survey the wreckage of my pride and joy. The lamppost had driven the engine block right up into the dashboard and, had I been going slightly faster, I'd have been crushed by the engine before the car jettisoned over the low bridge wall onto the tracks forty feet below. Still in a state of shock, I went into denial, trying to lift the car off the lamppost with live cables spitting electrical current all over the place, in order to drive it home!

So, whilst I'd pranged my car, completely writing it off, in actual fact I'd been extremely lucky to walk away from it unscathed, bar a sore thumb.

To rub salt into the open wounds of my damaged pride and crushing embarrassment, the couple I'd flashed and cursed minutes earlier came around the corner and into my eyesight. I recognised their car instantly, and they recognised me and what was left of mine instantly too. They slowed right down as they approached and, when level with me as I stood saturated and devastated in the pouring rain, the passenger wound her window down for the driver to shout at me:

"Stupid boy!"

Never have I felt so humiliated, blatantly culpable and stupid in my life!

I left the car where it lay, wrecked, on the path over the bridge. I called Andy when I got home and he arranged for one of his dad's mechanics to come and retrieve what was now really only describable as a Mark 2 Ford Scrapheap, to transport it back to his garage on the back of his flatbed tipper-winch truck.

It was a complete and absolute mess, with the headlights both looking at each other, but hey, at least the red, gold and green lights on the dashboard were still working!

Regardless of all the hiccups and push-and-pull factors, March 1977 saw me leaving home for a 'proper' reason and heading off to London to start my first six-month stint of psychiatric nurse training at the Maudsley Hospital in Denmark Hill. There was a huge nurses accommodation centre within the hospital grounds where the majority of student nurses lived, and I got a fantastically equipped and appointed fifth floor studio-flat overlooking the grounds. The flat was swept and tidied on a weekly basis, with shared cooking facilities, it was superb for my needs, it felt like a posh hotel room to me!

I even played one season for the hospital football team that played its home games in the grounds of our sister hospital, The Royal Bethlem, in Beckenham, south London. Originally built in 1247 on the site where Liverpool Street station now stands in London, it is the oldest extant psychiatric hospital in Europe. One of its nicknames was the 'Bedlam', a word which has become synonymous with madness itself. In fact, for a significant period of its history, not only were parents and families of inmates actively encouraged and allowed to visit their often chained and incarcerated relatives, so was the general public, who'd 'visit' in their droves to watch the patient-inmates for entertainment purposes!

Five or six other students had chosen the Mental Nursing option, all white, and all good people, there was even a middle-aged nun, Liz, who always dressed in a habit in classes, on the wards, and even eventually at uni and, although at times she reminded me of the Convent Mother in "The Sound of Music", she was great fun and had a heart of gold. I think we all fell in love with her!

I really enjoyed the first stint of student nurse training, working on general psychiatric wards while attending theory lessons one day a week. It taught me that, no matter how bad we may think we have things, there are many others whose lives are made far worse than ours by elements over which we have little or no control. I suppose I was slowly developing a new and different appreciation of life, my horizons were opening up, and I started to see things from a wider range of perspectives. I was working with people suffering from schizophrenia, depression, manic depression (now more often referred to as bi-polar disorder), and an array of neurotic and obsessive disorders, and I found it intriguing learning the theories that attempt to explain how people had ended up in these sorry states. It became very clear to me that there was an exceptionally thin line between sanity and insanity in all of us and, by virtue of a certain combination of genetics and environmental experiences, we are more or less likely to suffer mental health issues in our lives. It's estimated that one in four of us will require hospitalisation for mental health concerns at some stage during our lives, which I find scary!

Another thing I learnt was that, as human beings, intellectually, psychologically, physically and emotionally we *are* very complex, but slabs of meat nonetheless! Six weeks into our training we attended a post-mortem examination, and we were stood right up next to the occupied gurney, inches away from the unfortunate deceased occupant. A surgeon was present, and was being ably assisted by a grounds man/porter who I'd only seen previously attending the lawns and clearing rubbish! I was shocked. What the hell is he doing here?! My tacit question was soon answered when the post-mortem examination began. He was helping the surgeon to saw off the top of the cadaver's skull, before peeling the skin back off his face, then cutting a 'Y' from underneath the chin down to the groin, before peeling the chest cavity skin around to the sides then sawing off the chest plate. The internal organs, including the brain, heart, liver, kidneys, spleen, lungs and intestines were all removed right in front of us! I thought I was a tough guy, but this was beginning to freak me out!

On dissecting the brain it became evident that this guy had died of an embolism and, upon certifying the cause of death, they just slopped everything back into place and stitched him back up! It was just like watching two skilled, efficient, but emotionally detached butchers at work in an abattoir. It didn't make me feel sick, but I started to feel 'strange', a bit light-headed. I felt a bit stuffy and breathless behind the facemask I was wearing, and I thought maybe it was a bit warm in there as Dave, the only other male student ran crashing out of the abattoir, clearly distressed at the procedure we'd just witnessed.

My macho pride wouldn't allow me to follow suit, but I didn't want to do anything stupid like passing out and falling all over the cadaver! I didn't know what was happening as I began to feel progressively uncomfortable and worse for wear, and my eyes were hurting me, throbbing behind the facemask.

"Please don't let me pass out!"

That was all I could think of. I didn't want to compromise my reputation and self-image.

I suppose the scene had completely immobilised me as I stood rigidly motionless throughout the procedure, and I also think, to make things worse, my brain stopped functioning also. However, when I pulled my facemask down to try to catch a bit of fresh 'abattoir' air, I instantly felt fine. I hadn't noticed that I'd pulled the facemask up too high and it was putting pressure on the bottom of my eyeballs, making me feel uncomfortable. That was it. I nearly embarrassed myself over something eminently straightforward, innocuous and simple!

We all grew up very quickly after that experience, and started to adopt a more serious, mature and professional approach to our tutelage in psychiatric nursing care. I was even able to show compassion and empathy to Dave who'd run out of the abattoir when we finally made our exits into the glorious sunlight and real, sweet fresh air. To give him credit, he was fully in touch with his 'feminine side' and wasn't the least bit embarrassed. I was totally unaware at the time that men even had a 'feminine side', so I was really learning a lot about psychiatry and also myself!

The angry, rebellious, revolutionary and naively idealistic streetboy was beginning to be introduced to a new and interesting world and, as such, new approaches to and perceptions of life seemed high on the list of priorities for me. But I couldn't abandon my boys back home in Reading, where the street life still called and enticed me.

True to my commitment and pledge to the boys, I answered the call. I made sure I'd get back to Reading for some weekends and fell into the old routine of staying one step ahead of the law, borrowed cars, music, clubs, dancing, fights and girls. The excitement never waned, but my perception of risk and consequence started to alter. Given some of the situations we'd been through in the past, and some of the things we were planning for the future, it became abundantly clear that I had to make a decision that would irrevocably shape the rest of my life.

But the habits and practices of my past were *so* difficult to shake off.

Twenty-Seven

I found myself back in Ladbroke Grove again where I joined the Black Liberation Front (BLF), a group of young, angry, but organised 'politicised intellectuals' committed to fighting against police and governmental oppression. I likened it to the English version of the Black Panther Party in America, and was very excited at the prospect of participating in extremely radical activities to redress certain grievances and expose the inherently corrupt and racist British 'establishment'.

I was very quickly kicked out of the BLF for being '*too* radical'! On receiving and discussing news that some east-end racist thugs had beaten up a group of black people in east London, I advocated an immediate revenge attack. I insisted we drive straight to east London and beat up any white thug-types we happened to come across. I even offered to 'acquire' extra cars for transport purposes! But the BLF were obviously too 'intellectual' to dirty their hands pursuing such action, and didn't want to be associated with it either!

Shortly after being jettisoned by the BLF I participated in an anti-National Front march that took place in south east London. I was enraged at the thought that these thick racist white-trash thugs felt empowered enough to actually take their case to the streets. There were several hundred National Front 'demonstrators' draped in the red, white and blue of the Union Jack, voicing their 'political' concerns about blacks and 'pakis' taking their jobs and houses, and demanding they be 'repatriated' from whence they came, and many thousands of anti-NF marchers, blacks, whites and a few Asians, intent on shouting them down.

I joined the march as it snaked its way from Camberwell towards Deptford before its final destination of Lewisham, all of these areas being highly populated by first generation immigrants with their young families. Emotions were running extremely high, with a thin blue line of helmeted and riot-ready police keeping both sets of demonstrators apart. The inevitable skirmishes and scuffles began to erupt in Deptford, and became fully-fledged face-to-face hand battles by the time we reached Lewisham. Similar to Ladbroke Grove, Lewisham was undergoing early stages of urban regeneration and development but was, and still largely remains, a working class area.

Bottles, stones and bricks began to rain down on the NF scumbags, who retaliated from behind police lines with missiles of their own.

So, I'd taken great steps and made admirable progress to leave the streets, but the streets weren't leaving me in a reciprocal or synchronised manner, they were still deeply ingrained! Intrinsically I was still happy and comfortable with the concept:

"By Any Means Necessary!"

As introduced to popular culture by Nation of Islam and black political activist Malcolm X in a speech before he was assassinated in his last year of life:

> "We declare our right on this earth to be a man, to be a human being, to be given the rights of a human being in this society, in this day, in which we intend to bring into existence *by any means necessary*".

Whilst Malcolm X wasn't stating revolution *must* involve the use of violent means in his efforts to "internationalise the fight against racism", he wasn't excluding its use either.

Unlike one of his predecessors, Mohandas Ghandi, who sanctioned non-violent means only to bring about political change in India against imperial English colonial tyranny. Ghandi was also assassinated; and also unlike Malcolm X's American contemporary Dr Martin Luther King Jr., who advocated non-violent civil disobedience means only whilst orchestrating the American Civil Rights Movement to end the exploitation, oppression and disenfranchisement of black Americans. Dr King was also assassinated.

September 1977 saw my arrival on campus at Brunel University, where I got another self-contained bedsit in one of the several halls of residence, another more-than-decent 'bachelor pad'! The campus was relatively large and sprawling, with the library, refectory, student union bars and the majority of the lecture theatres in the centre. I was happy to see other black students and to find out during Freshers Week that there was an established and active African-Caribbean Students Society. Needless to say this was the first (and only) student society I joined! However, I was still football-mad and made sure I got the dates for the trials!

I loved Sociology 101 and Psychology 101. I loved learning the theories of Marx and Engels, Freud and Laing. Things began to fall into place for me. I started to understand how and why things were the way they were and, surely, if we all understood, then things ought to be able to be easily changed?! I began to understand the dynamics and history that lay behind the evolution and development of social, sexual and racial inequality, discrimination and oppression, psychological and emotional well-being and ill-health. I was actually able to start making links between theory and reality, *real* life.

My intellectualisation of *real life* experience was further developed and enhanced by a Yoruba student who was a year ahead of me studying one of the sciences, Tayo. He was six foot two, and, other than being bespectacled, a perfect physical specimen of West African manhood, and became a very good friend of mine. Chairperson of the African-Caribbean Society, I'd spend hours in his company discussing black history and politics. Despite his very pronounced stuttering impediment, he did most of the talking, and I was more than happy to soak up the information he'd lay before me. He seemed *so* informed, knowledgeable and wise for his age, and always succeeded in helping me to see things from a different perspective without forcing his opinions on me. He was analytical and balanced in his renditions and, whilst I thought I was pretty well informed, he was light years ahead of me and it felt almost as if he was throwing pearls before swine every time he spoke with me.

The university football trials took place in the second week of the first term, and I made a sufficiently impressive impact to be chosen for the first XI team. I was the only Fresher to be selected for the first XI during our first year, although there were many very good first year trialists and established first-teamers, the majority of whom had played at a decent part-time semi-professional level. I'd lost any real hopes of playing professionally, but I never lost a love of the game. I absolutely *loved* playing football, even if it was just for the sake of a kick-about, I'd be the first out there!

Whilst I'm on the theme of football (not for the first or last time I might add!), an uncle on my dad's mother's side of the family, Titus Okere, was a footballer who arrived with a Nigeria National team to tour England in 1949, which he captained. He must have done well, because he was signed to play for Swindon Town based on his performances whilst on the tour. He, along with his wife and son Chiedo, were regular visitors to our home as youngsters:

Uncle Titus – kneeling middle row
far left – with the Nigeria National
Football Team Squad at Everton
FC Training Ground (1949)

Unbelievably, Obi managed to unearth video footage of the tour on Youtube (the wonders of the internet never cease to amaze and thrill me!), just Google: Colonial Films Nigerian Football Tour 1949. It starts at the Everton training ground, then goes on to feature clips of two matches they played, the first against Marine Crosby FC in Liverpool, the second against Dulwich Hamlet FC in south London (who, coincidentally, my son Ike played with for three and a half seasons). Even I played on the same pitch, decades after our uncle!

As is the norm in the world of football I made a lot of friends-for-life, black and white, opposition players and members of my own team, through playing the game. However, I'd made friends with other first year students, especially Colin, a Law student from Antigua, and preferred to play with the second XI to play with him and my mates. Over the duration of my time at university we got to several regional and national cup finals, and during my second year I was selected to represented England Universities Athletics Union (UAU), which meant I went to the famous Lilleshall National Centre in Shropshire (next county Wales!), in the midlands, where the full professional England team trained.

A few things remain in my mind from this experience. Prior to leaving Camberwell in south London, to Lilleshall, I filled the tank of my Mark 2 Cortina for £8.00. *£8.00!* At today's petrol prices that would cost me close to £90.00. Secondly, I was stunned by the opulence of the centre. Set in secluded Shropshire countryside, it was like a 5-star hotel for the super-rich athletically gifted, with sumptuous individual rooms, communal games room with snooker, pool and table tennis, dining area, and the food! Sumptuous! I'd never eaten such a vast array of culinary delights, all of which were 100% nutritious and healthy! There was a physiotherapy clinic, well-trained (polite and docile but eager-to-please) staff, and the many practice and playing fields were in pristine condition. If you couldn't play on these surfaces, you couldn't play anywhere!

I was the only black player there which for me, though no surprise, was bitterly disappointing, but I'd developed the social skills to integrate effectively and, as footballers worldwide will state, there is only one language in football, and I was more than capable of letting my football do the talking for me. As is usual, when other players see your ability and rate you, all walls come tumbling down as your popularity and importance to the team rises. The coaches were brilliant, they really knew their stuff as they extended our ability and experience, taught us a lot about formations and tactics whilst making each session challenging, enjoyable and fun. Apart from my regular nocturnal street pursuits, I'd never before been on such a physical fitness regime, and I don't remember ever feeling so strong and fit before, or since!

Part way through the second session on the second day we took a break during training and whilst we stood in a huddle on the training pitch, all of a sudden, we looked up to see a black face trotting over from the centre to join us. I couldn't believe it, and I was so happy that Ray was in my group. We hit it off instantly and became friends for life. Ray was a dark-skinned quick and nimble right-winger who was studying Languages (French), at Leeds University, though his family lived in Tooting, south London. Like me, he was a first-generation British Black boy but, in his case, his parents originated from Guyana, South America, an ex-colony of the empire previously known as 'British Guiana'. We made a pretty effective partnership on the pitch, and established a very good and long-lasting friendship off it.

Whilst at Lilleshall we played against three famous first division (equivalent to the current Premiership), teams at the time, Wolverhampton Wanderers, Stoke City, and Birmingham City. Ex-Liverpool and England captain Emlyn Hughes played for Wolves, as did one of my early English league favourites, mixed-race Welsh central defender George Berry, he of the HUGE afro! We spoke quite a bit together after the match (they beat us 6-0!), and I found we shared a lot in common in terms of our shared experiences and attitude to life. He went on to play for Stoke City and Wales at international level. Our next game was against Stoke City, who beat us 2-0, with the young though now legendary Garth Crooks in their side. He was a powerful goal-scoring centre forward who went on to play for Tottenham Hotspur and England and, of course, he notched one against us!

In the final training session immediately prior to our last match against Birmingham City, in view of the previous two results, our coach didn't rate our chances too highly. At the end of the session he made us all take one penalty each, with no goalkeeper, because, according to him, this would be the closest we'd get to scoring on the day. As a centre forward and goal-scorer I wanted to go last, so the others all took their penalties, the majority of them simply rolling the ball into the unguarded net. I wanted to go last so as to leave a positive impression on the coach, but I wasn't going to be rolling the ball in, oh no, I was going to smash it into the top left corner of the net! 'Top Bins!' With all eyes on me I stepped up, placed the ball on the spot, took several steps backwards, ran to the ball, and smashed it over the crossbar! Everyone including the coach laughed as the ball 'came back down with snow on it' about 70 feet into the adjoining field. As the only player to miss from 12 yards without a goalkeeper, I should have been ashamed and embarrassed (but I wasn't, I was having fun!), so I took the ribbing in good spirit, but guaranteed the coach that, if I got a chance in the game against Birmingham City, I'd score.

We had a 'light' pre-match meal, but I was last in the restaurant and was forced to leave the table by my coach who told me I wouldn't be able to perform on a full stomach! I grabbed one more banana on my way out, confident I'd do well!

Birmingham City fielded an inexperienced squad of young hopefuls and first-year professionals. They were 1-0 up when they conceded an indirect free kick about 15 yards outside their penalty area. Me and Ray stood over the ball and I told him to just roll it short to me, my intention being to have a shot from 30 yards. I sensed quite a bit of reluctance not only from Ray, but other team mates also, but I was insistent. After telling him to just "roll it, roll it!" Ray dutifully obliged, and I dutifully obliged by smashing it 'top bins' from 30 yards! You *know* I just *had* to remind my coach of my pre-match goal-scoring promise! We went on to lose 2-1, but it was great being the only player to score against professional opposition.

England UAU – Lilleshall Hall National Sports Centre – 1978
Me and Ray – front row – you can't miss us!

At the end of the week Ray and I cruised back to London and vowed to stay in touch, which we did. However, I haven't mentioned that by this time I'd grown my hair into dreadlocks that swept down to my shoulders. My dreadlocks and rasta-look was the life-changing and life-saving decision I'd made the previous year.

In my mind, in order for me to break out of the virtually all-engrossing lifestyle of petty crime and violence that was steadily leading to more daring, high profile and dangerous escapades, I had to draw a line under it all, or risk almost certain death or prolonged periods of incarceration at Her Majesty's Pleasure!

Two incidents come to mind that epitomised my concerns, and both of them happened at the same venue, Skindles nightclub in Maidenhead, Berkshire, and both of them on separate Friday night excursions. On the first, me and the boys had borrowed a car to drive from Reading to Maidenhead. As we were driving over the bridge approaching the club, a guy shunted into the rear of our car. We all piled out of the car and made it clear to the boy that he'd need to pay an 'on the spot' repair bill for the damage he'd caused. He did so immediately and without even bothering to mention referring the incident to insurance companies. He knew he'd have been wiped out!

We were enjoying a great night out in the club, soul, disco and funk music pumping out of the speakers; we were all getting our groove on. Me and Smiffy went to use the toilets and, whilst standing at the urinals 'pointing Percy at the porcelain', I looked over at Smiffy. A couple of thuggish-looking white guys had just entered and I could tell by the look on Smiffy's face that they weren't going to leave the toilets without an altercation taking place. Little did they know they'd just walked into hell on earth! Smiffy confronted the guys with some false allegation about one of them having stood on his foot inside the club without apologising. The guy hotly denied the accusation and, much to his imminent demise, started getting into Smiffy's face. BIG mistake. Then he started pushing up his chest and pushing Smiffy whilst being encouraged by his mate. Even BIGGER mistake! Smiffy smashed him in the face, totally obliterating him. His mate flew at Smiffy, bottle in hand, so I had to intervene with a right hook to his jaw, and he crumpled to the floor to meet his mate. We were now both hot-wired, adrenalin coursing through our systems and, almost telepathically, decided to wait in the toilets for other victims to arrive to relieve themselves as the two thugs groaned and moaned on the floor.

The entrance door to the Gents opened and, as we'd instinctively guessed, mates of the thugs had come looking for them and, as they entered in twos and threes, they were met by a barrage fists and boots. In many ways they didn't stand a chance as they wandered unsuspectingly into the toilets which, fourteen guys later, resembled an abattoir. The white and chrome decor and tiling was covered in blood, *their* blood. Our mate Barry walked in and nearly suffered a similar fate as me and Smiffy were just about to jump him as we'd done the previous victims. Barry stopped dead in his tracks and gaped in awe at the Texas-Chainsaw-Massacre-like scene, blood splashed all over the walls and cubicle doors, fourteen white guys rolling around in agony on the floor, even Barry looked sick and disturbed at the carnage. We could tell just by the look on his face that enough was enough, so we made our hasty exits from the club to the car park, and waited for the boys to reassemble before we sped back to Reading.

The second incident went down in Skindles, and became friends and family legend!

We were all there, Smiffy and the boys, Ijem, Obi and their mates, it was a pumping night, the club was packed with 'faces' and strangers, and a tense undercurrent of tension added an extra vibe to the night's enjoyment! Previous arrangements had already been made for a fight to take place, with Reading teaming up with Maidenhead, against Slough who'd teamed up with London. Amazing, considering there was no such thing as mobile phones available to make such arrangements.

Looking very dapper in my short-leg two-piece suit, dickey-bow tie and sporting the BOAC badge I received on my return from Nigeria (1960)

Innocent, angelic, optimistic, before going completely off the rails (1968)

Off the rails, angry, disinterested, disenchanted, increasingly cynical, realistically pessimistic, rebel without a clue, soul-head but loving life! (1974)

Changed appearance and lifestyle, reforming character, saved!! (1980)

Settled, married, responsible, professional, family man – mid-1990s

Mellow, wise, old, fat, bald, more at peace (2009)

Proceedings kicked off according to plan and without too much rigmarole on the dance floor, when one of our Maidenhead 'members' got into a messy scrap however, it served its purpose and acted as the spark that ignited the litmus paper.

All hell let loose!

Within seconds chairs, tables, bottles and glasses (either full or empty!) were used as weapons by hundreds of clubbers to incapacitate their targeted adversaries. The scene was utter mayhem, girls screaming in fear as they whimpered and cowered looking for cover; blokes, mainly strangers, punching and kicking the shit out of each other; guys were getting knocked out left, right and centre in the running battles that now took over the floor where, minutes earlier, young happy people had been dancing with their partners; tables crashing over to the floor; chairs flying through the air; screams and thuds rang out as victims were pummelled with fists, feet, chairs and bottles. It was just like a bar room brawl from a classic western film starring John Wayne, Ernest Borgnine or Clint Eastwood. It was great!

The dance floor and stage had been transformed into a swarming mass of battling bodies. I even saw Obi attempt to deliver a Bruce Lee style kung-fu kick to a guy's head but, as some of the battling crowd swept into him, he was carried along in its tide, desperately hopping on one foot as he tried to make sure he didn't hit the deck. It was laugh-out-loud comical!

I had guys target me and got stuck into defending myself with gusto, knocking a few out and scaring others off. One guy jumped me from behind but I managed to swivel him round in front of me and punched him up a few times. We both fell onto a table from which I grabbed a pint glass to smash over his head and, when I did, the glass pin-wheeled off into the air. It was a plastic glass, typical of my luck, the first time I ever try to use a weapon in a serious fight and it turns out to be as much use as a chocolate tea pot!

To assuage my embarrassment, I battered him brutally before discarding of his limp frame on the floor. I looked up to identify another potential target and, in my peripheral vision, I noticed a white guy calmly leaning against the room-length bar. He looked maybe ten years older than us, and appeared very composed, almost serene, and seemed to have a disdainful smirk on his face as he returned my gaze. I tried to work out if I knew him from somewhere, or if our paths had crossed previously, but just couldn't picture him. His contemptuous composure unnerved me to the core. I decided not to take him on and continued my search for other victims. Every now and again I looked over at this enigmatic guy, and he'd never moved, but remained casually propped up at the bar.

I decided discretion (cowardice?) was the better part of valour and put the idea of taking him on out of my mind. The guy must be a freak, calmly standing there, unmoved, as total mayhem erupted around him! My survival instinct further kicked in when I just *felt* it was the right time to make myself scarce, so I fought my way to the long exit corridor, randomly swatting guys as I made my way through the heaving mass of pugilistic antagonists. As I reached the neck of the exit corridor about twenty policemen came pouring through the main entrance. I hobbled my way towards them, shouting at them and the club management team that it was Hell in there, whilst pretending I was lucky to get out alive as an injured innocent bystander victim.

They rushed past me as another ten came pouring in through the main entrance, scuffling with a mixed-race friend of mine from Basingstoke, Harry, who'd had the misfortune of arriving at the club just before the deluge in blue. He was completely innocent of any wrongdoing or participation in the melee, but they'd handcuffed and arrested him anyway. I sneaked past as they bundled him to the floor, his face crushed under their boots. Thankfully he didn't see me and, thankfully, I heard his shouted protestations:

"I'm not *fucking* Gus! I just got here! Get the fuck off me! Gus looks like me, but I'm not him! My name's Harry, not fucking Gus!"

If there was ever a clearer notification that my time was drawing near, this was it. It seems the boys in blue had intelligence that I, along with my boys, would be in the thick of things at the club that night and, by the skin of my teeth, I managed to worm my way past them without being detected. I left Harry trying to snitch his way out of trouble, and scarpered across the car park to our borrowed car. Smiffy and the boys managed to avoid arrest and, in drips and drabs, we assembled at the car before making our clandestine-by-way-of-back-road return to Reading and safety, guffawing our way through our individual anec-dotal accounts of the one-on-ones we'd enjoyed that night!

A couple of weeks later we learnt that the mysterious guy at the bar had just been released from prison on the very day of the fight, and had been at the club privately (psychotically?) celebrating his release after a long stretch, for murder. I was *so* glad I hadn't made the mistake of tangling with him, but the writing was very much written loud and clear on the wall. Change and get out of this lifestyle. NOW !

To make a successful change, I had to revamp my outward appear-ances, reinvent myself, move in a new and different circle of friends, and completely change my social 'commitments'. So I transformed myself from the biggest soul-head in town, to a deeper-thinking and more conscious roots-reggae loving dread.

As I mentioned previously, I totally loved the 'rastaman look'. But for me, more importantly, I also loved the philosophy that Rastafarianism stood for: a complete and visible rejection of established white Christianity as they looked to Africa for answers and explanations, attempting to perceive and understand the world from a black perspec-tive. I loved it! I didn't go in for the religious aspects that proclaimed Ethiopian Emperor Haile Selassie God reincarnate, but I was excited by, and soon grew to respect, their anti-establishment historical, social, economic, political and moral views, which were exceptionally Afrocentric, especially the centrality of Marcus Garvey to Rastafarianism.

Marcus Mosiah Garvey Jr. (1887-1940), was a descendant of slaves who became a Jamaican political leader, publisher, journalist, entrepreneur and orator who was a staunch proponent of the Black Nationalism and Pan-African Movements. He founded the Universal Negro Improvement Association in Jamaica, and African Communities League (UNIA-ACL) in the United States, where he became an inspirational figure in the Civil Rights Movement. He was also part of the 'Back-to-Africa' movement that promoted the return of the African Diaspora to their ancestral lands.

"Africa for the Africans, at home and abroad".

The concept of repatriation carried a very powerful message encouraging economic empowerment and independence, and inherent in Garvey's mantra, the removal of non-Africans from the continent. He even set up the 'Black Star Line' shipping company for the very purpose of repatriating African-Americans to Africa (the Black Star was later to become the central feature of the Ghanaian national flag, and the name of their international football team!).

His philosophy sounded great to me, and I'd have been happy if the message was absorbed, internalised, and acted upon. I couldn't help thinking Marcus Garvey *must* be of Igbo origin: intelligent, proud, confident, arrogant, multi-talented, entrepreneurial, typical Igbo! And interestingly, the tricolour horizontal Biafran flag of red, black and green charged with a rising sun over a golden bar was inspired by, and based upon, the pan-African flag designed by Marcus Garvey's UNIA organisation.

Marcus Garvey's
Pan African Flag

Biafran Flag

Sadly, Garvey was discredited by many black intellectuals and political thinkers, including W E B du Bois, who denounced Garvey for meeting with the Ku Klux Klan to discuss and eventually agree upon the need for racial separation and segregation, on the basis that it's better to know and recognise your enemies than to lie with white hypocrites who only operated to deceive and continue to exploit the 'black nation'. He praised the KKK for their openness and honesty.

But it's very difficult if not to say impossible to support the sentiments and politics of racial superiority and inferiority, segregation and apartheid, no matter which colour, black or white, is considered superior or inferior.

However, after having been educated in the English education system that either totally misrepresented or ignored the contributions of African and Caribbean people to British history, I couldn't help but find other accounts and theories utterly irresistible, particularly as they rejected the orthodox, white-washed, English-establishment view.

Very much like the Mau Mau anti-colonial rebellion that was orchestrated by the Kikuyu people in Kenya against their incumbent British colonial masters (between 1952 and 1960), in many ways both they and Garvey were doomed to fail in the face of the odds stacked against them. But their successes can be measured in terms of the impact they had in inspiring black people to challenge the prevailing white political exploitation and oppression, and the attendant negative notions of black servility, docility, and ability that expounded throughout 'the empire' at the time. I know I for one *fed* off such 'hidden' information, the type that didn't exist in our school history books.

Knowledge is a true liberator. Those who challenge the status quo are true liberators, true heroines and heroes of history. But we were never taught about *black* political leaders and innovators, scholars and inventors, civilisations and languages. Even Jamaica, apparently, was discovered by the white European voyager-cum-looter Christopher Columbus! To my knowledge, Jamaica had been inhabited by Arawak Indians for thousands of years before his accidental arrival on their shores, and I'm fairly certain they knew of the existence of their own island long before he did! Regrettably, they now no longer exist, after having fallen victim very quickly to white European violence and disease.

History in school was white history. A history of the glorious, heroic, victorious type that depicted the English, and Europeans in general, as buccaneering pioneers and adventurers, bravely venturing forth on epic adventures on behalf of (a Christian) God and the Queen. Blacks and Asians were always, without fail, depicted as pathetic, savage, uncivilised, thick, ignorant, dirty, barbaric, loincloth-clad, child-like imbeciles who joyously appreciated salvation from themselves by the wise and all-conquering white man.

I loved History in school, but hated being made to feel very much like I'd descended from second-class citizens, if not to say sub-human species. The history of black people was always portrayed in the negative light of slavery and/or colonialism. It was almost as if black history started and finished with Britain's lustful participation in the 'triangular trade'! Savage, ignorant, heathen black Africans were transported from the Gold and Guinea coasts across the Atlantic ocean on ships that had departed from Bristol, Liverpool, Swansea, Cardiff and London, to be deposited in the Caribbean and North and South America, where they 'produced' sugar, cotton and other valuable and sought-after commodities which were finally transported back across the Atlantic to Bristol, Liverpool, Swansea, Cardiff and London where they were sold, consumed or developed as 'finished' goods, for huge profits.

Even the media and popular children's books were saturated with such imagery, including golliwogs on jam jars and angry-deceitful-criminal-mugger golliwogs in Enid Blyton's world renown Noddy children's books! When would it ever end?!

I grew to learn and understand that such subliminal and not-so-subtle messages acted as the glue that kept their morally corrupt system together. How could the powerful white English establishment ever hope to maintain its credibility in the eyes of its populace if the truth were known? It couldn't! Has it ever declared that the gold and diamonds that bedeck the Queen's crowns, tiaras and palaces were stolen from Africa and India? Has the fact that England kidnapped and brutalised millions of black Africans into forced slavery and servitude ever been declared as the bedrock upon which industrialisation and modernism were based? No chance!

Their global debauchery, theft and exploitation had to be sexed-up by centuries of regally- and politically-appointed spin-doctors, in order to justify their disgusting theft and evil brutality. So the Africans became savages who needed to be saved from themselves. They were actually happy and grateful for the intervention and ministrations of the entrepreneurial slave traders and pioneer colonisers and settlers, honestly! Britain civilised these 'heathens' by introducing them to the Christian Bible and, in exchange for gaining empire and commonwealth citizenship and status, it was only fair for the blacks to work, surely? After all:

"We ARE British, play the White Man old chap!"

But it wasn't simply a matter of colour. England employed a similar brainwashing tactic with regards the Irish, and the 'Irish Problem'. The Irish were portrayed as characteristically thick, uncivilised, loutish, Catholic, child-breeding drunken sots whose lives required British organisation, development and administration. The Irish were brutalised by the English, but forcing Protestantism and 'the English way of life' on them would redeem their sorry souls. Indeed, the Irish became known and referred to as the 'Blacks of Europe', in recognition of the similar way in which England oppressed and exploited them.

So, for me, I respected and admired *any* black person who came out and selflessly contributed to the re-writing of history, and probably none more so than Nelson Mandela.

Nelson Rolihlahla Mandela, South African political activist, Chairman of the African National Congress (ANC), moral and social leader of the majority black population of South Africa in their struggles against the prevailing oppressive apartheid regime. Although he advocated non-violent protest and resistance, he participated in activities that included 'guerrilla warfare' designed and perpetrated to unsettle and destroy the symbolic pillars and bastions of apartheid, including the sabotage of military and government targets, government posts, machines, identity pass offices, native magistrates courts, post offices and other government facilities. He even resorted to crop burning! Eventually 'tried' and found guilty of sabotage and treason in 1962, he spent a total of 27 years in prison for the cause, many of these years on the notorious Robben Island with other black activists. Resolute and eminently dignified, a true national leader, he survived and outlived the vast majority of his detractors and persecutors to be released in 1990, an event that was broadcast live all around the world.

He resumed leadership of the ANC and led them into the first open elections in South African history in 1994, which he won with 62% of the vote to become the first black President of South Africa, thus cementing himself in my mind as an absolute legend!

I loved my hair in dreadlocks. I still dream that I have them every now and again, and wake up bitterly disappointed as I disconsolately rub my (now) bald head in the morning after having had such a dream! If, as Feud's Dream Theory argues, dreams are the windows to our unconscious wishes, thoughts and desires, then I certainly agree with Sigmund! A taller version of Bob Marley, my affiliations couldn't be more starkly evident. Much to the consternation of my mum and dad, and Smiffy and the boys, all of whom were bitterly unhappy with my conversion, for widely different reasons of course!

Dad, because people in Nigeria with dreadlocks were considered "mad pipple", and Smiffy and the boys because my conversion equalled my rejection of our 'bad old ways'. I felt desperately bad on both accounts, especially Smiffy.

Me and Smiffy spent a lot of time together, doing what testosterone-fuelled adolescent boys do and, more significantly, sharing many of our thoughts and feelings. I was happily surprised and impressed at the level of Smiffy's understanding about the relationship between Africans and West Indians. He understood and accepted the fact that we were separated only by history, and not by genetics or, to varying degrees, culture. To be absolutely honest, he gave me the impression that he actually embraced the idea that he originated from Africa. He was one of a very few 'West Indians' I'd met who seemed not only at peace with the concept, but embraced and revelled in it.

This was important because, other than among some schools whose teachers remained concerned and interested about the future of all of their charges, the majority of schools weren't great places to be for African kids. Not necessarily because of the teachers who, other than a passing awareness of the differences between African and West Indian pupils' names, didn't understand the differences between us to effectively discriminate against us. Schools were hard places to be for African pupils because of other pupils.

It was hard enough to be black in school, almost *any* school. But to be black and *African* was double-bubble! Not only were we (like all other black pupils), discriminated against by racist teachers, we were also discriminated against by our 'West Indian' peers. The last thing any pupil wanted to be in school, socially at least, was African! However, it was a confusing situation. West Indians would always make a point of referring to the "blackness" of Africans, Africans' accents, noses, food, clothes, lips. African anything! But we, my brother and sisters, *didn't* fit the description. For all intents and purposes, we were African in name alone.

In progressive schools, as far as the teachers were concerned, we Africans were more likely to be from integrated and supportive families and, as such, 'a better bet'. We were also lighter skinned, and as such we were more 'acceptably-black' blacks, 'the acceptable face of blackness'.

As far as our West Indian pupil peers were concerned, despite the fact that we were African, we were lighter skinned than most of them so, as a result, we were what they and their parents wanted to be themselves, 'the preferred face of blackness'.

Psychologically though, we made things pretty clear to everybody, we were black, we were African, and proud to be African.

We often discussed these issues at home with mum, doing so with dad seemed almost pointless at times, and she'd reinforce our stance:

"At least ye know where ye come from!"

Twenty-Eight

To this day I firmly believe that "knowing where ye come from", your origin and history, is an essential ingredient and defining aspect of being human. I never hesitated in letting my detractors know that I knew exactly where I originated from, the actual villages in Biafra and Eire, and I always very swiftly followed this assertion up with a conversation- and argument-winning question:

"Where do *you* originate from?"

Unlike many mixed-race children of our generation who suffered crushing identity crises, we were confident and often arrogant about our self-identity and knowledge of our backgrounds of origin and history. We made it abundantly clear that we'd *never* wish nor want to be anything different and that, in fact, given the choice, we'd remain exactly as we were. We were strong. Knowledge of our origins gave us this strength.

"Thank you mum and dad!"

All of our teachers and peers, black, white and Asian, quickly learnt there was no point in trying to knock us on our African or Irish roots, our identity, because we 'knew who we were', never hid from nor rejected either element of our roots, and never pretended to be anything other than African-Irish.

Black Shamrocks!

Though me and Smiffy used to 'go deep' in these discussions, it was never the case that I felt I had to *explain* things to him. He seemed to know and, when he didn't, he seemed to very quickly understand

237

and accept. When it came to issues of black identity, history and our relationships with white society we were on the same page, which made it so difficult for me to make my decision to change my lifestyle, because I didn't want him to feel I was rejecting him and turning my back on our friendship.

But I wasn't up for going back on my decision, despite the fact that I couldn't explain my position to dad without revealing my hidden life, the contents of which would undoubtedly have dismayed him no end. I wanted, needed, to get out of my secret lifestyle in order to pursue the 'right way'. So I stuck to my guns (and my dreadlocked hair), until I'd convinced myself there was no going back!

Much to the chagrin of our parents, my kindred spirit Ijem had also grown her hair in dreadlocks! We seemed to be following a similar path with regards many things in life, especially our views with regards how we presented ourselves to the outside world, rejecting the established status quo in favour of more obvious and positive black philosophies and imagery. We were resolute and happy to declare:

"Say it loud, I'm Black and I'm Proud!"

I sometimes wondered how mum used to feel about our very obvious rejection of white society, after all she was white! Were we being totally insensitive? Was she still as vehemently anti-English as she'd been during our early childhoods? Did she still understand and support our sentiments and motives? She'd still never made any attempts to contact or visit her family who'd rejected her, but somehow she was aware that some were living in Exeter, Devon. Whether or not she was emotionally affected by our increasingly more obdurate 'blackness', she never let on, and always supported us ideologically.

It dawned on me though, that she was becoming increasingly isolated. Apart from a couple of friends that she could count on one hand, and work colleagues, we were the only significant people she had in her life, her immediate family. She'd become the sole white face at the centre of a black domestic and social world. Was this healthy for her?

Virtually everybody who came to the house, other than the post-man, electrician, gas supply serviceman, and the police, was black! She never seemed to miss or pine for 'another' life. She seemed to live her life quite contentedly through those of her husband and children, sharing our thoughts, dreams, goals and aspirations; experiencing our disappointments, setbacks and pain as keenly as if they were her own; organising and making practical plans for achieving progress and development; advising and supporting us in our friendships and relationships; she was the core, the foundation stone of our family, the ever-present rock around whom everything evolved and upon whom everyone relied; she was happy in this role. In conversation she still expressed that deep, aggressive, passionate and protective fighting spirit that was her essence, and our safety blanket.

I say *in conversation* because things seemed to start to settle at home and in our lives generally. It felt like we'd somehow (and against all odds as a family of African-Irish first-generation immigrants to an oppressively racist and nepotistic 'host' nation), managed to turn a very long and perilous corner. As we'd driven around that hazardous bend we'd encountered resentfully bigoted landlords with their "No Blacks, No Dogs, No Irish" notices in their vacant properties; racist, doom-mongering negative-stereotyping teachers; "Jesus, God and the Angels are white" Sunday School teachers; thick, hate-filled, knuckle-dragging skinhead thugs; corrupt, anti-black, violent boys in blue; smug, arrogant, potential employers; in many ways, many of the elements that make up the 'core' and social infrastructure of British society and, almost miraculously, we were still together, still united, still strong, still driven and still purposeful. And, in their own individual ways, mum and dad had made this possible.

Battling to steer us in the right direction, they stayed together in the face of disturbing and frightening taunts and gestures; set us an admirable example of positive family and married life; taught and reminded us of the differences between good and bad, right and wrong; ensured we internalised the values and attitudes that would enable and empower us to survive and achieve in every aspect of lives;

provided us with shoulders to cry on; supported and advised us; and guaranteed a secure bolt-hole to return to!

I've never seen, known nor heard of other 'mixed-race' families of our generation that actually managed to stay together in the traditional 'nuclear family' sense. Separation and divorce among all-black and all-white couples was becoming increasingly 'popular' and 'socially acceptable', with the previous biases towards men having been stripped back to favour women, amid declining social stigma. The majority of our friends and members of our reference groups were raised in female-headed single-parent families, whose fathers remained significantly absent and, despite the cold-war that existed throughout my teens between me and dad, he never turned his back on me, he never turned his back on any of us. He always wanted the best for us, and always wanted us to make him and mum proud.

However, apart from the rubbish 'birds and the bees' chat he had with me when I was 10 or 11 years old (it was truly embarrassingly cringe-worthy and utterly useless as information I'd ever employ in the future!), I'll never forget another piece of advice he gave in my late teens. He'd been up to London to collect a certificate he'd gained from a course he'd successfully studied at the Hospital for Tropical Diseases just off the Euston Road in Kings Cross (dad was *the* epitome and living embodiment of the stereotypical perpetual Nigerian student!). I'd driven him up there and spent a while waiting for him in his Mark 2 Cortina Estate, to avoid him receiving a parking ticket in the event a traffic warden strolled past, along with the local pimps, pushers and prostitutes who populated the area.

He returned to the car with a schoolboy look on his face, smiling, happy at his success on the course, and I happily congratulated him as he proudly showed me his diploma. As I was negotiating our way through heavy nose-to-tail traffic down Grays Inn Road onto the Euston Road opposite Kings Cross station, he turned to me and said:

"Goz, whatever you do, never marry white".

It wasn't just *what* he'd said that stunned and shocked me to the core or, as mum would say, "gasted my flabber!", it was the *way* he'd said it, full of deep, thoughtful, solemn gravitas.

In the never-ending-split-second of silence that followed, I began to wonder if it had all been a sham, if dad had lived much of his life in regret, or he'd only stayed with mum 'for the sake of the children'.

"What do you mean never marry white? You did!"

He went on to talk about his deep and unerring love for mum, the constant prejudice and discrimination they'd faced throughout their lives together, the fears they'd encountered on our behalves, the fights they'd fought for us, the dreams they'd shared for us, and the joy we'd brought them through our triumphs and successes.

Dad had NEVER spoken with me like this before, as a man, with respect, acknowledging me!

My understanding of his advice was that he couldn't bear the idea that I, or any of his children for that matter, should suffer the experiences he and mum had endured as a mixed-race couple. I was astounded at the depth of knowledge and understanding dad had developed surrounding issues of race and racism, and his analysis and evaluation of these experiences. When did this happen? He never spoke like this at home! Had something happened that I wasn't aware of? Apparently not, this was coming from the heart!

He was blissfully and serenely happy and content with the family life that he and mum had forged together and, retrospectively, the only fly in the ointment, the only ever-present threat to destabilise and derail their efforts, was the ogre of racism. He didn't want us to go through similar experiences so, in his simplistic way of thinking, marrying within our own colour (mixed-race or black), would minimise if not eradicate the probability of negative racism impacting adversely on our future relationships.

I was *so* relieved with his explanation, and went on to reassure him that for me, the skin colour of my future wife wasn't the issue. I'd marry the person I loved, regardless of her colour, race, religion or creed. I'd learnt from my parents that, as far as relationships were concerned, unconditional love underpinned all that was good about family and marriage. It's an essential part of the glue that contributes to keeping things together, it stops things falling apart.

Late twentieth- and early twenty-first century social service provision ought, in my mind, to bear this in mind as they mount increasingly agonised, anguished and desperate advertising campaigns to recruit foster carers for the abandoned 'black and mixed-race' children in the UK, especially those of the inner cities. I'd squirm as I watched these earnest pleas and absorb the messages on bill boards around the increasingly depersonalised capital city. With unwavering certainty it's always *black and mixed-race* children who most needed foster care and adoption. In the typically simplistic and often dangerous minds of the unerringly right-on, politically-correct, progressive, left-wing, soul-searching, hand-wringing, liberal employees of the 'services', parentless *black and mixed-race* children can *only* go to *black and mixed-race* couples and families. Why? Because they wanted to ensure they received 'appropriate' cultural input from foster parents of the same or similar backgrounds.

Absolute tosh! Based on my experience I'd argue that the thing most abandoned children need and crave is love, unconditional love. All other requirements would fall into place if this cornerstone was in place for them.

However, this dilemma prompted me to question our own experience. Would our lives have been easier or 'better' if we'd been 'put up' for adoption or fostering (as was surprisingly quite commonplace among some Nigerian immigrants, even if only on a temporary basis, throughout the last forty years of the twentieth century), as opposed to staying with our white mother who shared nothing of her black husband's origins and culture? No chance! I couldn't imagine a more 'appropriate' mother than ours; she was the backbone of her 'black' mixed-race family and, like her husband, we benefited from the abundance of love she shared.

The point I'm trying to make is that true love, I've learnt, is truly colour-blind.

That's NOT to say we shouldn't 'see colour'. We MUST see colour in order to fully love, appreciate, understand and care for others, because different skin colours attract different types and levels of experiences in the UK. It would be socially, politically, economically, educationally, emotionally and morally devastating to pretend that skin colour *doesn't* matter. It does!

I hate hearing supposedly intelligent and sensitive souls espouse sentiments such as:

"I don't see colour."

as they sickeningly and pathetically attempt to curry favour, popularity and support before making their ultimately inane and pointless 'insightful' gestures of empathy and understanding, of 'being down' with 'the blacks'.

They're just as bad as, if not worse than, their less intelligent countrymen and women who stridently deny a racist bone in their bodies by profoundly proclaiming:

"One of my best mates is black!"

or:

"I've got a black neighbour!"

almost as if this type of claim automatically exonerates them from any remote possibility of *being* racist!

Bleeding heart politically-correct middle class white left-wing liberal, or thick white working class thug, there's very little if any difference between them; they're both as bad as each other, though quite often the more open honest racism of the working classes is more preferable than that of the covert middle class silent assassins.

If the truth be told, neither group would be happy at the thought of their daughters marrying a black man!

Twenty-Nine

May of 1978 saw me back at the Maudsley Hospital to continue my psychiatric student nurse training. We had a medical examination at the start of this six-month stint which revealed I had a huge lump at the base of my throat. I was referred across the road to Kings College Hospital for further investigation, which diagnosed an overactive thyroid, for which I'd need to be admitted and operated on. Mum was adamant this affliction was the prime cause of my wayward behaviour when I was younger, and I wasn't about to attempt to dissuade her from this notion, if it made her feel better!

On the morning of my operation the anaesthetist arrived at my bedside as scheduled to administer the pre-med at 9.00am, the intention being that they'd return at 9.15am when I'd be drowsy and ready to be wheeled down to theatre. They duly returned at 9.15am to find me sitting up on the edge of my bed, as perky as ever. The pre-med had failed to render me partly unconscious, so they had to order down for an emergency supply of pre-med, which I received at 9.30am. Within minutes I was woozy and wheeled down to the operating theatre, outside of which I received the full anaesthetic and was asked to count to ten. I got to about 7 when my lights went out.

They came back on again a little while later, but I was looking up at the ceiling and the surgeons were leaning over me. They were still operating on me!

I hoarsely asked them:

"Are you nearly finished?"

They were shocked.

"Yes, nearly finished."

One tried to reassure me whilst he whispered frenzied instructions to an out-of-vision theatre nurse. I picked up on his anxiety:

"Am I going to be alright, is it going to be alright?"

Again I was reassured and, within a couple of minutes, pumped full with more anaesthetic.

I next woke up as I was being transferred from trolley to bed back on the ward. I remember trying to fight the nurses and orderlies because I was aware the back-to-front theatre robe I was wearing had come undone, and I didn't want my arse hanging out for all to see! There were a couple of guys in there, about the same age as me, both waiting to be operated on for chronic piles, one white, one black (the guys, not the piles!). Prior to my operation we'd been chatting and become loose mates. When I'd made a full recovery they both ribbed me about my unglamorous return to the ward, and obviously exaggerated my scuffle with the nurses as they tried to transfer me onto my bed. It seems I have quite a resistance to medication and need larger doses than most! Unfortunately for me the surgeons removed two-thirds of my thyroid, which has left me under-producing thyroxin, and surviving on 200mcg on a daily basis to ensure I don't keel over and turn my toes up!

I was unable to do the six-month general nursing A&E stint due to the operation I'd had so, instead, did two three-month stints at the Bethlem between the adolescent and geriatric wards that were based there. I cared about elderly people because I'd been raised to be respectful towards them, but I didn't identify with them at all. However, I was more profoundly affected by the young people I worked with on the adolescent ward, some of whom were really screwed up! I thought I was bad! Psychotic, depressed, schizophrenic, neurotic, anorexic, bulimic and obsessive, and so young! I couldn't imagine them having had more difficult and trying early-life experiences than I'd had, so what could possibly had driven them to malfunction?

A toxic combination of nature and nurture, genetics and environment? Who knows?

Certain 'symbolic interactionist' theorists argue both these approaches are too 'deterministic', in that all human beings have an independent will and volition to decide to behave how they wish. This position dictates that we are fully equipped to make decisions as to how we behave, and that we are not docile recipients of different forms of influence, genetic, environmental or other. We are not blank canvasses waiting to be written on. In fact, they argue, we negotiate our way through the myriad of situations that life presents us with. Those who do so successfully are the ones who achieve their goals and 'self-actualise'.

This is quite commendable as a theory, it 'sounds right'. But can we reduce all our achievements in life to our individual abilities to successfully steer around life's obstacles? If this is the case, then we'd certainly be entitled to wallow in our triumphs and glories, and ought to expect appropriate recompense, reward and recognition for our efforts. However, we'd also need to take full responsibility for our failures in equal measure, which, in fair and equal circumstances would be fine. But do such circumstances actually exist? Are opportunities to advance in an unfettered manner truly available and open to the working classes, women, blacks, Asians, or does the glass-ceiling still exist to thwart progress and advancement at varying levels in society? Has the 'old school tie' really been thrown onto the clothes dump of veracious egalitarianism? Have the wealthy members of the power elite said a final unequivocal "No" to nepotism?

I don't think so!

Which means the very same obstacles that have existed for millennia to hinder, frustrate and block access to and opportunity for equality remain as powerful and pervasive as always. From a personal perspective, I fully identify with the young black men who are striving to achieve against all odds, which are stacked insurmountably high against them. But it's not just the young black men; it's also the working classes, women, immigrants of all nationalities, second-language speakers and virtually anybody who falls outside of the white upper/middle class predominantly male privately-educated uber-group!

Thirty

Having (unbelievably?!) passed the compulsory (though open-book) statistics exam at the end of my first year at uni, we were tasked with completing a piece of empirical (practical, in the field) research using Participant Observation as the primary research method. I managed to wangle a part-time job at the hippest record shop in Uxbridge where I was to 'do' my undercover research. There was a very attractive, young, fun-loving, outgoing and friendly Sikh woman who worked there on a full time basis, and we hit it off immediately. She wasn't traditional, I never saw her wearing anything other than trendy up-to-date fashion wear.

We became a bit of an item, and she'd sometimes stay over with me in my room on campus. She'd done so one Saturday evening and, at around 8.30 on the following Sunday morning I heard a knock on my door. I am not a morning person at the best of times, especially so at weekends! Who the hell could this be? Bleary-eyed, I opened the door. And there was dad! I nearly shat myself! What else could I do but invite him in? My guest shrunk under the bed-covers as I introduced her to dad, who was very cheerful and chirrupy at meeting her. He was also very tactful by taking his leave very quickly, and giving me a surreptitious wink and nod of approval as he made his exit.

Relieved, and I must say happily surprised at dad's reaction (though I'm not sure what I expected!), 'Sam' and I chatted for a while about mixed-race relationships. I felt as though she'd really fallen for me, but it seemed as if there was an underlying reserve and sorrow in the way she spoke. I didn't understand her demeanour at all, especially as she said she really liked dad. My feelings were confirmed when I mentioned the fact that I'd like to meet her family one day.

"No way! My dad and brothers would kill you!"

She went on to explain that under no circumstances could she be seen with, let alone *marry*, a non-Sikh guy, especially a black guy! Not that I had any notions of marrying her, but I found the differences between how my dad had reacted, and how her family would have reacted, very interesting! She detailed how, as men of the family, they would be duty- and honour-bound to dispense with me by employing their Kirpans, ceremonial daggers, to chop me to pieces. I began to question my sanity with regards any idea of prolonging this relationship and, very unceremoniously, dumped her very soon thereafter!

However, this episode brought into mind a variety of issues. Would the reactions of her dad and brothers been justifiable under the Sikh religion, or was this more a case of Sikh culture overriding that which is written in their holy book, the Guru Granth Sahib? Or would it have been more honest of her to say she didn't like me as much as I thought she did, so she used this as a tactic to destabilise our relationship? Either way it didn't really bother me, because I knew she wasn't 'the one', but it niggled me on a certain level. I felt it ironic that other visibly non-white people also negatively discriminate against black people. Asian people, the self same Asian people who, a decade earlier, ran to black people for defence against and protection from the 'Friday Night Paki Bashers'!

Just like the bleeding-heart white middle classes, and the knuckle-dragging white working classes, it seems, whilst Asians have black friends and neighbours, *they* wouldn't want their daughter marrying one either!

How and why did they develop this mentality? Yes, sure, everybody in England was competing for scarce resources, but this type of mentality doesn't become part of practice and culture within a generation, surely?! Surely there is some historical explanation.

Black Africans, Arabs and Asians from the Indian sub-continent have traded for thousands of years, from ivory, silk and spices, to gold, diamonds and slaves, human chattel. Each has had their periods of dominance and power, which is no different to the history, terms and format of trade in and around Europe. Where there was a significant difference is in the nature and form of human slavery that existed within and between Africa, Asia and eventually Europe. Whilst by no means trying to defend any form of slavery, that which existed in Africa was characterised by the slave owner being duty-bound to care for their slaves. Slaves had rights and were entitled to marry, have children and earn or buy their freedom at some stage in the future. Indeed it was not unknown for slaves to marry into their owner's family. This was comparable with the prevailing system of serfdom throughout Europe.

The European participation in the triangular slave trade introduced a new and more sinister dynamic. This new system of slavery was one which was previously unknown to Africa, one in which the illegally captured and sold slaves had no rights and actually became the property, the chattel, of their buyers. Brutalised, degraded, used and abused, the experience of slavery totally dehumanised those unfortunate enough to become enslaved. Again, without trying to justify or legitimate slavery in any way, Africans who participated in the trade were, in the main, totally unaware of the system they were selling their brothers and sisters into. So, in many ways, for Africans operating in the transatlantic slave trade, it was business as usual, only this time with new, white-skinned trading partners.

In order for the Europeans to morally justify the reality and mechanics of the trade, it was essential for them to dehumanise their captives; to present them as sub-human savages; to depict them as needing to be 'saved' from themselves; to salvage their souls with the introduction of the bible and Christianity; to uplift them with spurious notions of superior western civility; in essence, to de-monkeyfy them! Almost as if in exchange for these vital services bestowed and rendered, it was only reasonable to expect them to *work* to earn their salvation that only white Europeans could facilitate on their plantations in the Caribbean and the Americas.

Conservative estimates suggest approximately 12 million African people, aged from 16 to 24, preferably (but by no means exclusively!) male, were stolen from Africa between the 16th and 19th centuries. Five million were transported to South America, mainly Brazil, by the Portuguese; 6.5 million were dispersed among the islands of the Caribbean, mainly by English, French and Dutch traders; and approximately 450,000 to North America, the principal traders being the English.

The European triangular slave trade with Africa (not that Africans were equal trading partners!), was based purely on economic greed and debauchery. Human slaves were the equivalent of goods that provided an involuntarily free service that generated obscenely profitable and lucrative levels of wealth for the traders, owner-masters, private and government investors. The fact that this took place in relatively recent historical terms means that there is an almost automatic association between being black and second-class citizenship status.

Despite slavery being abolished in 1833 by the British government, trading in slaves continued well into the latter part of the 19th century. However, with slavery being illegal, but its practice still producing unimaginable wealth, the system *had* to be maintained in some form or another. Britain 'transported' thousands of poor white working class and Irish as 'indentured servants' to bolster the now illegal regime of black African slavery, to the point where it was quite commonplace to see white indentured servants working alongside black slaves across the slave-owning states of the Americas. But many died premature deaths as they rapidly capitulated to the excessively harsh and trying plantation conditions, often not living long enough to complete their period of servitude and claim their freedom.

Britain's colonisation of the Indian sub-continent provided the solution, in the form of the 'coolie' indentured servant. Over a million Indians were transported to various colonies of European powers to provide labour for the (now mainly) hugely profitable sugar plantations.

The Indian indenture system was an ongoing form of bondage in which (mainly) young men were granted 'free' travel, accommodation and feeding for between 4 – 8 years in exchange for their labour on the plantations. Upon successfully completing this period of contractual indenture, the servants would be fully and legally free to pursue their goals in life, usually after having received their 'freedom pack' comprising land and a cash payment for foregoing return travel to India.

In terms of status, indentured servants retained 'free' status throughout the period and self-determination at the end of it. Black African slavery, on the other hand, stripped its incumbents of all and any vestiges of humanity, dignity and status; they became the property of others, had no human rights and, in the majority of cases, remained slaves in perpetuity. This constituted not only a clear 'legal' demarcation between servant and slave; it also fostered and encouraged economic competition and social distancing between the two groups. To be an indentured servant, and the offspring thereof, was far better than to be a slave or a descendant thereof. The owning-classes fed into this divide-and-rule sub-text to the extent that in many slave-owning islands and states it was 'illegal' to be black and 'free'.

It made political and economic sense to avoid miscegenation, as to mix the bloodlines would be tantamount to mixing and watering down social privilege. Such was the importance of maintaining unpolluted racial inheritance that this mentality and philosophy became internalised. The 'coolies' didn't want to mix with the totally disenfranchised black African slaves and their descendants, and neither did the Irish, the impoverished white working class English trasportees and other 'white trash' Europeans.

This position was further compounded across the southern states of America where miscegenation was made illegal under the 'Jim Crow laws of the south'. Enacted between 1876 and 1965, and similar to the apartheid laws in South Africa, these laws were supposedly based on the theme of white and black African-Americans living 'separate but equal' lives. The laws involved racial segregation in public life including, for example, segregated housing, transport, education, restaurants, restrooms and drinking fountains. Inevitably, the 'coloured' facilities provided for African Americans were of far lower quality, standard and reliability than those provided for their white counterparts.

The nomenclature of the 'West Indies' is in itself inherently inaccurate, arrived at under totally errant circumstances. It seems Christopher Columbus set sail in a westerly direction in his mission to 'discover' India and the East Indies in order to open trade links with the host nations, especially to trade spices. On waywardly arriving in the Caribbean he assumed he'd arrived in India, and named the indigenous Carib and Arawak people he encountered 'Indians'. Sadly for these people, if they survived the initial violent incursions, they were very quickly wiped out by the gun, the common cold, syphilis, gonorrhea, smallpox and influenza which accompanied the European invaders everywhere on their empire-building looting and pillaging travels.

Similar to apartheid South Africa and the segregated Jim Crow southern states of America, plantation life across the West Indies was demarcated and determined on the grounds of race and colour. Essentially, the whiter you were, the more privileged you were. So again, it made sense to outlaw legal and recognised miscegenation among the plantocracy. For some slaves though, miscegenation became the key to freedom and improved privilege and social status.

The coolie man was never a slave, and was in time able to earn his freedom from contractual servitude. He even had straight hair like massuh! He too exaggerated the differences between himself and his black African slave counterparts, ensuring he'd always be perceived to be 'better than' them. So it's evident and understandable how and why East Indians have internalised the 'better than thou' attitude towards blacks and, even more so, their self-serving affinity with, and continued deference towards, their ex-colonial white masters.

Outside of the genetic 'red Igbo' characteristic, issues of colour became increasingly significant and all-pervasive in plantation life and culture. Jamaica became Britain's jewel of the Caribbean on the profits made from sugar production, with English planters becoming increasingly 'creolised' and unwilling to sever links with the 'Motherland', unlike their American counterparts. Jamaican settlers didn't want to risk jeopardising their excessively lucrative business and lifestyle by changing their allegiances or pushing for independent status.

An ever-present feature of the planter lifestyle increasingly involved (predominantly male, though not exclusively!) 'consorting' with the black African slave population (who had no choice in such liaisons), which often resulted in 'mulatto' or 'quadroon' offspring. Mixed-race children. Lighter in skin complexion, these children (especially sons), were often sent to the UK to be privately educated before returning to the island where, as the (illegitimate) sons and daughters of the white planter class, they had a stake and status in society, much to the concern of the British political establishment.

Racial stratification as opposed to class stratification slowly, but irreversibly, began to take hold in everyday social, political and economic life and, probably most importantly, in the minds of the island's inhabitants. Predictably, though making up the majority of the population, 'full' African blacks were at the bottom of the hierarchy which escalated upwards through varying degrees of lightening skin colour to the white plantation owner or political elite at the apex.

Obviously, for the emerging 'coloured' population, it paid social, political and economic dividends to remain towards the top of the racial hierarchy of privilege and relative security. The vociferous white-male-driven pace of sexual activity with black African female slaves and the resulting transculturation raised many concerns among the traditional slave owners. It also raised concerns among the black African slaves and their descendants who were now faced with another non-white echelon of potential beneficiaries and stakeholders.

Psychologically, racial mixing, miscegenation, was impacting on every strata in Jamaican society. Whites stood to lose power, influence and control; blacks stood to lose even more dignity, and suffer increasing levels of oppression from this newly-emerging 'yellow' class. This situation wasn't restricted to the confines of Jamaica, but was becoming an alarming cause for concern right across the Caribbean.

Interestingly, the descendants of the white Portuguese settlers and slave-holders in Brazil dealt with 'the problem of colour' in a very different way. With approximately 70 million inhabitants of African descent in Brazil, which is the second highest in the world after Nigeria for any one country, the Brazilian government introduced a policy referred to as "branciamento" (whitening) of the population, by importing 4 million white Europeans and 185,000 Japanese to dilute the black African population. Clearly, the policy failed, but Brazil has significantly 'repackaged' the issue by presenting itself as a nation based on 'racial democracy'. So, if you believe the hype about Brazil, it's a racially integrated and harmonious country. However, if you look at the racial stratification of 21st century Brazil, it still pretty much reflects the 19th century Jamaican plantation, invariably with the African blacks at the bottom, ascending through a myriad of colour combinations to arrive at the ex-European whites at the top.

Generation after generation of Jamaican slaves and ex-slaves have lived by, internalised and passed on this perception of colour and its relationship to privilege. Some resenting, mistrusting and rejecting their lighter-skinned countrymen based on the perceived and actual privileges they enjoy, whilst others bemoan their lot in life, and *really* wish they'd been born lighter-skinned as they suck up to and lick the arses of their light-skinned 'ideal types'.

Such skin-colour resentment and/or sycophancy are by no means the sole preserve of Jamaicans. It's widespread across Asia and the Indian sub-continent, Africa and the Caribbean, North and South America, where skin colour still determines to some extent a person's opportunities to maximise their life chances and achieve their full potential. Essentially, the whiter you are, the better the chances you'll get in life.

The complete reverse is the case in terms of your blackness. Indeed, so much so that a massively expanding market in skin whitening products, gels, creams, potions and tablets is proving an extremely lucrative venture for the modern day entrepreneurial skin-colour ghouls who avidly trade on the insecurities of the sad self-haters and -doubters.

As far as possible I've never allowed my skin colour to stop me doing the things I want to do. Having experienced racism from both black and white people, I feel I've developed the necessary interpersonal skills to help me deal with all that they may wish to throw in my direction. That's not to say it's easy though. Often, my natural inclination is to react emotionally, with both barrels blazing, but I've learnt this isn't always the best way to go!

Also, this is not to say that I've attempted to hide my colour, or lived in the hope that people won't notice I'm black. I always try to conduct myself with social and professional dignity and integrity and, if my skin colour is a problem, it's not *my* problem, it's the problem of whoever it is that's taken objection to it.

Thirty-One

For the majority of my time at university I was one of the few black students in lectures, seminars, and on the football pitch. We went on a football tour to West and East Berlin in my second year, and I was the only black face in the team, and the only team-member who could speak German, which saw my popularity ratings soar amongst my team-mates when it came to chatting up the frauleins in the bars during our leisure periods!

Never having lost my innate desire to work (I think I unwittingly internalised Max Weber's ideas of the 'Protestant Work Ethic'), I always endeavoured to get additional paid employment around my university and nurse training schedules. In the gap between the end of my second uni stint and before starting my third nurse training stint in 1979, I was working as an auxiliary nursing assistant in a facility for physically 'handicapped' and educationally 'subnormal' patients (society was far less concerned with issues and the accompanying language of modern day political correctness in the late 70s!), in south east London. I really enjoyed working in the caring profession. I felt as if I was 'giving back' to society in some way, helping those less fortunate than myself, and also recognising and appreciating the fact that I was of sound mind and able body!

Whilst working in this facility I became very friendly with a very light-skinned Jamaican woman who seemed to be mixed with African, European and Chinese. Pat was an exceptionally loving and caring person who worked long hours to not only help provide for her family, but to care for the patients in a sincere, considerate and dedicated way.

Like many people Pat thought that I was Jamaican, and I suppose my dreadlocks contributed to this perception even more so. She couldn't believe it when I explained I had no links, genetic, familial or otherwise, with the Caribbean at all. She seemed intrigued to hear about my experiences growing up in England, and I was equally as curious in her tales of her life in Jamaica before migrating to London. We developed a very positive and friendly relationship. Pat was another 'earth-mother' who sacrificed herself for her husband and family, and I made many parallels between her and my mum (a great honour!). She eventually began to talk with me as if she was talking to her own child, and that made me feel comfortable.

When it transpired, in discussion, that I was looking for accommodation for my final two years at uni, she asked me if I'd like to live with her and her family in south east London. We agreed for me to come to her family home where I'd meet the family so, one day after work, I drove her home and popped in to meet her husband, George, six of their seven children who were still living at home, and another friend of the family who was also living with them. Their three-level house was very spacious, but with all its inhabitants it felt crowded, noisy and chaotic, fantastic! I felt right at home straight away, and happily agreed to move into a box room on the top floor in September prior to returning to uni! Driving to uni for two or three days per week was no problem. I felt so at home and at peace with myself I even asked Debbie, their 13 year old daughter, to cut off my deadlocks which were by now, past shoulder length! Debbie was *very* nervous as she neared my hair with the scissors. I told her not to worry and to just get on with it, which she did, snip, snip, snip, and they were gone. I felt nothing at the time, which surprised me, I thought I'd descend into a deep depression, but that wasn't the case. All was well with me and the world!

I was 22 and becoming increasingly interested in finding out about 'home', Nigeria. I spoke constantly with Obi, dad and Uncle Sammy, and raised the idea of us going home for Christmas in December 1979. Dad wasn't able to go, but Obi and Uncle Sammy were up for the idea, so we made all the necessary arrangements, booked our tickets well in advance, and began to count the days to departure. The closer the date came, the more excited I became. I couldn't wait to get on that plane and touchdown in Nigeria. Pat and her family became increasingly concerned about my trip 'home'. They'd taken me in and treated me as a member of their family, something I truly respected and appreciated, and now worried about me as if I were their own son.

Finally, the day came, we were packed, ready and off to Nigeria, the far away country in 'deepest darkest' Africa that we'd heard and spoken about for so long! Actually checking-in our luggage, getting our boarding passes and boarding the flight were excellent preparation for Nigeria, it was mayhem! The Nigeria Airways ground staff at Heathrow Airport were completely and absolutely useless, lazy, slow and arrogant. This turned out to be customer service Nigeria-style which I'd soon become familiar with! Every step of the process was a monumental battle, with people (some passengers, some non-travelling family members), frantically trying to ensure they got on the flight, everybody trying to push in, the more well-heeled blatantly bribing the ground staff to get their boarding passes, and the *BIGGEST* suitcases and hand luggage ever designed, made and purchased, much of it stinking of stock fish!

For a so-called 'Biafran Soldier', Uncle Sammy was a complete and absolute coward when it came to flying in aeroplanes. He couldn't eat before we left Heathrow, but had several stiff shots before boarding, to the point where he was nearly rendered comatose for the duration of the flight.

This was the first time me and Obi had been in an aeroplane as adults, so we were exploring anything and everything, from playing with the angle of our seat recliners to working out the mechanics of the in-seat ashtrays. Uncle Sammy sat rigid in his seat, trying to scold us for mucking about and touching things, but really trying to mask his abject fear of flying! He did this all with typical good humour and the family sense of fun and idiocy. Everything was exciting for us, even making instant enemies during the battle to get on board, though I couldn't imagine most travellers and flight companies being prepared to endure such excessive exertions, annoyance, frustration, anger, panic, shouting, bribing, screaming, and tests of strength and will power on a regular basis, if ever! Apparently, the British army have only ever been called in to Heathrow on one occasion to quell a disturbance in a terminal and, you've guessed right, it was in the check-in area for a Nigeria Airways flight! Amazingly, once safely ensconced on board, the sworn enemies we'd made during check-in became instant best friends, happily greeting us and chatting the time away. I imagined this could *only* happen with Nigerians. Had the same been the case with English people, no doubt actual fist-fights would have developed between the passengers!

At the end of the six hour flight we were making our descent into Lagos, Murtala Mohammed airport. From the sky, Lagos looked massive, as did the Sahara desert (which is bigger than the United States of America!), which we seemed to be flying over for hours. It became evident we'd cleared the desert crossing when the scenery changed from an arid yellow-brown to the densely-forested green of sub-Saharan 'black' Africa. It occurred to me that it had taken hours to cross the north of Africa to Nigeria in the west, so the African continent in its geographical entirety must be immense! I tried to imagine trading caravans and slave coffles making their way across and through what appeared to me to be formidable terrain, and, try as hard as I could, I just couldn't even begin to comprehend how such journeys were *ever* completed on camels, horseback or foot!

The landscape and buildings of Lagos became larger and clearer as we approached the runway. I could see what resembled complete and utter chaos with regards the huge massed tangle of town-planning-less houses topped with rusting sheets of corrugated iron for roofs, crammed side-by-side and on top of each other; hundreds of yellow taxis darting here there and everywhere along their frenzied fare-catching routes of intertwined roads; huge vultures lazily circling in hot thermals no doubt looking for their next carcass to feed on; thousands of busy 'okadas' (motorcycle taxis) weaving confidently in and out of the incessantly busy traffic jams and traffic queues that make up Lagos.

And hundreds of thousands of people, *black people,* riding on the backs of the okadas, jumping on the rusting buses, haggling the taxi drivers to reduce their fares, and casually walking along the dusty and perilous paths, jumping over the open sewers as they made their way to and from their places of work and generally going about their business, and not a discernable white face in sight!

Thirty-Two

Emotionally it was an utterly overwhelming sight and experience for me. It meant *so* much to me to be in Nigeria, to be 'home' among my own people. I started to well up and allowed tears of joy to run down my face unashamedly. I quietly looked over at Obi to see how he was faring and, predictably, he'd managed to maintain his very British stiff upper lip. I don't know how he managed to remain observably so stoical, unaffected and unmoved by our prodigal return home!

The exit doors opened and, as we approached them, the heat and humidity started to seep in and hit us as it shoved its way down the fuselage. I say 'hit', by the time we'd actually managed to shuffle our way to the door behind the other disembarking passengers it battered us! And not only the heat and humidity, but the sights, sounds and smells of the pandemonium that is Lagos, with people shouting, screaming and singing in the distance; whistling and hissing through their teeth as they try to attract the attention of others; the acrid nostril-assaulting stench of armpit sweat of the ground crew dressed in the tattiest and shabbiest blue 'uniforms'; the whirring and chugging of the maintenance and cargo vehicles as they made their exhaust-spewing way around the airport landing strip and arrivals area; petrol and diesel fumes clogging the atmosphere; the clear bright blue sky; the green palm trees and shrubbery that bordered the airport confines and perimeter; the variously striated faces of Igbos, Yorubas, Hausas and Fulani flight attendants and ground officials; black faces in an array of uniforms, proud and dignified pilots and stewardesses; baton- and gun-toting army and police officers; passengers of all shapes and sizes (but predominantly one colour), wearing a mixture of western and traditional garbs. And I'd never before felt more alien in my life!

With beads of sweat popping out all over us and running down our backs, it was very clear who was in charge as we warily waited for the safe delivery of our luggage, the khaki-uniformed army, immigration and customs officers of the Federal Government of Nigeria! Nigerians LOVE a uniform and the unassailable never-to-be-questioned authority their uniforms bestow upon them! Imperiously strutting around the baggage claim and arrivals hall, they made sure to exude their authority with every measured step and searingly intimidating glance. As mum used to say:

"Woe betide the person who dares to cross these people!"

As, for all intents and purposes, newcomers to Nigeria, me and Obi were sufficiently impressed with their preening displays. We made sure to snatch our incoming luggage and dutifully opened them for customs searches upon request. The immigration officers, upon studying our visa-endorsed British passports, asked us why we had Nigerian names! I couldn't really comprehend what would prompt such absurd questions.

"Our dad's Nigerian".

"Eehhhh, is that so!?"

"Yes".

"From where?"

"Owerri, Imo State".

"Eehhhh! Kedu?"

"Odinma".

"You are welcome, wettin you dey bring foh my Christmas now?"

I didn't have a clue what the officer was asking me, but Uncle Sammy soon appeared at my side to palm him some notes. We very quickly learnt about the system of "dash" in Nigeria. Greasing peoples' palms to enhance the prospects of unhindered progress or completion of any project being pursued, be it waiting in a queue for service or buying flight tickets for the ridiculously over-booked Nigeria Airways planes. Bribery and corruption is endemic in Nigeria at every level (as it is in most other states of the world, including the 'civilised' west)!

After successfully negotiating our way through all the arrival duties and 'formalities', we stepped out into the cauldron of the landside arrivals hall, to be accosted from all angles by taxi touts desperately trying convince us to take their taxi as they grabbed at our suitcases and luggage, almost as if the 'possession is nine-tenths of the law' principal applies to them holding your suitcase means you *must* use their taxi! Both me and Obi found this quite funny, but Uncle Sammy wasn't in the least bit amused. I think he was concerned we'd have a suitcase stolen, but we weren't letting go no matter what!

Uncle Sammy had arranged for us to be met by one of his friends who, unbelievably for Nigeria, was actually there waiting for us *on time*. Nigerians, like virtually every other black people I know, are notorious for being late, for never rushing and, in this heat, I fully understand why. This doesn't, though, explain the same syndrome with black people in cold climes everywhere else in the world! We were taken to Suru-Lere where we stayed overnight in Festac Village, which was built in 1977 along the Lagos-Badagry Expressway to accommodate the participants and staff of the Second World African Festival of Arts and Culture. At the time it was quite contemporary with its well-appointed roads and amenities, but lack of maintenance since the festival had already allowed deterioration to start nibbling away at its foundations.

Driving through Lagos I was still impressed and emotional at the sights and sounds of Nigeria, **black** Africa. It was strange but uplifting to see nothing but black road sweepers and municipal workers, black taxi drivers, black bus drivers and their black conductors hanging precariously out of their vehicles shouting and hissing to attract more fares:

"Apapa, Apapa, Apapa!"
"Mushin, Mushin, Mushin!"
"Ikeja, Ikeja, Ikeja!"

"Marine, Marine, Marine!"
"Ajegunle, Ajegunle, Ajegunle!"
"Ikoyi, Ikoyi, Ikoyi!"

Black motorcycle riders, black families in cars, black people strolling, chatting and laughing, black people working in offices and shops, black children in their khaki and white school uniforms and dusty shoes making their way to and from school. Basically, black people going about their daily lives in just the same way as people do everywhere in the world. But for me it just meant *so* much more that this was all happening in black Africa!

Lagos hit me as being a massive, hot, reckless, lawless, chaotic, ridiculously overcrowded but vibrant capital city that pulsated with life and teemed with people. Named Lago de Curamo by the Portuguese explorer Ruy de Sequeira who visited the area in 1472, its previous Nigerian name was Eko. Lagos also became a significant slave-trading centre, with a holding and departure point located in Badagry, shipping the vast majority of the kidnapped captives to the Americas, particularly Salvador, the state capital of Bahia in Brazil.

Virtually every road vehicle seemed to be irreparably rusted, dented and totally un-road-worthy, with gaping holes and patched-up body work which, given the cavernously pot-holed and cantilevered roads bordered by open sewers, was little more than ought reasonably to be expected. Images of Fred Flintstone's rickety vehicle-cum-car-cum-mode of transport kept popping into my mind, and I bet none of them had anything that remotely resembled an MOT certificate! Despite all the obvious (to me anyway!) dangers, everybody just seemed to be getting on with things, getting on with life, dealing with the hardships and inconveniences they were relentlessly confronted with.

Uncle Sammy's friend's place in Festac village was reasonably comfortable though rudimentary. It was great just sitting under the ceiling fan as it wafted a steady breeze to cool us down from the stiflingly humid tropical heat, watching the TV as he and Uncle Sammy reminisced about the good old days. Sammy remarked on the changes that had taken place since his hasty departure, and indicated he was happily pleased and impressed by them. I'd have hated to have seen things in their previous state!

Boom! All of a sudden the lights went out, the TV went on the blink and the ceiling fan slowly but surely slowed down to a creaky squeaky halt. Then, after a split second of silence, a spontaneous and communal groan emanated from all the surrounding dwellings in earshot, followed by a groaning exclamation:

"NEPA!!!!!"

Uncle Sammy burst out laughing, saying that not everything has changed!

"NEPA done tek light-oh!!!!!"

The Nigeria Electrical Power Authority, NEPA, we were soon to learn, is notorious for "taking light" (stopping service), on an apparently random though reliably regular basis. Much to the angry but sometimes good-natured frustrations of Nigerians, electrical power service from NEPA, similar to the water authorities, street lighting authorities, and probably any and every other authority known to humankind supposedly provided in Nigeria, is at best chaotic, erratic and dysfunctional, and at worst totally non-existent, especially in rural areas. Nigerians have wittily altered the acronym to:

"NEPA – Never Expect Power At all!"

Whilst it's probably fair to say me and Obi didn't enjoy an upbringing that lavished comfort and convenience upon us every step of the way, it would also be fair to say that we'd grown used to certain standards and expectations of minimalist living requirements. Constant and reliable electricity and water supplies immediately went to the top of our list of expectations, though privately we were steeling ourselves to be disappointed on these expectations for the duration of our stay. If they couldn't get things right in Lagos, capital city of the Federal State of Nigeria, the 'giant' of Africa, where *could* they get things right?

After showering off the sweat and grit of the past twenty four hours early the following morning, we were on our way to Sabo Motor Park, Ikorodu, where we'd be chartering our taxi to make the twelve hour journey to the east, Biafra, home. Sabo motor park is huge, with hundreds of taxi cars queued up ready to fill up with passengers before heading off to destinations all around Nigeria. Teeming with people all intent on either cramming others into the taxis, or being crammed into the next outward-bound taxi themselves, Sabo is a hive of industrious hustle and bustle. The other main group of identifiable people were those women and children with trays of goods for sale balanced unerringly on their heads. Trays stacked high with boiled eggs, loaves of bread, bananas, groundnut, moi-moi, bar-soap, soap powder, bundles of chewing sticks, basically anything that the Nigerian traveller may deem essential for their journey, the vendors weaved their majestic way through the taxis, touts and trippers, shouting their wares for sale. Many of the women had sleeping snot-encrusted babies strapped to their backs in traditional wrappers to enable them to work and mother at the same time.

The majority of the taxis were clapped-out Peugeot estates, rusting relics that had clearly seen far better days. The thought of travelling so far and for so many hours in any one of these clapped-out vehicles was *very* daunting to say the least. Uncle Sammy was very circumspect with the touts hustling passengers, the drivers themselves, and the taxis also, making sure to fully 'inspect' the one he deemed safe enough for us to enter. Speaking Yoruba to let the driver know he wasn't green, he also interrogated the driver, ensuring he was experienced and reputable. Once satisfied, like our now battered and disintegrating suitcases, we were stuffed into the taxi and ready to go.

My heart was thumping in excited anticipation as we made our way slowly and carefully out of Sabo. The driver dutifully paid his dues to the necessary 'officials' at each point of our exit onto Ikorodu Road, whereupon he put the pedal to the floor and we were off, hurtling along at ridiculously breakneck speeds towards the east. The driver, constantly chewing kola nut with his stained teeth to help him stay awake and alert, developed a serious case of deafness every time Uncle Sammy berated him to slow down. It felt like he was on a mission that, come hell or high water, he'd be making it to the east in a land-speed record-breaking number of hours!

Me and Obi thought it was hilarious, we loved the speed and the recklessness of the driver's resolute attempt to gain a place in the Guinness Book of Records! Just as in Lagos, the main accessory used in driving on the expressway apart from the accelerator pedal, was the car horn. Driving in Nigeria isn't only reckless, it's also potentially deafening! Our excitement began to abate when we were approaching a steep and winding hill near Ibadan. Obi had nodded off to sleep when the driver informed us that he may have to slow down going down the next hill as there'd been an accident the day before and it was quite likely the road hadn't yet been cleared.

Accident?! The still-smouldering macabre scene we were about to witness looked more like an Apocalypse!

A petrol tanker had been driving up the hill and had clearly smashed head-on into a 'luxury' bus filled with up to 60 passengers, and an open-back cattle truck filled with namma (cows) for market in Lagos. The petrol tanker had exploded on impact, instantly incinerating all three vehicles, drivers, passengers and cattle, all of which was still visible and on-show for passing wayfarers! The charred bodies of the drivers were still seated behind their wheels, the luxury bus passengers were still in the rows of seats they'd no doubt fought tooth and nail to obtain, the char-grilled cattle carcasses (exceptionally well-done!) were still in the mangled wreckage of the open-backed cattle truck, and the vehicles themselves were a mess of molten and twisted metal.

Needless to say, the sight and smell was absolutely grizzly and shocking. I'd *never* seen anything like it before, and couldn't understand how, twenty four hours after the accident, the carnage was still road-side. I asked the driver why and both he and Uncle Sammy scornfully advised me the mere idea of Nigerian emergency services attending the holocaust was a joke. The driver even relayed a story about the

Nigeria Fire Service arriving at fires without water in the tanks to douse the fires, rendering them totally inept and ineffectual, capable only of watching the fire and its victims burn themselves out!

I very quickly sobered up and became intensely and neurotically aware of the speed we were travelling at. I winced as we approached each and every corner. Bracing myself rigidly in my seat I started to press imaginary breaks at every potential hazardous and hair-raising moment, I was now officially and unashamedly terrified for my life!

Hundreds of miles later (at least, that's what it felt like!), my nerves began to settle back to a palpable state of normality. I actually began to absorb and appreciate the sights, sounds and smells of Nigeria as we careered relentlessly towards the east. I was intrigued by the rich red soil; the density of the virtually untouched tropical rain forest that bordered the roads; the communities of thatch-roofed mud huts we'd flash by; the apparent languid disposition of the people as they strolled through the heat of the day with gracefully measured poise and nonchalance; the size and apparent robustness of the women's bottoms (nyash), for whom the buttocks of many were "not cooperating" (moving and jiggling independently); the resolute commitment and endeavour of the road-side entrepreneurs who rushed the vehicles for custom at any and every natural or man-made go-slow (traffic jam), on the road.

And I felt grossly intimidated by the regular police and army checkpoints en route, manned by dash-expecting officers who greedily but slyly left their palms open ready to be greased by the driver, AK47s slung loosely over their shoulders and pistols at their waists, arrogant and confident as they swaggeringly and contemptuously 'served' the nation. Both me and Obi expressed our concerns, and were immediately corrected by Uncle Sammy and the driver who explained that the soldiers and police officers are poorly and irregularly paid, so the only guarantee of some form of income was from drivers, commercial and private, as they made their way around Nigeria's clogged arteries of road systems and state checkpoints.

I was beginning to formulate an understanding that life in Nigeria wasn't easy. In fact, if the truth be told, it was exceptionally harsh and difficult! Nothing then, or since, has happened to change my perception of Nigeria. Sure, things have become a lot easier for those people lucky enough to succeed by hook or by crook; by grinding honest endeavour or 419 trickery; or by gaining from, and giving 'favours' to, influential people in local, state and national politics. However, these people are in the overwhelming minority. The overwhelming majority of Nigeria's population, conservatively estimated at some 150 million people, suffer considerably on a day-to-day basis, scraping a subsistence living in order to provide sustenance for their families, and totally reliant on consuming, bartering or selling their small-holding farm produce.

As my perception of Nigeria's geographical and demographic immensity developed I tried to imagine, to go back in time, to slavery days. I just couldn't fathom how the kidnapped slave coffles, their captors and drivers, actually managed to walk so many hundreds of miles in the heat from the dense interior to the holding forts along the coast. The forlorn and terrified captives *must* have been abnormally strong to survive such a trek, and the captors resolutely driven by insane, pathological, short-sighted callousness, ignorance and greed!

Thirty-Three

The closer we got to 'the east', the more dilapidated the roads became. Uncle Sammy explained that the roads, in his opinion, were still quite good!

"Wait until we cross the river Niger into Igboland, you will see."

He pointed out the entrance to the renowned University of Ile-Ife as we scorched past, Obafemi Awolowo University, famous for its high and exacting standards and expectations. Again, my thoughts drifted. University, normality, surrounded by irreverent chaos, things just didn't seem to add up or make coherent sense in my mind. I was later to understand that I was "too English", "too British", in terms of my own expectations of what ought to be considered 'normal'.

We eventually arrived at the natural border between the west and east of Nigeria, the mighty river Niger, and our progress ground to a shuddering halt. An incident had occurred on the bridge that traversed from west to east, and the traffic was reduced to crawling at a snail's pace on its approach to the bridge. Among a babble of heat-induced frustration, shouting and cursing, we inched our way onto the expansive suspension bridge. Cars, vans, lorries, trucks, okadas and buses were jostling at all angles in their attempts to gain the slightest advantage to inch their way off the bridge. At the height of the mayhem, a baton-wielding khaki-uniformed army officer screamed at a belligerent driver who'd had the temerity to creep ahead unauthorised:

"Ah beg, com ot foh road, if you no move dat your useless carton I goh divide your head foh Christmas!"

I wanted to piss myself laughing! It was hilarious and, looking at the miscreant's car (which wasn't observably any better or worse than virtually every other vehicle stacked on the bridge), I sort of understood the officer's rant. Me and Obi just chilled-out on the bridge, marvelling at the sights, especially the enormity of the Niger river and its convoys of log-hewn boats ferrying local sand for construction up and down the shores of the river, and sharing our impressions.

It's interesting how people can be reduced to identifying and exaggerating others' faults when in heightened emotional states, especially those of anger and frustration which in Nigeria is a highly combustible, though highly predictable, combination!

It took us hours to get across the bridge and into Igboland and, when we eventually made it, a curious sense of 'arriving home' descended upon us. Uncle Sammy was ecstatically happy as he showed us the sights of the huge and rambling market town of Onitsha, situated on the east bank of the river in Anambra State, and the birthplace of the famous Nigerian author Chinua Achebe. Like dad, he started to exaggerate all the good things about Igboland in the totally biased manner that is characteristic of our family!

After the initial euphoria, reality struck home, hard. The crumbling pot-holed and cratered roads were *even* worse than anything we'd experienced so far. When this was commented upon, Uncle Sammy said much of the damage was done during the civil war that ended nine years earlier. There was no evidence of repairs to the roads, nor to any of the buildings that were still pockmarked with bullet holes! He lamented the (conspiracy?) theory that the Yoruba-Hausa political coalition deliberately failed to regenerate the east, corruptly and vindictively favouring the west and north to the detriment of Igboland. He even went as far as to exclaim:

"The bloody government pours money into Yoruba land and Hausa land, how many Hausas dey sef? Hausas count and include their cattle when it comes to counting their population, idiots!"

Interestingly, the Yoruba driver agreed with Uncle Sammy on every point. So, was Uncle Sammy really speaking the truth, or was our driver being craftily agreeable? It was impossible to tell at the time, but later experiences and observations suggested that Uncle Sammy was, indeed, talking the truth! The deeper we got into Igboland, the more apparent were Uncle Sammy's claims of systematic discrimination against Igbos in the ex-secessionist state of Biafra.

If the roads and buildings were anything to go by, there'd been hardly any visible post-war redevelopment, regeneration or investment in Biafra, which was now part of the much-heralded Federal State of Nigeria again. Granted, nine years is a relatively short period of time after any war. Indeed, post-second-world-war Britain was a complete and absolute slum for the majority of its working class population, especially those living in London, Liverpool, Manchester, Birmingham, Newcastle, Sunderland and the other major cities of England (21st century Sunderland *still* doesn't appear to have developed much since!). But regeneration was visible, with declared redevelopment drives uppermost on the political agenda. Britain went on to 'enjoy' a massive expansion of post-war development that prioritised housing, roads, civil amenities and services, which included spectacular growth in newly-created middle class jobs. The National Health Service was established, as were the State Education Service, Welfare Services, the Social Services and Transport services.

Peoples' lives and life chances, including their hopes and aspirations, were beginning to improve relatively quickly. This was especially so among the working classes who began to become increasingly geographically and upwardly socially mobile.

The same could not be said for Igbos in post-war Biafra. The quality of the roads was disgracefully hazardous, and buildings in general still appeared to be war-ravaged and deteriorating. In the absence of government-provided social or welfare services anywhere in Nigeria, survival is down to individual and community effort. In life everybody needs a 'leg-up' every now and then, but evidence of this was manifestly non-existent as we made our way deep into the heartlands of

Biafra. This prompted the release of repressed television news images into my conscious mind. I could imagine the extent and depth of the starvation-induced suffering and disease that Biafrans were forced to endure and survive during the war. Malaria, kwashiorkor, cholera, yellow fever, diphtheria, pneumonia and hunger, starvation, it *must* have been hell! But, thankfully, mercifully, unbelievably, survive they did!

I believe in the saying:

"It takes a lot to keep a good man down".

I also believe this sentiment can be applied to nations of people. In essence, Biafrans are 'good people'. So I believe the saying applies to us also.

They also say that:

"The good die young".

Well, notwithstanding the geo-historical fact that Biafra existed many centuries before Nigeria, it's also true to say that the new independent post-colonial State of Biafra, the 'Land of the Rising Sun', lamentably, died young. Actually, it died in its infancy.

We eventually arrived 'home' several hours behind schedule due to the Niger Bridge go-slow. Late in the night we negotiated our way through the haphazard and dimly lit streets of Owerri, the state capital of Imo State. Much if not most of the house and street lighting was provided by stinking and smoky oil lamps, and this included the roadside businesses that were clearly central to survival in the east. Small family groups huddled around their rickety home-made wooden stalls that were piled high with small and portable wares; matches; mosquito coil; bottles of thick red palm oil; small packets of soap powder; candles; bottles of kerosene; foaming recycled bottles of fresh 'pammy' (palm wine); plastic jerry-cans of 'kai-kai' (palm wine extra-fermented into illicit white gin, similar to Irish 'moonshine', Poteen); in short, an array of sundry items that were essential to help maintain rudimentary everyday life and, as far as possible, comfort and convenience. Essentially, all those things we take for granted!

Our journey wasn't over though. Our actual home, our dad's place of birth in Egbelubi village, was a thirty minute drive from Owerri. This was a drive Uncle Sammy was not prepared to take at this time of night. Apart from the perilous state of disrepair of the roads, he was fearful of us being hijacked by 'armed robbers', so we waited in the safe haven of the Owerri motor park until day break. Though disappointed we wouldn't be seeing home that night, we were shattered, exhausted, filthy and covered in red dust and motor exhaust fumes, the detritus of our sixteen hour drive through the heaven and hell that is Nigeria. The idea of us making an even more dangerous half hour drive as potential victims of armed robbers didn't appeal to us in the slightest, so we were happy to bunker down and exercise a little bit more patience until Uncle Sammy declared it safe to set off.

Thirty-Four

Igboland, Biafra, truly is the 'Land of the Rising Sun'!

At six o'clock in the morning the sun made its eagerly anticipated and glorious appearance, instantly warming our minds, souls, hearts and bodies, accompanied by the crowing of cockerels; the spluttering of car, bus and motorcycle engines; and the sights and sounds of people waking and preparing for the day that lay ahead.

Thoroughly enjoying the opportunity to speak Igbo with everybody now, Uncle Sammy chartered the local taxi that was going to take us on the final leg of our incredible journey. The taxi was in far worse condition (if that were ever conceivably possible!), than that which transported us from Lagos to Owerri. Fred Flintstone's conveyance was now looking quite appealing in comparison, at least a lot safer. The rust was widespread, hardly anything actually worked, and the brakes seemed alarmingly non-responsive, which appeared to be a pretty standard and acceptable condition for most forms of transport in Nigeria, but the engine eventually managed to cough into life after several prompts involving manually wetting the carburettors with petrol, and we were off.

Exiting Owerri onto the Aba-Port Harcourt 'expressway', Biafra had woken to a new day, and for us it was a day that would change our lives forever.

Uncle Sammy explained that it was protocol for us to first visit the Egwuonwu family, my maternal grandmother's family, in their village Umubachi, about a couple of miles away from dad's. We survived *the* most horrifying half hour drive along the Aba-Port Harcourt expressway before safely diverging onto the minor village roads. I hated the

Aba-Port Harcourt road, it was in a terrible condition, rutted and pitted with mortar craters, crumbling at the edges, and strewn with virtually-invisible-til-it's-too-late potholes. Astonishingly, the local and familiar drivers raced its length at death-defying-if-not-encouraging, speed, and the vast majority of their vehicles were totally un-roadworthy! It felt like I was hardly able to draw breath until we were actually off it.

Incredibly, the local village roads were even worse! They were over-whelmingly made of graded and compacted red earth which in the dry seasons turned into dustbowls and, in the rainy seasons, glutinous quagmires of swampy almost-impossible-to-navigate sludge. The hot and dry caress of the Hamatan wind that marks the change between the dry and rainy seasons ensured that the roads were dry and passable. Our taxi tilted and wobbled, kangarooed and bounced over the roads' unyielding baked surfaces on its mission to deliver us, and deliver us it did to our maternal grandmother's village, Umubachi, deep in the lush, leafy and marginally cooler village environment.

Enquiring eyes set in quizzical dark faces watched our slow approach to the compound of our grandmother. People stopped and stared wide-eyed at the two 'white' faces of the young strangers in the back of the taxi, children, adults and elderly stood and gazed in apparent awe-struck curiosity. We stepped out of the taxi and me and Obi became instantly conscious of the fact that we were the centre of attention. As people and faces started to emerge from their predominantly thatched-roof mud huts, the older ones began to recognise Uncle Sammy.

"Dede, is that you?!"

Dede (pronounced Deh-Deh, or the abbreviated version Deh), is a term of respect that a younger person will use to address an older person of the family and kindred, such as an older brother, uncle or member of the community.

When it became clear that yes, indeed, this was Deh Samuel, Innocent (his middle name that it appeared he was often [inaccurately?] referred to as), Biafran Soldier, saviour and hero of his people, there was instant uproar. Crowds gathered as the women wailed in their spine-chilling high-pitched ululating screams of joy and welcome;

singing and rhythmic clapping erupted among the young and the children; his age-grade mates with knowing and excited glimpses in their eyes swooped on him to shake his hand and clap him on the back, shouting their approval and welcome; and the elderly women sat and smiled their joy and excitement as the elderly men of the village approached him with dignity whilst exuding seniority and trying to quell any evidence of their excitement.

I felt Uncle Sammy was happy and excited, but there was a definite reserved restraint in his demeanour which I didn't understand. However, I would later in the day!

I can't speak for Obi but at first I felt like the proverbial 'spare prick at a party' as we stood quietly observing from the periphery. As the initial furore began to subside, I'd started to get emotional again at the unrestrained and spontaneous welcome that Uncle Sammy had received. Damn! I *so* wished I could have been more like Obi and maintained that stiff upper lip!

Uncle Sammy held centre-court and, as the dust settled, was asked to identify the strangers he'd brought with him. It was interesting that, although I couldn't speak Igbo, I was able to 'follow' conversations and get the gist of much of what was being said.

His reply was something along the lines of:

"Kawo omo Deh Mike".

Which I understood to mean:

"These are the sons of my senior brother Mike".

Instant pandemonium ensued as we were mobbed by every able-bodied person, all of whom took turns to grab and embrace us, to shake our hands and welcome us whilst staring in awe-struck disbelief.

We didn't fully appreciate what Uncle Sammy had just told them nor, in fact, what he had just done. The implications of his one-line introduction were immense. In effect, he was introducing the grandsons of a highly respected woman of the village, and re-introducing her son to them. Dad had left home for London over thirty years previously, and nobody had heard from him since. In their eyes they never expected to see Uncle Sammy again, so it was a miracle he was actually standing in front of them again since he disappeared after the war, but the rein-carnations of Deh Mike *also*? It was all too much! The joyous singing, clapping and dancing escalated exponentially as me and Obi ingrati-ated ourselves with our maternal relatives and village people.

It was strange, emotional, and surreal. Being stared at by hundreds of elated eyes and ridiculously happy faces in unrestrained joy and welcome made me feel like I 'belonged' to a community, for the first time *ever* in my life, albeit thousands of miles away from my place of birth and home in the UK.

Uncle Sammy then completed all the traditional and necessary duties of showing respect to the community by taking us around to every house (hut), to formally introduce us. I loved it! All the things I'd wondered, thought, imagined and dreamed about Nigeria was actually happening to me. I started to see and understand dad's obsession with showing respect; of conducting yourself with dignity and honour; of following centuries-old traditions and customs that, to me until this point in my life, were mainly distant and abstract. Now it was for real!

Everybody wanted a bit of us and Uncle Sammy, so we couldn't make the mistake of missing certain houses, and in each house we were invari-ably greeted with kola nut which, though disgustingly bitter to taste (it's no wonder one of its effects is to help keep you awake, it would be impossible to sleep after chewing and ingesting its sourness!), we wouldn't dare insult or offend our hosts by refusing their offers. We even had to learn *how* to accept the kola in the proper and respectful way. Usually, two or three whole kola nuts and some alligator pepper are brought in on a plate, with an invariably rusty knife. The plate is passed to the youngest male in the group, who must only accept and take it with his right hand, and then pass it on to the next oldest, who does the same until it reaches the right hand of the oldest male in the group. He then has the choice to cut the kola into segments and disperse it accordingly, or signal his acceptance by almost regally hovering his right hand over the proffered dish before allocating the duty to another senior male family or community member of his choice. It's considered an honour to be given such a duty.

Though it was intriguing to participate in this ritual, after having done it a few times and the dire taste of kola had seeped into every pore of my body, the novelty very soon wore off. By the time we'd finished the rounds I felt like I was tripping on speed! I couldn't imagine myself ever falling asleep again! Thankfully, we were being supplied with a constant source of soft juices to wash away the overpowering sour and foul-tasting kola nut residue.

And as for the sinister-looking black and furry "alligatoh peppeh", which was supposed to enhance the palatability of the kola, yukkkkkk!

Later into the afternoon Uncle Sammy, still seemingly tense and distracted, started to prepare us to leave for the ten minute drive to Egbelubi, the village dad was born in. Amid promises to return and maintain contact, we made our emotional and heartfelt farewells to our new-found family, then we bundled into the waiting taxi to make our departure down the rutted, ululating and sun-baked village roads. I liked the village scenery. Dense and shady palm trees rustled by the much-appreciated gentle Hamatan breeze; the rich red soil; small 'farms' of cassava and yam; sporadic drumming, both distant and far; chickens and goats scratching and grazing their way through the day; half-naked children playing everywhere under the watchful eyes of their guardians; elderly men off to farm or hunt, carrying their glisteningly-sharp machetes nonchalantly at their sides; graceful women somehow managing to carry everything on their heads, from bundles of fire wood to huge ten-gallon jerry-cans of water fetched from the river; and people of all ages riding huge rickety old bone-shaker rod-brake Raleigh bicycles; the excessively numerous local Christian churches, the biggest buildings on view bar none throughout the community. The pace of life, in comparison to the towns and cities we'd glimpsed during our epic journey, was slow and peaceful. Everybody said hello and greeted us and each other as we passed on our way to Egbelubi.

And I wasn't prepared for what lay ahead.

Thirty-Five

It was late in the afternoon when we finally arrived in Egbelubi, home. Aside from the flaky and garishly blue painted tin-roofed colonial style 'main house' of the compound, the majority of the dwellings surrounding it were wattle and daub mud huts thatched with compacted palm leaf roofs.

We pulled up outside the main house, Uncle Joshua's house. We climbed out of the taxi, hauling our suitcases out with us, before paying the patient driver and bidding him farewell. People, approaching from all angles, began to stop and stare. They'd recognised Uncle Sammy instantly and started to shout his name in incredulity.

"Soldier!"

"Biafran Soldier!"

"Dede!"

"Innocent!"

"Samuel!"

"Chineke!"

Cue instant unbridled jubilation, mayhem and pandemonium. He was swamped by all these people who shared similar characteristics to him, and dad. It seems they just couldn't believe he was still alive or at liberty after his civil war heroics and stealthy though ignominious departure from Nigeria. Amid the incredible scenes of excitedly disbelieving shouting, screaming, crying, and joyous back-slapping, I was quite happy to melt into the background as an unannounced observer. I was beginning to feel even more emotional than I ever had been since landing at Murtala Mohammed Airport, including

Umubachi, and I really didn't want this to be the first impression my family would have of me.

Predictably, Obi was still managing to maintain his now concrete-stiff upper lip!

Uncle Sammy was equally excited and, with tears brimming in his eyes, he was going berserk also, enjoying his return home to the maximum, wallowing in the unrestrained attention and adulation! He became the Uncle Sammy that we'd grown to know and love again. I began to feel like a bit of an interloper, an uninvited and voyeuristic gate-crasher to an intimate (though public) reunion of a much-loved prodigal son's return.

As the decibels started to abate and as the euphoric clamour began to dissipate, quizzical eyes started to twitch in our direction and the inevitable question regarding our identity was raised and, on the same reply as before:

"Kawo omo deh Mike"

Cue total and utter chaos.

Obi and I were immediately engulfed by disbelieving, deliriously happy, shouting and screaming faces, all wanting to touch us, almost as if to make sure we were real. We were being pulled here and there by everyone, all wanting to introduce themselves to us. Though totally unfamiliar with such outpourings of emotional welcome and, as a result, a little embarrassed, we were beaming our joy and pleasure in return.

The fact was, and for all intents and purposes, we were meeting our actual first cousins for the very first time. It was surreal. I was able to identify family characteristics and traits that I thought only existed in my immediate family in England. Dad's nose, Chi-chi's chin, Ijem's soft brown eyes, Kele's cheeky grin, it was incredible. The noise levels shot through the roof again. Our uncles, aunties and cousins didn't expect to see dad again, let alone his two sons! It was almost as if God, Jesus, the Virgin Mary, Bill Gates and Santa Clause had arrived unannounced all at the same time in our sprawling sub-Saharan village in rural Igbo land!

Though I could see the shared family similarities, there were obvious dissimilarities. Me and Obi were much taller than them; we were bigger-built than them; we were a lot more fair-skinned than them; we didn't have the short, nick-type facial striations on the cheeks or temples; and obviously we were dressed western-style as opposed to traditional Nigerian garb. That's not to say all wore traditional, but many did. Of those who wore western clothes, it was abundantly clear the clothes were old-fashioned and had seen far better days in Europe before being shipped as used, second-hand garments to the 'bend-down' boutiques of Biafra (a bend-down boutique is the affectionate name given to second-hand clothes outlets in Nigeria, where the clothes are displayed on the ground and paths alongside main roads in the towns and cities. In order for garments to be viewed before purchase, the prospective purchaser must bend down!).

I felt like a Hollywood superstar being mobbed by adoring fans (Nollywood was yet to take off in Nigeria at the time), and I was filled with an intense pleasure and satisfaction I'd never before experienced. The euphoric reception we received totally eclipsed that which we'd received earlier in the day in Umubachi. Each of our cousins, both male and female, wanted their own time with us. They wanted to interrogate us about our lives in London:

"What of deh Michael?"
"What of mum?
"What of your sistahs?"
"What do you do in London?"
"Are you married?"
"You get pickin?" (Do you have children?)
"How life dey foh London?"

Both me and Obi were very happy to answer all the questions thrown at us and, although English is the official language of Nigeria, we found we had to slow down our speech in order to be understood, and concentrate very closely in order to understand!

Uncle Sammy's father, Papa Wilson, was the oldest man in the compound so had first dibs on conversation with us whenever he wanted to talk. He was a lean, wiry and wizened elder whose rheumy eyes conveyed experience and understanding, with a hint of impish fun. After introducing himself, he proudly informed me:

"Am di eldest man foh village. Am di fada to Innocent, na him
mi pickin".

He told me that he was the eldest man in the village (the implication being that, with such status, he is to receive unquestioned respect!), and that he was Uncle Sammy's father. I nodded and spoke my confirmation that I understood, which pleased him:

"Sorry I noh spik English well well. I noh go school"

He apologised for not speaking the Queen's English, explaining that he never attended school in his life!

I was impressed, I liked him, and I could tell he'd been a bit of a lad in his youth and adulthood. It was evident he had a rascally sense of humour and, for that alone, he had my utmost respect. A sense of humour is a 'must-have' in our family!

So as to avoid causing insult and offence, and as with our previous visit to dad's maternal village, we were required by tradition to go around the compound and village on a house-to-house basis, meeting with the eagerly expectant families that made up our kindred. This meant more personal introductions, more handshaking and, unfortunately, more offers and consumption of *even* more kola nut!

It was strange that we'd left England having only known a very isolated nuclear family, to arrive in Nigeria to be surrounded by hundreds of extended family. That feeling of 'belonging' is priceless.

Even more significant, we were actually in dad's place of birth. Pointing at the big (on a village scale at least), flakily-painted blue house, Uncle Sammy made a big thing of emphasising the fact that:

"This is where your father was born, this is where he belongs, this is where *you belong*!"

Papa Wilson went on to confirm:

"You are both sons of the soil, this is your birthright".

To be confirmed a 'son of the soil' in Igboland is to be bestowed with a very prestigious status. Igbo society is patrilineal and, as such, all familial status, wealth and property rights are inherited by the sons of the family. According to Igbo tradition, women 'marry out of the family', losing any claim of inheritance. Whilst politically very incorrect, I understand the philosophy. Far be it for me or any westerner to criticise other people's traditions. In countries where property, wealth and status are extremely hard to come by, and where there is no form of welfare state support, such traditions operate to ensure survival of the family unit, local community, and a structured and organised wider society in general.

Well, that's my excuse and I'm sticking to it!

As daylight ebbed from the sky at night's approach, we were back in the family compound, where the stifling heat of the day had subsided in deference to a slight evening chill under a clear and cloudless star-spangled sky. We'd been made aware that a formal welcome had been arranged, to commence after nightfall, and we were intrigued as to what this may entail.

Summoned into the compound interior, surrounded by mud huts and staring eyes, me and Obi stood side by side, confused and unsure as to expectations of tradition. Again, I regretted the fact that we were unable to speak Igbo, but was gladdened by the fact that we could sort of 'follow conversations'. The only sources of available light, other than the multitude of stars in the sky and the fireflies that signalled their darting routes by tail illuminations, were a wood fire in the centre of the compound and kerosene lamps dotted around inside and outside of the huts.

All of a sudden, and at the appropriate and appointed time, Papa Wilson emerged from his dark single-roomed hut that quadrupled up as his bedroom, living room, kitchen, and en-suite bathroom and toilet, in short, it was pretty much a hovel and, with the utmost respect, it stank! Like all of the abodes in the compound, there was no electricity or running water, and the majority of his furniture was handmade of local wood and foliage. The waste and sewage system comprised of a whole dug from the inside of his bathing area to the outside of his hut, where it would freely run its course to its lowest level, wherever that may have been!

It was dark. Pitch black. To the accompaniment of frogs croaking and the chirruping of crickets in the background, there was a lot of murmured conversation and a palpable increase in tension and expectation. Me and Obi didn't have a clue about what was going on, nor what was about to happen. Papa Wilson started to address the assembled clan in what was clearly a very profound and intense 'call and response' type oratory, with our family and village members interjecting and contributing, chanting and vocalising their understanding and agreement at every step of the uttered ritual. He made several libations to our ancestors by throwing Schnapps and kai-kai on the ground and at our feet (such a terrible waste of perfectly good alcohol!).

Throughout the early stages of the ritual me and Obi were quietly prompted by Uncle Sammy to respond where and when appropriate. I was quite happy to imbibe the high-alcohol-content kai-kai when instructed to partake, though far less enthusiastic when those damned kola nuts reappeared! All was going well, me and Obi were blagging things quite admirably, then one of our uncles appeared with a frantically clucking white chicken (it was making a very good impression of Andy during our fight with the Geordies in Torquay!).

As my now quite ample middle-aged girth will attest to, I'm ardently partial to fresh meat and vegetables, but I thought it was a bit late to start cooking at this time, plus this chicken needs to be slaughtered and de-feathered before any form of cooking could take place! However, the chicken obviously knew its impending fate. It was presented to Papa Wilson who proceeded to incant traditional messages and invocations, before cutting its head off right in front of us! With hot chicken blood squirting everywhere, he then raised it to our head-height, smearing the still-pumping gore on our foreheads and chests while continuing to beseech our ancestors on our behalf.

This was some crazy stuff! I never imagined I'd be involved in anything so raw and 'rootsy' in my life. I'd only ever seen this kind of thing in anthropological documentaries on the television. It never dawned on me that I'd actually participate in it! A ritual sacrifice! This was heavy! I was struck dumb and rooted to the compacted mud that we were standing on. With instructions not to wash away the blood until the following morning, we were allowed to return to the blue house where we'd sleep for the duration of our stay.

Uncle Sammy told us the following day that, among other things, Papa Wilson had 'called on the spirits' to protect us throughout our lives, proclaiming:

"Our juju is the strongest, nothing will harm you now!"
Juju!

I didn't even believe in God, and now I was being reassured that I was protected by *Juju*!

This stuff was freaking me out! It was clear by the number of churches in the community that Christianity was the prevailing doctrine and faith. Yet we were being offered the 'protection' of obiah, witchcraft, the 'black magic' that we'd heard about in derogatory terms growing up in the UK. But it was *real* to them, important to them and, as I'd later learn, life-defining to many.

As the Nigerian author Leo Igwe asserts in his 2004 article 'A Skeptical (sic) Look at African Witchcraft and Religion":

"Witchcraft is a prevalent belief and practice on the African continent. It permeates and controls the thinking, perception and lives of nearly all Africans, both educated and non-educated. It is an integral part of Africa's traditional religious heritage."

He goes on to explain that the belief in witchcraft in Nigeria is common among people of all ethnic and religious backgrounds, Christians and Muslims alike. He observes that witchcraft exists with equal force and ferocity, claiming even science in Africa is infused with witchcraft and sorcery, making much of it a unique form of African pseudoscience. Ritual killings and human sacrifices are still made in Nigeria today. It was blatantly evident to me that witchcraft and established religions are practised in juxtaposition in Nigeria with equal commitment and devotion. My atheistic view is that both forms of belief constitute an irrational pre-science that Nigeria, like many other developing societies around the world, even today still struggles to develop away from. Indeed, transported by slaves to the Caribbean and the Americas, the belief in witchcraft, obiah and juju is still practised among their modern-day descendants.

Apparently, a distinction is made between 'negative' (harmful) and 'positive' (harmless) witchcraft. Predictably, negative witchcraft is associated with women and children, whilst men are said to possess the antidote, positive witchcraft, hence they are called 'witch doctors'. Both witches and wizards are believed to have magical powers. Witchcraft is believed to be manifested and exhibited in a variety of medical and social ills including, for example, prolonged and complicated illness, incurable diseases, misfortune, business failure and sudden and mysterious death. Central to the belief in witchcraft is the claim that some people have magical powers and can use them to inflict harm on others. However, is it credible to believe witchcraft, as dispensed by such holders of magic, can cause death, infertility, diseases, miscarriages, business failures, accidents and so forth?

It occurs to me that, again similar to the supernatural claims of the established world religions and in agreement with Igwe, these incidents have rational, scientific and naturalistic explanations that do not require the causal power of witchcraft and sorcery. To further agree with Igwe's assertions, I support his position that:

"Witch doctors possess some skills, manipulative tricks and techniques through which they may exploit ignorant, gullible and credulous folk."

In much the same way that the dextrous 'three-card-trick' merchants of the west extort money from their gullible and unsuspecting roadside punters; and the universally popular TV illusionists who impress and amaze their millions of viewers and innocent volunteer participants in their weekly prime-time entertainment slots; and priests, rabbis and imams spell-bind their fawning congregations in religious gatherings, the deft exponents of the reverentially perceived 'dark' arts of juju and witchcraft to me, merely provide a different version of the same theme.

Juju, voodoo, religion, superstition, horoscopes, the occult, fortune-telling and tarot cards all amount to pretty much the same thing in my eyes and experience, the exploitation of the weak, needy, ignorant and dispossessed that live in hope for a positive change in their circumstances. According to Igwe, African witchcraft relies upon certain underlying assumptions and ingredients:

> These are fear, ignorance, poverty and religion, all four of which thrive in Africa in abundance.

Fear is the driving force of witchcraft and the cruel act of witch killing.

Ignorance, lack of knowledge, especially of nature and basic medical science has been at the root of the belief in witchcraft, which is a pre-scientific belief and constitutes part of traditional medicine. Unfortunately, according to Igwe, this pre-scientific mentality has refused to go away despite phenomenal discoveries and breakthroughs in modern science.

Due to the unyielding endemic and systemic poverty throughout the villages, towns and cities of continental Africa, many sick people cannot afford to go to hospital for medical treatment, so they resort to consulting witchdoctors and fortune-tellers, and in so doing voluntarily become potential receptive victims to the whims of the 'person of magic'.

Religion provides the subsoil in which the belief and practice of witchcraft thrives. As previously mentioned, witchcraft forms part of traditional African religion and most Africans retain their witchcraft mentality even when they embrace the alien faiths of Islam or Christianity. Even many imported religions have reinforced the belief in witchcraft. For example, Pentecostal Christian groups, of which there are thousands spread over the length and breadth of Nigeria, let alone Africa, in the Naira-driven promise to "help people identify, fight and defeat the witches and wizards".

In retrospect, and with reference to countless visits home over the past thirty years, I also fully recognise and agree with Igwe's observation that "nobody dies naturally" in Nigeria. There is a tradition among Africans of applying spiritual or supernatural explanations and interpretations to anything that happens. Every dead person was killed by someone. Every misfortune is the spiritual handiwork of some enemy. Thus, fetish mentality has greatly undermined the growth and development of reason, science, logic and free enquiry on the continent. And it has made pseudoscience, dogmatism, occultism and mysticism the mainstay of African thought and culture.

Just as importantly, fetishism has led to needless suffering, hatred and conflict in families, and torture and maltreatment of innocent people. The African continent must rid itself of the irrational belief in witchcraft and sorcery if it is ever to join the developed world any time soon!

However, it would be disingenuous of me to deny that, after having been 'protected', I felt strangely safer and more assured, because I did, instantly. I now understand, though, that I *wanted* to feel safer and more assured, especially given the fact that I was out of my comfort zone in a strange and unfamiliar land. Also juju, like Rastafarianism, represented another authentic alternative to the established order of the racist white society within which I grew up, so there *must* be something in it, surely?!

Our first night's sleep took us back to the good old days when we were kids, with me and Obi sleeping in the same cramped bed, leeching off each other's body heat to stave off the surprising tropical night chill. Though stiflingly hot in the early night hours, things definitely got colder later in the night. We also had to contend with the smoky stench of the mosquito coils which we lit before going to bed. As yet we were still to experience the avid attention of the marauding mosquito squadrons, but we didn't have to wait too long for them to detect sweet fresh blood!

We were woken, moderately refreshed, by the early morning sounds of rural village life at the sun's prompting. I've never grown used to the early morning awakening and rising to start the day in Nigeria! People just don't seem to treat themselves by having a 'lie-in' every now and again. They just get up and get on with things. I suppose when you consider getting through the day in Nigeria, for many, rarely involves the use of labour- and time-saving conveniences such as running water, electricity, kettles, washing machines, tumble driers, TVs and other taken-for-granted domestic appliances, it's necessary to start the day early if you have any realistic wish of achieving that day's goals!

As creatures of habit, we tend to follow our daily rituals wherever we are in the world. Our early morning ablutions are on the list of our rituals. For me, I need a nice cup of tea and a cigarette, which is usually followed by a dump before I wash and set about my daily commitments. I rarely if ever eat breakfast. I fully appreciated the efforts our relatives made on our behalves in order to cater for us, but the tea, Lipton's on a string, was the weakest I'd ever tasted, with the damp and crumbly ant-infested sugar cubes and clotted powdered milk failing to make the tea any more palatable.

Far more important for me is the early-morning dump, the eagerly-anticipated and consistently satisfying evacuation of the bowels that clears the body (literally), and mind (metaphorically), enabling us to prepare for the forthcoming day. I asked Uncle Sammy where the toilet was:

"You want to ease yourself?!"
"Yes."
"Ok, follow me".

He led me through some bushes to a humming pit-toilet which, apparently, had been specially erected and reserved for the exclusive use of Papa Wilson and invited VIP guests. Enclosed by wattle-and-daub mud walls, there was barely enough room to swing a cat. The toilet consisted of a pit dug several metres into the soil, above which there was a roughly-hewn expanse of hardwood, at the centre of which a hole had been hacked, through which urinary and faecal effluence was to be disgorged!

It was obvious Papa Wilson and previous 'VIPs' were crap (excuse the pun!), at aiming accurately. The wood reeked of stale piss and visible discolouration. This evidence suggested probably tons of piss and shit had hit the sides before either drying out in the heat or being slooshed away by an appointed attendant! I almost developed an instant case of total urinary and faecal retention! However, after nearly 48 hours of anal retention I *had* to let rip.

Men are often criticised for an inability to multi-task in comparison with women. I refute that allegation! Squatting precariously over a rotting wooden slab holding your breath in order to avoid death by ammonia asphyxiation whilst trying to accurately despatch shit and piss through a hole through which hundreds of disturbed and angry flies were making their escape and smashing against your exposed asshole without passing out and retaining your balance is a feat, if executed successfully, to be awarded a medal for!

After making my contribution to enrich Nigerian agricultural subsoil, light-headedly, I made my meandering way back to the blue house where I warned Obi about his future date with dumping-destiny! Though we laughed about it at the time, a serious realisation was starting to hit home for both of us. We'd need to forget the luxuries and conveniences that we take for granted in London, and get our heads around dealing with life at its very basic and subsistence levels. For example, even after having completed the dumps-from-hell, there was no running water with which to wash our hands. This meant we washed our hands by transferring water in a succession of bowls and a variety of receptacles ranging from clean to dirty. It was evident that even the water itself was a scarce resource that wasn't tapped 24/7 through the community.

Apart from a very unreliable single standpipe situated on the road that bisected the village, the main source of clean fresh water was the

stream and river that demarcated our family land from the Ngwa people's land, about a two-mile walk away! This trip was made several times
per day by young children before and after school, and the stay-at-home
women who spent the overwhelming majority of their days catering for
their families without recourse to labour- and time-saving mod-cons
and devices.

In short, and to put it mildly, these were *strong* people who took all
that life threw at them in a determinedly stoical not-to-be-beaten way.
I could do nothing but marvel at their daily achievements and admire
their positive approach to life. I couldn't imagine how other people
around the world would cope in similar situations. That's not to claim
that Nigerians, Biafrans, don't experience frustrations and react negatively to adversity, but given the excruciatingly high levels and variet-
ies of their daily grind, these people are *real* survivors. It came as no
surprise to me that Biafrans had survived the civil war, just in the same
way that it was no surprise to me that so many millions survived the
arduous 'middle passage' and the abominations of European slavery
in the Caribbean and the Americas.

One of the Nwanokwu compound
houses in Egbelubi village (1979)

Thirty-Six

Uncle Sammy arranged with another one of our uncles for us to drive to Aba town (now Abia state capital), a vast, sprawling and industrious commercial centre approximately forty five minutes drive from Egbelubi, in order for us to change our pounds sterling into Naira. He ushered me and Obi into the bush to the rear of our compound where we met with the appointed driver and there, strangely covered and camouflaged under tree foliage, was a car waiting for us to use. We asked Uncle why the car was hidden, and he told us that he didn't want anybody stealing the car. It later transpired that the car was in fact stolen and being hidden by him and his boys!

There's a lot of truth in the sayings:

"Ignorance is bliss".
and
"What you don't know won't harm you".

Unsuspectingly, me and Obi blissfully and ignorantly climbed into the car and were ready to visit Aba. Once off the village roads past Okpala, the central focal point of our Eziama area, and after having successfully negotiated (bribed) unhindered passage onto the Aba-Port Harcourt expressway, we were up and running. The driver drove like an experienced 'get-away' driver at reckless irrational speeds, but slowed to 'normal' speeds well in advance of the remaining police and army checkpoints, all of whose palms Uncle Sammy surreptitiously greased!

Bombing along the (at best) terribly and (as standard) non-maintained roads was frightening enough, but the sight of yet another dead body left decaying by the roadside added to our already rising sense of fear and impending danger. Apparently this person had been knocked down by a vehicle and just left there to rot until anybody who may have recognised him or a random local search party came across him. I've since seen many similar sights in Nigeria over the many years and visits I've made, and have never quite reconciled this feature of life in Nigeria with the many positive aspects of actually celebrating life that I've witnessed.

My overall feelings were that Nigeria is a land of obscenely ridiculous contradictions. It's a land where the daily fight for life and survival seems to acquiesce at the loss of life which, at death, appears cheap; where people conduct themselves with utmost propriety and pride in public, yet are reduced to miserable levels of poverty and deprivation in hand-to-mouth domestic survival; where people profess their love and devotion to their Christian God on Sundays, their Muslim God on Fridays, and the traditional Gods of their 'spirit world' on every other day of the week; where life and death exist cheek-by-jowl on either side of a very slim kobo coin; where Pentecostal Ministers and Muslim Imams berate their devoted audiences with the scriptures of the righteous whilst dipping their fingers into collection boxes filled by the poor, and their penises into the pussies of their adoring flock; where education is revered yet students are forced to survive and continue their studies by selling their bodies to beer-swilling oil-worker expats in the seedy hotels and motels of the university towns......

Yet life goes on, testimony to Charles Darwin's theory of 'survival of the fittest'.

It's true, only the fittest of the fit have a chance to survive and prosper in Nigeria, the remainder, and in Nigeria's case, the overwhelming majority, suffer on a daily basis. So much so that the 'lowest of the low', those forced to eke out a living combing the flotsam and jetsam deposited on the stinking city refuse tips, or those pulling stacked and loaded handcarts piled high with weighty wares, are referred to as "suffermen".

I suppose they provide a yardstick for others to measure themselves by, with the grim determination never to allow themselves to sink to such depths.

On our arrival in the outskirts of Aba after what felt like a ride on an out-of-control big-dipper along the treacherous expressway, we approached a small traffic jam leading up to a bridge. The landscape that dropped away from the bridge about forty feet below consisted of a small river, a couple of streams, and quite a crowd of seemingly agitated people, and what appeared to me to be a large bonfire. I wondered if they were all enjoying a Sunday afternoon barbecue, and asked if this was indeed the case. The driver had overheard some of the shouted exclamations from some of the crowd, and explained to Uncle Sammy that:

"No, it's pipple wey dey burn inside fire".

As we slowly approached nearer to the bridge and looked more closely, it was abundantly evident that what he'd said was true! I could see the arms and legs of a few people in what I'd innocently thought was some sort of celebratory bonfire. Apparently, a woman and two men had burgled somebody's house the night before. The three of them had been walking through Aba market when they were recognised as the perpetrators of the burglary. At which point the victim of the burglary shouted:

"Hollam! Hollam! Na de teef wey dey boggle me last night!"
(Stop them! Stop them! They burgled me last night!).

It seems the mistake they made was to start running when the accusations were levelled at them. By so doing they were, by their attempted evasive actions, admitting guilt. A medieval hue-and-cry ensued, and if there's one thing Aba market traders (and Igbos generally), detest intensely, it's thieves. As the traders and shoppers were alerted to the cause, the stopwatch on the lives of these hapless burglars started ticking. It didn't tick for very long. The pursuing crowd descended upon them, beat them mercilessly, and frogmarched them to their date with destiny. After hanging them for their crime, their still-breathing bodies were chopped down from the tree, tethered to old car tyres and doused with petrol, before being set alight.

Summary justice meted out in its most brutal and death-defining worst.

Uncle Sammy soberly advised us *never* to run if somebody shouts "Hollam! Hollam!" at us.

He also advised us *never* to stop if we accidently (or otherwise), knocked someone down on the road. In either case, the likelihood is the same outcome, instant death by enraged suffering people who don't appreciate being robbed or losing a member of their family by (clearly by virtue of owning a motor vehicle), a more affluent citizen!

I went cold at the thought. What about the rule of law?! What about human decency and responsibility?! What about applying a sense of humanity?!

Not interested.

In a harsh environment where everybody lives or dies by their individual effort, where their life chances are determined by their toil against relentless pressure, where life is considered a precious but vulnerable commodity, the prevailing sentiment is that life is hard enough as it is, and we don't need thieves or reckless people making our lives even harder!

Whilst shocked speechless and stunned to the core, I understood the feeling, I understood the thinking. But I struggled to envisage and understand a society where life seemed so cheap. Granted, Nigeria doesn't suffer from a population shortage by any stretch of the imagination, but that shouldn't negate the value of any one individual's life, surely?

In post-war Biafra, it felt as if we were as close as possible to living in a lawless state of anarchy! Whilst exiting our Okpala Local Government Area (LGA), the first township is that of Owerri-Nta, in Ngwa. Uncle Sammy explained to us that people in this area were reduced to cannibalism during the war, and that they already had a reputation for eating the human sacrifices they made to their juju spirits well before the war! The saving grace for Biafra at the time being the grim determination of its inhabitants to return to established peace and tranquillity, and self respect and dignity. In the horrific event that this drive and resolution had been irretrievably lost, Biafra would have been hell on earth.

Something else struck me on our drive to Aba, it was something that I'd become increasingly aware of since our arrival in Nigeria, especially in the east. This 'something' was the very noticeably high number of albinos among the populace. I'd only ever seen two or three white albinos in England, and was totally unaware that black people, African people, produce albinos also! They made a strange and incredible sight, with their totally African features but white, non-pigmented, sun-sensitive skin and eyes.

"Unfortunate Oyibos" (unfortunate white people), is the crassly insensitive term with which they are described by their clearly more fortunate darker skinned brothers and sisters. However, they *are* African, they are perceived as African, and they see themselves as African. Both Obi and I were incredulous and, if truth be told indignant, when even the albinos referred to *us* as "Oyibos". This served to remind me that in Nigeria people will describe you as they see you which, in our case, is as foreigners. We were often incorrectly described as 'Black Americans' and other variations of non-Nigerian origin. Despite Igboland having thousands of lighter skinned people than ourselves, albinos were instantly identifiable as being indigenous, whereas we were most definitely 'alien'. Their comments were not necessarily a reference to our skin colour, and when they learned we were 'sons of the soil' this usually resulted in shocked and initially disbelieving responses, generally characterised by them first asking our names and then speaking to us in Igbo! This was generally the case for all Nigerians, not just the albinos.

We met with Uncle Sammy's friend James who, though he'd since become a lay preacher, was obviously one of Uncle's 'boys' in pre-war

Biafra. Reading between the lines of their conversations it was clear that much murkiness had transpired among and between them. Also, I never hesitate to question the motives of lay preachers, whose often miraculous 're-births' that lead to them setting up money-spinning Pentecostal places of worship never ceases to astound, shame and disgust me. I remember reading (somewhere) that Nigeria and Jamaica have the highest 'church-per-square-mile' statistics in the world. This doesn't surprise me in the slightest. It would appear Nigerians and Jamaicans are not only very spiritual people, they're very gullible people also.

Aba was a huge commercial centre of hustle-and-bustle hustlers. It seemed as if everything was for sale, from petrol- and diesel-powered generators, to handkerchiefs, plastic plates, bread, biscuits, stockfish, car tyres, local furniture, 'bed foams' (mattresses), you name it, Aba would sell it! We went to a bank where one of our Aunties worked, to exchange our sterling for Naira, then later went to visit another one of Uncle's boys who'd 'done well' since the war by opening his own restaurant.

Respite from the heat and dust of the graded and compacted mud roads, his restaurant was paradise, blissfully cooled by a very effective air-conditioning unit. Obi and I luxuriated in its comfort whilst enjoying a wonderful chicken-and-rice meal and a few 'on the house' cold Star Lager Beers. Stepping out into the heat on our departure was reminiscent of stepping off the aeroplane, with the heat and humidity instantly descending upon us to remind us where we were!

His restaurant was situated on a hilly junction, one of the exiting tributary roads leading to Ikot Ekpene and Calabar (as previously mentioned one of the busiest slave-holding departure points in West Africa during the transatlantic trade). Ikot Ekpene is famous for its basket weaving, sculptured artefacts and raffia cane furniture, and was of strategic military and political importance for both Biafra and Nigeria during the war, which had a severe impact on this Niger Delta city. Uncle Sammy made a pretty impressive tour guide as he explained and discussed the history and traditions of each of the towns, cities and communities that featured during our trip. He explained that the father of legendary mixed-race Welsh singer Dame Shirley Bassey, Henry Bassey, was from Calabar, and that her family was a large and important family in Calabar (a later trip to Calabar confirmed that this was, in fact, the truth).

Virtually every meeting with one of Uncle Sammy's boys was loud and boisterous and, regardless of the differing levels of success they'd achieved since he left (absconded from) Nigeria, every one of them without fail attributed their success to him. He clearly was a very resourceful 'fixer' who was happy for others to benefit, gain and develop alongside him and as a result of his personal 'entrepreneurial skills'. It seems he made much of his initial profits whilst employed as a manager by Leventis Stores in Port Harcourt which, at the time, was probably comparable to the modern-day Marks & Spencer type chain of supermarkets. The upward rise in his personal profits tallied in exact proportion with the firm's losses. He didn't just sit on the money though, but invested it in his own transport company and other causes, including those of his mates who he helped get established. It also probably financed his eventual clandestine exit from Nigeria when things got too hot for him!

I very quickly learnt that, in Nigeria, village life is very much for me. Every town and city I've since visited has been ridiculously over-crowded, disorganised and chaotic. That's not to say I don't enjoy the vibrancy and energy of the hustle and bustle of Nigerian city life, it's just that I enjoy the relative peace and tranquillity of the village even more.

Thirty-Seven

After the initial euphoria of our arrival, things eventually settled down in Egbelubi. We became less of a novelty factor and more relatives with whom to become more acquainted. It felt almost as if they'd arranged a turn-taking rota to sidle up to us and start chatting. Our cousins were intrigued about our lives in London, and were literally starry-eyed at our stories. Putting London in a bad light seemed impossible, because nothing could be worse than the everyday stresses and strains of trying to make life in Nigeria. A female cousin asked me how many wives I planned to have. When I explained only one, she was shocked. She couldn't understand how any man would only take one wife, and went on to further explain that she didn't want to be the first wife of any man, but would prefer to be the second so as to avoid the onerous overall responsibilities of managing the husband's household(s)!

Our male cousins appeared far more concerned to discuss more 'manly' matters with us, like education, employment and political issues as they affected us in the west. Obi and I tried to be as open and honest as possible. But, in the same way I found it difficult to believe it was so hot in Nigeria while in England it was so cold, I thought it would be quite difficult for them to believe the negative things we had to say about living life in a racist country. They demonstrated no concept of racism and seemed to dismiss the points we were making as irrelevant. It eventually dawned on me that they saw us as light-skinned, "yellow", and as such we should be making the most of our 'privileged skin-status' in London. The underlying sentiment was that, if they were light-skinned, they'd capitalise on any and every opportunity that came their way. This may well have been applicable in Nigeria where lighter skinned people were afforded preferential treatment, but it didn't apply in London, where light-skinned people are considered and treated as black like every other black person. Yes, the 'acceptable' face of black, but black nonetheless.

Our cousins also confronted us with their concerns about our surname, Egwuonwu. To be frank, they were vociferously peeved at the fact that we weren't answering Nwanokwu, because this was our family name! They passionately questioned us as to what had led to dad changing his surname, and at the time of their interrogation we weren't sufficiently informed to provide an adequate explanation. Uncle Sammy filled them in with the details, and they left us with no uncertainty that they were unhappy. I resolved to speak with dad, mum and our sisters on our return with a view to changing our family name, reverting back to Nwanokwu. In the event, this is indeed what happened. Dad was very open, honest, and listened to our accounts of the discussions we'd had with our family in Nigeria. He agreed with my assertion that we should change our name back to Nwanokwu by deed poll, and this is what we did. Dad was a very proud man, so relinquishing his stance was quite a major event for us, a decision we all respected.

Whilst on the subject of name-changing, as part of the process we had to go to a law firm in Reading to complete the deed poll documentation. I'd already entered the street level reception area to the solicitors' office where I stood waiting for dad, who'd lagged behind a bit. I watched as he approached the glass doors with his customary very purposeful stride however, he didn't appear to be slowing his stride down! I said to myself a few times 'he *must* slow down soon before entering, surely!'

He didn't.

He hadn't seen or noticed the fact that the doors were all glass and walked headlong into them! With the doors reverberating loudly on impact with his face, he was instantly stunned, confused and embarrassed when he realised what he'd done. I went through a series of emotions, from concern about his well-being, to shame and embarrassment on his behalf, and then when I saw him laughing at himself, I burst out laughing also. I've learnt that being able to laugh at yourself is a very valuable characteristic and, in dad, given his stiff 'authoritarian' approach to the way he raised his children, it was very endearing and made us love him even more!

This was probably the first indicator I'd had of dad's degenerating eyesight. Whilst he wasn't too proud to refuse to wear glasses for reading and other indoor purposes, he rarely wore them in public and, on this occasion, much to his detriment. Whether it was due to pride or vanity I'm not too sure but, like many Nigerians, he didn't like to appear to be disabled or debilitated in any way.

Interestingly, mum had similar 'public concerns'. From the age of 16 she smoked every day of her life, but "wouldn't be seen dead smoking on the streets or anywhere else in public".

Sadly, for both of them, these problems were to feature highly later on in both their lives.

Our first visit to Nigeria continued in much the same way as it started, so over the remainder of the two weeks we were subjected to more mosquito bites (they obviously loved us 'freshies'!); more handshaking family meets with disbelieving but ecstatic shakers uttering the now inevitable exclamation "Is that so? You are welcome!"; more hair-raising stomach-churning heart-stopping reckless-though-exciting drives along treacherous roads; more Star Lager Beer; more fufu, yam, and wiry chicken; more kai-kai; more pammy; more grit-crunchy rice; more banana and groundnut; more new sights, sounds and smells; more learning and understanding of Igbo tradition and culture; and even more mosquito bites and disgusting kola nuts!

Our 'holiday' was a life experience. I've since learnt that there's no such thing as a 'holiday' in Nigeria. Holiday *time* can be spent there, but to regard that time as a holiday is totally inappropriate. On my very many visits home since then it's become very evident that Nigeria is FUN, especially in the east, Biafra. Things are always hectic, in a constant state of, at times, almost rabid pandemonium. Nigerians don't 'do' queuing, but will try to find the slightest of angles to push-in, whether it's on the road at traffic lights or in a bank waiting to be served. Amidst all the impatient rush and mayhem, nothing works (in British terms at least) quickly, reliably or efficiently, including people; traffic lights; electricity (NEPA!!!!!) plumbing; the roads; the government, the list could go on forever, yet it's fun!

The people are warm, loving and welcoming, and will always smile and say "Hello sah, morning sah!" as they beam genuine warmth through their eyes to accompany their greeting. The bars and clubs are places where people *really* de-stress and get happy. Excluding the tragically high incidents of fatal road traffic accidents and being robbed by armed robbers, life is valued and valuable in Nigeria. Village life is slow, safe and peaceful. There's nothing better than walking along the sandy village roads and paths under shady palm trees, strolling into family homes to chat and laugh, or rolling into More Day's bar in Okpala to drink copious amounts of Star Lager Beer before making our way home to sleep off the excesses of the day.

But Nigeria is not a holiday! Every subsequent visit we've made has been equally eye-opening, and we've never returned since without the inevitable question on our arrival:

"What did you bring for me?"

A particular feature of expectations in Nigeria is that everybody from London (abroad) is stinking rich and, as a result, ought to "bring something for me" on every arrival home. The concept of people working abroad, struggling to make ends meet, saving every penny in order to be able to afford their 'holiday' back home in Nigeria is complete anathema to them. The more familiar they get with you, the more they expect you to bring something. It doesn't have to be money, but 'something', anything. The expectation becomes irritating eventually, so we often spend time ducking some people or developing and refining excuses as to why we've brought nothing. However, I understand things from their point of view, so I've always made a point of bringing things to 'dash', especially clothes that I no longer wear. It's a constant source of fun and pleasure to see so many items of my old clothes being worn by so many different cousins and friends in and around the village!

Uncle Ben visited home one Christmas time and arrived back in the freezing cold at Heathrow airport with nothing but the T-shirt, shorts and sandals he was wearing, and his passport in his back pocket! He'd left on his outward bound flight with two suitcases full of clothes and belongings, some of which were for dash purposes, much of which was *supposed* to return with him!

Nigeria is a country full of contradictions where life appears, to me at least, to be lived quite publicly, with obscene wealth living alongside excessive poverty; the ostentatious privilege of the minority elite prevailing over the completely disempowered and comparatively destitute masses; infuriating frustration alongside satisfying achievement; a massive abundance of natural resources alongside embarrassing under-development and creaking-at-the-seams infrastructure; survival of the fittest existing hand-in-hand with a genuine love for humanity; where shameless pompous pride is flaunted over abject and pitiful humility; materialistic greed fighting against (and often prevailing over) humanistic values; centuries-old custom and tradition pushing back the tidal waves of western 'disrespect'; Muslims and Christians paying homage to their Gods on Fridays and Sundays respectively, then paying Naira to the juju man throughout the rest of the week; outlandish fun alongside forlorn misery and anguish; unrestrained and sometimes naive hope alongside immeasurable and grinding despair; astounding academic brilliance, ingenuity and intelligence alongside astonishingly low levels of common sense and practical initiative.

Thirty-Eight

The following twelve months saw us return to London, change our surname, dad retire from work and return home to Nigeria, and me and Obi speaking excitedly and in awe about our Nigeria 'experience' at any and every opportunity and family gathering, so much so that the following Christmas all five of us children went home for Christmas.

Dad had been appointed Head of Psychiatry at Port Harcourt Prison, and was provided with a house in the area of Rumuola in the city outskirts. Mum stayed at home that year to look after Ijem's young children, son Uchenna and daughter Chidinma. 16 year old Kele fell in love with Nigeria instantly and resolved to return for good as soon as she'd finished school in Reading. Our sisters loved home, but Ijem found it difficult at times as she was, as a young single mother, understandably missing her children.

When she did return to Nigeria for good after completing her education in Reading, Kele threw herself into making a life for herself at home in a way that surprised us all. I don't think any of us would have guessed that she'd make such an enthusiastic and successful transition in the strange new land that was Nigeria. She managed to get a job as a radio presenter with Radio Rivers Port Harcourt, which brought her almost instant popularity and fame, locally at least. Over thirty years later and she's done everything from radio presenting to government contracting and private investments. Financially and socially, she's done extremely well, and we're all proud of her achievements.

As for the rest of us, we were unable to dive in and make such life-changing decisions. Chi-chi was still developing her career in music,

Ijem had her children to raise single-handedly, and Obi was in the process of completing his A Levels with the aim of going on to university.

Despite the lure of home, I resolved to finish what I'd started and get my degree. Still living with my adoptive family in West Norwood, I was enjoying every aspect of my life. University was good and I did a lot of travelling with the football team around England and Europe, scoring goals and winning trophies along the way. My psychiatric nurse training went well and I qualified as a Staff Nurse in 1981. I was having a great time living with Pat's family. I loved her and her husband George, as well as all their children, who were like brothers and sisters to me. George, a very dark-skinned Jamaican (based on his nature and characteristics I'd bet everything he descended from Ghana), worked as a Post Office manager, but had also been an avid sportsman himself in his younger days. Like many Caribbean people, he had a passion for cricket (especially when the West Indies were playing against England!), followed by football. In fact, he actually managed a very high profile Sunday morning league team that had become famous across south London – YABAC FC.

George had started the team with a very close friend of his, Ben, another Jamaican who, like my parents, Pat and George, and thousands of other African and Caribbean people, migrated to London during the 'Windrush Era' of the 1950s to make a life for themselves and their families.

Apparently, at its inception YABAC was an acronym for 'Young And Black And Christian', but by the early 1980s this had been altered (principally by the players!) to 'Young And Black And Cool'! Football aside, I think the latter interpretation accurately reflected the position of black youth from the 1970s and onwards in Britain. Outside of the (racist) education system and police service, it was, indeed, 'cool' to be black! 1970s America exclaimed:

"Say it loud, I'm black and I'm proud!"

In England, particularly the larger towns and cities, Black 'culture', especially Jamaican music, idiom and fashion, was 'cool'. Everybody wanted to be, look or sound like a sticksman or a rudeboy, a Rasta or a soulhead, even the white kids, some of whom tried desperately to '*be* black'! The very few who succeeded did so only up to a point. They kept up with the buying of the ska and reggae, soul and lovers 7" and 12" inch music. Their parents were forced into buying their children the latest clothing fashions, from the two-tone stay-pressed and Oxford Bags high-waister trousers, to the sleeveless tank-top jumpers and butterfly collar shirts, to the stack-heeled and platform shoes, but they still couldn't *dance* to save their lives! Even for those who'd 'been accepted' by their 'naturally cool' black mates, things always fell apart for them on the dance floor!

However, for me, the cynical side of all of this was the fact that black-inspired music and fashion was systematically being hijacked by the established mainstream producers. So instead of Desmond Dekker and Johnny Nash making millions from their talent, it was copied and replaced by the more insipid covers and replications of the likes of UB40 and Boy George's 'Culture Clash', who went on to make the millions.

As for fashion, there's always been the Haute Couture industry to serve the rich and famous, but street fashion, urban fashion, was increasingly being driven by black youth who could make virtually anything look cool simply by wearing it! This too has been jumped on by the 'fashionista piranhas' who have developed a multi-million pound industry from mimicking and mass-producing the 'cool black urban look' without promoting it as such.

I suppose such is the history of most things popular. Like ska and reggae in Jamaica, jazz, blues, rock and roll and soul developed and thrived in the black African American community for decades, yet only came to prominence and mainstream acceptability, and commercial viability, when Elvis copied the beat and style. No disrespect to Elvis though, he was a white boy who could sing *and* dance, most definitely a brother from another mother! The same can't be said though for the overwhelming majority of others who followed in his wake, including the likes of Buddy Holly, Shakin Stevens and, dare I say it, The Beatles and The Rolling Stones, all of whom made millions!

During my first year with the Pat and George I'd committed myself to playing football for the Maudsley Hospital staff team, and felt I couldn't renege on the agreement, so I joined the all-black YABAC FC a year later than I'd have liked, but I still enjoyed playing for the hospital and we won the league that season. Playing as the creative midfield lynchpin I scored about 18 goals, and set up loads for my team mates, so it was a good year nonetheless.

Life at the Cacoes was great, and both Pat and her husband George could cook! Wonderful rice and peas, chicken, curry goat and beef, truly home from home. I tried, and sometimes succeeded, to be sensible and act like an older brother in front of their children. Spending quite a bit of time with the oldest sons Gary and Colin, we'd go out together and Gary played football for YABAC juniors, so we were inextricably linked on the most important fronts. I felt very protective towards them, though probably didn't always show it. This may have been because I felt they needed room to grow and become the people they wanted to be. At times I felt both Pat and George put me on a bit of a pedestal, which irritated their own children at times, but they didn't hold back from putting me in my place as and when necessary!

I remember on one occasion during the season before I started playing for YABAC, the team went on a friendly tour to France. Pat and George both went on the tour so, for us left at home, it was a case of 'while the cat's away, the mice will play!' We organised a house party for the Saturday prior to their return the following Sunday - *not* the brightest idea by any stretch of the imagination, and certainly not a wise move for a supposedly responsible and mature 'older' brother. Well, the party rocked, everybody had a good time, and no damage was done, but George sensed something had happened the minute he stepped through the front door after getting back from Dover. After conducting his investigation, none of us dared lie to George, so we admitted to holding the party. Both he and Pat took it in good spirit, but deep down I wondered if they were disappointed in me, because I felt disappointed in myself. I felt I'd abused their trust in me and, quite rightly, would have expected more of me. However, in my defence, I suppose I was still relatively young, and it *was* a great party!

Me, George and Pat

When we didn't have anything on our private weekend agendas, the oldest son Gary and I used to go out partying together every now and then. Gary was a very handsome, light-skinned, blue-eyed, bandy-legged charmer who really rated himself with the ladies. And, in many ways, he had the right to. He was outgoing, gregarious, and loved to be the centre of attention in any company, he was a fun guy who, other than playing football, didn't take too many things in life that seriously. We rolled up to a party in the Croydon south London suburb of Thornton Heath where some of the YABAC players were all headed to for one of "the firm's" birthday celebrations.

It was a nice affair where most people were either local or knew each other. Then I noticed a slim, pretty and petite black woman who, to me, looked beautiful on the outside and going by the radiant smiles and laughter she freely shared with her two friends, beautiful on the inside also.

The only problem was Gary had spotted her as well and, true to form, he moved in for the kill! I knew at first sight that I was going to marry this woman. I knew she was the woman who I wanted to have my children with and who I wanted to live with forever. Don't ask me how I knew, I just did.

Within a split second of the next lovers' rock record seeping seductively out of the speakers, Gary made his move and confidently schmoozed over to her and her group of friends. He asked her to dance, and she accepted, and I was so pissed off! (Irrationally) pissed off at Gary for dancing with my future wife before I'd even had the chance to speak with her, and totally pissed off at myself for being so bloody slow out of the blocks! Most men were extremely cautious at blatantly declaring their interest in a woman by making that long, lonely walk to approach a stranger and ask her to dance. The fear of rejection and public humiliation on refusal can, at times, be too much for any man to bear as he makes the *even* longer and lonelier walk back to his starting position (usually propping up the wall), across the other side of the room!

Whilst I'd never really had to work too hard with women, to be honest, I'd never really developed the skill of confidently pulling off a cold approach and then chatting them up. My approach, usually, was to try to make eye contact with the woman and, if the signs were favourable or reciprocated, then I'd summon up the courage to ask for a dance and, if accepted, chat her up whilst dancing. Gary was a master at both and, at this precise moment, I regretted my failings, bitterly! It was the longest three minutes I'd ever been forced to endure but, thankfully, the record came to an end and Gary moved on to his next target. I now had to leave things for a little while as I didn't want to steam straight in after Gary, I had to make *some* effort at appearing cool, even though I was in turmoil.

After what I thought was an appropriate amount of time had elapsed, and encouraged by a popular slow record, I made my move. Others were also pairing up, so it was now or never. Heart thumping, the long and lonely walk began. The fact that she'd already danced with Gary increased the potential humiliation and shame if she refused my proposal, but I just *had* to do it. She and her friends spotted my approach and, though the music was playing, it felt like everything went deathly quiet and time had stood still, with all eyes focused on me. Gingerly, but politely, I extended my hand in her direction whilst leaning into her earshot with my request. I was a total bag of nerves because, in my mind, so much (the rest of my life), all seemed to hinge on this one moment in time. The sense of relief that flooded my every pore was indescribable as she accepted and I took her into my arms. I tried to be as cool as possible, tried not to miss a beat, tried to get the conversation started, tried not to appear desperate!

We danced, and we thanked each other at the end of it. Her name was Yvonne, she lived locally, and was friends with one of the party hosts. I'd explained my more tenuous link to the hosts, and felt that we'd 'clicked'. We had a few more dances during which we established a far more comfortable and easy patter. Part way through the night she disappeared upstairs with her friends, Hazel and Diana. After what seemed like an eternity I went in search of her whereabouts. The bathroom door was open and they weren't in there (why is it that women always go to the bathroom in twos and threes?!), so they had to be in one of the bedrooms. I knocked on the first door and it was answered by Hazel. I felt like that naughty little schoolboy standing on the headmaster's mat as I meekly told Hazel that I wanted to speak with Yvonne. Hazel shut the door in my face and, after a short while during which I assumed they'd convened and completed a hasty and impromptu conference, Yvonne opened the door. She revealed that they were in the process of getting ready to leave, at which I panicked. I didn't even have her telephone number!

So I asked her for her number, and she reeled it off to me, and I felt relieved and happy that I'd be able to contact her at a (not much) later date - happy days!

Wrong! After she left with her friends Gary and I stayed for a while longer. I wasn't in the least bit interested in dancing with any other woman, but enjoyed the music for the rest of the night. I called Yvonne the next day, and couldn't get through. She'd given me a bogus number. I was gutted! I even tried different combinations of the number she'd given me, hoping against hope that I'd get through, but still got nothing. I couldn't believe she'd given me a bogus number. I thought we'd got on well at the party and was sure we'd meet up again soon after. I was crushed!

A couple of months of no contact later there was another party taking place at the same house. I went along with Gary and others of the YABAC crew, not expecting that lightning would strike twice in the same place, but it did, she was there again, with the same two friends Hazel and Diana. I had mixed emotions because, whilst I was happy to see her again, I felt confused and betrayed by her also. I decided to put the devastating 'bogus number blow' to one side and asked her to dance again, and she accepted.

We got talking again, and she was the kind, gentle natured person I'd met previously, and she seemed a bit more relaxed. It transpired that, when we first met, she was actually already engaged to another man, hence the bogus number and her subsequent Lord Lucan act! She explained that she'd felt uncomfortable with the situation at the time and didn't want or mean to mislead me, then she apologised for giving me the bogus number. She was a really decent young woman and I understood her dilemma. She gave me enough to work out that she was interested in me, so I pushed things there and then, not wanting to miss this chance to firm things up with her.

I made it clear that I wanted to pursue a relationship with her (to hell with her fiancé!), and went into overdrive with my charm offensive. It worked. She said the feelings I expressed were mutual and reciprocated, and she committed herself to ditching Mr Fiancé, which she did, and we became an item.

My initial first-sight feelings proved to be true. We married on August 14th 1982, and thirty-odd years and three children later we're still together! I *never* thought I'd meet anyone who'd fully satisfy my hopes and expectations for my wife, and certainly didn't think I'd meet anyone who'd want me for a husband!

Thirty-Nine

I continued playing university football on Wednesdays, and started playing Sunday morning football in the top division of the Morden and District League for YABAC during my fourth and final year at uni. It was a fantastic feeling playing for an all-black team. There was no greater feeling than going to play away games in the traditional white working class enclaves around south London where, at times, the resentment and racial hatred were almost palpable. Beating them in their own back yards was the high point of my weekends, and winning league titles and cups was the cherry on the cake for us all.

George was a great manager, he really understood football tactics. Also, just as importantly for me, he acted as a role model and mentor for many of the players in both the senior and junior squads. He was clearly a very principled man who wouldn't compromise the stance he adopted in order to curry favour from others, regardless of their status in either the team or club. He always did what he felt was right for the team, and was prepared to back his decisions without prejudice or favour. He even kept Gary in the junior team when it would have been easier for him to select him for the senior team squad!

I played in various positions for the team, but mainly down the middle. Centre forward, central midfield or central defence. YABAC had a reputation for being a club with talented players, which was largely true. I think if several of those guys were coming through today they would have played professional level football, and some at the very highest (Premiership) standard. But those were the days when there was only a smattering of black professionals in the football league;

when white scouts were reluctant to 'take a punt' on young black play-ers; Cyrille Regis, Laurie Cunningham and Brendan Batson made up the 'Three Degrees' at West Bromwich Albion FC at a time when it was virtually unheard of for more than one black player to be in a team, let alone three!; and ten years before the likes of Ron Noades, Chairman and owner of our local club Crystal Palace FC, who in 1991 stated:

> "The black players at this club lend the side a lot of skill and flair, but you also need white players in there to balance things up and give the team some brains and some common sense".

Alan Pardew, the current Crystal Palace FC manager and ex-Crystal Palace player under Ron Noades, played for Morden Nomads FC in the Morden and District league before going on to play for Whyteleaf FC and a number of other non-league clubs before breaking into Crystal Palace. We played against him and his brother in a cup semi-final which, according to pre-match speculation and warnings, supposedly, we were going to lose *because* the Pardews played for Nomads. We battered them. We gave them a real football lesson as we knocked them out of the cup in a game that we never even remotely looked like losing. I couldn't believe the hype surrounding Pardew who, in my opinion, was a very ordinary player compared to every player in our squad, but he went on to further his career, and to eventually play and manage at the highest level, enjoying fame, fortune and security for life in the process!

But we were, very much, unwitting pioneers for the future of black footballers in the UK. We contributed to changing the thoughts and expectations of the established order at grass-roots level. We helped to make it almost impossible for pro clubs to continue to ignore the abundance of talent in the black community, to a point where it would be tantamount to financial suicide if clubs resisted the recruitment of black players for much longer.

I learnt a lot from George about the importance of pride and integrity, the principles of man-management, and just being a decent and honourable human being in general. I grew to love and respect

George in the same way that I loved and respected his wife Pat (my second mum), and will always do so.

I recommended Ray to George, as well as my younger brother Obi, both of whom impressed enough to be signed by the club. They both did well, especially Obi, and both integrated into the club seamlessly. I really enjoyed playing in the same team as Obi for the first time. We understood each other's game after all those years of kicking a ball around on the streets and in our back gardens! Between the pair of us we scored lots of goals for YABAC and I think George saw us as reliable players who'd always contribute. However, after being a regular selection over the three seasons that I played for him, I was aware George was coming under increasing pressure from some players and club hangers-on *not* to play me. It seems I'd developed a reputation for being George's 'blue-eyed boy' which, in my opinion, was very far from the truth. George stuck to his guns and continued to play me, at times to the dismay and consternation of some members of the team, who had their own favourites and their own ideas as to who they thought should be first team starters.

George taught me the importance of showing loyalty in return for effort, and I never shirked on the effort side of the game. In fact George made it abundantly clear that, despite the references to 'superstar' YABAC players of the past, my statistics were comparable with the best, and better than most (and Obi's were even better!). But it must have been hard for him at times, because his integrity was being put at stake. I understood this and endeavoured never to let him down, so I put myself under pressure to perform to the best of my ability every time he selected me. I'm fairly certain I never disappointed him and justified my selections.

Sadly, George resigned as senior team manager at the end of my third year with the club. An 'old boy' ex-player, 'Budgie', took over the reins. He, in my opinion, didn't have the strength of character that George demonstrated. Budgie sat on the fence with me, so much so that he must still be pulling splinters out of his arse today! He was swayed by the grumbling minority in his team selections and, when he wooed another 'old boy' centre forward to sign, I knew my days were numbered. But I determined that it would be on my terms and nobody else's. Over the first four games of the new season Budgie picked me to start two, and brought me on as sub in two, on an alternating basis, in the other two. I scored six goals in what were effectively two full games. The 'old boy' ex-YABAC 'superstar' didn't score at all. This pissed me off as I knew my performances warranted starting selection, but I also knew that Budgie wasn't a strong enough character to do what was blatantly the right thing.

Our fifth game was a Surrey Cup match against Queens Park Rangers Supporters FC. We lost. An argument erupted in the changing room afterwards and, when I voiced my opinion, for some reason people thought I was going to get aggressive, which wasn't the case, I was just speaking my mind. The mutterings of discontent spilled over into midweek training, before which we met and were encouraged, as a team, to say what was on our minds, in the hope that things would improve. Again, I said what was on my mind, as did Obi.

Similar to the way our mum refused to suffer fools gladly, neither myself nor Obi were willing to do so either. It became clear during the contributions our team mates made that maybe it was better for us to leave the club. When the 'clear-the-air' discussion ended, and after the rest of the team had left the changing room to commence training, I held Obi back and told him I was leaving. He instantly agreed and said he'd leave also. That was it. We told George of our decision and asked him to de-register us when we'd found a new team to play for. George was devastated, and so were many of the team when he announced the news. Some actually ran after us to try to persuade us to change our decision. But it was too late. Enough was enough.

It seemed to me that the club needed a reality check. They were playing in the Morden and District Sunday League Premier Division, not in the first division of the English professional leagues! Sunday morning football is to be played and enjoyed for the love of football, to hell with the politics and shenanigans of some small-minded people! We weren't Real Madrid or Barcelona, we didn't have Christiano Ronaldo or Lionel Messi rocking up to play with us! We didn't need this shit and couldn't be persuaded by George or anyone else to return.

A couple of weeks later we went on to sign and play for a local rival club, Wandsworth Parks FC, which was made up mainly of black players and a few white guys. This club was far more fun to play for, they didn't take themselves too seriously, and we really enjoyed each other's company, and just as importantly, we could play! For me, the most important thing was to get good results against YABAC during that first season, which we did. We drew our first league match against them 3-3 (after being 3-0 down with five minutes to go, Obi scored two in our last-ditch revival, Hughie scored one and missed a one-on-one with their keeper as well (we should have ended up winning it!); knocked them out of the Morden and District cup semi final 3-0; and beat them 2-1 in the second league game - happy days! Race wasn't an issue at Parks. We'd all take the piss out of each other regardless!

The most hilarious moment came after our cup win against YABAC. Our captain Gary Rich was a fantastic left-footed white boy who was strong, could play, and didn't give a damn about race. As far as he was concerned, if you could play and you were on a level, you were all right by him. The cup game was, at times, brutally contested with emotions running high. We were down to the bare bones with Obi out injured (from the previous league match against YABAC!), and our first choice right back Smudger also sidelined. We were the underdogs who were expected to get a beating. However, the strength of character and camaraderie we shared proved too much for the YABAC superstar back-biters, who left the field at the final whistle bedraggled and bemoaning the decisions that didn't go their way, including a disallowed goal for blatant offside. In the shared changing room after the match, Gary Rich started talking in a Jamaican accent, which had us all cracking up with laughter to the point that we were pissing ourselves. The YABAC boys didn't see the funny side of it at all, but were too ashamed, embarrassed and deflated to raise any objections!

If my memory serves me correctly, Parks went on to win the league that season but we lost in the cup final. However, the only thing that mattered to me was that we didn't lose to YABAC that season!

Forty

Apart from a potentially difficult situation when Yvonne's ex-fiancé tried to intercept her at Thornton Heath train station (whilst I waited outside for her in my car), in a desperate possessive effort to win her back, our relationship developed very smoothly. We'd both met each other's families, her parents migrated to London from Guyana in South America and, like most first generation immigrants, they did so with the intention to improve the opportunities and prospects for their children. My parents fell in love with her instantly, and I think her parents felt the same towards me. I was shocked when both sets of parents met for the first time and both dads battled it out to offer libations to our relationship by throwing alcohol on the living room floor as they made speeches. I'd learnt in Nigeria that libations are par for the course when wishing and hoping for success, and didn't realise that it was yet another tradition that had survived the middle passage.

My mum even warned me that:

"If anything goes wrong between the two of you, don't come to me, I'm on Yvonne's side!"

Even more importantly, Yvonne's parents and family were really good people, and I could tell that she, and they, were the type of people I wanted to commit myself to forever.

Graduation Day – 1981

Forty-One

As a final year assessment for my nursing qualification we were required to produce and submit an independent research piece on a topic related to psychiatry. I chose to research the phenomenon of the high incidence of black African-Caribbean people being referred and admitted to psychiatric institutions. My impression was that black people were admitted at a far higher rate than any other group of comparison for the southeast London 'catchment' area. Not only were their admissions vastly disproportionate in terms of numbers, but also in terms of nature of diagnosis, especially and specifically, schizophrenia.

To cut a long story short, my findings were that these figures were quite likely to be the result of a toxic combination of contributory environmental factors, including: inherently racist police; the inherently racist education system; inherently racist employment trends; and inherently racist referral procedures and practices which, when combined with any possible genetic factors, led to a higher likelihood of mental breakdown.

Essentially, *pressure*.

It wasn't the case that black people, genetically, are more likely to become schizophrenic than any other group but, given the prevailing socio-economic and political pressures they endured, acute breakdown was more likely to be the outcome. Though potentially controversial at the time, my research was well received and I went on to qualify as a psychiatric staff nurse.

1981 saw me complete my degree at university. I got a 2 (ii) with honours which, in all honesty, was no more than I expected. I didn't really care much either. I could have got a first class honours degree, but that would have probably meant me foregoing the football and social side of university, spending my head buried in tomes, which really didn't appeal to me. Mum and dad were exceptionally proud of my achievement, which was far more important to me and it pleased me to see them happy. It hadn't dawned on me until many years later that I was the first person on either side of our family, Nigerian and Irish who, to our knowledge, had gained a university degree. Mum, dad and Yvonne accompanied me for the graduation ceremony which took place on campus, and I could tell dad was pumped full of pride as he strutted around campus as if he was a Dean of Faculty!

So, armed with a Joint Honours degree in Sociology and Psychology, and being a newly qualified psychiatric nurse, I started my first 'real' full-time job as a staff nurse on the 'Villa' ward at the Maudsley Hospital. This ward, at the time, was a locked ward for the 'criminally insane', so in some ways I felt quite at home working there!

I spent eighteen months on the Villa, and had a wide variety of experiences that served to both inspire and deflate me. I was a young, idealistic 24 year old who still felt he could put the world and its inhabitants to rights. How naive and wrong could I have been?!

The ward had communal sleeping arrangements for the more 'stable' patients, as well as lockable individual bedroom cubicles for the less stable, more florid and volatile patients. There were constant fights and attacks on the ward, committed against other patients and staff by patients suffering schizophrenia and 'manic depression' (bi-polar disorder in modern parlance), and regular suicide attempts by those suffering depression. I found the work fascinating and fully committed myself to the daily quest of treating the conditions that were presented by patients who I always saw as people with families who loved and cared for them.

The essence of the person always surfaced throughout the stay of each patient as they survived their interment. But for me it was impossible not to identify and empathise with each patient on a personal level. With the depressed and suicidal (mainly female patients), who needed constant supervision and monitoring; the floridly manically depressed patients who were either ecstatically happy or suicidaly low and, during these troughs, a very real danger to themselves; the schizophrenics experiencing auditory, visual, tactile and olfactory hallucinations, often zombified by a cocktail of heavy sedatory drugs as they pill-rolled their hands on their circuitous Frankenstein-type laps of the ward; the overly-sensitive and often self-deprecating neurotics who were in what seemed like a constant state of anxiety and self-doubt; and the psychotics with whom you were never quite sure whether they were smiling at you because they liked you, or because they liked the idea of killing you!

Every day was an interesting day at the Villa, full of highs and lows. It was an indescribably rewarding and satisfying job when patients you'd spent months treating, rehabilitating and preparing to return to the community, actually left. We were always full of hope for their future. It was equally as crushing when they returned, often just as 'mad' or as 'bad' as they'd been previously! For every success story, there was always at least one failure.

I remember arriving on the ward for an all-day (7.30am-7.30pm) shift, when I was met by a virtually fully-recovered female patient at the rear security double-door. Looking at her through the windows I could see that there was something wrong with her face. I could see her teeth which had been exposed by another patient who'd bitten her top lip off because God had ordered him during the night to cast the Devil out of her by so doing. She tried to explain what had happened to me but I couldn't understand her, because she couldn't speak properly. I went into the locked staffroom to find the whole night-staff team in shock and cowering in the safe haven that the room provided. I asked what had happened, and was told that a schizophrenic male patient who'd been transferred from the Bethlem Hospital for stabbing a nurse during the night had bitten her lip off. Not only hers, but another Turkish male patient's lip, and for the same reason, to cast the Devil out of him! I was then told that the lips had been placed in a petri dish in the medicine cabinet, in the hope that they could be sewn back on later! (I checked the petri dish, and there they were, the two lips, one with moustache still fully evident!). They were in fact taken over the road to KCH later that day, both patients and their lips, but to no avail, the lips couldn't be reattached successfully.

I asked about the newly-admitted 'biting' patient, and was told he was on his own in a locked cubicle. I felt uncomfortable with that, so I went up to the room. He was lying on his back in bed, gazing at one spot on the ceiling. I entered the room and sat beside him. I was shitting myself as I introduced myself to him. He introduced himself to me in return, before going on to talk me through the night's events as I held his hand. He was a small, wiry, dark-skinned Jamaican man in his mid-thirties. We chatted for up to an hour before I left him, and he was cognisant and contrite about what had happened. He felt he'd been ill-advised by God!

He remained on the ward with us for about three months before he was transferred to an open ward, and then back out to resume his previous life in the community. A couple of years later whilst walking up Denmark Hill I saw him walking towards me. I couldn't tell what state he was in, and was shitting myself again just in case he remembered me with any malice. He walked straight up to me and my heart leapt into my mouth. I didn't know what he was going to do, but I knew I didn't want him chewing my lip off!

He grabbed me, hugged me, shook my hand, and thanked me for being the only person who spoke with him 'like a human being' when he was going through his 'hard times'. I was *so* happy he'd made what appeared to be a full recovery, and so relieved that he hadn't bitten my lip off. But for every success, there's a failure, the stories don't always have happy Walt Disney-type endings.

Like the story of Big Cyril. Big Cyril was a well-built six foot two inch brown-skinned Jamaican guy who was brought in under section by six police officers who were struggling to control him. The emergency hospital restraint team (much like an armed forces SWAT team), was rushed to the ward to help the police restrain him whilst he received a forced sedative injection, and it just so happened to be my turn to administer the injection. I stayed on the periphery of the melee, jockeying for a position, waiting for the optimum opportunity to deliver the medical knock-out. This guy was *powerful*, and the struggle continued for a while until my opportunity arose. Feeling like a 'Great White Hunter' armed with an elephant gun (and I swear the contents of the syringe would have knocked out a bull elephant from one hundred metres!), I made my approach from behind, like a thief in the night, and plunged the syringe into the upper-and-outer quadrant of his backside, and just as I did so he turned round and stared deep into my eyes.

I've never forgotten the signs of complete hatred and contempt in that look, which was animalistic in its intensity and full of bad intent for the future. *My* future!

He spent several months on the ward before being discharged. He never spoke a word to me in all that time.

Six months later I was stuck in a traffic jam on Coldharbour Lane in Brixton, and who should I see walking along the path towards me on my driving side?

Big Cyril!

Instant terror and panic gripped me as my heart-rate soared to ridiculously high life-threatening levels. If he saw me I *knew* he would kill me! He'd rip the car door off its hinges, drag me out screaming for mercy, before ripping me to pieces! I saw the whole scene unfurl before my eyes, and saw the next day's newspaper headlines in my mind's eye:

"Ex-psychiatric patient murders nurse in Brixton walk-by assassination".

Not wishing to bring attention to myself from the already frustrated and irate drivers behind me, I could do nothing but duck down as low as I could get whilst still trying to manoeuvre my car inch by inch towards the traffic lights and salvation. As he came abreast of my car door he was inches from me, thankfully unwittingly so. He hadn't spotted me. A mere glance through my window would have been all that was necessary for his memories to come flooding back, and for him to bring about my inevitable demise! I could feel the blood pounding through my heart, coursing through my veins and thumping in my ears, sweat was pouring down my face, and anybody who may have seen me at that point in time would have wondered how this panic-stricken shrivelled dwarf of a hunch-backed Quasimodo looka-like was actually managing to drive a car!

Even up until today, if I saw Big Cyril, I'd run screaming!

I found it a bit disconcerting when I noticed that I'd started to emulate some of the mannerisms and behaviour traits of some of our patients. There's obviously an exceptionally thin line between sanity and insanity, 'normal' and 'abnormal'. I fully appreciated that concepts of 'normality' and 'abnormality' are culturally and socially determined, and vary within countries and over time, so something that may have been considered abnormal in 1970s Britain may today be considered normal. However, I started to think about other possible forms of employment that I might enjoy. The feeling of failure brought about by the constant revolving-door returns of relapsed patients was one thing to contend with, but copying some of their behaviour traits was *really* worrying!

The idea of teaching sounded great to me. Dedicating my life to enhance the prospects of others was, to my mind, a noble gesture and one that I thought would motivate me as a sustainable career. I liked the idea, so I researched teacher training programmes and, after fourteen months working as a psychiatric staff nurse, I resigned from the Maudsley Hospital to take up a place I'd been offered to start a one-year PGCE (Postgraduate Certificate in Education – Secondary level) teacher training course at Avery Hill College in New Eltham, southeast London, in September 1982.

Forty-Two

1982 was a momentous year for me for an even more important reason – Yvonne and I got married on August the 14th! I'd proposed to her the previous year and, when she accepted, I did the traditional thing and asked her parents and her Auntie Eileen (who was on an extended visit from Guyana at the time), for their daughter's hand in marriage. They were all happy to 'give their daughter away' to me, and my parents were equally, if not even more happy, to accept Yvonne into our family. So, we'd received the necessary 'blessings' from each other's families, everybody was happy, happy days!

Yvonne, who was working at a major American international bank in the City of London, did all the wedding plans. For months on end I worked and did a lot of minicab driving to make sure we had enough money to pay for our wedding, often for up to twenty hours a day. The only problem I had was that the ceremony was to take place in a church. Yvonne and both of our families wanted and expected the 'Full Monty'. I'd wanted the ceremony to take place in a registry office but, in the face of mounting pressure and to avoid disappointing others who I cared about, I relented. I understood that certain types of rituals are important to many people, and sometimes you just have to go along with the ritual to keep individuals and communities happy – so church it was!

It was a fantastic day, Smiffy was best man, and both families turned out in large numbers, along with many close friends and relatives. Yvonne exercised the bride's traditional prerogative to be late, by 45 minutes, so I was left nervously leg-shaking at the front of the church until she arrived and the ritualistic ceremonies proceeded. I had 45 minutes to do a runner and didn't take the opportunity. I was in this for the long haul!

Throughout the ceremony, vows and wedding-ring ritual (I gave Yvonne a ring, but didn't want one for myself), I couldn't help imagining the huge wooden effigy of Jesus nailed to 'The Cross' erupting away from its mountings high at the front of the church, in a shower of sparks, flames, lightning and thunder, arcing down to impale me as a sinner and one not worthy of marrying in this holy place! Needless to say it didn't happen and, after the photographs were taken amid a blitz of camera flashes (which was the only time I've ever felt like a famous superstar!), we all went to the church hall for the reception.

I enjoyed this part of the day most, with parents, brother and sisters, uncles and aunts, friends and relatives, all of whom made well-wishing speeches which were really appreciated by me and Yvonne (although I got a bit tense when Uncle Sammy referred to "you West Indies pipple" in recognition of our wedding symbolising Africa and the Caribbean coming together). Smiffy was *so* nervous he only managed to bumble partway through his speech, but considering the things we'd been through together in our adolescence, this was irrelevant to me. We'd survived 'the trenches' of the streets and had each other's backs through thin and even thinner, so flopping on his best man speech was nothing!

Auntie Eileen organised the catering, and the food was sweet! Rice and peas, chicken, roti, dumplings, fish, beef, it was glorious and so sweet that it was ravished very quickly so, 'belly full', the guests got straight into the drinking and dancing. The reception and music went superbly well, so well that strangers attending a house-party across the road actually left the party to join our reception!

Yvonne and I had already bought a terraced three-up-two-down in nearby Thornton Heath, where we spent our wedding night with mum, dad and Uncle Sammy, before we went off for our honeymoon in Devon the next day. For me though, the most important thing was that I'd married the only woman I'd met who I thought I could live with for the rest of my life, and wanted to have children with. I *really* used to worry about this because I'd had *so* many girlfriends that I thought I'd never meet 'the right person', and then, thankfully, I met Yvonne. I always wanted children but it had to be *only* with my wife, who I imagined I'd stay with forever. I'd learnt the importance of strong family bonds from our parents who, against all the odds, had set us a fantastic example, and I couldn't bear the thought of either having children outside of marriage (which to me is a public statement of commitment), having children with more than one woman, or having children with someone who I wasn't permanently living with (I hate the thought of another man exercising authority over my child).

I'm also certain it was probably even more important that my wife-to-be could actually bear living with me!

14th August 1982 – Our Wedding Day

Forty-Three

The teacher training course went well. I made a few good friends in the class, all of whom, though very different in terms of backgrounds and personalities, were idealistic and well-intentioned. It also helped that Avery Hill College had a very good football team. Again, I was the only trialist who made it straight into the first eleven to become a first-choice starter as centre forward. I ended the season as top goal scorer as we won the League and got to the final of the SEETECH cup which we lost 1-0!

The course itself, for me though, was pretty disappointing. In terms of content, some of it was based on refreshing our subject knowledge, so going over stuff we'd learnt at university. The remainder of the course was centred around the theory of teaching which, though useful to know in an abstract way, didn't really prepare us for what we were to meet whilst on our teaching practice stints which started in the spring term.

I was allocated to Kingsdale Comprehensive School which, at the time, was a typical inner-city post-war four-storey metal, glass and plastic prefabricated edifice, with some grassy areas to the front but surrounded by concrete playgrounds to the sides and rear. Incongruously, it was built on a very posh suburban street named Alleyn Park in Dulwich, a very salubrious area of southeast London. Many of the houses on the road were million-pound residences. Indeed, the famous Dulwich College was a five-minute walk around the corner, and Dulwich College Preparatory School was immediately next to Kingsdale.

It was obscene.

The prep school taught very small classes, whilst in Kingsdale a class wasn't thought viable unless it had at least thirty pupils! Even more obscene was the comparison of the grounds in which Kingsdale and Dulwich College were situated. Essentially, Kingsdale was modelled on a post-war inner-city design with what there was of the (high-rise) site surrounded by concrete. Dulwich College sits in acres of what appears to be rolling countryside, with expansive sports playing fields and tennis courts. It even had its own swimming pool and museum housing priceless artefacts of international renown!

If there ever was a case of the 'haves' and the 'have-nots' existing cheek-by-jowl in society, this was a prime example of exactly that. Dulwich College privately educated (to the tune of tens of thousands of pounds per year), the sons of the political elite, the rich, the powerful and the famous. Whilst 'mama' and 'papa' drove their precious little offspring to school in their Volvos, Mercedes and Land Rovers, they'd pass the hordes of mainly dishevelled, loud, unruly and unkempt-urchin-like Kingsdale pupils making their own way to school on packed London buses, or 'trodding' in stolen Nike trainers!

The extent of the inequality that existed between the two institutions couldn't have been made more explicit than one day when an armed robbery took place directly outside the Kingsdale school gates. Apparently, on the basis of a tip-off from a nark, the police were aware that a robbery had been planned to be executed outside the school, so they made a set of arrangements: closing both Dulwich Prep and Dulwich College, whilst not even bothering to *inform* Kingsdale! Timed to take place during a break time, with the playgrounds packed with pupils enjoying themselves, the robbery still went ahead. The cash-stuffed Securicor van was corralled and brought to a halt outside the school gates and, whilst in full swing, the armed police surrounded and cautioned the thieves, but they weren't prepared to come quietly, so started shooting, and the police returned fire. Worryingly, rather than run away petrified and screaming in terror to the safety of the inner school, our pupils ran to the perimeter fences to get a closer view of the action! Thankfully, none were harmed in the crossfire or by stray bullets, and they clearly totally enjoyed the excitement!

Even more worryingly was the fact that the police and 'the relevant authorities' were quite happy and prepared to jeopardise the safety of the comprehensive school pupils by not even bothering to give the school a 'heads-up', but they made sure the private schools in our immediate location were warned and closed for the day. Absolutely disgusting!

I *loved* my teaching practice at Kingsdale. The pupils were from very disparate backgrounds including Africans, African-Caribbeans, Indians, Pakistanis, Vietnamese, Irish, Turkish and working class white English. Virtually all of them were from working class backgrounds, and the majority lived in inner-city sink estates and council houses. Many of them were from single-parent families (though nowhere near as many as today!), and just as many were already alienated from and disaffected by the state school system. The school had a very small sixth-form centre, which largely existed to cater for those who actually managed to achieve the required number of GCSEs, so the class sizes at A Level were very small!

Initially I observed classes in the PSRE (Personal Social and Religious Education) Department, before I started to teach sessions independently. Essentially, I taught GCSE and A Level Sociology, with a bit of 'Social Issues' type enrichment classes. I was astounded by the apparent lack of social consciousness and awareness that seemed to prevail among the pupils. How could young people be born and bred in the inner-city and be *so* unaware of issues such as racism, sexism, prejudice, discrimination, inequality, differential opportunities and life chances *and* the importance of education as the tool to liberate themselves?

They all seemed blissfully or naively ignorant of the impact of differentials in power that would affect their lives directly one day. Of course they were aware 'life wasn't fair', but they never really understood, nor seemed interested enough to understand, the dynamics of privilege and power, and the relationship they had with these two aspects of life.

I was particularly dismayed with the almost total ignorance of 'black history' among the African and African-Caribbean pupils, who seemed quite happy to sit back and absorb without question the contents of the abjectly and overtly racist curriculum and delivery methods. It wasn't just that they received, absorbed and internalised stereotypical accounts of slavery, colonialism, innovation, and exploration without challenging these warped accounts, but that when confronted with alternative 'pro-black' accounts they appeared to resist, reject and be offended or embarrassed by them.

In essence, they just didn't want to talk about their 'blackness'.

They didn't want to talk about their origins.

They didn't want to talk about their history.

A sentiment often cited is that:

"Without knowledge of your past, you cannot determine your future".

Probably unsurprisingly, I subscribe to this sentiment.

In my view, people who are unaware of and disinterested in their past, their origin, their history, approach life from a position of weakness. Those who *reject* or feel uneasy with the idea of their ancestors having made vital contributions to the development and evolution of humanity and the human race are even more critically disabled. Such was the mindset of the majority of the young people I met at Kingsdale during my teaching practice. The overwhelming majority were bright, enthusiastic and had a real zest for life, but they didn't have questioning minds that challenged the power-elite-imposed status quo of 'truth and knowledge'.

In actual fact the complete opposite was the case. The thought, the idea of Africa and Africans, black people, having played any significant part in the evolution of humanity, was anathema to them. I got the distinct impression they were ashamed and embarrassed by their blackness which, in comparison with their white counterparts, was something that negatively affected their ideas of self-worth and dignity. In fact, when the intention was to insult and offend each other, they'd do so by *referring* to each other's blackness:

"You African!"
"You chief!"
"Nigger!"

And it wasn't just the black African-Caribbean pupils, mainly of Jamaican origin (there were very few African pupils attending the school at the time), who'd use such terms as a put-down, they were also just as liberally hurled by the Greek, Asian and white kids, at *anyone* they were rowing with. Such was the disdain 'blackness' was held in that it was used casually and pejoratively by *all* irrespective of racial or cultural background, without censure or reprimand!

'Blackness' associated with negativity had become normalised, accepted, expected.

Thankfully, I was able to relate to the pupils quite easily, probably because we shared many similar background characteristics and experiences. However, I wasn't prepared to compromise my integrity with regards issues of race and racism, and was always happy and ready to engage any interested young people (and members of staff!), in conversations and discussions that explored the issues. But it wasn't all heavy stuff. I had a laugh and a joke with them also, and wasn't afraid to pull them up on disciplinary type issues where necessary, and I like to think I successfully integrated equalities-type issues in my teaching that effectively began to break down barriers in their minds, and encouraged the students to start asking questions also.

Whilst I freely admit by the time I got to Highdown Comprehensive School in Reading my general approach to school had slipped, I still loved education and learning, and I never confronted or openly disrespected teachers in lesson or around the school. I couldn't believe how things appeared to have changed in such a (relatively) short space of time. The vast majority of Kingsdale pupils were openly resentful, disdainful, rude and contemptuous towards many of the teachers. It seemed they'd developed, for some reason, a debilitating sense of entitlement; debilitating in the sense that they hadn't developed a sense of responsibility and accountability to balance their sense of entitlement. The pupils knew their rights but had no idea or interest in fulfilling any tangible sense of responsibility for their actions.

It felt like a madhouse at times, with marauding disaffected pupils charging up and down the corridors with scant regard for either themselves or others. Apart from the crème-de-la-crème pupils who'd actually passed a sufficient number of GCSEs to progress onto sixth form to study their A Levels, the rest were very much members of the burgeoning counter-school, counter-education culture. Significantly, the A Level classes were very small, rarely reaching double figures in size per subject, and the majority of A Level students were white, from the (aspiring?) working class and established middle class (of whom there were very few), Asian (Indian especially), and one or two African-Caribbeans at most.

I found my lesson observation both amusing and interesting. Amusing because they took me back to my own schooldays and I imagined which of the pupils most reminded me of myself; interesting because of their attitude towards their education, which was disinterest and lethargy at best, and outright resentment and hostility at worst. Apart from those who were planning to join their dads' firms as electricians, plumbers, painters and decorators, or follow their mums into shop work, most of the pupils didn't seem to have an idea as to what they wanted to do in the future, and didn't seem to care particularly either.

Most alarmingly, rather than actively participate in their education, they seemed happier to absorb whatever they were spoon-fed like sponges, as if it were gospel. They rarely if ever questioned anything, rarely challenged that which was presented as 'the truth', or objected to anything they may (or may not) have found credible or acceptable. This was particularly the case with the portrayal and imagery of black people in history and general resources across the curriculum. Black people were invariably represented as slaves, servile, comical, underachievers and ne'er-do-wells (or a combination of all five!), or totally absent by their omission from academia. Even the A Level students were more concerned about 'being told' what to remember, think and do rather than making the effort to question so-called theories and truths.

Towards the end of my placement I was teaching A Level Sociology classes as well as a variety of PSRE lessons with the 14-16 year old pupils. I also volunteered to do after-school sessions in the school youth club, where you'd see an extension of their fun and ill-disciplined approach to life, school especially! It became abundantly evident that many had survived horrendous experiences, domestically and socially. Broken homes, alcoholic and drug-addicted parents, physical, emotional, psychological and sexual abuse, gang involvement and activity, petty theft, asylum-seeking (especially in the case of the Vietnamese 'boat people'), and rape (male and female).

Much like my school days, there were arguments, fights, thefts and confrontations virtually every week. Unlike my school days, the pupils appeared to do their utmost best to avoid culpability at all costs. Very rarely did I see a pupil 'put their hands up' and take responsibility for their actions. There was also a very elaborate 'shaping' ritual where pupils would, on the surface at least, get inordinately wound-up and angry, and *promise* and *threaten* to batter the shit out of each other, then fail to back it up with any action (unlike my school days!), but at least they'd been seen to go through the ritual!. Or they'd lose it completely and bring knives, bottles, snooker cues and cousins in to batter the shit out of each other (unlike my school days!).

Probably worse than all of this though, was the *state* of state education that these young people were being subjected to. Forget the obscene comparisons and contrasts between Kingsdale Comprehensive School and Dulwich College, poor and rich, powerless and powerful, insignificant and influential, have-nots and haves. While, in my view, the fee-paying public school sector remains an offensive insult to the masses, the sons and daughters of Mr and Mrs Bloggs, Mr and Mrs Reid, Mr and Mrs Begum, Mr and Mrs Ozdemir, Mr and Mrs Uddin and Mr and Mrs Nguyen, and more latterly Mr and Mrs Owusu, Mr and Mrs Ofori, Mr and Mrs Jokubaityte and Mr and Mrs Tomascinski, it is no less an insult when we look at the state school sector in isolation.

Despite decades of comprehensive schooling in the state sector, within which young people were supposed to receive an education that would enable them to achieve their highest potential regardless of their backgrounds, we still see the white(r) more middle-class pupils in the top streams where success is almost guaranteed, and the dark(er) more working class pupils in the lower streams where failure is almost guaranteed in equal measure.

Back at the Avery Hill teaching college I raised the issue of the differences between what we were being taught there, the 'theory', and the reality of what I'd seen in the classrooms. Some of my student teacher colleagues had similar tales to tell, but none seemed to be as intense as mine. It seemed demography plays a huge part in education: the more inner-city the school, the more intense the problems. Several of my colleagues were teaching in less inner-city, more suburban schools, and the rest in the leafier suburbs of commuter-land. None reported either the same extent or range of problems that I did.

Before completing the course we did another placement at other schools with the intention to broaden our experience. I was assigned to the Sacred Heart Catholic School for Girls in Camberwell, southeast London. Another inner-city institution situated down the road and round the corner from the Maudsley Hospital, where I'd trained as a Psychiatric Nurse.

I was beginning to wonder if I'd been typecast as some sort of 'inner-city' teacher!

Sacred Heart was a traditional red-brick single-storey building that looked like an old alms house next to Camberwell Green bus garage. It had very little greenery and was surrounded mainly by concrete playgrounds. If my memory serves me correctly, they only taught up to GCSE/O Level, after which the pupils who wanted to progress on to studying A Levels would need to do so in Further Education Colleges or other schools' sixth-form centres.

Whilst I'm aware that girls do much better in single-sex as opposed to co-ed schools, I didn't feel comfortable with teaching girls only. The feeling of discomfort and concern was exacerbated even further by the sight of the flock of pious nuns as they wafted around the school classrooms and corridors in their flowing black habits. I kept expecting them to burst into song every five minutes like Julie Andrews in The Sound of Music. Even more disconcerting and worrying were the smug, permanently self-satisfied (lecherous?) smiles (grins?) on the puffy red and alcohol-bloated faces of the male teachers. I've *never* worked in a place where everybody seemed so happy!

So I didn't trust the people, the teachers, who worked in the school. The pupils seemed fine and, despite the fact that they were being educated in a supposedly highly sought-after school, they appeared very similar to the pupils at Kingsdale, only less troubled and more self-disciplined (religiously-sedated?).

I really *couldn't* take the regular morning assemblies and evening masses that all teachers and pupils were required to attend, almost at the fear of excommunication from Heaven and everlasting paradise sitting at God's right hand if you should dare to miss one! If such a place exists, you just know it will be populated by a grey-haired white God, sitting on fluffy white clouds, listening to 'white people music' all day long. I bet there's no Bob Marley or Delroy Wilson blasting out from inside Heaven's Gates, with St Peter nodding his head in time with the beat, bass and ryddim!

I remember standing dutifully in the Chapel, attempting (on behalf of the pupils) my very best to look as if I was actually interested and 'believed'. This *really* made me feel like a sinner! Even more, it made me feel like I was being dishonest to myself, hypocritical, a thing I struggled to live with. I'd already jettisoned the Religion shit seventeen years earlier as an eight-year-old Conscientious Sunday School Objector, and I had no plans of picking it up again, either sincerely or insincerely, later in life as an adult.

Also, I didn't want to contribute to the dogmatically oppressive indoctrination process that religion (in general), and Catholicism (in particular), imposes on young people under the suffocatingly-cloaked guise of religion. Increasingly, divorce and marital breakdown was affecting Catholics in the increasingly secular 'modern' British society. Rather than succumb to such breakdown and be excommunicated, many families 'stayed together', which resulted in increasingly high levels of domestic violence and abuse of all family members (though mainly wives, mothers and children), through the resulting frustration.

As I looked at the huge and very graphic centre-piece image of Jesus on The Cross, blood flowing freely from the stigmata-inducing nails hammered into his hands and feet, from the crown of thorns on his head, and from the life-ending spear wound to his side, I wondered...

I mused that there's no surprise that domestic violence is on the rise these days if such iconic images of violence are internalised and become normalised through religious iconology.

I also wondered whether God, in his infinite wisdom, power and glory, had set us all a very good example, because even *HE* didn't get it right with his own people!

He set Adam and Eve up in Paradise, where they begat two sons, Cain and Abel. Eve (devious, conniving, not-to-be-trusted woman), fucked things up by enticing Adam to eat the forbidden fruit from their garden, which pissed God right off! He got the hump and, like any self-respecting profit-obsessed Peter Rachman-type rogue land-lord, He evicted them from the Garden of Eden (a great address if you can afford it, remember, location, location, location!). Then, to make things even worse, Cain was jealous of Abel, so he lured him out one day to farm the fields, where he proceeded to murder his younger brother in a fit of rage.

I'm sorry, but this sounds more like a poorly scripted episode of Eastenders than a credible account of the origins of humanity!

No plausible explanation is provided to explain how the earth became populated, other than the idea that God's totally dysfunctional nuclear family comprising a gormless and hapless Adam, deceitful Eve, murderous Cain and gullible Abel 'met with others' outside the Garden of Eden. Well who the fuck 'made' these *others*?!

And people are expected to believe this shit!

Just as sickening is the fact that denominational schools are considered to be *the* schools to get our young people educated in. People actually move house in order to fall into the right catchment area for highly sought after denominational school places! The birthplace and origin of the British education system was in the churches, where priests taught the privileged sons of the nobility. But times have changed, things have moved on. It should no longer be the case that a 'better' state education is associated with receiving denominational (preferably Church of England) education. Surely this only exacerbates social division, suspicion, resentment and unrest?

The solution, to me anyway, is fairly straightforward and simple. Get rid of the private schools, get rid of the denominational schools, invest our education budget into improving the state school system and, in so doing, remove the obscene advantage and privilege of the rich whilst improving the educational experience and life chances for *everybody*, regardless of social background. It seems to me that, if the sons and daughters of the rich, famous and powerful were educated alongside those of the 'less fortunate others', the education system and its provision would be improved immeasurably, because the rich and powerful wouldn't want to gamble on their own children's education, and would ensure *all* schools were up to scratch!

So, to hell with private and denominational education of any type or persuasion, I knew I'd receive far more intrinsic satisfaction and sense of purpose by teaching in the mainstream state school system.

On successfully completing my PGCE, I was assured by the attendant officiating dignitary at the graduation ceremony that I was:

"Exactly the 'type' of teacher that inner-city schools need."

Was this a back-handed compliment or what?!

I was offered a full-time teaching job back at Kingsdale Comprehensive School immediately after obtaining my PGCE as a Grade 1 (newly qualified) teacher. Within eighteen months I'd been promoted to Head of Year and Head of PSRE Department, which was one of, if not, *the* quickest promotions in ILEA (Inner London Education Authority) history. So I must have been doing something right!

I like to think I was setting a good example and role model for *all* the pupils, and enjoyed the steep learning curve I was experiencing.

In addition to encouraging high academic achievement, I also invested a lot of time and personal effort (voluntary and unpaid!), into developing other aspects of the school, like organising fund-raising events for a young black boy who was an exceptionally talented and gifted canoeist of Olympic standard potential; we raised enough to buy him a new competition canoe and accessories; writing the school's very first Equal Opportunities Policy; setting up and establishing a Black Parents Association; helping with the school football teams etc., which were all admirably worthy and, to my mind at least, vitally important requirements.

My early years of teaching were punctuated by Margaret Thatcher's austerity Britain, political turmoil and unrest, including, among other things, the continued application of the racist sus laws; the Falklands war against Argentina; the protracted miners' strikes led by Arthur Scargill, and the sympathetic and supportive teachers' strikes that followed; union-bashing; and a resurgent 'greed is good' culture. In short, it was a very politicised era that would change the face of Britain forever.

Other than the teacher-strike-induced days and weeks off school, the Kingsdale pupils didn't really show any awareness of, or interest to understand, the 'changing times' they were living in. I suppose like most young people, they were far more interested in fashion, music, and generally being young. Unfortunately for many, their parents didn't earn enough to be able to provide their children with all the latest must-haves, which resulted in many of our pupils robbing other young people of their Nike trainers and any other accessory considered desirable. Imagine, actually physically robbing another young person for their trainers, actually taking them off their feet!

I think the Thatcherite 'greed is good' mentality exacerbated perceptions of 'want' and 'need', and contributed to this type of behaviour among the young, which was soon to spiral into fights, gangs, and contemporary concerns regarding postcode violence. The concept of *relative* poverty was now beginning to replace that of the *absolute* poverty which I'd experienced as a child and young person. However, it would never have crossed my mind to rob somebody for their trainers, or anything else for that matter, but the 1980s were beginning to see in a totally new and different-minded young person who felt entitled to take that which they couldn't afford, but wanted, by any means necessary.

Among the many highs and lows I had in my early teaching experience, a few stand out in my mind.

First, after our Headteacher had left I happened to bump into a tall, light-skinned Jamaican black woman who was in school for interview. I *so* wanted her to be appointed, and wished her all the best of luck in her interview. She was successful, and was appointed. Greta Akpeneye was a very liberated, confident, strong, conscious, outspoken, intelligent, independent and politically aware woman who changed the philosophy of Kingsdale School forever and, eventually, aspects of my life.

The second experience wasn't so fondly remembered by me, but had a profound and long-lasting impression on me. I was in my second floor office eating my lunch. My office window overlooked one of the school playground exits onto the main road. I saw a puny little first-year white pupil being followed out of the school by a gang of excited and animated black male fourth-year pupils, who were clearly intent on terrorising him at best, and at worst beating the shit out of him.

I alerted my colleagues and was out of the office in a flash in order to intervene and stop the inevitable. By the time I'd crossed the road and entered the throng, the little kid was panic-stricken and traumatised, being held by the throat by DB, a slightly bigger bully, who was black. The white kid wouldn't say "Boo!" to a goose in and around the school on a good day, which probably made him the perfect victim for this baying bunch of cowards. I stood in between the two boys, telling the aggressor DB to release the little kid, which he did.

However, buoyed by his hyped-up crew, he grabbed me around the throat with both his hands instead!

I shouted at him to let go, but he was too full of false bravado, avidly encouraged by his 'boys'. When it became obvious, at the increased pressure he started to apply around my throat, that he didn't intend to let go, I grabbed both of his hands and pushed them down and away from me, and as I did so I felt both his thumbs snap in my hands.

DB wasn't known to me. I neither taught him nor was he in my year group, so I wasn't aware he suffered from brittle bone disease. He crumpled into a sobbing, quivering heap on the ground as his boys stepped back as one. On spotting his thumbs at odd and unnatural angles to his hands, I escorted him back into the building in order to call an ambulance and care for him until its arrival. The ambulance arrived, and he left, never to return to the school again.

However, his parents *did* come into the school the following day. Head teacher Greta called me to her office to let me know that DB's parents were on their way, and wanted to speak with me. Just before I left my office enroute to hers, she called me again to tell me they'd arrived early, and were fuming about what had happened to their son, and cautioned me *not* to meet with the parents. This perturbed me deeply. I felt it important for them to know exactly what happened, especially in terms of their son's bullying behaviour, so I made my way to Greta's office despite her request to the contrary.

As I approached the office I could hear a heated monologue of complaints being hurled at Greta. Not only were DB's parents angry that he'd been injured (despite the fact he'd been the bully and aggressor towards both the pupil and me), they were patently even more incensed at the thought that an '*AFRICAN*' teacher had intervened to stop their son from injuring and robbing another pupil!

"What! A bloodclaat *African* do dis to me son!"

This increased my desire to speak with the parents. Apart from the fact that what their son had done was *wrong*, how would *they* have felt if it was their son who'd been bullied in exactly the same way, and heard that teachers saw and ignored the incident? I have no doubt they'd have been equally incensed.

Greta saw me making my approach to knock on her office door. She sidled out and pleaded with me *not* to enter. She agreed 100% with my actions and motives for wishing to speak with the parents, but assured me it would be to no avail. I deferred to her advice and went back to my office, disappointed and frustrated.

DB never returned to the school. The last I heard of him was that he'd received a four year sentence for stabbing another youth relatively shortly after his last day at Kingsdale.

The third experience evolved in 1987, when I was informed of the opportunity to apply to participate in a teacher exchange programme to the Caribbean. The League for the Exchange of Commonwealth Teachers organised a programme of exchanges whereby UK teachers would go to the Caribbean (Jamaica and Trinidad), to teach in schools and colleges, with teachers from those same schools and colleges coming over to the UK to teach over a one year period. The idea of teaching for a year in the Caribbean appealed to me, especially Jamaica (and tax free!), so I applied. I was shortlisted for interviews, which were conducted on group, then individual bases. I was fortunate enough to get one of the sought-after places, and needed to plan for an August 1988 departure.

In my mind, I'd be tying up some loose ends. I'd lived virtually all of my life in England, I'd travelled to and been influenced by Nigeria, West Africa, so going to Jamaica would complete my travels throughout the triangular trade route.

I was excited, intrigued and, once my place had been confirmed, impatient for the exchange to commence. I'd be teaching A Level Sociology to 16-19 year olds in the Pre-University Department of Excelsior Community College (Exced), Mountain View Avenue, in the capital city of Kingston, Jamaica.

Forty-Four

A far more important event had taken place four years before my departure to Jamaica though, in the form of the birth of our first child, Kelechi, in March 1984.

Yvonne had had a fairly straightforward pregnancy, other than when we were involved in a car crash on Clapham Common when she was three months pregnant. A car smashed into the back of us, which led to Yvonne bleeding heavily and extensive clotting. We were in despair. We'd only recently revealed to our families that Yvonne was expecting, so the thought of losing our first child in this way was tragic for both of us. She was hospitalised and scanned, upon which we were reassured that the baby was still alive, thankfully!

She went full term and, in the early morning of 27th March 1984, Yvonne nudged me awake to tell me:

"Gossy, I think my waters are breaking".
Now, *I AM NOT A MORNING PERSON!*

So, despite the magnitude of the message Yvonne was delivering, it didn't register immediately. My early morning brain slowly started to click into gear.

'Waters', 'breaking'? The penny eventually dropped in my morning-befuddled mind.

"Your waters are breaking!"
"Quick, get out of bed, you'll mess up the sheets!"

At which she clambered out of the bed, and her waters broke all over the floor.

I sprang into action like a micro-waved slug, getting dressed and gathering Yvonne's pre-prepared antenatal hospital bag. I phoned Mayday Hospital to inform them that we'd be on our way and, within the hour, Yvonne was safely ensconced on the maternity ward, when I also informed both sets of parents.

Twenty one and a half hours-worth of contractions, gas and air, back-rubbing and general cajoling later, and still no sign of the increasingly distressed baby, it was discussed and agreed that the safest option was for Yvonne to deliver by caesarean section. This meant I wouldn't be able to witness the birth of my first child, which had been my dream, and I was gutted! But it was far more important for Yvonne and the baby's health to be prioritised, so I readily and happily greed.

Yvonne's parents, sister and several of her brothers had arrived during the day, and assembled on the grass verge outside the window of her room. Mum Daniels was especially anxious and became increasingly concerned and impatient as Yvonne's labour appeared to go on forever.

"What the hell is going on in there? Can't she hurry up?!"

Typical of that old-school hard-back 'get on with it!' approach to most things, including childbirth!

Our beautiful daughter Kelechi Sarah was delivered safely by c-section, and I can't fully explain the feeling when I first held her, my first child, in my hands.

I was instantly overwhelmed by an all-pervasive sense of responsibility and a powerful urge to protect her, it was unreal! She had a little button nose and a shocking mass of thick curly black hair. I was *so* proud and happy! My wishes had come true. I'd always wanted a girl as a first child, in deference and respect to our older sister Chi-chi, who ruled us with a rod of iron. That's exactly what I wanted for the sons who I wished would follow!

Yvonne returned to the land of the living after the effects of the anaesthetic wore off, and both our families were ecstatically happy at the news of Kelechi's safe arrival.

'Kele J' ceremoniously announced her arrival to the family by pissing all over the face of a junior paediatrician as he held her up to examine her, soaking him in urine delivered via a perfect golden shower!

As things transpired, we were informed by the attendant midwives and delivery doctor that Yvonne had a twin placenta. It seems her twin (likely to have been a boy), didn't survive the car crash at three months, which probably explained the excessive bleeding and clotting Yvonne experienced as a result.

To be honest, I was thankful for Kele J's safe delivery and arrival, and I've loved every day of being a father to her. She's beautiful, kind, intelligent, considerate, level-headed and exceptionally talented. She makes me feel proud and I'm happy to be her father.

Forty-Five

Sunday 14th August 1988, my departure date for Jamaica, eventually arrived. I went downstairs to notice something attached to our front door, which I went to investigate. On opening the door I was greeted by the site of a plastic life-size naked blow-up doll, a prank that my mates thought appropriate and hilarious, which it was. Probably like most young couples with children, Yvonne and I had made many friends with other young families in a similar position, some of whom lived on the same road as us. We'd developed a fantastic social life within our community of mixed, though mainly African-Caribbean, friends and neighbours.

By the time I was ready to leave for Gatwick airport, a large group of mates and their wives and partners had arrived to see me off, back-slapping and joking as they gave me their heart-felt advice. I wasn't expecting them all to follow us to Gatwick, but they did, in a convoy of about ten cars, it was mad, but I really appreciated the sentiments, and asked that they make themselves available to support Yvonne and Kele J if needs be. It was a promise they all made, with all sincerity.

The plan was for me to spend about a month in Jamaica to sort out suitable accommodation before Yvonne and Kele J came out for the remainder of the year. In the meantime, we'd rented our house out, so they'd stay at Yvonne's parents' home until they left for Jamaica.

I met up with the other teachers, three females, who'd also been offered places on the exchange in the check-in area. They were accompanied by only one or two family and friends, so my entourage of well-wishers felt a bit excessive and over-the-top, but I appreciated their support nonetheless. Two of the other teachers were black, of Caribbean origin, one was white English who, like me, had no familial links (or otherwise), with the Caribbean at all.

Our flight was delayed by several hours, so we had the time to get to know each other, share our experiences of applying through the exchange process, and our hopes and concerns for the year ahead. Once airborne, the flight was problem-free, and I, along with most of the other passengers, made full use of the complimentary rum being served throughout its duration! These were the days when smoking was still permitted in aeroplanes, so a very convivial bar-like atmosphere very quickly developed among us all.

Nine hours later we started our descent to Norman Manley International Airport, Kingston, Jamaica, which is situated on a peninsula that juts out into the Caribbean Sea, very close to Port Royal, a small town famous for its history as a pirates' Sodom-and-Gomorrah-type haven, as well as its defensive fort, and slave-holding centre. At night, the descent is beautiful, with the lights of Kingston twinkling through the tropical darkness. Very much like our arrival in Lagos, Nigeria, I was once again struck by the intense heat and humidity as soon as the doors were opened. Again, like Nigeria, I was profoundly impressed and affected by the site of so many *black* people, ground staff, officials, stewardesses and pilots, going about their working lives.

It occurred to me that 'what else should I expect?!'

And probably more significantly, 'why should I expect anything different?'

Probably as a direct result of 31 years of insipid, covert, subliminal psychological conditioning?

Growing up in racist British society in which the overwhelming majority of positive, important, powerful, influential, authoritative role models are white?

More than likely.

We were met at the airport by the exchange coordinator from the Ministry of Education, who would be responsible for our settling in to the system, including overseeing our accommodation arrangements.

She was a very pleasant brown-skinned black woman, very prim, proper and correct, her features suggesting a mixed African and Chinese heritage. She explained that we'd be taken on the Ministry minibus to the Shortwood Teacher Training College where we'd stay for the first week before going to our respective accommodation.

Having passed the many waiting families and friends of arriving passengers in the external arrivals area, with their eyes peering closely at each and every tired traveller, we bundled our luggage and ourselves into the waiting minibus. I couldn't help but marvel at the sea lapping against the sandy shores of the peninsula as we drove down it towards Harbour View on Norman Manley Boulevard and into Kingston. The peninsula was, at some stages, only about fifty metres wide (at most), and I couldn't help thinking that it wouldn't take much of a high tide to submerge the road that ran its length. Turning left at the Harbour View roundabout and heading past the Mineral Baths at Rockfort towards Kingston, I was impressed with the state of the roads and cars, and was also aware of sporadic reggae music emanating from clusters of communities while we made the twenty minute drive to Shortwood. The closer we got to 'town', the more populated the communities became, and the blaring of music amplified even louder.

Though late in the night, just like in Nigeria, it appeared much life was lived publicly, with people out on the roads, propping up bars, listening and swaying to music and generally enjoying themselves. We hooked a right off the Windward Road onto Mountain View Avenue, a long road cut into the Wareika Hills (famous for its reputation as being the main area where the gunmen hid their guns!), that linked old Kingston to new Kingston, traversing the Old Hope Road. Halfway along the road the coordinator pointed into the dark to tell me "That's where you'll be teaching, that's the Excelsior Community College campus". I couldn't see anything in the dark of night and the poorly lit roads, but it was clear 'Exced' was in a 'semi-depressed' area (a common euphemism used in Jamaica for ghetto!).

We settled in for the rest of the night in individual student teacher rooms at Shortwood and, just like Nigeria, the mosquitoes obviously smelt fresh blood, and descended in swarms to feast upon us. We'd been given some mosquito coils by the coordinator, but it seemed as if the mosquitoes had developed contempt for them, and they gorged on us!

We were up after a few hours sleep, and had breakfast, before waiting for the coordinator and Ministry driver to pick us up. One of my colleagues had been directed by her bank in London to open her account at a particular branch of Barclays on King Street in downtown Kingston. We'd been on the island for five or six hours, and already the morning sun was shining, with temperatures soaring through the eighties, it was hot!

Relaxing in the minibus on our way downtown, enjoying the soft breeze flowing through the open window, I soaked up the sights and sounds as we made our way: the blue, cloudless sky; the bright sunshine; the tropical flora; humming birds refuelling with nectar, and "John Crows" (carrion crows, turkey vultures), as they circled lazily on warm thermals on the hunt for prey; the houses; the people; the square Lada cars; the area "dargs" (dogs) that made aggressive barking, feinting runs at the minibus in defence of their territories; and the scruffy little boy who shot a finger-pistol-gesture directly at our bus behind dark, deadpan eyes.

I asked the coordinator to confirm that Kingston *didn't* have an underground tube system, because I'd heard and felt rumblings during the night, at the Shortwood hostel. She reassured me that "No, we don't have an underground rail system like London. What you felt last night were little earth quake tremors, which we haven't had for years".

She said it *so* casually, "little" earth quake tremors!

"Little!"

Fucking hell! I had no previous idea that Jamaica, indeed the Caribbean, suffered from earth quakes! Let alone us sitting right on top of an active earth quake fault line! On the surface I made light of it, and joked about my reaction, and we all laughed, but secretly, deep down, Yvonne's and Kele J's faces were flashing through my mind, I couldn't bear the thought of anything happening to bring trauma to our lives!

Looking at the faces of people as we passed, apart from the light-skinned and obviously mixed, I couldn't see many differences between them and West Africans, Nigerians especially. There were no visible clan striations, but many with grotesque and often keloid facial scars, acquired as a result of knife and machete wounds by the looks of them.

We passed National Heroes Circle (sometimes referred to as 'Park'), where Bob Marley famously bought together the warring factions of the Peoples National Party (PNP – leader Michael Manley), and Jamaica Labour Party (JLP – leader Edward Seaga) political parties at the 'One Love Peace Concert' in 1978; then the Education Ministry building on the left as we entered downtown.

'Downtown' is designed and built on very similar bases to the American grid system of street planning, in blocks running north, south, east and west. The architecture, in the most part, consists of many dilapidated and deteriorating colonial and post-colonial edifices, with crumbling verandas and previously ostentatious though by now cracking concrete steps and balustrades. Dingy and unkempt, though nowhere near as badly maintained as those in post-civil-war Biafra, the buildings, houses and work places of downtown Kingstonians were in desperate need of repair. The ravages of historical and systemic poverty and political unrest were clearly evident on many of the buildings, and on many of the faces of people, downtown.

We parked immediately outside the entrance to the bank. My three teacher colleagues went inside with the coordinator, who maintained her very conservative but pleasant, prim and proper (PPP) countenance at all times with us, she was very 'school-marmy'. She Miss PPP warned us *not* to go downtown, *ever!* It was, she went on to advise us, *too* dangerous, so dangerous in fact that 'uptowners' rarely, if ever, ventured further south than Cross Roads, let alone all the way down Slipe Road to downtown. She warned us about so many things, dos and don'ts, all of which I decided I *must* do as soon as the opportunities arose.

I chose to stand outside the bank on King Street with the Ministry driver and 'take in' Jamaica, my first experience of the Caribbean. Whilst chatting with him it soon became clear I'd need to 'develop an ear' to enable me to understand '*Jamaican*' Jamaican, proper, real, raw Jamaican, not the fake version I'd become familiar with in the UK.

Prior to arriving in Jamaica, I *thought* I could understand Jammohs!

I was almost in a trance-like state, absorbing the new and alien sights, sounds and smells: car horns hooting; people shouting, talking and singing; heavy bass music thrumming from battered roadside speakers; scrawny dogs lolling in the heat; school children, 'schoolers', laughing and skipping in their khaki, blue and pristine white school uniforms; lorries coughing out plumes of rancid black smoke; 'higglers' operating their own version of Nigeria's 'bend-down-boutiques' selling second-hand used clothes on corners and sidewalks; ingenious home-crafted trolleys piled high with goods for sale being gracefully steered by their inventive owners, darting in and out of the downtown throng; "box-juice" and "bun-and-cheese" being shouted then sold; fresh coconut water vendors hacking the tops off the kernels with their sharp, glistening machetes; the general hustle and bustle of a Caribbean capital city's commercial centre.

And I plummeted into an even deeper trance-like state when bullets started fizzing past me, front and back, missing me by inches as they slammed into and ripped up their targets standing mere feet away from me.

Gunshots are *loud*, especially when they're discharged at such close range, and the smell of cordite is distinctively choking!

A security van was in the process of delivering money to the bank and, as soon as the delivery guard stepped out, gunmen appeared from nowhere and began shooting in their desperate bid to rob the guard of the money he was delivering. He returned fire as both sets battled it out.

And I froze. I just stood there as war raged around me. I don't know how I wasn't shot, gunned down as an innocent bystander, it was incredible! I still remember the feeling; it was like I had a front-row seat at a four-dimensional gangster movie, or a John Wayne-type spaghetti western. Everybody else 'got flat' (a term used to describe ducking down when shots were fired in order to avoid being hit).

And I just stood there like a complete and absolute knobhead!

Though, in all honesty, I was exceptionally lucky to be alive! I seem to remember at least two people dying in the exchange of hot lethal lead, but the gory image of lead-induced blood and guts remains with me til today. What an introduction to Jamaica!

I was left thinking:

"Fucking hell, it's true what they say about Jamaicans, they're all bloody bad or mad!"

I was later to learn that there was nothing further from this 'truth'.

Miss PPP (Pleasant, Prim and Proper), and my three colleagues were totally oblivious to what was happening outside. They took hours setting up the account (nothing gets done quickly in Jamaica or Nigeria!), and, when they eventually emerged to meet us at the mini-bus, they didn't believe what I told them. Miss PPP asked the driver for confirmation, which he gave her and then, right on cue, the incident was announced over the car radio. Miss PPP still struggled to believe it:

"I've lived in Kingston all my life and I've never witnessed this sort of thing. Gus has been here ten minutes and he's been right in the middle of it!"

I wasn't sure if she was telling the truth, or delivering a perceived much-needed PR pitch on behalf of Jamaica, or she may well have been one of these uptowners who'd never dream of going downtown! I wasn't to know, and didn't particularly care, she was a decent person and meant well.

The following day, and several mosquito bites later, Miss PPP arranged for us to complete our induction at the Ministry of Education. We met with Ministry 'dignitaries' and 'notables', and it struck me how formal Jamaicans are when addressing each other. First name terms clearly wasn't the done thing, it was "Miss This", "Miss That", "Mr This", "Mr That", and I wondered why this was the case? Was it that Jamaicans actually were extremely formal for formality sake, or was it a throwback to some distant time-frame where showing a deferential attitude when speaking with others was necessary, the established order, custom and practice? If it was the latter, then, yet again, another relic passed on from slavery days. It would have been a life-saving essential for a slave to show such fawning deference to their master, but 150 years later? Notwithstanding my 'downtown experience' (which was *the* topic of conversation at the Ministry!), I was developing the impression that, far from its risqué reputation, Jamaica was, in fact, a very conservative member of the Commonwealth!

Miss PPP then arranged a two-day trip for us to visit 'country' (basically, anywhere and everywhere outside of Kingston), which would include us staying overnight in the tourist resort of Ocho Rios after visiting the famous town of Accompong, a historical Maroon village located in the parish of St Elizabeth, approximately forty miles south of Montego Bay in the northwest of the island. The name Accompong derives directly from the Ghanaian family name Acheampong, and the town was consolidated by a treaty in 1739 after runaway rebel slaves (maroons) fought for, won and maintained their freedom and independence from their plantation owners and, more significantly, British military rule. We all looked forward to the trip.....

Jamaica is BEAUTIFUL. As a country, *the* most beautiful place on the face of the earth (of those that I've visited anyway!).

We left Kingston via Marcus Garvey Drive onto Spanish Town Road, passed Racecourse before entering Spanish Town, which for 300 years was the original capital city of Jamaica. Much of the scenery on the route is characterised by sugar plantations and, again, I couldn't help wondering what things would have been like in slavery days for those toiling under the glare of the relentlessly blistering hot sun, in fear of the overseer's relentlessly blistering hot whip. Spanish Town is now the historical and administrative centre, and the location of the national archives. As might be expected, Spanish architecture is prevalent in the old town which, again, was built on a very tight grid system. The national archive centre was particularly interesting, especially with regards providing a snapshot of slavery and the slave trade as it impacted on the island. The Spanish were the original invaders, pillagers and looters of the island, hence the name of the old capital city, and were responsible for the genocidal slaughter, enslavement, and eventual death-by-European-disease and forced labour imparted on the island's original Arawak inhabitants. Jamaica was 'lost' by the Spanish to the conquering English in 1655 as part of the British expansion of empire.

In fact, England's first foray into trading in African slaves materialised as a result of English pirates ransacking a Spanish ship in the Caribbean Sea, upon which (and among other items of commercial value and worth), were eight African slaves, all of whom became the property of their new European captors.

After Spanish Town we set off for Accompong, the maroon village located in the hills of the parish of St Elizabeth. Off the beaten track, the minibus bounced its way through the rutted terrain, deeper into the densely forested cockpit country of the island.

Accompong was unbelievable; it was almost as if time had stood still deep within the hilly, mango-tree-shrouded community. It didn't take any effort to imagine this secluded maroon retreat during the days of slavery. The houses were very basic, and the overwhelming majority of the people were undeniably of direct West African descent. In accordance with West African tradition, one of the village elders took main responsibility for educating us about the history and struggle of the maroons.

It was awe-inspiring listening to his tales of the Accompong family of brothers, and their sister Nanny, who'd been stolen into slavery from Ghana, and how they ran away from their plantations to set up a retreat high in the hills of cockpit country where they could mount successful resistance against their owners and the might of the British military by employing guerrilla war tactics that led to their independence and autonomy. He even stated that, in their 250 year history (up to that point), they had never experienced crime in their community!

As we left Accompong I felt totally uplifted, proud of their achievements, and impressed with their resolve and fortitude, though a little disappointed at the knowledge that they eventually signed a peace treaty with the British authorities which involved them no longer providing sanctuary for future runaway slaves. What price freedom?

Our circuitous trip took us through Mandeville, down the infamously steep and swirlingly dangerous Spur Tree Hill, through Bamboo Avenue and Savannah-la-Mar, into Montego Bay and on to Ocho Rios, where we stayed in a tourist hotel overnight.

I knew I hadn't yet seen all of Jamaica, but I'd already made up my mind that it is incontestably *the* most beautiful place on the face of the earth. It was impossible for me to imagine anywhere else that could match Jamaica's natural beauty, including: standing on Hope Road in Liguanea and peering up at the Blue Mountains keeping an almost regal watch over Kingston; the ornate Spanish architecture of both downtown Kingston and Spanish Town (previously known as St Jago de la Vega); the vast and rustling-in-the-breeze sugar cane plantations; the cooling island breeze itself; crossing over the Rio Cobre on 'flat bridge' in the steeply-wooded Bog Walk; the sweet yet overpowering smell of citrus as you tunnel through Porous; the life-affirming warmth of the sun; the big-dipper descent down Spur Tree Hill after leaving the cooler climes of Mandeville (popular for 'returnees' due to its cooler climate); hurtling through the mesmerising majesty and hauntingly whispery shade of Bamboo Avenue; the smell and taste of freshly caught fish being fried to gastronomic perfection at any and every stop-off point; the crystal clear blue and turquoise sea that laps against the soft yellow and white palm-tree-fringed seven miles of sandy beaches in Negril; sunset off Negril Point; the spectacular sites of Runaway Bay and Discovery Bay on the north coast; the babbling brooks of Dunn's River in Ocho Rios as it cascades into the Caribbean sea; the three-mile long rocky gorge of Fern Gulley in the parish of St Ann's (slippery when wet!); the eerily daunting edifice of the Rose Hall Plantation (of 'White Witch' notoriety); the wild and rugged coast of the banana-producing area of Oracabessa; taking a dip in the Blue

Lagoon, where cold fresh river water meets warm salt sea water; salivating deliriously over the open-pit charcoal-cooked pimento- and scotch bonnet-flavoured jerk chicken (and pork) in Port Antonio; marvelling at and reminiscing over the statue of Paul Bogle in Morant Bay, who led 200-300 slaves in a major rebellion against slavery in 1865 that changed the history of Jamaica and featured highly in the emancipation debate; the historical fort and sinking 'Giddy House' of Port Royal; luxuriating in the mineral baths of Rockfort; eating the succulent fried fish, bammy and festivals at Hellshire Beach. *So* many wondrous attributes in such a small island of potential, perfect paradise.

I've since visited Barbados, Trinidad, Haiti, St Lucia and Cuba in the Caribbean, and Guyana in South America, and none come anywhere close to matching the natural beauty and awe of Jamaica.

Forty-Six

We spent the remainder of our first week in Kingston completing our induction, and finalising accommodation arrangements which, for me at that point, were non-existent. Accommodation for my three colleagues had been successfully arranged, and I was scheduled to meet with a senior female member of the Education Ministry staff who'd be taking me to view a bedroom in a family house located in Papine, a community partway up the Blue Mountain, situated directly adjacent to the University of the West Indies.

I met her at the appointed time, and we walked to her car. Before she got in, she said a prayer. As soon as she was strapped firmly into her seat, and after having instructed me to use my seatbelt, she switched on the ignition, and said a prayer, beseeching The Lord to ensure our safe deliverance at the address in Papine!

As you can imagine, I was shitting myself at this point! I was now entrusting my life in the hands of a person who was *so* devoid of confidence in her driving ability that she actually appealed to The Man Big Man Upstairs for our safe guidance and delivery!

As we stuttered and kangarooed out of the Ministry car park, I understood exactly why she'd performed the ritual. She was *the* worst driver I'd *ever* had the life-endangering misfortune to be driven by, including my reckless teenage 'boy-racer' mates and an assortment of Nigerian taxi drivers! We had *so* many near-misses on the 30 minute drive out of downtown to Papine (it should only have taken about 15-20 minutes, tops!), it was ridiculous! Nevertheless, we reached our destination and, on switching the engine off, she said *another* fucking prayer, thanking The Lord for delivering us safely. I was a sweating, hyperventilating, heap of a nervous wreck who, once out of the vehicle, used a few seconds to compose myself before meeting my potential landlords.

It was a lovely house and I liked the area and family, but they wanted to impose too many restrictions on me, including curfews, friends, drinking etc. – no way! I was a 31 year-old married man with a 4 year-old daughter. I wasn't about to accept being treated like a teenager again. But the realisation began to dawn on me that Jamaica was, or appeared to be (on the surface anyway), a very reserved, conservative country, within which much of its culture and relationship-dynamics were based on the formal traditions of a by-gone era, which was *not* for me!

Disappointed, disillusioned, and despairing at the thought of re-entering the car, we left, for me to be dropped off at Shortwood after several more near-misses and worryingly profound prayers of deliverance! I was quite cool about things though, as I felt certain my accommodation issue would soon be sorted out.

Our first Saturday saw my three colleagues leave Shortwood to their accommodation. We arranged to meet that evening in New Kingston, and caught a taxi to Liguanea where we had a drink in a run-down local bar. Reggae music thumping through outdoor speakers, we relaxed, chilled out and swapped notes on our first week's experiences. It wasn't long before we were approached by a rum-soaked gravel-voiced regular of the bar:

"W'appen don..... evryting cool?"

I assured him that everything, indeed, was very cool.

"You a police?"
"No".
"Oh, sarry sah, mi did tink you a police true you a brown and big soh and wear that certain type a ganzi (shirt), you look like police. Be careful where you ah go, some people might not ask first!"

This unsettled me slightly. The thought that I generically resembled a plainclothes police officer due to my skin colour, size and the way I dressed was worrisome enough, but the thought of 'some people' not asking first before 'acting' concerned me even more!

He went on to explain aspects of life in Jamaica, Kingston in particular, and his version presented a far more cautionary and sobering account than that offered by Miss PPP. We enjoyed his company, he enjoyed ours, and the drinks we were buying! Several Dragon Stouts, Red Stripes and White Rums later, he conspiratorially leaned over to whisper in my ear:

"A you one control all tree a dese ooman?"

He was very impressed at the idea that I was 'controlling' (having affairs with) my three colleagues! I assured him that wasn't the case, with any of them, which led us into a discussion about our purpose in Jamaica. It was clear he was bitterly disappointed in the knowledge that I wasn't 'controlling' them!

I liked the less formal dynamics of the rum bar, with music, dominoes, and shouted conversations erupting everywhere around us. I felt far more relaxed in the company of spontaneous, non-pretentious people. We each hailed cabs home after our first 'independent' night out, my 'home' being back at Shortwood.

With nothing to do on the Sunday, and on my own, I thought I'd take a walk, downtown. After surviving the bank raid shoot-out I'd noticed an old harbour at the bottom of King Street, and couldn't resist the urge to stroll down to the harbour and generally 'take Kingston in' on my own. So I took off, unaccompanied, on the half-hour walk downtown. I'd remembered the route by vicarious learning, and strolled past National Heroes Circle after looking at all the commemorative statues of Jamaica's heroes of historical note, and the mango tree strangely festooned with weather-worn strips of paper.

The deeper downtown I got, the more I began to realise that places look and feel different than they do from the safety of the inside of a minibus. I didn't realise that King Street was *so* dilapidated and 'ghetto' – *real* ghetto, nothing like the so-called 'ghettos' that dispossessed council estate dwellers in England often complain about and provide as reasons to justify their underachievement and social exclusion. I'd unwittingly walked into Trench Town, notorious for its drug activity, gang activity, and violence. Looking back I often wonder what was going through the minds of the Trench Town inhabitants as they watched me stroll (affectedly) nonchalantly through their midst.

Had it been they thought I was 'a police', I don't think I'd have got out alive.

So they must have thought I was either a relatively well-dressed madman, or that I was somebody 'from farrin' who'd obviously got *way* lost.

I made it to the old harbour after crossing the Harbour Street intersection, deep downtown, where I "sat at the dock of the bay, watching the tide roll away". I took a few photos, smoked, and generally daydreamed some time away. A ganzi-less young man in his mid-twenties had been sitting twenty or thirty yards away from me. He was tall, slim, wirily muscular and clearly a Trench Town resident of the most dubious type. He ambled over to me to sit next to me and started making small talk.

It very quickly became evident to me that he was sizing me up to rob me. So I got up, ostensibly to bid him farewell, but really to ensure I was ready for his attack, which very quickly ensued. He flashed the ratchet knife that had been in his cut-down-jeans shorts, which glinted in the sun's rays as he slashed at my throat area. My fight-or-flight survival mechanisms sprang into action, pumping much-needed adrenalin around my tense and coiled body. Somehow, I managed to evade his potentially fatal lunge to deliver a wild right-hander to his temple, which only succeeded in stunning him slightly. This guy was a desperado with lethal intent! His second lunge, again at my throat, missed but caught the 18-inch gold rope chain that I was *stupidly* wearing around my exposed neck. I don't know how I made it walking all the way through Trench Town down King Street with it on display. It snapped into several pieces before hitting the dusty concreted ground and, even more stupidly, I stooped to pick it up. As his knife arced high from the sky it occurred to me that he'd settle for the possession of my rope chain without having to murder me for it. So I dodged the knife's trajectory and made good my scampering escape to the forecourt of a run-down hotel on the corner of Harbour Street.

I'm *so* glad my common (Igbo?) sense kicked in when it did. Any later, and I'd have been stabbed, skewered to death over a rope chain. But it wasn't just any old rope chain. Yvonne had bought it for me.

I've never, ever, related the truth about this incident to anybody since.

In retrospect, it was my fault. No way on earth should I have walked downtown, in fact anywhere that I was unfamiliar with, wearing an exposed gold chain around my neck, let alone in the ghetto of the dispossessed. Yvonne was later to ask me what had happened to my chain. I told her I was wiping the sweat off my head and neck when it got caught in my hanky, snapped off and fell into a roadside storm drain. I didn't want her worrying about me.

After the shock had worn off and the adrenalin had settled, composed, I began the long, lonely, and now knowingly far more dangerous and intrepid walk back up King Street towards National Heroes Circle. Feeling intensely vulnerable and sweating like a Christmas goat (Christmas turkey in England!), I was now even more acutely aware of the bemused, inquisitive looks I was attracting on my excessively paranoid ascent to safety. Everybody, in my mind, was a potential assailant with murderous intent. On reaching Cross Roads I at last felt safe, stupid, but safe!

Forty-Seven

In view of my continued homeless status, Miss PPP had made contact with a senior lecturer at Exced, Ivor who, very kindly, agreed for me to stay at his fairly new-build bungalow-style house off Constant Spring Road (on a temporary basis), 'uptown', for which I was exceptionally grateful. The student teachers would soon be returning to the Shortwood campus to continue their studies, so I could no longer stay in residence there.

Ivor was a very dark skinned man of mixed African-East Indian descent. He talked me through the expectations at Exced, and took me out to a few bars and places of interest during the lead-up week to my arriving at Exced for student enrolment, which was due to commence on Monday 5th September. Ivor was well-known and respected in the area, and even more so in the more semi-depressed area that he originated from. During the first week that I stayed with him and his live-in girlfriend, we received a couple of visitors one evening. They'd come to report to Ivor on their attempts to avenge the robbery of a female community worker in their area. The three robbers had been identified, ensnared and attacked by these two guys and their accomplices. But the guys were disappointed. They'd failed to actually *murder* the robbers and expressed a huge sense of regret, shame and guilt at their ultimately vain and frustratingly futile attempts to finish the job off! They graphically re-enacted the scene:

"Boss, we did jook dem so much time, mi cyan believe dem no dead, cyan believe it! We jook dem, jook dem, jook dem so til, and dem still nah dead. Mi never see a man get wet up so much and dem still nah dead!"

I went cold as I tried to portray a cool, calm, composed and familiar exterior, nodding in agreement with the sentiments they'd expressed to justify their attempted predetermined multiple murder. Based on my own experiences after a couple of weeks, I knew I had to be extra-vigilant throughout my time in Jamaica and, at the very first opportunity, I bought myself a ratchet knife that never left my pocket for the whole duration of my stay – just in case.

Monday 5th September 1988 and we were driving down Mountain View Avenue, cut into the Wareika hills, past the rear of the National Stadium, towards the Exced campus. Big Ivor pointed out the communities in the area, Nannyville around the arena, and neighbouring Back Bush on the northern side of Mountain View Avenue. Apparently, the two communities, 'garrison towns', were constantly at war with each other over divergent political affiliations, Nannyville PNP (red), Back Bush JLP (green).

We entered the rusty iron gates at the top of the entrance drive to Exced. It was manned by a grizzly, old, shiny-skinned black guy wearing a fading khaki uniform that had clearly seen far better days. He stood his watch with his even older and grizzlier security dog, and both he and the dog were far too pleasant to provide serious security. The college was built of yellowish-brick, of which there were two large main buildings of two floors, where the majority of teaching and administrative work took place, a single-storey library-cum (obsolete) computer and IT centre, and a few stripped- and shelled-out converted old buses, which were hitched up on breeze blocks and used as make-shift classrooms.

Ivor introduced me to some of the members of staff I'd be working with, including Earl (Head of Humanities), secretarial staff and other lecturers waiting to commence the interviewing and enrolment process with new and returning A Level students, one of whom, Charles, 'looked' *very* Igbo. Earl showed me around the campus and gave me a brief induction before I joined the others in the interview room. Overhearing Charles during several interviews I was convinced he actually was Igbo, though he'd developed a bit of a Jamaican twang to his pronunciation. I couldn't resist asking him:

"Charles, are you Igbo by any chance?"
"Yes, why do you ask?"
"I'm Igbo too".
"Which part?"
"Imo State".

At which he dived out of his seat, totally ignoring the student he was in the process of interviewing, grabbed me laughing and screaming, shook hands, and then the inevitable.
"Kedu?"
"Odinma".
Our friendship and inseparability were cemented on the spot.
Charles had been living in Jamaica and teaching Science at Exced for the previous eighteen months. He lived a 10-minute stroll away from the college gates down Mountain View Avenue in a notorious area of Back Bush. Typically Igbo, he'd converted part of his rented flat into a shop selling used, second-hand car parts! He was mischievous and had a real sense of fun. I asked him what had brought him to Jamaica. He said after teaching in India he got bored and frustrated, but he didn't want to go back to Nigeria, so applied for work in Jamaica. He once regaled me with a story about him and his Igbo friends in India who'd take great fun in:

"slaughtering and chopping dat dere sacred namma!" (killing and eating their sacred cows!).

He was totally irreverent and gave me the impression he respected nobody, other than other Igbos. Aba boy!
I'd received advice and inductions from a variety of well-meaning people during my early days on the island, but Charles's induction was the one that seemed closest to the reality that I'd witnessed and

experienced. He told me how he'd been dodging bullets the week before as gunmen fought a running battle outside his flat.

"Enyi, be careful oh, dese pipple no fit love themselves, dey crez!"

"Brother, be careful, these people don't love each other, they're mad!"

I'd planned to visit Montego Bay on the northwest coast of the island at the end of that week's enrolments, Charles already had previous commitments, so on the Friday I jumped on a minibus and went by myself, with no idea where I'd be staying. The drive from 'town' was mad as we hurtled across 'country' at break-neck speeds down hills and along straights, and crawled painfully up any and every hill we encountered due to the weight of the packed minibus.

News on the radio was that a hurricane was heading towards Jamaica, which was predicted to hit the island on Monday the 12th of September.

Had I known better it might have occurred to me that my fellow passengers were intent on getting home safely to 'country' before the hurricane hit.

Anyway, I spent the Friday and Saturday nights on the beach attending a couple of sound-system clashes, which was heaven. *Nothing* beats being on the beach in Jamaica hearing and feeling heavy bass reggae music! I slept on the beach during the day time. However, I was becoming increasingly aware of the weather reports and, come the Sunday, people were at a fever pitch. Hurricane Gilbert was picking up speed and intensity, and was due to hit Kingston in the south of the island on Monday. Warnings were *not* to travel under any circumstances. Sensing peoples' anxieties, the thought of being exposed to the ravages of the hurricane on a beach really *did not* appeal to me, so I made every effort to make my way back to Kingston.

I was lucky. I managed to fight my way on to the last country bus that was daring to attempt the trip back to town. 'Daring' because an eerie squally wind was beginning to pick up as evidence of the forthcoming hurricane, and the normal sounds of people, cars, animals and birds were noticeably increasingly on the wane and absent. As I was shoving my way up the steps of the bus, I felt a hand on my back pocket where I kept my wallet. I instantly tuned to confront the potential pickpocket who, due to my reaction, melted back into the maddening crowd. Despite the fact that *he* was trying to pickpocket *me*, the look on his face was one of anger and frustration, as if I'd had the temerity to deprive him of rich pickings. Following up on this altercation wasn't my priority. I hadn't had my pocket picked, and it was far more important for me to secure my seat on the bus, which I did.

However, another lesson learned, I never used my wallet from that point and on and always kept my loose cash in my front pockets!

The country-bus trip back to town was tortuous! Packed like sardines, we were all becoming increasingly concerned and afraid of the worsening weather, and worried about the bus's ability to arrive safely at its destination in the country-bus stop in downtown Kingston, behind Coronation street market and near to the now virtually defunct single-track railway station. The wind was howling and gusting, and rain started to lash the bus in ever-strengthening torrents. This was probably the only time ever I used a bus of any description in Jamaica when music wasn't blasting through the speakers! Radio RJR was our constant companion, keeping us updated on Gilbert's imminent arrival.

Somehow, we made it back to town, and I jumped on a town TATA bus up Constant Spring Road to Ivor's and safety.

Hurricane Gilbert introduced itself with full force on Monday 12ᵗʰ September, and *what* an introduction!

I couldn't help but think back to the 'great storm' that hit the southeast of England nearly a year before in October on 1987 (the English really do have to get off labelling everything and anything about themselves as 'great'. It really wasn't *that* great!). However, it made front page news for ages, and TV weather forecaster Michael Fish, who complacently pooh-poohed a viewer's concerns about the incoming storm, has never been allowed to forget his monumental national weather broadcasting fuck-up. The storm even reduced the town of Sevenoaks to Zero Oaks in Kent! But compared to Hurricane Gilbert, it was a mild breeze!

The temperature dropped noticeably on Gilbert's arrival. *The most fierce and intense winds accompanied torrents of lashing rain* as I stood watching the carnage unfolding outside from Ivor's parlour. Centuries-old massive mango trees were being ripped out and dashed aside; palm trees bent double under the crushing, relentless hurricane-force gales; zinc roofs were ripped off peoples' houses and somersaulted through the air as they were flung unceremoniously to their final resting places; parked cars and houses were smashed by falling trees and telegraph poles; even the satellite dishes of the wealthy went to meet their brother- and sister-satellites in the sky!

This went on for hours! It was incredible. I still find it impossible to adequately explain the experience. Another lesson learned; *never* underestimate the strength, power and mercilessly destructive force of Mother Nature. Gilbert helped me realise that we, as humans, are totally insignificant in nature's path. It will do whatsoever it wishes, and there's nothing we can do to stop it. Partway through the early part of the hurricane one of Ivor's awnings started to come away. I felt duty-bound to try to secure the fittings, so I went outside with this in mind. Like Kingston, I got battered by freezing wind and rain, but successfully managed to secure the awning, and raced back inside, soaked through and shivering. Ivor's partner insisted on rubbing some Wray and Nephew white rum over my back and chest to reheat my body which, whilst I fully appreciated the gesture, I still thought was a terrible waste of perfectly good alcohol!

The eye of the storm arrived eventually. The winds dropped and the rain ceased. We were surrounded by an eerie silence and complete wreckage. I understood there'd be a couple of hours before the storm would return in the opposite direction, so I took the opportunity to take a stroll and view the local wreckage and havoc that Gilbert had delivered. I walked down to Red Hills Road, where I saw a man lying dead in the gutter, the top of his head had been chopped clean off by somebody's flying zinc roof, leaving his brains splattered all over the road. This sight sobered me up instantly, and I returned immediately to the relative safety of Ivor's.

If previous hurricanes prompted the Welsh author Richard Hughes to write his famous novel 'A High Wind in Jamaica', then he definitely under-emphasised the wind bit. '*Wind*' doesn't get anywhere near an apt description of hurricanes. Trust me on that!

After the eye had passed, the second half of Gilbert was just as devastating as the first, the only difference being the winds were gusting in the opposite direction. So, trees, cars, satellite dishes, zinc and all forms of other debris that had been blown down in one direction were lifted up again and thrown down in the opposite direction.

Needless to say, Kingston, like the rest of Jamaica, was totally smashed up in Gilbert's wake, which caused 4 billion USD worth of damage to buildings, crops, power and water services, communication lines, poultry production, and aviation. It was estimated up to 80% of houses across the island lost their roofs, hundreds of miles of roads and highways were severely damaged, and 49 people lost their lives.

And I fully understand why. The power of Gilbert was *immense!* Even worse for me, the likelihood of getting suitable accommodation for Yve, Kele J and I was even further diminished, if not to say totally obliterated. So many people were made homeless or were forced to survive in extensively damaged properties that once were their homes.

As soon as Jamaica Telecommunications (JTC) had salvaged its service, I phoned home to reassure Yve that I was fine, but accommodation was proving extremely difficult to procure for the three of us. She was relieved to hear from me, and told me she'd seen the devastation on the news in England. Apparently my dad, who was in Nigeria at the time, was apoplectic with worry. He thought he'd lost his 'Opara!', so I asked Yve to let the whole family know that she'd heard from me and that I was OK.

It was good speaking with her. She reinvigorated me to tough it out!

Somehow, in the face of such adversity, the students arrived, punctually, when classes started in the third week of September. I'd been allocated a desk in the main staffroom, and had received my teaching timetable of Year 1 and Year 2 A Level Sociology students. Built in between two warring ghetto communities, Exced was mainly populated by students who'd failed to gain entry to the esteemed Kingston College (KC), or Jamaica College (JC), either because their grades weren't good enough, or their parents couldn't afford to send them there. Many came from ghetto areas around Kingston, and the island in general.

I was *so* impressed by them! They all made their best efforts to arrive on time, fully equipped and prepared to work! This was *very* different to the attitude of pupils of comparable backgrounds I'd grown accustomed to in London, who seemed to resent education as an inconvenient imposition on their lives. Jamaican students actually *appreciated* education, *respected* their teachers, they were highly *motivated* to achieve and took great *pride* in their academic accomplishments. The overwhelming majority even produced and submitted their homework on time and to the best of their ability! Much like young people in Nigeria, they were also confident and able to speak eloquently and articulately in public.

To cut a potentially long story short, they were an absolute dream to teach. I couldn't help but reflect that, whilst I thought I'd been doing a great job in London, I realised that I spent only some of my time actually *teaching*. The rest of the time I spent playing a variety of roles, including surrogate parent, policemen, social worker, counsellor, youth worker, welfare officer, careers guidance adviser, security officer, and then a bit of teaching.

At Exced I *taught*, and I loved every second of it!

The students were bright, inquisitive and receptive, willing and able to discuss, debate, analyse and evaluate concepts that were presented in an alien context to their own culture and experience; the syllabus taught was AEB Sociology, the content of which emphasised sociological theory as it applied mainly to England and the USA. This didn't deter them though but, rather, seemed to inspire them even further. They were hungry for education and, it seemed for many, for an education that focused on life in England and America. No doubt they were able to apply the knowledge they gleaned to their own experiences and life in Jamaica in a constructive and positive manner. This satisfied me that they understood the concepts. I *knew* I was going to enjoy this teaching year!

However, I was becoming increasingly desperate to sort out my accommodation situation. Whilst I fully appreciated Ivor's help, this was only ever going to be a temporary solution, and I didn't want to become an imposition on him. Earl, the Head of the Pre-U Department, took me to a potential place near to the college in Vineyard Town which, though convenient, seemed very expensive for one room in a family house, but I'd run out of options so I took my suitcases and dumped them there before taking off for another weekend trip of discovery to 'country'. My heart and mind weren't really sold on the arrangement though, and I spent a troubled weekend considering my (depressing lack of?) options.

Bearing the devastation of Gilbert in mind, even Miss PPP was encouraging me to go back to the UK, but I didn't want to do this. I wanted to complete what I'd started, and I was already beginning to fall in love with Jamaica. My weekend trip only lasted a day, due to the state of the hurricane-ravished island. By the time I got back to Kingston I was hot, hungry, thirsty, parched in fact, but couldn't find water to drink. I got off the bus at Halfway Tree and got another to Liguanea, enroute to Vineyard Town. Whilst in Liguanea I walked past a guy watering his lawn with a hose, which I thought was *so* unnecessary and decadent given the fact that tens of thousands of people were struggling to get clean drinking water. I'd never felt so forlorn and wretched in my life. I felt like kicking his head in!

I couldn't bear the thought of going to Vineyard Town to unpack my stuff and settle in. Greta, head teacher at Kingsdale School, had given me the number of her younger sister, Joan, who lived in Kingston, 'just in case'. So I called her. She'd been expecting to hear from me since my arrival, and gave me directions to her house on Windsor Avenue, off Old Hope Road near the National Sports Stadium. Bedraggled and weary I turned up at her gates, to be greeted by a pack of frenzied, barking Rhodesian Ridgeback dogs.

Not wishing to antagonise them by walking through the gates, I stood and shouted. Joan's husband Maurice came to the window and told me just to walk through, the dogs wouldn't harm me. So I did, and they didn't, thankfully!

Timing, at times, is everything in life. I arrived just as Joan, Maurice and their sons Daniel and Benjamin were about to eat, so I accepted their invitation to sit and eat with them! Accept? If the truth be known I would have eaten everything on the table! They were a beautiful family. Joan was an independent freelance journalist who wrote for women's political organisations across the Caribbean. Maurice was a prominent barrister in Jamaica, one of a long line of prominent Jamaican barristers in his family. Daniel was the same age as Kele J and about to start his first year at school, and Benjamin was a few months old and keeping Joan busy!

Their house was beautiful, built in the old colonial bungalow style. When they learnt I still hadn't managed to arrange accommodation for myself, let alone Yve and Kele J, they immediately invited me to live in the unused bedroom (with en-suite WC and shower!), to the rear of the house, which also had its own entrance door. When I explained the rent I was being expected to pay in Vineyard Town for far more inferior accommodation, they were appalled. As soon as we finished eating Maurice bundled me into his car and drove straight to my prospective landlords, who he thanked very much for their offer as we gathered my things and left.

Maurice was disgusted by the rent they'd asked for:

"A tief dem a tief!"

We made the ten minute drive back to Windsor Avenue, where I unpacked and settled in instantly. It was surreal. One minute I was effectively destitute and homeless, the next I had my own room with en-suite facilities with a family I felt *were* family.

Unbelievable!

Just as important for me, they were by no stretch of the imagination the stuffy conservative types or wannabes who seemed prevalent among the aspiring or already-established middle classes of Jamaica. They were ordinary 'normal' people, on a level, intelligent and liberated, confident and outspoken, and clearly in possession of very acute social consciences.

I felt *so* lucky, and truly appreciated their offer.

Furthermore, their house was a five minute bus ride to Exced, so really convenient also.

For the first few weeks I used to walk to work through Nannyville past the National Stadium. I also used to have a drink every now and again at a bar on the outskirts of Nannyville, where I quickly got labelled with the nickname "Resident Cowboy!" Don't ask me why! Interestingly, I'd later be given a nickname by residents of Back Bush, where I'd soon be spending lots of time with Charles. "Teach". This moniker was far more logical.

I'd been at home with Joan and family for a week when there was to be a big concert held at the nearby national stadium. I managed to contact my two black colleagues who were keen to attend, but couldn't find our white colleague. Apparently she wasn't happy with her accommodation, had met an English contractor living in a plush hotel in New Kingston, and had shacked up with him for the rest of the year! Either way, we only saw her once again after the concert, when she told us she'd been mugged and robbed of her purse, passport and other belongings whilst she was in the guy's car as they were stationary at traffic lights.

Reggae superstars Maxi Priest and Dennis Brown were headlining at the concert, so we were looking forward to going. The whole stadium area was packed with revellers, mainly ghetto people intent on enjoying themselves. I thought we'd arrived in reasonable time but the crowd of people forcing their way to the turnstiles was massive. I didn't think we stood a good chance of getting in. With my colleagues behind me we dived in, inching our way towards the turnstiles which seemed miles away. All of a sudden, the guy two people in front started shouting and swearing at the guy between him and me. It seems this guy was in the process of picking Mr Angry's pocket who, in turn, started shouting his accusations at Mr PP (pickpocket). *Very* similar to Aba in Nigeria, Mr PP made the mistake of running past me and back through the crowd (amounting to an assumed confession of guilt), at which Mr Angry drew a gun from somewhere on his body. Virtually using my shoulder as an armrest, he shot Mr PP twice in the back as he was trying to make good his escape. He slumped to the floor dead, the crowd started shouting and screaming and, due to force of habit, 'got flat' and, ears ringing, I saw this as our chance to surge forward to the turnstiles. I grabbed my screaming colleagues and rushed for the stadium as the crowd were still scattered and flat.

We got in. No problem!

Maxi Priest was big in the UK at the time, a very popular exponent of the Lovers' Rock reggae genre. But he didn't go down at all well with the majority of the crowd, who preferred more raw reggae, and felt cheated of their entrance fee when Maxi was on stage doing his best to entertain. The crowd weren't having it, and started pelting him with rocks, cans and bottles. I couldn't believe it. Why were they *so* angry? This was like a black version of the Reading Festival hippies. It took Dennis Brown to come out on stage and beg on Maxi's behalf. He even did a duet with him to get the crowd onside. Dennis Brown was mega in Jamaica, and soon soothed and seduced the 'batty-rider' clad throng into tolerating, and eventually appreciating, Maxi Priest, who I think couldn't wait to get off stage. Dennis Brown smashed it! He sang all his 'big tunes' that we were all familiar with, and turned the concert into a fantastic night out.

Forty-Eight

Yve and I decided to shelve our original plans in favour of her and Kele J coming to visit me in Jamaica for two extended six-week holidays over the 1988 Christmas period, and July and August of 1989. This would enable Kele J to start primary school in London.

Also, another consideration was required. When I'd left for Jamaica Yvonne was pregnant again. In October, and shortly after Hurricane Gilbert, her waters broke four months early, and it was clear she was going into labour. I explained my position to Earl at Exced, and every member of staff was very concerned and totally supportive of my plan to return to the UK to be with Yve.

I managed to get the next flight from Kingston to Heathrow. It was a ghost flight. Due to the impact of Hurricane Gilbert on travel out of Jamaica, I was the only passenger on board. It was weird.

On arrival in London I went straight to the maternity ward at Hammersmith Hospital on Du Cane Road, west London, to find Yvonne cradling our newly-arrived son. She was singing him a lullaby, and it broke my heart. I guessed his chances of survival were exceptionally slim, but I could sense Yvonne's maternal instincts desperately hoping for his survival. She has such a strong maternal instinct. He was tiny, beautiful, but tiny. In my absence and on his premature arrival, Yvonne named him after me, Ngozi. He fought and survived for five days but his lungs weren't strong enough to sustain him, and he died.

It was tragic. It ripped us both to pieces. But we had to stay strong for ourselves as individuals, for ourselves as a couple, and for our daughter Kele J. There's nothing worse than having to register the birth and death of your child at the same time. We tried to be as 'normal' as possible, but it was difficult. I even played a game of football with my mates at Kaieteur FC, which helped take my mind off things a little, and it was good to see family and friends again, but not a 'happy' good. However, two weeks after landing in London, I was on a sparsely-populated flight back to Jamaica.

The staff and students were really *so* genuinely sympathetic and supportive, and that helped me so much, as did living with Joan and family.

In addition to making my way around Kingston and Jamaica using a combination of taxis, town and country buses, I now also had at my disposal the use of two cars, Maurice's low-riding automatic Mazda, and Joan's red Niva Jeep which, when they had no plans to be using them, I would. I got to see so much of Jamaica. I think I got to know Jamaica better than most Jamaicans. I was often told by many of the things I'd done and the places I'd been and seen, that they'd never done them. Obviously it helped that I was being paid, tax-free, from my job in London. The currency exchange rate between the Jamaican Dollar and British Pound Sterling was 10:1 at the time. My gross, tax-free income was £1,000.00 a month, equivalent to JS10,000.. At the time it was impossible for me to spend this in Jamaica! The principal of Exced was being paid JS2,500 per month before tax, so I was taking home at least four times his salary. I asked Yve only to send me money when I asked for it.

Even more embarrassingly, teachers in Jamaica are paid quarterly bonuses, which they insisted on paying me. I told them that I really didn't want or need the bonuses, but this concerned them. They understood my position, but insisted that my not taking the bonuses might jeopardise them receiving theirs, so I took it. I felt bad in doing so, but I'd have felt even worse if they lost theirs as a result of me refusing mine. Before I returned from London after Ngozi's funeral, I packed and shipped a few crates worth of educational resources and materials that I knew would benefit the faculty and students. I felt better when they eventually arrived and I was able to make the donation to the faculty. It was very much appreciated by all.

I tried desperately not to flaunt my position of privilege, and always treated everyone with respect. I think this stood me in good stead, as I soon became a very popular member of staff with teaching colleagues and among the students, all of whom wanted to get to know me and speak with me, even if they weren't in any of my classes! For the first time in my professional career I actually felt valued and appreciated both professionally and personally, and I didn't want to abuse this relationship, because I too also gained so much from the experience.

A young Indian teacher named Lakshman arrived shortly after I did to teach at Exced. In his mid-twenties, he was good fun and also popular, though less reliable than me at times. He, Charles and I would make up a 'terrible trio' at times, heading out to the bars and generally creating havoc in the evenings and over the weekends. It surprised me how often people would shout at Lakshman:

"Hey! Hindu!"

This was in order to attract his attention. Again, another example of how Jamaicans describe things as they see them.

However, Charles and I were the main combination. When we didn't fancy eating a box-lunch from the college canteen, we'd stroll down to the campus gate for a liquid lunch of Dragon Stout, soaked up with ample-sized bun and cheese. At the end of the day, we would walk to Charles's flat in Back Bush, before hitting the local rum bars in the area. This was all good fun. We'd chat, backslap, and have a laugh. Charles was *hyper*-critical of Jamaicans. He'd clearly absorbed, internalised and retained the Nigerian attitude towards 'Jammohs'.

It became quite a regular thing for us to be drinking at a bar, when in would walk a squad of Jamaica Defence Force (JDF) servicemen, AK47s slung loosely over their shoulders and pistols at their wastes. This unnerved me slightly. I couldn't help but wonder what would happen if they got drunk on their white rum and started 'lickin shots' around the place. Even scarier was when the 'Eradication Squad' would arrive, tyres screeching to a halt as they parked up outside the bar in their unmarked vehicles. They were big, hefty, black-shades-wearing semi-automatic- and pistol-packing guys who were virtually tasked with shooting first, and asking questions second! Trained and detailed to break politically-affiliated gangs, druggists (drug runners) and area boys, these members of the Jamaica Constabulary Force (JCF), have often been accused of extrajudicial executions in their 'clean-up' operations, a task they attacked most zealously. They were definitely a frightening sight.

We'd also regularly see drunken fights, domestic fights, woman-on-woman fights, essentially every type of fight that would, invariably, end up in stabbings, acid attacks (women in Jamaica and Nigeria are particularly fond of this practice against each other!), and generally random, horrific, maiming violence. Every time this happened Charles would be prompted to lament:

"Dese pipple eh! They don't love themselves! Ah!"

If truth be known, such laments were consistent with the Nigerian attitude towards Jamaicans. Delivered ostensibly as a concerned observation, in actuality it was a damning indictment of Jamaica and Jamaicans. This troubled me, because it represented, for me, further evidence of the deep psychological damage that has been inflicted on black people on either side of the Atlantic, which has survived and perpetuated for many hundreds of years.

That's not to say Charles and I didn't have great fun, we did. He was always up for a laugh and, again in that typically Igbo way, he was also able to laugh at himself as well. When his car parts business allowed, we'd travel around the island, go to shows, dancehall parties, the beach, fishing, eat jerk chicken and fried fish (he'd also cook fufu, meat stews and egusi soup occasionally, which went down a treat!), and even more rum bars! We became great friends and really enjoyed each other's company, but at times his attitude towards Jamaicans was *so* embarrassing for me, and whoever it was directed at.

Colourism was rife and rampant in Jamaica at the time. It was abundantly clear to me that skin colour dynamics was endemic among

Jamaicans. It was the done and expected thing for lighter-skinned people to dominate, and darker-skinned people to be subservient. This was evidenced everywhere, from the virtually white skinned JLP and PNP political party leaders, through the very light-brown-skinned front-of-house bank tellers, all the way down to the dark-skinned road sweepers. Skin colour equated unequivocally to differential levels of status, power and privilege. I *never* saw little light-skinned children begging at roadsides, outside restaurants, or rushing cars at traffic lights to wash windscreens for a pittance. Such practices were the sole preserve of the disempowered and dispossessed darker-skinned black people of Jamaica.

Overwhelmingly, it was darker-skinned people who populated the run-down, overcrowded, under-resourced, zinc, wood and cardboard built ghettos and shanty towns, and lighter-skinned people who populated the hugely sought-after private, gated, security-defended communities around town. Police brutality and extrajudicial murders were invariably perpetrated against the darker-skinned by brown-skinned and dark-skinned government forces, at the command of their lighter-skinned superiors who preferred to keep their hands clean.

Similar to Nigeria, colourism was rife.

It's inevitable that, where socio-economic and political advantage exists, and life chances are enhanced exponentially by virtue of being born lighter-skinned, psychologically, nations' populations will wish to be born lighter-skinned. Those who *are* lighter-skinned live and work to maintain their unassailable status and privilege, and those who are darker-skinned live and toil every day of their lives to minimise the socially-imposed ravaging effects of their darker skin colour.

My feeling is that herein lies the source of division, derision, resentment, hostility and corruption. In a competitive world, human beings are forced to compete for scarce resources, and most will use any and every perceived, actual or assumed advantage to enhance their position and opportunities in life. Consequently, in general, lighter-skinned people will be more inclined to maximise on this perceived advantage, and darker-skinned people will be inclined to resent them for this, and their lowly status.

Obviously, there are exceptions to this rule. There are conscious, historically and socio-politically aware lighter- and darker-skinned people who won't play the 'colour game' within and among themselves. Rather than contribute to the nauseous cesspit of colour politics, the enlightened among us will strive to generate and maintain unity of identity and purpose, particularly in white-dominated western societies where we're all perceived as the same, in terms of skin colour, if we have a visible drop of black blood in us.

Rather than aspire to join the ranks of liberated black thinkers, the ignorant at each end of the colour continuum remain entrenched in their battle for the crumbs that may fall off the high altar of colour. Light-skinned people will continue to self-serve and gorge on the benefits over which they had no control, but just happened to be born with; darker-skinned people will continue to stew in hatred and resentment, whilst at the same time applying skin-lightening cream and pill-popping by the bucket-load in their forlornly pathetic quest to become lighter!

In many ways, both groups are as bad as each other. They both suffer from deeply entrenched insecurities and vulnerabilities but, rather than pull together for the mutual benefit of all, each chooses to magnify the differences between themselves in a desperate bid for an ill-conceived and perilous form of random genetically-based survival.

And *oh* how massuh must still be laughing; laughing up his sleeve. He no longer has to worry about creating division among his niggers. They have become expert at doing it to themselves!

Hell, massuh is now *so* relaxed and *so* far removed and detached from the process, he can even afford the luxury to save up and look forward to his two weeks in the holiday sun every year, after which he can return to work and show off his sun tan. Massuh not only *wants* to be darker (even if only on a temporary basis for some), he even wants to show it off, safe in the knowledge that his position is secure, whatever shade of brown he may be! Many massuhs spend fortunes in tanning salons up and down the UK in order to maintain and top-up their 'perma-tans', while black people run to buy skin-lightening creams and pills, wigs and weaves from Mr Patel's and Mr Akbar's cosmetic stores, and blue eye contact lenses from Boots, in sorrowful denial and shameful rejection of their blackness.

UK- and western-born mixed-race people will feel they rarely need to risk being trampled in the rush to Mr Patel's, Mr Akbar's or Boots, but that's not to say we're all happy and comfortable in our skin.

I'm of the opinion that it's lazy and inaccurate to *assume* that *all* mixed-race people have shared the same experiences as each other and other black people. This may be as a result of either *perceived* or *actual* experience (positive and/or negative) of racism, or the apparent lack thereof. However, the prevailing *tendency* is to make such an assumption. Based on my own experiences, I cannot conceive of a UK-born and bred mixed-race person *never* experiencing racism, but many mixed-race Brits claim that this is, in fact, the case.

So the question needs to be asked: Is this a matter of denial, self-delusion, or fact?

Whilst I'd hesitate to claim with any degree of authority or certainty that *every* lighter-skinned mixed-race person *has* experienced racism in the UK, I can't imagine otherwise; which means (from this perspective), that any racism they may have experienced is either not perceived as racism in the first place, or their ego defence mechanism of denial works *so* effectively that it's registered, but goes unrecognised. Freud suggests the mind develops and employs automatic ego defence mechanisms to filter and deal with perceptions and experiences that are too painful to deal with in the conscious mind. So it may well be the case that the perception of racism, an exceptionally painful and potentially devastating experience for its victims, is swiftly and efficiently funnelled aside or away, deep into the subconscious mind, in order to enable the denying victim to continue to operate effectively.

My experience is that black people are equally capable of acting in a racist manner towards mixed-race people, as do white people. Similarly, mixed-race people are capable of the same against black people. I suppose, in short, we're *all* capable of being racist and treating each other differentially regardless of whatever race we may 'belong to'. This may well be part of the 'human condition'; a sad and daunting trait that we've been unable to cast off, due to our genetically-predetermined survival instinct.

If this is true it is, again, a sad indictment of humanity. According to popular contemporary science, that *thing* which separates us from the rest of the animal world is the fact that, in comparison, we have far larger brains. It strikes me we should make more and better use of our 'super' brains to embrace each other, regardless of the happenstance of random genetic encoding that we may have inherited as individuals or groups that determines our skin colour. But we don't. We *choose* not to. We choose to exacerbate irrelevant differences between ourselves, in a manner that elevates some to privilege; keeps others vainly squabbling to join the privileged; and subjugates most to disempowerment, resentment and frustration.

Forty-Nine

My time teaching in Jamaica flew past. Yve and Kele J visited in December 1988 and July 1989 for six weeks on both occasions. It was fantastic having them with me. In addition to making circuitous trips around the island, taking in the sights and experiences, we also managed to visit Barbados, Guyana, Disney World in Florida, and generally enjoyed immensely our time together. During the final leg of a trip around Jamaica we were approaching downtown Kingston along the Windward Road. I mentioned to Yve that:

> "Every time I come down here something happens, usually a gun fight of some sort or another."

As soon as I'd said this, gunshots started firing within yards of the car. I've *never* seen Yve move *so* quickly as she dived between our front seats to push Kele J flat on the back seat. It goes without saying that I beat a hasty wheel-screeching exit to the safety of Parade, up through Cross Roads to Half Way Tree and on to Windsor Avenue. What prompted me to make this remark to Yve was we were at exactly the same spot where, whilst on the bus from Exced one afternoon heading downtown on exactly the same route, we got embroiled in a traffic jam. The cause of the jam became evident when we passed the spot. Apparently, two homosexuals had been 'caught at it' and were instantly dragged from their love nest by an enraged and baying mob into the street, where they were summarily hacked, beaten and stoned to death for their indiscretion. It reminded me quite a lot of Aba!

Jamaica, at the time, was probably *the* worst place on the face of the earth to be a male homosexual….. a "batty bwoy!" I understand things have changed significantly over the last quarter of a century or so since I first arrived in the island. In fact, there was one student who I taught who seemed exceptionally effeminate in comparison to the exceptionally macho stereotypical Jamaican male. Though at the time I wasn't 100% sure of his actual sexuality, I was 99% certain her was gay. This didn't concern me in the slightest. If the truth be known, though at times I felt slightly conscious of his outward persona when he was in my company, I really admired and respected him for his psychological and emotional strength, his independence of thought, his sense of (at times self-deprecating) humour and fun, his academic intelligence, and the way he saw things in general. It *must* have been *so* tough for him though, but he survived, succeeded and prospered before leaving Jamaica to complete his university education in America, after which he became a freelance photographer and author.

Kele J even started to develop a bit of a Jamaican accent as she accompanied Joan's son Daniel to school for a few weeks across both visits. She even went to get her hair done in notorious semi-depressed ghetto areas by Miss Joycey, Joan's trusted home-help. My view was if you're being brought into the ghetto by a resident, you're safe. Every time I went into the shanty towns around Kingston I never felt intimidated or threatened but, possibly because of my early experience, I made a point of remaining alert at all times, ratchet at the ready! Despite the dauntingly shabby external appearances, the shanty dwellings were surprisingly clean and cool.

Jamaicans are sports-mad, especially athletics, cricket and, more recently, football. It's incredible how such a small island of approximately 2.5 million people consistently manages to produce so many Class A athletes, Don Quarry and Usain Bolt to name but two. If there's one thing I regret about my time in Jamaica was not getting involved with the Exced football team. They had a really good athletics team though, which did well at Champs 1989 in the national arena where, with unbridled passion, pride and commitment, the island's schools' and colleges' athletes compete. Exced would have done a lot better had *all* their team been available to compete. Twenty one students left Exced to compete in Miami prior to Champs, and only one returned. The other twenty took the opportunity to 'go missing' (start another life) in the States!

This is a common phenomenon among 'third world developing' countries, where many of their members enter other 'first world developed' countries on legitimate, organised grounds, only to abscond and disappear in hot pursuit of the Dollar or Pound Sterling. West Africans have been doing this for decades, usually after first having taken 10 years off their dates of birth when entering the west, especially footballers! To be fair though, many of the older generation literally didn't know their own birth dates. Dad didn't know his, so mum gave him December 5th, 5 being her lucky number and December being the month they met (knowing mum, that's what I'm assuming).

However, Nigerians are particularly fussy about age. During their middle years they go to great efforts to shave off as many years as possible, so as to extend working life etc. Yet when they're buried their families tend to, almost miraculously, add about 20 or 30 years, in order to emphasise the seniority, wisdom, statesman-like status and standing in the community of their departed loved-one. One thing is true though. Black people seem to 'age better' than white people. I've been informed this is due to higher levels of melanin in black skin, which also makes us more resistant to skin cancer.

I never personally experienced any further life-threatening situations during my stay, though I had a few near misses, especially whilst out driving! The worst I can remember was arriving at a crash-scene shortly after two private cars had met in a head-on collision as I was approaching the outskirts of Spanish Town. Nobody was at the scene other than the driver of one of the vehicles. Both his feet were up on his driver seat, his head lay on the lay-by's hot, dusty, blood-splattered concrete surface, and his brains were running out of his nose.

Charles and I used to go to all the reggae shows and generally arsed around in Kingston's many roadside bars.

Pat and George Cascoe even visited with Richard, a family friend whilst I was still there, so we hooked up a few times and, at one stage, we drove up into the coffee-producing Blue Mountain, where there are spectacularly breathtaking views overlooking Kingston. We also went to Port Royal to visit the remnants of the slave-holding fort (similar in its construction to Elmina Castle on the Ghanaian coast, though far smaller in size), and walked through the Giddy House, which was built as an artillery store housing gun powder and weapons, but partially sunk during the 1907 earthquake. Try standing straight or walking in a straight line from one end to another. Virtually impossible!

I even won the Exced Pre-University Department Teacher of the Award in May 1989, an honour I wasn't expecting at all! I was actually stood at the front, camera in-hand, waiting to take some photos of the winner when my name was announced. I felt really embarrassed. I've never really won anything in my life (either before or since!), so my acceptance speech was totally adlibbed! It was, for me, a great honour though, and in my mind as much to do with the way the students inspired me as it was recognition of my teaching ability. To be honest, the teaching was pretty easy, with much of the theory being UK- America-based, I was able to provide a sense of first-hand reality to the theories I taught. I think the students also enjoyed my irreverent, non-Religious, anti-monarchy stance whilst teaching as well. I don't think they'd ever been taught by a non-traditionalist teacher before. Thankfully, the A Level results were excellent that year, the best in Exced's history to that point. The students even wrote, signed and submitted a petition requesting my appointment be extended for another year. Sadly, to no avail!

As the saying goes, "all good things come to an end", and twelve months after my arrival Yve, Kele J and I were on the plane heading back to London in August 1989, at the end of what was probably one of the best years of my life. Not that I'd 'gone native' whilst in Jamaica, but I truly loved everything about my experience and the people I'd met, so readjusting to grey London was problematic for me initially, especially having to return to teaching at Kingsdale school. I'd already decided I couldn't continue teaching at secondary school level (my year teaching in Jamaica had helped me make my mind up on that issue!), so I spent the year keeping an eye out for

Graduation Day, Excelsior Community College (1989), left to right: Lakshman, Me, Earl, Charles and Business Studies lecturer (my apologies, but his name has escaped me over the years, but he was a fantastically intelligent and inspirational man).

lecturing jobs in Further Education (FE). I spotted and applied for an A Level Sociology Lecturer vacancy at South Thames College (STC) on Tooting Broadway in southwest London. I was interviewed and got the job, starting in September 1990. FE teaching was more straightforward and similar to teaching in Jamaica, but still not as rewarding or satisfying. UK students, in my mind, have a distorted sense of entitlement which, when combined with the all-encompassing availability of the welfare state safety net, produces some young people who often lack drive and ambition, and the ability to think independently.

But I enjoyed teaching 16-18 year olds and adults at FE level. In my time at STC I contributed to writing the first Access to Higher Education programme and was very quickly promoted to a Senior Lecturer post as Head of A Levels and GCSEs and Cross-College Coordinator.

1991 was another great year in my life. It saw the birth of our first son. After Ngozi's premature birth and death, Yve had experienced several miscarriages. This alarmed us to the extent that we sought the intervention and advice of the world renowned Professor Winston at the Hammersmith Hospital on Du Cane Road in West London. He didn't identify any specific problem other than bad luck, essentially. We were cautiously optimistic when Yve carried past the first trimester, that period of foetal development most likely to result in miscarriage. I got even more excited when a later scan revealed she was expecting another boy. I couldn't help doing a 'thumbs-up' behind the nurse's back as she scanned Yve's gelled lump.

However, it seems it was written somewhere we were never to experience and enjoy a straightforward childbirth. Yve's waters started to break towards the end of the second trimester, on the 21st November, three months early! I was devastated, as heart-wrenching memories of Ngozi started flooding back to me. She was rushed into Mayday Hospital and, despite the efforts of the staff to slow things down, this boy was adamant about making his entrance to the world!

Within minutes of Yve arriving on the maternity ward it was evident that his arrival was immediately imminent. I was able to be present for his birth, but couldn't help desperately thinking:

'No, no, no. Please. Not yet!'

But he had different ideas. He'd had enough and wanted out.

And he shot out!

Apart from his head, he was *so* small! At 3lb 6oz he looked like a huge-headed tadpole, with the rest of his body straggling off his head. He came out so quickly we nearly needed the services of a running wide receiver to catch him before touchdown!

Like Kele J, he was whisked off to an Intensive Care Unit incubator. Thankfully, all his vitals were strong and the prognosis for survival was good. I worried, due to his three month prematurity, whether he'd be either physically or mentally disabled, or both. Neither was the case. He was soon breathing under his own steam, and it was clear he was a fighter and survivor.

We named him Ikenna, Igbo for 'Strength of the Father'. Obviously, as first son (Opara!), his middle name is Michael, after my dad and me. Hopefully, if he is lucky enough to have sons in the future, he will name his first one Michael also, to maintain the family tradition. 'Ike' has grown up to be a very intelligent, deeply principled, pleasant, popular and decent young man who has always made me proud and I am glad to be his father.

I took a break from teaching for a year in 1994, when I started trading with Ijeoma's partner, Derron. We did reasonably well, were paying the bills, and eventually went into partnership with another company. We'd broken into tobacco trading; procuring and selling cigarettes for export through our community contacts, and were doing very well.

Life was good, and Yve was expecting again; another boy.

I got a call out of the blue from Ray who told me a contact of his was looking for young black couples who were expecting children at the time. The idea was for the BBC to film and interview three young couples as they advanced through pregnancy to the birth of their babies. The focus of this episode of the 'Black London' documentary series, inspired by the London-based black author Patrick Augustus, was to examine the role of the (black) fathers. Augustus had written and published his book 'Baby Father' earlier in 1994, which highlighted the issue of the rise of female-headed single-parent-families in the UK black community, and the effects of the growing numbers of absent black fathers.

The producers visited to discuss the project with Yve and I, and we agreed to participate. They made it quite clear we were to be portrayed as the 'stable' couple who were most likely to remain intact, with the predictable benefits and advantages ensuing for our children as a result. The other two couples, by default, were considered less likely to remain together.

After agreeing, we met with Patrick. Lo and behold I knew him already. He'd been a peripatetic music teacher at Kingsdale School! The music department building wasn't part of the main school so we'd never actually met or been introduced, but we both recognised each other instantly.

The camera crew started to turn up and film us going about our daily lives. It was strange at first but it's amazing how quickly you become familiar with their presence and de-sensitise, to behave 'normally' when the cameras were rolling. To some degree, we were in the vanguard of the now very popular 'reality TV' genre. The crew were put on notice as to when our new son was to arrive, *if* Yve went full-term this time, which thankfully she did.

Unlike Ike, this boy either didn't *want to*, or *couldn't*, get out! He was massive! After what seemed like ages of pushing, ripping and cutting (to avoid both Yve and the baby becoming even more distressed), he forced his way out. Like Ike, his head was huge, but unlike Ike, his body was also huge. At 8lb 10oz he already looked like a ripped and muscle-bound body-builder. Because he was distressed he, like Kele J and Ike, was rushed to an ICU incubator in order for him to de-stress and stabilise. He looked ridiculous alongside the other tiny incubator babies, like some sort of moon-headed mutant neonate!

He very quickly stabilised and was returned to us on the maternity ward. We named him Obidike Isaac (O-B-D-K, we call him 'Dee' for short), an Igbo name which means 'Warrior', 'Brave Heart' or 'Strong Heart'.

He has grown up to be a very affectionate, sociable, popular, clever, talented and decent young man who has always made me proud and I am happy to be his father.

My three beautiful, talented and gifted children
– Kele J, Dee and Ike – my three gifts

The BBC camera crew was on-hand to film his arrival live and broadcast it to the watching nation as part of their Black London series. The other two couples, according to the producers, 'didn't get it together enough' to inform them of their new arrivals, so they weren't filmed. It was funny. We were told we'd be portrayed as the more mature, settled, reliable couple, and that was exactly how it turned out! I'm not sure if the other fathers are still together with their partners and playing a part in the lives of their children.

I was a bit concerned about how we were portrayed and perceived by the public. However, my fears were assuaged nearly a year later when Yve and I took the kids to the 1995 Notting Hill Carnival. We were recognised by groups of people who'd obviously watched the series, and it was clear they were not only happy to see 'that couple off the telly', but also happy to see that we were still together! We received 'the thumbs up' and congratulatory smiles and positive affirmations all-round. It was a nice feeling. I felt as though we were helping to set a good example.

I met Patrick socially about eight months after the broadcast, and he told me his phone had hardly stopped ringing from women asking him to 'fix them up' with me! He also mentioned that he could barely go out without receiving the same request. Whilst complimentary, this was also a bit disturbing. It was clear from the broadcast that I was married and committed to my family, so *why* would women be keen to get 'fixed up' with me?

A few weeks after Dee's birth we were awoken by a very assertive and impatient rapping on our front door, at about 6.00am in the morning. Yve went down to answer the knock, to be met by two car loads of plain-clothed police officers in the process of executing an early morning raid. Yve called me downstairs.

"Are you Gus Nwanokwu?"

"Yes."

"You're under arrest for evading import duty to the value of £2.5 million."

"What are you talking about?"

"Import duty that should have been paid on cigarettes you're selling. Now, we know you've got children upstairs, and we don't want to wake up the neighbours, so can we take you to the station peacefully and question you there?"

I was in a state of complete and utter mind-numbing shock. Unpaid import duty? Impossible. We were selling for the *export* market only, not local sales.

I agreed to his request and, after being handcuffed, was marched out of my house into an awaiting unmarked police car. The arresting officers were actually from HM Customs and Excise who, unbeknown to me, were even more powerful than regular police. I sat quietly as we wended our way through the early morning traffic of people making their way to work. It felt strange, looking out at the 'normal' world whilst being whisked away for the inevitable interrogation to which I'd soon be subjected. As we slowed down in heavy Brixton traffic, I wondered what other drivers and pedestrians thought they were seeing. One miserable-looking black guy in the back seat of a car full of white men, I'm certain many would have guessed (based on the familiarity of such a sight), that I wasn't a colleague or willing passenger. So, in my mind, they probably quite rightly assumed I was a prisoner under arrest. I felt *so* miserable, afraid and confused, and started to try to work out what had happened, and failed to come up with any plausible explanations. If I couldn't do this for myself, how could I do it in answer to the interrogating officers' questions?

The head honcho driving the car tried to develop a "chummy" relationship with me, trying to suck me into revealing incriminating 'evidence' under the guise of a matey chat. I wasn't going to be sucked in by anybody, so was very circumspect with my responses, intent on keeping my powder dry and not incriminating either Derron or myself.

We eventually arrived at Snow Hill Police Station, situated on the north side of the river Thames in the City of London. After decamping I was booked in by a wizened and craggy looking desk sergeant who attempted to destabilise me with a witheringly disdainful look of contempt as he confirmed my details. I had flashbacks to my "wog comb" beating at the hands (and fists) of the Henley desk sergeant in my youth over two decades earlier.

Manacle-free and ensconced in a cold, bleak and sparsely furnished cell (*not* for the first time in my life!), I paced up and down still trying to make sense of the situation. What could I tell them other than the truth?

Mum always used to tell us that she couldn't stand liars, and warned us that:

"Once ye start lying, ye'll only get deeper and deeper in the lie, and deeper and deeper in trouble. The truth *always* comes out in the end!"

With her words ringing deafeningly in my ears, my strategy was clear, I'd tell the truth.

And so I did. In my view I had nothing to hide, I hadn't knowingly or deliberately broken the law and I certainly hadn't benefited to the tune of £2.5 million!

Interrogated separately, I had no idea what Derron might be saying, so I could only say what I knew.

It transpired that twelve people would be in the dock facing charges of conspiracy to defraud Her Majesty's Treasury of £2.5 million, and a substantive charge of actual fraud. With Derron and I positioned firmly in the middle of the defendants, our alleged co-conspirators included one of the top sales executives of the British and American Tobacco Company, another partner procurement company, and on the buyers' side, one of our 'community' contacts who headed up the eight purchasers. I engaged my tried and trusted solicitor Mr Harazi for the preliminary committal proceedings in the magistrates' court, where we were committed to trial at Wood Green Crown Court in north London, to commence November 1995. Mr Harazi appointed barristers to Derron and I. Whilst Derron and I were effectively, going to be prosecuted as the same entity due to our business partnership, we both required our own personal barrister. We were all given bail, but had to surrender our passports to avoid us 'doing a runner'.

The intervening months were tortuous. I didn't, couldn't tell my family, parents, brother and sisters or friends about my predicament. I really didn't want to put them all under so much strain and pressure, so I resolved to deal with the situation privately. I learned that HMRC were a crack outfit. Apparently, as far as the government is concerned, there's nothing worse in their book, no bigger, more heinous crime, than Her Maj's Treasury being ripped off!

For me, there's nothing worse than being innocent but presumed guilty, and having to prove your innocence which, in all honesty, is how the legal system works. Sod the 'innocent until proven guilty' bullshit. When you're in this situation, guilt is *presumed*, and you have to get yourself out of the shit!

I felt terrible for my family, Yve and the children. I began to under-stand how certain types of pressures can push people to act irrationally (at best), and commit suicide (at worst). I began to regret ever having left the security of teaching and getting into the shark-infested world of business. But I *was* in it. Right in it!

I reached my lowest ebb when mum and dad announced they'd be celebrating their 40th wedding anniversary in Nigeria. I knew I wouldn't be able to attend as I'd had to submit my passport, and no way would the Crown Prosecution Service (CPS), agree to my being given special dispensation to attend, for fear of my absconding. I had no option but to make up a cock-and-bull(shit) story about my pass-port being lost at the Nigeria High Commission after applying for the relevant visa. Given the ineptitude of the Nigeria High Commission at the time, this constituted a totally plausible excuse, and I was never questioned on it. I have never felt so low having to lie to my family, and to miss my parents' anniversary celebrations. I was totally and utterly gutted! Never before, or since, have I felt *so* wretched, and I've never fully overcome the feeling of disappointment and betrayal that I felt I'd bestowed upon my family.

Totally isolated from my whole family whilst they were in Nigeria, I drank myself to oblivion virtually every night. Despite spending some time with my mates Francis, Joe, Johnny and co I don't know how I managed to get through the days. I was at complete rock-bottom.

On their return I started to perk up and become more positive then, closer to the trial date, I slipped back into a negative depression-like state. My problem was that I didn't trust the UK system of law and, after having seen the other co-defendants who, apart from two white guys on the sales side, every other defendant was either black African or Pakistani Asian, apart from Derron who was London-born black of Jamaican parentage. I didn't rate our chances of gaining a 'not guilty' verdict at all highly!

The trial took place as planned at Wood Green Crown Court just before Christmas. Every morning I drove to Balham, parked the car, and took the tube all the way up to north London. Twelve defendants in the dock, I *knew* we must have looked like a bunch of criminals! The jury, to my recollection, was made up of nine white jurors, one black, one Turkish, and one Asian. So much for being tried by your peers!

As the evidence began to unfold, I found the whole thing intriguing. At the close of the fourth day, one of the Pakistanis on the buyers' side, headed up by Derron's Ghanaian 'friend' Eugene, change his original not guilty plea to guilty. He was Eugene's right-hand man, which to me suggested Eugene was involved to some degree. He was instantly taken to the cells, to be convicted separately from our proceedings. He received a significantly reduced prison term of eighteen months due to his change of plea, but because he'd already appeared and participated in the early stages of the trial pleading not guilty, he wouldn't be cross-examined on the basis that he'd already lied to the court.

So, a potential ally who knew what *really* happened couldn't provide the evidence that Derron and I needed to prove our innocence. Great!

Both the white sales guys gave testimony in the witness stand and proved their innocence. They were totally exonerated and freed to leave the court, due to insufficient evidence. The case for the CPS also became very clear. Their intention was to portray Derron and I as the primary movers in the £2.5 million scam. It was unbearable. Derron went to the stand to give evidence about a week or so into the case, and gave an excellent account of our unwitting involvement.

I was then called to the stand and immediately became hyper-sensitive to everything, even the fact that I knew I couldn't be a hypocrite and swear on the Bible, Koran, Torah or any other holy book. I worried how this might be perceived and interpreted by the judge and jury as I made a non-religious vow to speak the truth.

We knew the two white sales people and ourselves were innocent of any malpractice or crime, but couldn't see or understand exactly where the skulduggery had taken place.

Explanations began to materialise when the CPS provided copies of mobile phone calls and texts between Eugene and his guys. This was further supported by CCTV footage of his whole gang arriving at the bonded warehouse, under the pretence of collecting their consignments for despatch to Heathrow and exporting abroad, to load up the vans and drive them out of the warehouse. It was evident they were diverting the loads, not sending them abroad, and selling them on the UK market, making their profits by undercutting the market price.

The whole situation came on top when a notorious thief and burglar had been stopped whilst driving his van in Scotland. His van was searched and he had a carton of export-only cigarettes. When challenged, the carton was confiscated and the police were able to trace the sales history by batch code of the carton.

Eugene's modus operandi was also further revealed to me when I'd been excused to use the toilet. Just as I'd finished one of his guys, a Nigerian guy who was a complete stranger to me, entered, so I hung around to speak with him. I expressed how frustrated and concerned I was with the whole situation, then he turned to me and said:

"Goz, you really don't know what happened?! Eugene was the mastermind. He set things up so that we'd divert the goods to sell them on the market here!"

I wanted to punch his lights out.

I wanted to rip Eugene's face off!

So, from Eugene down they were all *knowingly* involved, yet all had submitted 'not guilty' pleas, meaning we'd all have to endure the trial and hope that the jury would work out the truth. Even more enraging, these guys were prepared to let Derron and I go down as total innocents in the vain hope that they'd get off!

I informed my barrister at the first opportunity as to the confession of Eugene's accomplice. The jury was dismissed for the afternoon in order for the situation to be discussed in closed court. It was decided the new evidence wouldn't be admissible due to the dishonesty of Eugene's boy. *So* frustrating! The guy even told me that one of the guys was a mate of his who'd turned up to meet him at the warehouse. He *innocently* offered to help with loading the van and, as a result, totally unwittingly implicated himself in the conspiracy. I actually felt sorry for the guy, a totally innocent Igbo guy who didn't have a clue what was going on, and *still* his 'mate' was prepared to let him go down rather than admit the truth and implicate himself.

Despicable!

All ten of us were held in a holding cell prior to returning to court to hear the decision as to whether the new evidence would be admissible. I was struggling. I couldn't bear being in the same room as Eugene and his boys any longer. So I challenged him:

"Euge, is that how it really ran?"

He just smiled a sickening smirk of guilt, didn't say anything, but it was obvious it was true.

"Euge, you're prepared to knowingly let innocent people get banged up?"

He smirked again, and I lost it. I lunged at him, I wanted to batter the smirk off his slimy face, but Derron and the screws held me back. I was livid. Our return to the court had to be delayed for half an hour in order for me to 'calm down'. On our return I felt all eyes on me. It felt as if the reason for the delay had been explained to the court and, in my mind, this represented another nail in my coffin. Not only was I being portrayed as an embezzler of HMRC funds, I was also a 'thug' embezzler who was happy and willing to resort to violence as part of the time-honoured judicial process.

I was cross-examined for three days, by the crown prosecutor and then by my own and other defending barristers. I stayed focused and concentrated on telling the truth, and made no attempt to embellish it. The crown prosecutor tried his best to lead me down several paths, accusing me and asking me a battery of questions in a variety of ways, but I wouldn't be outsmarted by sticking to the truth. He became exasperated and at one stage he paused, and said:

"You're a very intelligent man aren't you?"

I didn't answer, I just smiled, and I noticed several of the jury smiling with me.

After three days I was exhausted, but prepared to continue if necessary. When I was released from the witness stand I heaved a huge silent inward sigh of relief. I thought I'd given a good, true and honest account of myself, and hoped the jury saw my testimony in the same light.

Eugene and his junior partner in crime, another Pakistani, chose not to give evidence, which was their prerogative. 'Toilet-boy' gave evidence which was totally incredulous, and followed up his innocent pleas with the support of a Nigerian community church 'pastor' who came to provide a character reference on his behalf. It was nauseating to sit and listen to his dishonest eulogising. It made me sick. He either *knew* Toilet-boy was as guilty as the day is long; or he didn't know, in which case Toilet-boy was cynically using his lay-preacher, and thus religion, to provide him with a fake character reference, which gave me even more reason to despise religion and all the corruptions it stands for!

I got the feeling, I 'sensed', that nobody in the court found the pastor's testimony credible. Shame and embarrassment on them, their 'church' and their religion!

The poor innocent Igbo friend was the only other person on the 'buying' side to go into the witness stand to be cross-examined. His testimony made it quite (embarrassingly) clear that he didn't have a Scooby (clue) what was going on, and that he'd innocently walked into a nightmare of somebody else's making. I felt *so* sorry for him.

Three months of nerve-jangling court proceedings later, we arrived at decision time. After my cross-examination I actually began to enjoy the proceedings. It may sound crazy, but it was almost like an out-of-body experience whereby I was watching, and being thoroughly entertained by, the whole procedure, the cut and thrust, the truth, the lies, it was truly intriguing.

I was snapped back to reality when all sides began their summing-up, and it began to dawn on me that, in the next day or so, I'd either be a free man or banged up for years.

I asked Yve to drop me to Balham station. I didn't want her to be in the court if I was found guilty. The week before the verdicts I tattooed my children's name on my arm, because that would be the only way I'd see them for years. I didn't want anybody visiting me in prison. Other than the suit I was wearing, I had nothing on me. I'd removed the jewellery I'd grown accustomed to wearing, and only had enough cash on me for a cup of coffee on arrival. I was expecting to be found guilty and didn't want to be stripped of any personal belongings on arrival in prison, other than the clothes I was wearing.

On the day the verdicts were to start being announced by the jury foreman, Eugene didn't turn up. He'd done a runner. By this time it was blatantly obvious (to me anyway), that he was the true kingpin and mastermind of the conspiracy. Clearly, he didn't have the balls and wasn't prepared to face justice and the inevitable sentence. It later transpired that he'd somehow managed to abscond to Ghana. He probably had a British as well as a Ghanaian passport!

This, in my opinion, *did not* help us! I understand how easy it is for people to group everybody together, and treat them the same, doing so makes things easier, but for Derron and I that would mean us being lumped in with the guilty guys!

The verdicts started. Poor innocent Igbo guy, not guilty, free to leave the court; every one of Eugene's boys including Eugene (in his absence), and Toilet-boy, were rightly found guilty. We learned they received incremental custodial sentences, starting from two years for Toilet-boy, right through to nine years for Eugene's Pakistani second-in-command; had he been present, Eugene would have received twelve years.

It was incredible. Eventually, only Derron and I were left in the dock, and I felt it totally unlikely that the correct verdict would be made on all twelve defendants which, up to this point, was, unbelievably, the case. I felt the jury couldn't or wouldn't get it right on every defendant, therefore I was prepared for the guilty verdict and, on my summation given the sentences already dispensed, Derron and I, as the so-called 'kingpins' of the operation, were looking at sitting down for about fifteen years!

The suspense was unbearable, but I was prepared to meet the fate that loomed ominously.

"Would the defendants please stand?"

'Here we go.'

Standing ram-rod stiff but quaking with fear, I knew that I'd receive the same verdict as Derron because our roles were inseparable, and we were treated by the prosecution as such.

"How do you find against defendant Derron H on the first charge of conspiracy to defraud?"

"Not guilty your Honour."

I couldn't believe it. *NOT* guilty!"

"And how do you find against Ngozi Nwanokwu on the first charge of conspiracy to defraud?"

"*Not* guilty your Honour."

As waves of emotion surged through my mind and body, I made a quick assumption that, if we're not guilty on the conspiracy to defraud,

400

then surely we can't be found guilty on the substantive charge of fraud, to the tune of £2.5 million!

"How do you find against defendant Derron H on the substantive charge of fraud?"

"*Not* guilty your Honour."

That was it, I knew I would also be found not guilty, I knew in a matter of moments I'd be allowed to leave the dock, I knew I'd be free.

"And how do you find against defendant Ngozi Nwanokwu on the substantive charge of fraud?"

"*Not* guilty your Honour."

Though I knew this verdict was coming, I still could *not* believe it. *Not* guilty! I tried to maintain my dignity in order to convey a visible contempt for the police and judiciary, but failed. I cried like a baby. I looked over at the jury and thanked them. I wanted to praise them for achieving what seemed to me to be the impossible. To get the *right* verdict on *every* defendant! What were the odds of this happening? Incredible! I noticed one or two members of the jury were crying also, and they all looked totally spent but relieved, after having deliberated for over two days on the verdict for Derron and I.

The Crown Prosecutor looked momentarily gutted, but then gathered his thoughts, papers and demeanour quite casually, with a wry smile on his face. Just another day at the office for him I suppose! It dawned on me that we weren't, in his eyes, human beings with families, but numbers. It felt to me as if barristers adopt a competitive 'game' approach to their work in which they attempt to score points against each other by winning on behalf of the Crown or their clients, thus gaining, or losing, kudos, reputation and status. I couldn't help but think about the number of innocent people who've been found guilty and incarcerated over the centuries, cast away like pawns to be eaten up by the system which, invariably, is stacked hugely against them. Countless lives destroyed, but this meant nothing more to the barristers and the system than a numbers 'game'.

I learnt during post-trial discussions with our barristers that our case had set a record for the longest trial at Wood Green Crown Court.

Three months! Also, apart from the fact that we were innocent of all charges, it seems the fact that both Derron and I answered questions on arrest and provided statements, as well as giving open and honest testimony in the witness stand during the trial, went massively in our favour, because the truth is, we could have become another miscarriage of justice. Telling the truth throughout from first arrest to trial also meant our testimony was consistent and clearly not fabricated or designed to cover up any criminal activity.

As we walked out of the court and emerged into the sunlight, all smiles and back-slapping, I felt like Rocky Balboa at the top of the steps in front of the Philadelphia Museum of Art in Pennsylvania. Sylvester Stallone's character *Rocky Balboa's* run up the 72 stone steps to the tune of "Gonna Fly Now" is now universally seen as a metaphor for an underdog or an everyman rising to meet and conquer a challenge.

We'd certainly done that!

Fifty

I decided to end my dabbling in the dog-eat-dog world of business and look for lecturing work in FE again, and was very quickly appointed to a post at Waltham Forest College in Walthamstow, east London. Within a few months I was promoted to manage A level Humanities 16-18 and Adult Access in Sociology and Psychology. I also started up, on a voluntary basis, a football team at the college, which ran BTEC Sports courses, but which didn't facilitate the students engaging in competitive sports! The boys were mad keen on setting up the team, so I set it up with one of the lecturers I managed, Steve, who was also football mad (though a Manchester United supporter!).

Our first game, which was a friendly against our local rivals Sir George Monoux Sixth Form College, ended in a nail-biting 5-4 away win to us. More importantly though was the passion that the boys displayed. They were desperate to win and, after trailing throughout the majority of the match, we pulled back to overturn the deficits and win. Like the boys, Steve also went berserk at the final whistle, running onto the pitch like a demented banshee, shouting and screaming in delight. We were *so* under-resourced, we even had to borrow our kit from SGM! The boys' view was:

> "To hell with the embarrassment of not having our own kit, it was more important to play and win the game!"

Bragging rights firmly in-place, that team went on to beat all-comers and, during my four years at the college, won the Essex County League and Cup competitions, and progressed to the quarter-finals of the national cup. At the end of our first season I was actually given time on my timetable, and a budget, to cover all football-related expenditure. Many of the boys during my tenure went on to represent Essex at county level and, if truth be told, a few should have made it into professional football. However, in football development terms, they'd missed the opportunity, and it was now probably too late for clubs to 'take a gamble on them', even on a trial basis. Based on our results, I was soon appointed co-manager of the Essex County representative team, and was made Essex County delegate to the final England Under 18s Schoolboys match against Hungary at the old Wembley Stadium.

Walking into the huge reception room, situated between the legendry twin towers of the old stadium of 1966 fame, where the pre-match speeches and dinner was to be held, it dawned on me exactly why so few black players were chosen to represent England, and possibly why so few black players, at least historically, had made it into the professional ranks. About 2,000 'honoured' guests had been invited to attend this auspicious occasion, and I was *the only* black face in the house. The room was filled with mainly old, white 'suits' who, in my view, would have been so far removed and detached from the overwhelming majority of inner-city black boys in school or going through college.

For me it was a very disturbing sight to behold. The thought that the hopes and dreams of hundreds if not thousands of inner-city working class boys was in the hands of these 'suits' was depressing. They held so much power and influence, and, no doubt, didn't particularly engage or identify with 'my type of players', real 'ballers' who played with passion, ability, athleticism and skill.

It also didn't help when, as I was walking through the college one day, I bumped into the principal. I'd never spoken with him directly before, but I'd put the college very firmly on the map, and it was now *the* college to attend if boys wanted to achieve competitive success whilst on their sports courses. Applications and enrolments went through the roof and, as a result, even better players arrived to study and play. I was earning the college a fortune in enrolment fees, for very little in return in terms of salary, resources and time!

He stopped me to talk and to express his gratitude for what I'd provided the college 'on the cheap':

"Gus, you know you've done a fantastic job with these boys."
"Thanks."
"You know if you were doing this in an American college or university, you'd be on about 100K per year!"

I stopped listening and made my excuses to scurry away to a fictitious meeting. I didn't want to tell him to "Fuck of!", so thought it better to end the conversation prematurely, discretion being the better part of professional suicide!

Plus I was enjoying life, and wasn't particularly money-orientated. I still gained intrinsic satisfaction from enhancing the life chances and future prospects of the young people that I worked with. Also, family life was fine, Yve and the kids were doing well, and we'd developed a really enjoyable social circle of friends that added to life's joys. At certain stages I busied myself with setting up event initiatives: 'Big Belly Man' Promotions, or BBM for short. A good Guyanese friend and neighbour Joe B and I put on family fun days and coach trips to the seaside that catered for hundreds of friends and family. These events also put some money in our pockets which didn't go amiss at the time! I also set up a similar enterprise, 'NiJam' (Nigeria-Jamaica), with another good Jamaican friend of mine, Johnny M, which put on 'big people dances' for our age group. This was very successful also. So life, and things, was fine. And of course, I had my two close friends and wing-men, Francis J and Delroy P to roll with and confide in also.

Mum had retired by now and spent much of her time living between Nigeria (where we'd built a family house), and her flat in southwest London. She spent approximately six months of the year in Nigeria, usually during the winter months here, and six months in London during the summer. She enjoyed her independence and privacy much of the time, and totally adored her grandchildren. *All of them*. It struck me as almost miraculous how both mum and dad indulged their grandchildren in a way we never experienced as their children! Maybe that's an integral part of being human and the life-cycle that we all follow.

It was interesting how they'd take their grandchildren's sides on many issues, and support them even in the face of our objections as the child's parents. They seemed to be far more amenable towards their 'grands' than they ever were towards us at the same age!

I never really got to feel dad ever reflected on his fatherly role and how he played it, but his love for us never wavered and, in many ways, the older he got, the more emotionally dependent he got on us as his children.

Mum seemed far more able to reflect and often expressed a fear that she hadn't been a 'good' mother. This was a notion I refused to discuss with her at any length, other than to reassure he she was the best mum I could ever have hoped for. This despite the fact that one day, when we were having a chat in our lounge in Thornton Heath, she turned to me, totally randomly and out of the blue, to announce:

"Gos, you know, you were the ugliest of all of my children when you were young"
"Oh. Cheers mum. I love you too!"

And we had a good chuckle. If there was one thing, mum was always consistent, always spoke her mind and, if she thought for whatever reason she might have to hold things back, she couldn't keep it up for long and would eventually let you know what was on her mind.

In 1991 I was also managing a Sunday morning football league team, Spencer Park FC, in the self-same Morden and District League that I'd played when I was younger. We were very successful, winning league trophies and cup competitions. The team was made up mainly of inner-city black and mixed-race players, and a couple of white players, both of whom were indelibly part of the team's core and fabric.

We attracted the support of a sponsor who happened to be Irish and owned and ran his own paper-shredding company, Jack. He was a family friend of one of our white (Irish) players Chris. Jack suggested the team go on a long-weekend tour to Ireland, which materialised over the weekend after St Patrick's Day. We were to be staying in the city of Limerick (known as 'Stab City' at the time, now known as 'Uzi City'!), and Pike Rovers FC (Poik Rovers!), were to be our hosts. The games would be staged at their ground.

Given that I'd travelled to and visited Nigeria so many times, it was ironic that after thirty-odd years of life I'd be going to Ireland for the first time ever. Ireland being a mere hop, skip and jump away from London across the Irish Sea; Nigeria being thousands of miles away! Not just Ireland, but Limerick, mum's home county! I couldn't wait!

Chi-chi had already visited Ireland with mum in August 1984. She took it upon herself to suggest the trip to mum, who, after considerable cajoling on Chi-chi's part, reluctantly agreed. They drove over and Chi-chi arranged accommodation near Upperchurch, the small village in north Tipperary where mum spent much of her childhood and adolescence growing up. Lying in the green and golden Slievefelin Hills between Thurles and Limerick, this was where most of mum's legendary children's stories originated.

On their return I remember feeling exceptionally anxious, as I'd felt before they left. I didn't want either mum or Chi-chi to face any sort of insult, offence or trauma. I was hugely relieved when Chi-chi reassured us that everything went really well, as did mum. Other than mum's miraculous ability to remember road routes and directions in her corner of the Limerick-Tipperary border area of her youth (miraculous because mum was notoriously rubbish at remembering directions in *every* area that we lived in England!), Chi-chi recounted a particularly tense and poignant moment on their arrival at mum's village home in Upperchurch.

Mum was also concerned about the possibility of not being received in a respectful and cordial manner. She was prepared to give anyone a tongue-lashing if they made this mistake. She was dreading Chi-chi being abused by anybody and, in keeping with her powerful mother's instincts, wanted to protect her from any such abuse. After having driven up the narrow tree-shrouded hilly lane to where her mum worked as a children's nanny for the Purcell family, she ordered Chi-chi to remain in the car, outside the entrance gates. Walking purposefully towards the front door, mum was intercepted by Sean, the son of the family who'd been cared for by our grandmother as a child. They both stopped and stared at each other, like a scene from 'Gunfight at the OK Corral'.

Sean broke the silence first:

"Missy? Is that you Missy?"

Missy was the name Sean and his siblings used when referring to my grandmother when she cared for them as children.

"No, it's her daughter. You must be Missy's daughter! Ah, to be sure you're the spitting image of her!"

"Margaret?" "Margaret!"

At which he beamed with genuine delight and welcomed her with open arms. He was equally as welcoming towards Chi-chi who, tears streaming down her face with emotion and anxiety, left the safety of her car to join the reunion.

Sean remembered everything. He was shocked at the spitting-image resemblance between mum and our grandmother, his childhood carer. In the ensuing discussion he said much to dispel the notion that mum was disowned by her parents because dad was black. He felt it was more the case that he wasn't a Catholic!

This assertion appeared to be supported by another relative who they met, Jack Hogan, who mum thought was her uncle, but in fact either he or his father was our great grandmother's second husband. This meeting took place in Cappamore Lackabeg, the village where mum was actually born. Sadly, he died shortly after their return to London, and it felt as if our last chance of meeting any of mum's side of the family had died with him.

The legendary hayloft where mum and her sister Joan slept was in the roof of the tiny converted outhouse where our grandmother lived on the Purcell's farm. It was also, as I mentioned previously, the hayloft where the local IRA militia hid to avoid the attentions of the Black and Tans when they were operating in the area!

I was happy and satisfied that both mum and Chi-chi returned with positive feelings about their trip. Anything else would have devastated me, given the fact that mum had had no contact with any member of her family for so long. I think mum was pleased also, though she still exuded a certain low level contempt and disdain for her family of origin. Effectively, for the vast majority of her life, we were the only family she had, knew, loved and cherished.

The team, Jack, Chris, Obi and I bundled onto the tour bus and, amid maximum raucous banter, excitement and hilarity, we were on our way. After having made the ferry crossing from Holyhead to Dun Loaghaire in County Dublin, it felt strange to be in Ireland. We arrived late afternoon early evening, and would spend much of the remainder of the day making our way across country to Limerick, in the southwest of Ireland.

Obi and I sat together on the bus and exchanged our thoughts and feelings. He too found it strange, weird, being in Ireland. We both remarked how we were imagining mum growing up in these surroundings. Once we'd got out of the port town, we were in rural Ireland, and it was pretty much as we'd expected it to be, green! Lush green rolling hills and farmland, demarcated by centuries-old dry-stone and slate walls; narrow winding country lanes bisecting each glen and dale; new and dilapidated Gaelic crosses and iconography littering each and every small community; crumbling rustic stone peasant farmsteads giving a hint of the harsh lives its occupants must have led prior to succumbing to the potato famine, or joining the exodus fleeing Ireland to far-flung destinations and destinies around the world in search of survival.

We got lost in our own private thoughts, daydreams and imaginings. I for one couldn't quite put together the legendary stories mum told us as kids with the sights we were seeing. It was difficult. We were strangers on a bus packed with twenty black faces and four white. It was hardly the case that we could learn anything meaningful from any of our party, all of whom were on a 'jolly' or, as they say in Ireland, enjoying 'the craic!'

We arrived at Pike Rovers FC stadium in Limerick City where we were met by officials and local media reporters before making our way to our accommodation. We'd arranged a couple of training sessions before the matches we played, so the following morning we were out on the pitch going through a few pre-match routines.

"Neggers! Neggers!"

A small group of ginger freckle-faced kids, peering over a wall, were watching the boys easing through their paces, and couldn't help but express their ignorance. I'm not sure if I didn't want to hear what they'd shouted, or didn't want to believe that they'd actually shouted it, but I knew what I'd heard. Some of the boys reacted negatively, telling the kids to "fuck off out of it!", while others laughed and wound each other up over it. I got the feeling that these kids were in awe of us. It was probably the first time they'd seen black people up-close and in real life, and didn't have any other frame of reference to address us with, other than that which they'd been exposed to on television.

My suspicion, in my mind, was to be proved true later during the tour.

We had a photo session before our first game, which was reported on by the local media. We went into town on the Saturday night and everywhere we went people knew us. We were getting stopped in the street, being sincerely and warmly welcomed by all, with people asking to have photos taken with us and so on; we were made to feel like superstars, and lapped up the attention.

We ate out together before going on to spend the night at a local disco. Here again, we were the centre of attention, and the lads didn't waste much time standing on ceremony. The boys hammed it up in the club and on the dance floor, ensuring to suitably impress hordes of local girls. In actual fact a couple of the team, who shall remain nameless, needed to be picked up from young ladies' homes the following morning. According to one as he climbed aboard the bus, he'd 'scored' last night and was intending to score in our next game later in the day!

Pike Rovers put on a 'club night' for us that included music and food in their clubhouse. Their hospitality was excellent, warm, sincere and genuine. They really enjoyed hosting us. It's a pity I, like the majority of the team, couldn't say the same about the traditional food they prepared for us. A massive pot of boiled cabbage and pork! No chance! The smell of it alone was nearly enough to put you off food for life!

The Guinness was superb though!

We did a bit of sightseeing also, part of which included a trip to Blarney Castle, Blarney, approximately 8 miles from Cork, where I kissed the legendary Blarney Stone. The Blarney Stone is a block of blue stone which was set into the highest tower of the castle in 1446. Legend has it that kissing the Blarney Stone endows the kisser with the 'gift of the gab', great eloquence or skill at flattery. Generally speaking, the Irish have developed this ability in great abundance; they are eminently eloquent and articulate. 'Dem can talk sweet!' Especially when enhanced with the soft Dublin burr. The word "blarney" has come to mean "clever, flattering, or coaxing talk". I like John O'Connor Power's succinct definition:

> "Blarney is something more than flattery. It is flattery sweetened
> by humour and flavoured by wit. Those who mix with Irish folk
> have many examples of it in their everyday experience."

Our experience was very much in line with Power's definition. We found our hosts extremely welcoming, genuinely pleasant, witty, humorous, accommodating, genial and enjoyable company. Essentially, they were 'good people'. Ireland was a 'fun' place to visit which, notwithstanding the gawping and gobby ginger freckled-faced kids, appeared to actually be at peace with itself and others.

We left Ireland feeling uplifted after having really enjoyed our tour-cum-jolly-up. Football tour aside though, I didn't feel as though many, if any questions were answered with regards mum and her early life in Ireland. Our time there was busy and we didn't really get the chance to 'go off-piste' to start any other form of investigation. I certainly didn't feel any rootsy sense of home-coming that I'd experienced overwhelmingly in Nigeria, but my first trip to the enchanted Emerald Isle, though frustrating on this particular issue, was a very positive one.

Fifty-One

June 2001 was a time of celebration for the family. Chi-chi was awarded an MBE for Services to Music in the Queen's Birthday Honours list. She actually received her award from Her Maj at Buckingham Palace. Mum and dad were *so* proud! And, in all honesty, her achievements in the world of classical music have been astounding, considering how and where, as a family, we started out in life, and the trials and tribulations that dogged us throughout (though Chi-chi, somehow and inexplicably, less so).

Obviously I'm totally biased, but in my opinion, she's the best thing that's happened to the world of classical music for donkey's years. Unlike her contemporaries, she plays classical music with and from her soul; with passion; with expression; she entertains and stirs emotions in equal measure; she enjoys her craft as an expression of her being; she reaches out and communicates whilst on stage where all eyes are inevitably drawn to her. Not just because she's invariably the only black face in the orchestra or ensemble, but because she's so good, and loves her instrument and music. She's travelled the world many times over in the performance and delivery of her craft and passion, and is always fully booked to play well in advance. She's famous, well respected and highly regarded. She's appeared on national TV, has had her own BBC Radio show and, more importantly than all of this, she's still our big sister.

She knows better than to try to Lord it with us, and never does so intentionally. Given that she's still a 'family girl', with her heart still in the family, I felt free to register my concerns about the MBE

Award at the award party she held at her house in the speech I made. Essentially, and as politely as possible so as not to 'spoil the vibe', I mentioned the fact that I wasn't sure about the 'British Empire' shit and the connotations it carries with it. But I made it abundantly clear that, as recognition of her ability, achievement and professionalism I, like my brother and two other sisters, was immensely proud of her.

Proud day for the family – Chi-chi's MBE at
Buckingham Palace (October 2001)

L-R: Obi, Phoebe (Chi-chi's daughter), Dad, Chi-chi, Mum, Jacob (Chi-chi's son)

The thought of me being awarded an MBE for Services to _____ (whatever, fill in the blanks with anything that may come to mind!) is, quite clearly, a very far-fetched and fanciful notion. But I'd love to be offered it, just to reject it.

MBE – Member of the Most Excellent Order of the British Empire.

In my opinion and for what it's worth, these pompous awards are throwbacks to, and reminders of, a disgusting system of privilege and status, irrefutable evidence of jingoistic cronyism at its worst, serving to ensure the perpetuation of the British 'jobs for the boys' mentality and the 'old school tie' network. I am not saying that some people who have excelled in their field ought not to be recognised, and recognised most highly at that, but is it really necessary to append the reference to the British Empire?

The institution of the British Empire means so many different things to so many different people. I fully understand why a white 'English' person would be inclined to revel in the accolade, and tub-thump about erstwhile achievements of empire; however, I don't quite understand how and why so many non-white people 'of other origin' do so in a similar, if not more ardent manner. Have they become *so* assimilated by 'all that is *Great* and *British*' that they fail to consider the implications of the 'Empire' reference?

Does 'Empire' actually mean anything to them?

Should it?

Maybe they've got it right. After all, we're here and here to stay.

But *glory* in the 'Empire'?

An empire that attacked, raided, looted, abducted, debauched, abused, enslaved and exploited innumerable multi-millions of people, *my* people?

I couldn't. I'd feel like a complete and utter traitor to all those who went before me, a sell-out. This is not to disrespect or demean Chi-chi's achievements, but an expression of how I feel as a completely different person to her.

I now formally propose a 'British Peoples' Award' to replace the tainted, blood-stained, discredited and meaningless current award.

I like the idea of this and would definitely be up for receiving one!

I'd be up for an award that recognised remarkable commitment and endeavour in service to the community all day long! Though I won't hold my breath!

The British Peoples' Award would mean *so* much more to me because, after all, I *am* British. Not English. British.

Citizenship is a creation of socio-geo-political circumstance, an entitlement. I was born in England, in the UK, a part of Britain. Therefore I'm British.

But I'm not English.

I know where I 'come from' – Biafra ('Nigeria'), and Ireland.

Do the English *know* where they come from in such unequivocal terms?

For the majority, I doubt it.

However, I'd be happy to accept recognition through the British Peoples' Awards system, particularly on behalf of my family, ancestors, friends, and all the heroes of the now defunct British Commonwealth who selflessly gave so much to 'the Empire'.

I'm still not holding my breath though!

Fifty-Two

I spent the Easter period of 2004 in Nigeria with Kele, her now ex-husband Ifeanyi and dad, mainly in Port Harcourt, the 'Garden City' capital of Rivers State. Dad's eyesight had steadily deteriorated over the years and he was now extremely visually impaired, if not to say blind. Having known him as a proud man for all his life, it was horrible to see him so dependent. He'd developed diabetes and glaucoma, as well as cataracts, but was very obstinate and reluctant to make any real attempts to change his lifestyle habits and diet, preferring to blag his way through his remaining days rather submit to and confront his frailties.

Within a few weeks of returning to London we received news that dad had died a natural death on Friday 28th May 2004, at the ripe old of age 92.

We were all devastated. This was the first time we'd experienced death in our family. Yes, Ngozi had lived for a week but we didn't get the opportunity to watch him grow and become attached to him. Dad was there from the beginning, and throughout our lives. Like my brother and sisters I was totally inconsolable. I didn't know how to be anything else. I did know, though, that I'd have to 'deal with it'. Death is an unavoidable part of life. In fact, once there is life, death is the only *guarantee* in life. Bearing this in mind, as people, we remain shockingly unprepared for it when it happens.

Experiencing and coping with the death of a loved one, is *such* a traumatic but important event in our lives, similar to parenting, but, also like parenting, it remains an aspect of our lives that we're not taught about. Nobody teaches us how to be good parents, and nobody teaches us how to deal with death in the family.

As an 'Eze' (Chief), of our local Eziama area, dad would have to be buried with full honours in a traditional ceremony. Yve stayed in London with mum (who was not well enough to attend), Ike and Dee. I travelled with Kele J, Chi-chi and her two children (Jacob and Phoebe), Obi, Ijem and her two children (Uchenna and Chidinma).

The ceremony and ritual reconfirmed to me that death is, very definitely, for the living. The survivors have to 'deal with' death. As a family, we dealt with it; the arrangements, the catering, receiving the invited guests, and feeding the hundreds of villagers who attended. Obi and I dressed and prepared dad in the mortuary for his final journey, tears of grief streaming down our faces. But the most abiding memory I have is of Chi-chi riding in the hearse with dad, as tradition dictates, holding a large laminated photograph of him at the head of the cortege, inconsolable with grief, tears pouring down her face. My heart *so* went out to her.

They say time heals and, to a degree, there's a lot of truth and wisdom in that adage. But, no matter how many years pass, in the quiet moments, I still think of dad every day. I still see and hear him, I laugh at the jokes and good times we had together, and wonder about the things I never understood about him. I wish I could have spent more time with him, talking and learning from him, and about him. It's interesting though. The older I get, the more I appear to be morphing into him. People have commented about my increasingly similar looks and mannerisms, and I'm inwardly aware of my increasingly similar thoughts, feelings and opinions. Whilst I remain a committed atheist, a total 'non-believer', I do believe in a certain concept of the lasting spirit. *Not* in a religious manner, but more in terms of an idea that there are certain things about the essence of significant others that we adopt and pass on to our own children.

For example, I like the idea that, in the future, people will say:

"Kele J, she behaves just like her dad in those types of situations."
"Ike thinks just like his dad."

"Obi relates to people in just the same way as his dad."
And so on.

In essence, I suppose what I'm saying is that our 'spirit' lives on in our children. Being compared with my dad in this way is, to me, a great honour, and I hope my own children feel similarly at some stage in the future.

A couple of months after dad's funeral I'd just dropped a Cameroonian friend of mine off at Heathrow airport. I'd held a FIFA Players' Agents' Licence for a couple of years, and we'd done some business together. I'd reached Streatham Common, about a three-minute drive to our house, when I started shaking violently. Within seconds I was sweating profusely and I'd virtually lost all control of my body.

'What the hell is going on?!'

Somehow I made it home without crashing the car, but struggled to stay still enough (my whole body was body-popping by this stage!), to guide the key into the front door. I had to knock to get the au-pair to let me in. After just about managing to make myself a cup of tea, in the hope that I'd settle down, hands still shaking I called Yve. She told me to call for an ambulance but, typical working-class 'bloke', I waited until she got home, by which time I'd developed a fever, felt exceptionally nauseous, and was still involuntarily mimicking a James Brown slide. Yve took me to Mayday Hospital where, after providing a blood sample during a particularly severe break-dance routine, I was quickly diagnosed as having contracted a very virulent new strain of malaria.

I was admitted immediately whilst the parasites were still maintaining their assault on my nervous system, liver and kidneys, and was hooked up to a variety of intravenous drips which, after a few days, started to have the desired effect. I remained in hospital for a further eight days, at the end of which I was told I'd been very close to dying! I didn't understand *how* I'd actually contracted the disease though. For years I'd been travelling to and from Nigeria without having taken the necessary anti-malarial tablets, and never suffered. For some reason I decided to take them before, during and after returning from dad's funeral; and got infected! It didn't make sense. Anyway, all I knew was that I was happy and lucky to still be alive!

Chi-chi had spoken for a long time about trying to track down and meet up with any remaining and accessible members of mum's side of the family. She attacked the project with admirable gusto and indefatigable enthusiasm, to the point where it seemed she'd become obsessed with the idea. She'd excitedly relay every snippet of information she discovered to us as she relentlessly investigated mum's family tree. She made unbelievable progress and, after many significant and emotional ups and downs, eventually established the fact that mum still had a younger brother, Patrick. Not only was he alive and kicking, he was also living in the south western UK county of Devon, near Exeter!

We'd heard rumours that mum had relatives in the region, but wouldn't have known where to begin tracking them. Chi-chi's research in pursuit of mum's family had taken her all around the world, from the UK to Ireland, Zimbabwe, Australia and America. We *didn't* really expect her sole surviving sibling to be living relatively so close to us in Devon! Apparently Patrick, 'Uncle Paddy', had moved to England after mum and worked as a builder, on roads and Exeter airport. It also transpired that we had first cousins living in and around Devon, as well as Southampton and Cheltenham on Aunty Joan's side.

Possibly spurred on by mum's increasingly debilitating state of health (her smoking was beginning to catch up with her as she began to suffer emphysema), Chi-chi was now like a dog with a bone, totally resolved to reuniting mum with her brother, and us with the cousins we'd never previously met. She'd already facilitated our meeting up with Patricia, Aunty Joan's daughter, and she'd invited Uncle Paddy and his children, three sons and a daughter, up to London to meet at her house ahead of a massive reunion with all the Nwanokwu-Hevey clan.

Mum on the rear veranda of the family home in Egbelubi
village – beer on the table and fag in hand!

We met Uncle Paddy, his daughter Maggie and two of his sons, Sean and Derrick, as arranged. The family resemblance between mum and her brother was striking. They both had the same thick head of hair, and the same grey-blue eyes. They recognised and embraced each other immediately and, within minutes, it was almost as if they'd never lost contact, reminiscing over days and things gone-by.

For me, it was strange meeting 'white family' other than mum. I was happy and interested to meet them, but didn't really feel the overwhelming sense of emotion that I expected. Maybe, like mum, I'd become hardened to the idea of meeting with them. Throughout my life I'd wondered about what mum's side of the family were like, and whether or not we'd get on, and if there'd be any similarities between us. However, having resigned myself to never meeting them and therefore never finding out, I'd adopted the 'you don't miss what you don't have' feeling towards them. But, out of interest, I'd always *wanted* to meet them, if only just the once.

They were all really pleasant, down-to-earth people, with a very similar family sense of humour to ours, and both the sons played football, one to semi-professional level. The daughter, Maggie, was whacky and irreverent, and it soon became clear she nursed a partiality to alcohol to dispense certain demons. It seems when she was a child she was the best friend of

Genette Tate, a thirteen year-old who went missing whilst on her paper-round in Aylesbeare, Devon, on the 19th August 1978. The as-yet unresolved case made headline national news and even today features regularly on cold-case programmes, but sadly her fate remains unknown, and body unfound. It appears Maggie never really came to terms with the trauma, and found escape in the bottle. She died 18 months after our reunion.

Mum was glad she'd met her younger brother after all the years that had passed, but never became emotional about it. Emotionally, I suppose, she'd maintained an impervious defence against emotive intrusion by her family, so remained steadfastly stoical; pleasant and polite, but stoical.

Mum's 80th Birthday and Reunion Celebration
(her brother and nephew are to her right)

Psychologically and emotionally she was strong, but physically she was becoming increasingly weaker. I often took her to see the specialists at St George's Hospital in Tooting with regards her emphysema, and she was spending more and more time staying with us at home, rather than in her flat. I received the phone call I was dreading on the morning of Thursday 13th April 2006. Mum had been staying with us for the previous two weeks, and she'd been happy. However, her breathing was becoming increasingly laboured and she needed to be admitted to our local Mayday Hospital for observation. Her strength and resistance was low and she developed pneumonia. However, she eventually succumbed to a rapid cancer which forced her to give up the fight. She was aged 80 when she left us.

Kele happened to be in London, staying at mum's flat, and went to visit her in the morning, to be met with the news that she'd just died. She phoned me frantically and I raced to the hospital. I disintegrated when I saw her lying lifelessly on her bed. Mum, the rock of the family, was gone.

She was still warm when I kissed her 'goodbye'.

We flew mum back to Nigeria and buried her next to dad, as is tradition, in front of the new family house that we'd started to build.

I struggled to write about dad's death and funeral, and I can't write any more about mum's. Even today, it's still too raw and painful for me. Needless to say, I think about her every day.

It never dawned on me until after losing both mum and dad that we, my brother, sisters and I, were all that was left of the original, 'pioneer' mixed-race family unit. The ones that fought our way up against all the odds that poverty and racism conspired to throw at us, and, to some degree, survived and won. We did so as a family united. We prevailed.

It also dawned on me that each one of us had very different relationships with our parents. We each remember certain things about them that were special and personal, that were unshared by others. Our perceptions, thoughts and feelings towards them, though they were both loved and appreciated by us all; were also different. These differences are difficult to identify or quantify, but significant nonetheless. I am in no doubt that each one of us carries around these 'things' of mum and dad in our everyday lives, to be passed on to our own children, and their children, ad infinitum.

Uncle Sammy was equally forlorn at the loss of his brother and sister-in-law. It was almost as if he never recovered from the shock. He too, our 'Biafran Soldier', died of an acute cancer of the spleen and, like mum and dad, was flown home to be buried in front of his house in Egbelubi village.

Chi-chi's relentless pursuit of making contact with mum's relatives didn't abate in the slightest and, if anything, escalated to a more fevered level of intensity and commitment. In July of 2008 she was scheduled to perform with a chamber orchestra in Bantry House, Bantry Bay, situated on the south west tip of Ireland in County Cork. She thought it would be a good idea if members of the family could meet up to spend a few days together after the concert, so put the message out there. Our second cousins flew in all the way from America (June), and Australia (Rosie with her daughter Dani), as well as two first cousins from England, Patricia and Chris Hevey, and other second cousins from England including another Chris Hevey. It just so happened that a TV production crew was partway through filming a documentary on Chi-chi's life, and had followed her to Ireland also.

I flew to Cork airport in the southeast region of Eire where I met up with Patricia. We got a taxi from Cork to Bantry Bay, and on the way passed places that, for me, summed up my fantasies of Ireland. In particular, I was enchanted by the name of one town, Skibbereen; it just 'sounded' and 'felt' *so* Irish. Skibbereen, referred to as 'Skibb' by locals, is a town in County Cork. Its Gaelic name is *An Sciobairin*, meaning 'little boat harbour'.

Established in the 14th century, fifty years after being decimated by the Black Death in 1350, apparently by 1600 most of the land in Skibbereen was owned by the McCarthy clan. Today, McCarthy is the most common name in Skibb. 500 years after the scourge of the plague (between 1845-52), a time referred to as 'An Gorta Mor' (The Great Hunger), it's estimated that between 8,000-10,000 people perished during 'The Great Famine', the victims of which are buried in the Famine Burial Pits of Abbeystrewery Cemetery.

Skibbereen is also the name of a song about the potato famine, and the impact it and the British Government had on the people of Ireland. The song, known as *Dear Old Skibbereen*, takes the form of a conversation between a father and his son, in which the son asks his father why he fled the land he loved so well. The father relates to the son how the famine ruined his farm in Skibbereen, and killed his wife. As the man was unable to pay taxes:

"..... the landlord and bailiff came to drive us all away.
They set the roof on fire with their cursed English flame.
And that's another reason why I left old Skibbereen....."

In the final verse the son swears he will return to Skibbereen to take vengeance on the government he holds accountable. The town has a permanent exhibition at the Skibbereen Heritage Centre that commemorates that tragic period in Irish history. Also, the Phoenix Society was founded in Skibbereen in 1856, which was a precursor to the Fenian Movement that developed in America and, which was itself, a precursor to the 'Irish Republican Brotherhood' and, eventually, the Irish Republican Army (IRA).

The historical and strategic coastal town of Wexford is also in the southeast region of Eire.

History relates that the so-called 'Irish Problem' did not suddenly occur in one set year in the Nineteenth Century. Ireland's problems go much further back. Oliver Cromwell, who governed Britain in the mid-Seventeenth Century and at the time when Britain was a republic, detested Roman Catholicism and believed that the Irish could "never be trusted". His attempts to 'solve' the 'Irish problem' (as he saw it), was to send to the island his 'New Model Army' and coerce the Irish into obedience. This included the sieges of Wexford and Drogheda where the defenders in both towns were executed after being offered terms of clemency if they surrendered to Cromwell's forces. Cromwell also believed that the best way to bring Ireland to heel in the long term, was to 'export' children from Ireland to the sugar plantations in the West Indies as armies of slaves to toil alongside the similarly enslaved Africans, so that Ireland would suffer from a long term population loss, making it less of a threat to mainland Britain.

Hence the plethora of centuries-old Irish communities across the Caribbean, particularly in Jamaica, Montserrat, Barbados, St Kitts and Nevis, St Barts, Antigua and the rest of the English speaking Leeward islands, as well as Guyana in South America. Many of the Irish, who were exiled to the 'West Indian' islands, if they survived their servitude, left the islands to forge a new life for themselves in the colonies of North America.

In the Eighteenth Century, farming land in Ireland became more and more the property of English landlords. The bulk of these were absentee landlords who showed little if any compassion for the people who worked the land. The rural population of Ireland, which was the large majority of the population, lived lives of extreme poverty.

The extent of poverty and the issues surrounding it were well known in the British establishment. Even a stalwart Tory like the Duke of Wellington commented that:

"There never was a country in which poverty existed to the extent that it exists in Ireland".

Europeans who went to rural Ireland (though they would have been few in number) were shocked by what they saw:

Kohl, a German visitor to Ireland in the early 19th century, commented:

"Now I have seen Ireland, it seems to me that the poorest among the Letts, the Estonians and the Finlanders lead a life of comparative luxury".

Many years later when Gladstone wrote to the government of Naples to complain about the state of prisons there, he got a reply stating that what existed in Ireland, outside of prisons, was much worse and that he had no right to complain about prisons in Naples when Ireland was in such a state for people *not* in prison.

The poverty that existed in rural Ireland is relatively easy to explain and centres around land ownership.

First, the people who owned the land were frequently absent landlords who paid little attention to the state of their land. Their only concern was rent. Those who could not pay were evicted and there was no safety net in place for these people when this happened - as it frequently did. Absentee landlords were responsible for much anger among the rural population of Ireland. They crammed as many families onto their land as they could. No family who worked the land they had could produce enough to feed their families. Landlords enforced their authority through thugs or via the police or army who could be called in to evict families if the landlord requested such help. Even in the Nineteenth Century, it would still be possible to describe those who lived in rural Ireland as leading the lives of peasants, a term that would have been used in Medieval England. They had no rights, the power rested solely in the hands of the landlords and those who upheld law and order were frequently in league with the landlords.

The second problem the rural population had was the fact that their annual food harvest was based on the potato and not a crop such as wheat or corn.

The famous agriculturist, Arthur Young, once wrote:

"I will not assert that potatoes are better food than bread and cheese, but I have no doubt that a belly full of one, being better than a belly full of the other".

Potatoes were notoriously susceptible to disease, and famines due to a failed potato crop had occurred on a number of occasions in Nineteenth Century Ireland. However, the potato blight of 1845 eclipsed all that had passed before and its impact on Ireland is impossible to quantify outside of simple statistics.

Why was the potato grown? When it was not blighted by disease, a good harvest could be expected. Also the vegetable could produce a high yield with little intensive care. With protein from the dairy produce found in rural communities, those who used the potato as the basis for their diet, could get a reasonably good diet. However, when the potato crop failed, those who relied on it faced very serious problems.

The most infamous example of potato failure was in 1845. Its impact on Ireland was nothing short of catastrophic.

Ireland's population growth in the first half of the Nineteenth Century had been great. Disraeli even claimed that it was higher than the growth rate of China - but this is debatable simply because of the lack of statistics. From 1780 to 1840, Ireland's population grew at an estimated 172%. For comparison, in mainland Britain, it is estimated to have been at 88% in the same time period. By 1845, before the Great Famine, the population of Ireland was 8 million.

Why did Ireland's population grow so quickly in the first half of the Nineteenth Century? The impact of the Catholic Church cannot be overstated. The Catholic Church ruled against contraception and abortions (in whatever forms existed then), and preached about the value of large families. Also, many did believe that a large family would provide 'insurance' in old age as your children would look after you. Therefore, the more children you had, the more comfortable you would be in your later years (a concept very similar in African-Caribbean culture). However, a large family faced many problems when food was in short supply. When there was no supply, as in 1845-1847, the situation became catastrophic.

The Irish were alienated from the British mainland up to 1845, but after it, this feeling of alienation grew. It was after the Great Famine that secret organisations grew and they simply wanted the British out of Ireland and a republic set up free from the rule of Westminster. The most famous were the Fenians and the Irish Republican Brotherhood. The tactics of such groups were brutal including the murder of Lord Cavendish, Chief Secretary for Ireland, and T. Burke, the Permanent Under-Secretary in Ireland, in Phoenix Park, Dublin, in 1882. This one event horrified Victorian England but seemed to confirm to many in England that the Irish simply could not be trusted. Despite the murders, Gladstone continued with his Home Rule campaign, but without success in the 19th century. While Gladstone tried to push through many acts for Ireland, the basic issues of poverty and land ownership were never addressed.

Little did I know I was soon to be given local oral accounts of some of these issues, based on the experiences and tales of our family's ancestors, long since departed either by vessel or the end of life's course.

Patricia and I arrived at Bantry House early on the Thursday evening, where we met Chi-chi and our other cousins in a small marquee outside the main house. It was a very interesting meeting but, again for me, not one which stirred *deep* emotions. I was really very happy to meet with relatives of mine 'on mum's side', and I was keen, inquisitive and interested to work out and assimilate the family connections, but that all-powerful surge of emotion that I'd experienced on meeting my paternal relatives in Nigeria just didn't happen. Maybe this was due to the increased age, maturity and experience I'd since gained, or maybe it was a case of my being more able to identify more with my black African relatives than my white Irish relatives. I just don't know. I liked them all instantly and, in the short period of time we were together in Ireland, grew to love and respect them, and we keep in touch via social media. I suppose what's missing is not having shared experiences growing up together and being a part of each other's lives, hopes, dreams and aspirations, formative links, bonds, connections and dependencies that last for lifetimes. I'm certain they probably feel the same way too.

Differences in colour aside, we set about identifying and discussing shared physical characteristics, looks etc, before going on to chat about ourselves, lives, children etc. It was a very pleasant reunion and one which I'm so glad I was involved in. Everybody was happy to meet, and we definitely all shared a similar sense of humour and fun. Amid the hourdouvres, canapés, wine and champagne, early nerves and apprehensions were soon dispensed with and a relaxed atmosphere developed, before we went in to watch Chi-chi perform.

As per usual, she was outstanding, a true entertainer which, for most classical musicians (in my opinion), must be a very difficult if not impossible feat to accomplish!

Bantry House is very plush and ornate, festooned with historical artefacts and clearly exceptionally very valuable if not to say priceless trinkets, murals and paintings depicting its glorious past. It stank of history, old-money, lasting wealth and importance.

After the performance we all piled into a local pub on the bay, which was far more in-sync with my natural comfort zones! I can, however, make myself very comfortable and at ease in most settings and in most types of company. I very rarely feel ill at ease in other people's company, regardless of their social, racial and cultural backgrounds. I'm adaptable and versatile though, probably like most people, have my preferences. I've often been told, exclusively by black people, that I have this ability *by virtue* of being mixed-race. Sometimes it feels like an accusation being made against me, that I can *only* do this because I'm mixed-race, and for no other reason!

Hmmmmm. I'd like to think that I've developed the skills and confidence that enable me to operate in *both* the black and white worlds, if such entities actually exist.

The pub, and the Guinness, was great! We were able to really relax and get to know each other socially, *and* to establish the fact that we shared so much in common. This, I think, is true of us all. Superficial differences like skin colour are, or ought to be in my mind, irrelevant. But as human beings we seem unable, or unwilling, to let go. We *want*, if not *need*, to exacerbate surface and socially-constructed differences between ourselves, and then structure societies and relationships based on power differentials associated, among other attributes, to race.

The Irish are definitely the coolest white Europeans out there! The pub regulars, as well as the passing Irish trade, were so relaxed, warm and welcoming, and up for a good time, it was infectious. Everybody seemed to be smiling and, when the music started to take a hold, people laughed, sang and generally enjoyed 'the craic'. It was a wonderful affirmation of the human spirit and evidence of true brotherhood and goodwill to all. Unlike some of the times I've spent in pubs in London, where I've made the conscious effort to ensure I'm not sitting with my back towards the door. I'm only ever comfortable when I'm seated in a position where I can see who's coming in and going out!

After downing a steady flow of the creamy 'black stuff' and enjoying the 'feel-good factor', we made arrangements to meet the following morning before taking off on our quest of discovery that was to start in Upperchurch, the village mum lived in as a child.

After breakfast the following Friday morning we set off. We'd hired a 7-seater with ample storage space for luggage, so transport wasn't a problem. Mum had always spoken about a town called Thurles, which we headed for and passed through along the way. It's the second largest town in North Tipperary, which is probably why mum made so many references to it as, when she was a child, it was probably the 'London' of Tipperary. We also stopped in Cashel, in the south of Tipperary, where we stocked up on provisions. Tipperary is situated in the heart of Ireland, Eire, and like Limerick, is surrounded by rolling green countryside, made up of resplendently rich and loamy soil.

We arrived in Upperchurch in the mid- to late afternoon, and I couldn't believe the fact that it looked *exactly* as mum had described it; a few houses, two pubs, a church, and a village variety store to which her pet pig followed her every time she was sent on an errand to purchase. We were booked in to stay in an apartment above one of the pubs, the landlord of which was very welcoming. It just so happened that we'd arrived on a day when the villagers, once a year, always returned for a remembrance gathering in the graveyard to commemorate their ancestors. So, after settling in, we moseyed over to the cemetery, which was beginning to fill with patrons who'd travelled from all around Ireland to assemble and remember their beloved departed.

Strange, but I couldn't help making comparisons with the similarity in the rituals and mindsets of people in Nigeria and Ireland, and their obvious sense of duty and commitment to their community and village of origin, it was uncanny. Apart from the differences in skin colour, language and weather, the respect and significance proffered to their ancestors was immediately apparent. Also, the way in which they all returned to Upperchurch was very reminiscent of the way my relatives in Nigeria return to Egbelubi at Christmas and other significant times during the year, to dutifully commune and be together.

The Catholic priest led the service and singing, after which the assembled throng mingled and chatted as we looked at the gravestones.

If I remember correctly, there were Hogans, Hickeys, Flynns and Heveys buried in the graveyard. Sean Purcell, who my grandmother had looked after as a child, was there, as well as a second cousin we'd never met before, Mary Gleeson. Sean introduced her to us, and, after learning about the purpose of our visit, I felt she was itching to speak with Chi-chi and I. She very cautiously, though purposefully, hovered around us, before sidling up to offer us a wealth of knowledge and advice on our relatives.

It soon became clear that Mary was the oral historian of the family. She made all the links and provided us with all the 'secret' information that enabled us to unravel and make sense of much of my mum's family history. She explained who was related to whom, and how. She made it clear that 'certain things' were socially unacceptable 'in those days', such as single mothers, divorce, *and* marrying non-Catholics! A single woman with no children herself, she seemed very deep, strong and intense. She explained that she worked championing women's rights, about which she was passionate, almost as passionate as her disgust and distrust of the Catholic Church.

We were so impressed by Mary that we arranged to meet with her the following day for her to accompany us to Cappamore Lackabeg, mum's birth village, to which she agreed.

We spent that night in the pub below our apartment. It was *the* best night out I've ever had surrounded by white people. The Guinness was flowing, the landlord had hired a local group of fiddlers to entertain us with revolutionary riffs and reels, and he even sang and played a couple himself; inspirational centuries-old rebel songs of love of country and overthrowing English tyranny and oppression. Chi-chi even did a rendition of 'Danny Boy' on the piano, which got everybody in the pub up and singing along. It was a fantastic, magically beguiling night spent in great company, among family and friends who were genuinely sincere and loving people. Several of the drinkers remembered mum and our grandmother. The proprietor of the general store in the village also confirmed her stories of being followed by her pet pig wherever she went!

Just across the road from the cemetery entrance was a shrine dedicated to the memory of those from the community who'd been killed by the English during their sadistic occupation of Ireland and throughout 'the troubles'. The tricolour was prominent in the heartlands of the IRA, as were the effigies of the saints, especially St Mary, and the Gaelic Cross.

I found it interesting again, the fact that both our parents were from 'heartlands' of resistance; dad Biafran, mum Irish, both committed to achieving independence and sovereignty, international recognition, national pride, self-determination and dignity. Maybe this has also in some way contributed to our psyche and our achievements. Who knows?

I went to bed feeling warm and comforted that night. I felt as though I'd begun to connect with mum and her past at long last, and was eagerly awaiting meeting Mary again the following day. In the morning Chi-chi, Chris and I walked up the lane to the Purcell farm, where our grandmother worked. It was a single-track lane that ended at the entrance to the farm at the top of the hill. Sean met us and we had a chat. He showed us where one of his relatives, a 16 year old boy, had been shot dead by the Black and Tans for trying to help resist against his dad's abduction by them. There's a small shrine in the ditch where he fell. Scan gave us carte-blanche to stroll around the farm, and to enter the converted brick shed which was once our grandmother's home.

It was a small single-roomed brick-built and rudimentary enclosure more than it was a 'house', the ground floor of which was shared by the whole family as living quarters, where cooking and sleeping took place. The girls (mum and Aunty Joan), slept in the small hayloft unless the Black and Tans were in operation in the area, in which case the IRA boys would hide in the hayloft. It felt weird actually being somewhere *so* intimately connected to mum's childhood and teenage years. Virtually nothing had changed; little nick-knacks survived, crosses, a bible, the inevitable St Mary on a wall, a face mirror, a cup, a little table, a kettle, a sofa and a bed, all evidence of human occupation that was directly related to us. The view of the surrounding country-side from the vantage point on top of the hill was spectacular. You could see for miles over the lush green Slievefelin Hills. It was truly awesome, and our visit gave me the opportunity to 'imagine' mum as a child running, skipping, playing and doing chores around the farm when 'home' at weekends and extended holidays from the gloom and savagery of the orphanage.

Mary arrived to pick us up at our pub 'home' at the appointed time back down in the village, and we set off down the myriad of meandering lanes and roads that dissected the countryside to Cappamore Lackabeg. Just before we reached the outskirts of mum's birth village, we came across a man busy cutting the hedges and trimming the verges around his farm. Mary pulled the car over to the verge, stopped, and said:

"That's your cousin Bill Hogan. He's a policeman in Limerick".

We got out of the car and she introduced us. He was *really* happy to meet us, and invited us in for tea and biscuits, after which he strolled around the farm with us. We entered what was clearly an old cattle pen surrounded by crumbling and dilapidated pigsties and cattle sheds. He pointed to one and said:

"That's where your grandmother and her sister worked ragged and barefooted like slaves trying to survive before she left to work for the Purcells in Upperchurch".

I couldn't believe what he was pointing at. I couldn't imagine animals in there, let alone human beings. He told us how the English had brutally crucified the traditional way of life in Ireland, and the Irish themselves, during their occupation. He was clearly angry at the memories and thoughts as passed down to him by his own parents, but still retained a caustic and droll sense of humour:

"It would have been a duplex if they'd had a hayloft!"

434

The Irish sense of humour, fit for the gallows at times, never ceases to amuse and impress me!

We thanked Bill for his hospitality before re-entering the car.

Five minutes further down the road and we were entering Cappamore Lackabeg, mum's birthplace. The village was small, built on a crossroads, all four of which provided passage away from what was a very small and intimate community. Mary pulled up to the house where mum was born. Another cousin was outside tending to his hedge.

Mary introduced us as mum's children and he instantly beamed with delight and invited us in and, like Bill, insisted we take tea and biscuits. He proudly proclaimed and confirmed that this, indeed, was the house where mum was born, before going on to explain as best as he could, the family tree. He confirmed that our great-grandmother had emigrated to America with other members of the family due to the crippling levels of poverty that previously prevailed in Ireland, but that she'd returned to marry locally into the Hogan and Hickey family. Her daughter, our grandmother, married into the Hevey family. He also confirmed that Errol Flynn, legend of the Hollywood big screen was, in fact, mum's second cousin. It seems his branch of the Flynn family had arrived as convicts in Tasmania, where he was born.

It means *so* much to me that I've actually, literally, walked in the steps of both my mum and dad; that I've sat down in the places of their births; and that I've breathed the air they breathed as children. Being able to place oneself in this world is a very empowering phenomenon. I was now happy, satisfied that I could now talk about Nigeria and Ireland with equal knowledge, experience and authority, and the significance and importance of my heritage.

Chi-chi was hot-wired. She wanted to visit and explore graveyards, and talk with parish priests in the hope that they'd forward us official records of births, deaths and marriages, especially with regards a mysterious 'Uncle Patrick' who, as family myth and legend suggests, was a loveable rogue and scallywag who'd been to sea and travelled the world (no doubt with a girl in every port!), and could look after himself in a fight.

We left mum's place of birth with the intention to meet with a parish priest. On the way, Chi-chi insisted we stop at graveyards to check headstones bearing the family names, Hevey, Flynn; Hogan and Hickey. As things transpired, we found several, and Mary was able to place them in terms of their relation to us. We met with the parish priest who gave us a bit of background and committed himself to maintaining contact with Mary and Chi-chi in the event he came across the sought-after parish records.

Mary wanted to show us some places of interest on our way back to Upperchurch. First, we stopped beside a megalith protruding ten feet in the air by the side of the road. Apparently, this grey great stone had been in situ for thousands of years, and was in line with a set of equally impressive stones strategically placed throughout the countryside. Much like the arrangement at Stonehenge in the UK southwest county of Wiltshire, these stones were associated with fabled pre-historic tales of myth and legend.

Second, we stopped at a conical shaped pre-historic burial mound that had been overgrown by grass and trees. She explained the significance of these mounds in terms of their location and probable meaning to those buried within and the ancient communities they ruled over. Our discussion about deaths and burials seemed to trigger off a harrowing history lesson that Mary clearly had every intention to deliver and share with us.

I think she, quite correctly, sensed that Chi-chi and I were 'all ears' and keen to listen and learn something about the *people's* history and experience of Ireland. Many of these tales are often left untold or, when actually relayed, coated with euphemistic accounts to soften the harsh and disturbing blow of brutal reality.

Citing examples, Mary told us about the tyranny with which the Catholic priests and sisters sadistically dispensed throughout their dominion. It was commonplace and practice for them to abuse their positions of status and authority by terrorising their deferential parishioners with the threat of excommunication and eternal damnation for the slightest infringement, real, perceived, imagined or concocted.

Physical and sexual abuse of their flock was routine and rife in the parishes, schools, work places, homes and orphanages. Excessively harsh and sadistic corporal punishment was meted out for the most trivial offence. They were lauded and feared in disturbingly equal measure and, possibly most tellingly, mistrusted as 'collaborators' with the prevailing political powers-that-be.

It was abundantly clear Mary had no truck with religion, Catholicism especially. She spoke from the heart, with feeling, as she communicated personal anecdotes and oral history with first-hand pain and anguish.

The same was equally evident when she went on to educate us about the impact of 'the troubles' in Ireland's heartlands. She told of the atrocities that were committed by the English against the local Irish, including English Government-sponsored theft of traditional family and community land, wide scale evictions and enforced homelessness, burnings, looting, pillaging and torture. In the 17th and 18th centuries, Irish Catholics had been prohibited by the penal laws from owning land or leasing land; from voting; from holding political office; from living in a corporate town or within 5 miles of a corporate town; from obtaining education; from obtaining a profession; and from doing many other things necessary for a person to succeed and prosper in Irish society, any society, at the time.

A particular tale I remember her recounting was of a favourite method of torture, used by the English and their lackeys, which involved the pouring of boiling hot tar over the heads of locals who'd 'offended against the Crown'. They were left to die an agonisingly long and humiliating death in full view of the cowed and cowering public. She spoke of disease, poverty, famine and hunger as the constant companions of generations of rural Irish folk, which led to their eventual exodus in droves.

Grim-faced, she described the roles of strong, brave Irish women who supported and underpinned the never-flinching steely resistance movements throughout Ireland's history, and the armed struggle of their menfolk that was the vanguard of open and hostile resistance and organised movement to fight for independence. Mum was very definitely cut from the same cloth! With more than a hint of pride

Mary informed us that the IRA had its roots not so far away from where we were stood discussing its history.

Far from the 'happy-go-lucky' and laid-back view that the Irish are often stereotypically portrayed with by the British, Mary expressed and demonstrated a very different national character, one of fierce patriotism, loyalty, grit, determination and sacrifice, to achieve self-determination and independence. I was moved by her stories, and couldn't help but wonder why the British don't understand why they're detested by so many of the ordinary folk of their ex-colonial and Commonwealth denizens! It seems to me we don't have to travel too far or cross any borders with a passport to find evidence of this. A trip down the M4 to Wales, or the M74 at Gretna Green into Scotland would doubtless deliver us into the company of millions of like-minded people who deeply and passionately resent their homeland's history and relationship with the covetously conquering English!

I was definitely getting the message. Ireland suffered horrendously for centuries at the hands of the English, and such suffering hasn't been forgotten. Martyrs were made, and heroes were born, generation after generation, in the fight against poverty, famine, hunger, and tyranny of both body and soul.

Our cousins were, at the same time, making similar forays into the community to chase up links to their own strands of the Hevey family, so we discussed our findings later in the day. We went on a bit of a sightseeing trip around Tipperary and County Cork, where we visited Blarney Castle and I, again, kissed the stone (that's twice now. I should be able to talk myself out of any situation now!).

The following day, after thanking our landlord and his family for their very generous and much appreciated hospitality, we set off for the Galway coast in the east, before traversing the peat-bound breadth of Ireland to Dublin on the west coast. Amid earnest promises to return, I felt sad leaving mum's childhood village, but I know it's never left my heart and mind, just like Egbelubi.

I loved Galway, and Galway Bay, as much as I loved the people and the warmth of welcome with which we were always greeted. After meeting and lunching with cousin Chris Hevey's mum and dad, we returned to our hotel to rest before hitting the town later that evening.

Yet again I was pleasantly encouraged by the sociability of the Irish, who seemed happy with their own and others' company. So long as they were enjoying the craic, all was good.

We pitched up in Dublin the following day. Dublin was massive compared to any other town we'd visited or passed through during our stay, a very cosmopolitan metropolis. We even saw other *black* faces, the majority of whom resembled typical Nigerian student-types! Built on the mouth of the River Liffey, it was originally founded as a Viking settlement in the 9th century, but later developed into the most populous city in Ireland after the Norman invasions of the 12th century. Despite remaining the economic centre of Ireland, all forms of population, economic and political growth stagnated in Dublin during the 19th century following the 1800 Act of Union. However, following the Irish Civil War and the partition of Ireland in 1922, Dublin became the capital city of the Irish Free State and later the Republic of Ireland.

I loved Dublin. It has a really bohemian air about it, with the *actually* laid-back people, the coffee shops, art, history, buildings, museums, music oozing out of every corner, and its welcoming aura of all-inclusive friendliness. We took photos around the statue of Molly Malone on Grafton Street, otherwise known colloquially as 'The Tart with the Cart', or 'The Dish with the Fish'! Our musician cousin Chris said there is history of the Hevey family trying to orchestrate an overthrow of the city rulers 'back in the day'. Apparently, they conspired to storm the relevant building to overthrow the powers-that-were at the time, but they all got drunk the night before. Nevertheless, they *still* went ahead with their attempted coup, and were slaughtered in the process! Typical! He also claimed that the Hevey family had invented and produced Guinness, but were so regularly inebriated imbibing their own product that the Guinness family patented the brew and the rest, as they say, is history. Again, typical!

We did some more graveyard searches in and around Dublin in pursuit of our ever-elusive 'Scarlet Pimpernel' of a sea-faring Uncle Patrick, but to no avail.

Dublin certainly deserves its reputation as a 'fun city'! We spent our last night in Ireland in a Dublin pub-cum-restaurant-cum-cabaret-cum-karaoke establishment where the food was great, the Guinness even better, and the punters superb. It was a really enjoyable night out, one that I'll never forget, a great craic!

After saying our goodbyes to our cousins, Chi-chi and I drove to Cork from Dublin to catch our respective flights back to London. It was actually nice just having the time between ourselves to talk together about our experiences and feelings as we made the drive. We were both so happy to have made the trip and to have found out a little bit more about mum. I suppose, for me, just being in places where she'd been as a child and young woman before emigrating to England and meeting dad was sufficient. It meant that I could identify more with her, understand her a little bit more, and see things through her eyes a little bit more. It was impossible for me to love her any more than I already did.

Fifty-Three

Time and tide, as they say, wait for no man. Time has certainly moved on since our trip to Ireland. Yve and I are celebrating 33 years of marriage this August (2015). Well, I suppose I can only talk for myself when it comes to the 'celebrating' claim! I'd like to think she's equally as happy though.

Kele J, Ike and Obi have become wonderful young people and adults in their own right. They're all still living at home, and I'm happy with that.

The family has grown bigger though, with eleven children between my brother, sisters and I. The first UK-based Nwanokwu clan have produced the second generation who, in turn, have started producing the third. I'm yet to become a grandfather though! Everything in its own time, and time will tell.

So what *has* changed?

Not a lot really.

I suppose over the years I've mellowed and become less fiery and passionate about those things that used to 'light my fire'. I'm still just as passionate about the issues, I'm just less likely to demonstrate this passion in quite the same way as I used to! I've travelled quite extensively with my work in football, to Brazil, Cairo, Tunisia, Egypt, Cameroon, France, Jamaica, Sierra Leone, and Ghana to name but a few; and holidayed around much of Europe and North America. I think I've developed a more accurate sense of perspective with regards people, places, and relationships, about which, unfortunately, I'm significantly less naive, idealistic and hopeful, but far more cynical.

There has, however, been massive technological change in the world since mum and dad met, and my abortive attempt to fly by launching myself off the climbing-frame at Dr Barnados children's home!

These changes include modes of transport and communication especially (I remember watching Star Trek thinking the idea of such space travel was stretching the imagination a little bit too far, their flip mobile phones were a ridiculous flight of fancy, and those automatic doors swishing open seemed a preposterously ludicrous idea!); supersonic jets; super liners; bullet trains; electric cars; the worldwide web; emails; conference calls; cyberspace; Facebook; Twitter; iPhones; iPads; text messaging; instant messaging; saturation 'reality' television in high-definition *and* three-dimensional; instant news; and the expectation of instant gratification, if not stardom, merely examples of many.

But what, in essence, has *really* changed?

Since the 1976 Notting Hill Carnival 'riot' that I experienced, each decade has featured riots and civil unrest, significantly, with the relationship between the police and black communities at their core. These include, for example, the 1981 Brixton riots, the 1985 Broadwater Farm riots in which PC Keith Blakelock was murdered whilst on 'riot duty', riots in Chapeltown in Leeds, Moss Side in Manchester, Handsworth in Birmingham, Toxteth in Liverpool, St.Pauls in Bristol, Oldham and Burnley in Lancashire, in Oxford, Cardiff and Tyneside; right up until 35 years after Notting Hill Carnival when in 1976 we saw inner-city areas implode across the UK in response to the fatal police shooting of a young black man supposedly 'known to be armed' in north London. Violent clashes with the police, widespread arson and looting rumbled on for days. Did this provide evidence of very little change with regards racist relationships between the police and black youth? It was definitely a causative factor. But, like many of the preceding riots, it wasn't *only* black youth involved. Youths of every description and background participated, black, white, Asian, male, female, young, middle-aged, employed, unemployed, working class and middle class. The catalyst, though, was the fatal police shooting of a black man in north London.

However, in my eyes, what followed was opportunistic and wanton looting, vandalism, theft, chaos and anarchy, all (understandably?) committed under the guise of 'righteous riots'. Many rioters justified their actions in terms of poverty-induced feelings of disempowerment and anger as a reaction to grindingly high levels of unemployment combined with low or non-existent employment prospects.

Bullshit!

These things are relative, and I struggle to accept the position that today's young people are worse off than we were in our youth. Yet we didn't riot to loot, nor to acquire a new flat-screen plasma TV, or Nike trainers, or a mobile phone, or a cheeseburger!

So, apart from the *reasons* for rioting, in essence, there hasn't been much change; but there has been massive change in riot-communication on both sides. In the summer of 2011 rioters used mobile phones, especially Blackberry BBM-ing, to coordinate and dovetail their marauding activities, whilst the police used mobile communication in their anti-marauding activities, supported by CCTV for identification and prosecution purposes. Sadly, for me, one of the most abiding images was a row of smashed, gutted and looted city-centre stores. Mobile phone shops, sportswear shops, fried chicken shops, a McDonalds outlet, fashion shops, jewellery shops; electrical appliance shops; all raided and looted; only *one* store was left totally untouched - a Waterstone's Bookshop!

This begs a few questions, for example:

Is rioting the sole preserve of the poor?
Has materialism displaced philosophical ideology as the root cause of social upheaval?
Are books the sole preserve of the middle classes?
Does anybody care enough to encourage change?
Who stands to lose from change?
Who stands to gain from maintaining the status quo?

Social, political and economic inequality remains rife, and has probably become worse. The rich are forever getting richer, and the poor are getting poorer. The privately-educated political elite remain brazenly corrupt despite the constant allegations and confirmations of sleaze of every variety in the media. Major bankers and business fatcats who recklessly brought about the collapse of the world economy remain in position, and *still* receive annual million-pound bonuses, subsidised by the innocent poor and devalued workers. Health, education and public services are increasingly being put out to tender to private sector organisations to preside over. Welfare benefits and care services are being enthusiastically and hugely trimmed, if not to say decimated and withdrawn. Old age pensioners are expected to work for longer while being groomed to accept lower pensions and less care in their more senior years.

So, after years of developing towards a more caring, sharing, inclusive and tolerant 'Big' society, it seems we're fast reverting to increasingly fractured and bitter divisions between the hooray-Henry-haves and the who-the-fuck-are-you have-nots.

Religious wars are still being fought with gusto around the globe, and festering religious hatred and intolerance remains alive and flourishing in the UK. After decades of Equal Opportunities awareness and enlightenment, we're spiralling back down the gaping abyss of racial distrust, hostility and scape-goating. We're far more 'politically-correct' than we ever were, and we won't 'call a spade a spade' (well, to his face anyway), but we'll continue to disenfranchise him as a spade (nigger, coon, black bastard etc) covertly, behind his back, to inflict maximum damage on him and his 'sort'. Essentially, it might not be unreasonable to suggest the UK has adopted a far more sinister 'racial destruction by stealth whilst smiling at you in the face' approach.

Decades of tinkering with the education service to improve the prospects of underachieving, at-risk, socio-economically deprived young people has resulted in diddly-squat. The very same groups of virtually illiterate, under- and mis-educated students, especially black boys of Caribbean and now African backgrounds, continue to fail miserably, along with white working class boys and Bangladeshi students generally. As historically deprived and disempowered social groups, these young people are those who can least afford to under-achieve.

But there has been improvement. Now, far more black students and those from the previously oppressed white working class are managing to successfully navigate their way through the education system to university level. However, any analysis of the unemployment statistics for black male graduates will show they are still least likely to gain commensurate employment, and are four times more likely to become medium- to long-term unemployed. Might this provide proof that endemic racism is alive, well and flourishing in the myriad of corridors of power in our contemporary 'enlightened' and 'tolerant' UK.

As Programme Manager (Head of Department) for Health & Social Care in a very large inner-city London Further Education College, the overwhelming majority of students I am responsible for are female. Generally speaking, black and ethnic minority students make up the main student body of the whole college. However, inevitably, in and around the college I'm in regular contact with black male students, many of whom seem to be totally disaffected by, and uncommitted to, education. This cohort still tops the permanent exclusion and academic failure league tables. They appear loud, brash and, to many of my teacher colleagues (especially the white ones), aggressive, intimidating and threatening. As a result the temptation and most regular practice is to turn a blind eye to their misconduct and under-achievement. The staff fail to realise that by adopting this 'head-in-the-sand' approach they're not helping the young men and are, by default, contributing to their perennial failure.

This doesn't only apply to white teaching staff. 'Black' staff can be, and often are, equally as culpable. Significant numbers of white staff don't live in the inner-city, which in many ways is alien to them. They commute to work, where they 'don't see' differences in colour, and return to their prevailingly white middle class suburbs and shires at the end of the day. 'Black' members of staff, in the main, still live in the inner-city. We haven't quite yet made it in significant numbers to infiltrate the fortress-like bastions of white middle class suburbia. However, many *have* adopted a white mentality towards black students, they've bought into the mainstream moral panics and stereotypes that 'the system' has generated over the years to demonise young black people. We are failing these students ourselves!

Who, or what, do they turn to? Do they act out the self-fulfilling prophecy? I can fully understand the inclination and temptation to do so! Or do they continue to 'play the white man' and try to beat the odds? I totally respect and admire those that try and, even more so, those that succeed.

Not only has there been little or no change in the racist education system, it's evidently alive and kicking in the police force also. The issue of contemporary 'racial profiling' and police practices clearly demonstrates that police are still more likely to stop, search and arrest young black men than any other group in UK society. Yet so few of these arrests lead to prosecutions, let alone convictions. It's still the case that if you're a young black man 'you fit the profile' and, as such, you are disproportionately targeted for police harassment. The impact remains the same. Feelings of anger, hurt, victimisation and alienation have become second-nature to young black people in general, and men in particular. These things don't happen in isolation. Young black girls and the families of young black men are constantly challenged to live and deal with the consequences of such persistent racist police intrusions.

Sadly, I think a major mistake that young black men continue to make is that they live up to the stereotype. Not only do they live up to it, many revel in the notoriety of their situation. So rather than try to beat the system, and overcome the odds to succeed, they take the easy option. They become the under-educated 'losers' that the system defines and treats them as, and they themselves then build on this status to include criminality and lawlessness as extensions of their personas and the street-cred they seem to so desperately crave in order to boost their 'ratings'.

It's no wonder little has changed on the mental hospital admissions statistics, or the school and college exclusion statistics, or the unemployment statistics, or the prison population statistics, with regards the disproportionately high figures for young black men. So, again, little change there also!

The situation regarding the proliferation of single-parenthood among black British people hasn't changed either, in that they are still the group at top the charts, by a country mile. These families tend to be female-headed with the father either unidentified or totally absent from the lives of his offspring. Again, it would appear no wonder that their children, especially their boys, go off the rails. This is by no means a criticism of the mothers, many of whom I know work extremely hard under very trying circumstances, often with high levels of success given their circumstances, but surely their load needs to be lightened! It seems unequivocal that dads need to step up to the plate.

But this also begs a further question. My experience, and no doubt that of many black boys whose fathers *do* hang around, was one of excessive corporal punishment. Beatings! What is it about black fathers that seems to encourage them to resort to such violence, especially with their sons?

Do they not know any different or any better?

Do they honestly think it worked for them, so it must be OK?

Does this practice represent a deep, subconscious insecurity against which they feel they need to guard themselves by demonstrating their domestic superiority?

Does their violence, in their minds, confirm that they truly are 'the kings of their castles'?

I never got the impression that my white male friends, whilst growing up, were beaten *so* regularly by their parents, especially their dads. Does this reflect a possible higher level of confidence and security among their fathers? Indeed, is this a truly cultural phenomenon? Where corporal punishment is used as a regular means of discipline in the home by white people, it tends to be more prevalent among the working classes than the middle classes.

Are white middle class fathers more confident and secure than their working class counterparts? Possibly.

Whilst I say I 'deserved' the majority of the beatings I got, and 'they helped me become the person I am', exactly who and what *have* I become? Having experienced, seen and survived many types of violence, I know I'm not afraid of it, but I don't like it, and nor do I agree with its use as a means to resolve issues. Consequently, despite my children's claims to the contrary, I very rarely (in comparison to my own experiences), beat my children. I find 'the psychotic stare' far more effective. That's not to say I *didn't* beat my children when they were young. I did. I never felt good about it, but did it nonetheless. Not to the extent that they were ever wounded, scarred or marked either physically or psychologically (I hope!), but certainly enough to convey my displeasure, disapproval or concern regarding their actions. I'd like to think they've grown up as very loving, stable, balanced and decent young people.

I 'celebrated' my 56th birthday a couple of year ago, and received a card from my three children, the front of which read:

"To a brilliant Dad on your birthday
With lots of love and special wishes"

Inside, they each wrote the following separate messages:

Kele J:
"Dear Dad, I just want to say you are the best Dad a daughter could ever ask for. Always encouraging, helpful and supportive in every way. Full of words of wisdom. Thanks for being you – I'm such a lucky daughter! Happy Birthday!! Lots of love always, Kele xxxxx"

Ike:
"I am very lucky to be your son as you are the perfect example of a Dad that is there for his kids. I have learnt how to be a man under your guidance, you are my role model. I appreciate

everything you have done for me and it is my goal to repay you and mum. Happy Birthday!! Loads of love, Ike xxx"

Dee:
"Dear Dad, I just want to say thank you for all the love and support you have given me over my lifetime. You've stuck by me through my good times and my very bad times and you haven't given up on me; happy birthday dad, I love you so much, you truly are the best dad in the whole world!! Love from Obi xxxxx"

I'm man enough to confess their words moved me to tears. Totally unexpectedly I was, for the first time, overwhelmed with a sense, a feeling, that I'd 'done alright by' my kids, and it choked me up that they actually said as much. I felt complete. I felt happy and proud of my achievements as their father. Their words meant *so* much to me.

As a parent I've learnt that you worry about your children at every stage throughout their lives. You always want the best for them, regardless. However, there are chronological concerns about their health and safety as they start to explore their environment, as well as the outside world and whether they'll be able to make friends and interact successfully with others their own age. You want them to achieve academic success whilst developing their own interests and abilities to the highest and most fulfilling levels as possible. You worry about them going out at night, and coming back safely, without being robbed, beaten up, and assaulted or worse. And eventually you hope they meet and choose partners who they'll be happy with forever so as to start the next generation.

There *are* differences in the nature of the concerns though. With Kele J I worried about her being abused in any way by a boyfriend or potential suitor (for which I'd have to kill him!), or teenage and/ or unwanted pregnancy. With the boys, the concerns were (and still are), quite different. I worry about police brutality and racism, both of which I hope they don't *suffer* from, but I'm certain they'll experience at various stages throughout their lives. They've both managed to avoid or survive negative interaction with the police so far, and have done very well academically, but I also worry about their job prospects. I really don't want them to contribute to the disproportionately high unemployment statistics for young black men in this country. Worst of all though, is my anxiety regarding them falling prey to street violence, meted out by other young men their own age who operate in gangs, a phenomenon which seems to affect young black boys in particular.

Invariably, where gang warfare and 'postcode' violence is reported, it is young black boys who make up the majority of participants and concern.

This represents a *massive* change compared to my teenage years. We fought, and we fought a lot, but it was mainly against abusive white people, thugs and police. When, as black youths, we fought amongst ourselves, it very rarely involved knives and guns, and in my experience, never ended fatally. Today's statistics provide a completely different scenario. It 'feels' like the majority of inner-city postcode and gang violence is perpetrated exclusively by black boys. The images we constantly see on television news and the general media of victims and their murderers are invariably black. Equally notable, it's not solely a West Indian or Jamaican problem. It now also includes young boys of African descent, all of whom regardless of their origins, seem to be sleepwalking to oblivion whilst cultivating and pursuing their allegiance to 'the gang'.

This represents yet another issue whereby 'the system' no longer needs to brutalise, murder and write-off black people. We've become more than proficient at doing it to ourselves. I can categorically state that, in my experience, this would *never* have happened back in the day. In comparison, our fights seem glorious, righteous and purposeful, for the benefit of the greater good. What do today's young black people fight and kill themselves over?

A postcode?

A piece of pavement?

Their 'ends'?

Something they'll never, ever own or have influence over?

Inevitably 'getting Ps' (pounds, money, cash), through illegitimate and criminal activity including drugs, theft and prostitution; as well as 'ratings', social status and reputation, is central to their cause, their raison d'être. So central, and now so ingrained, that the government established and developed 'Operation Trident' in 1998, a specialist arm of the police service dedicated to dealing with the issue of 'black-on-black' drug-related gun crime. Maiming and murder is an everyday, commonplace inner-city event. It's nothing new, and our young people glory in the associated notoriety they accrue in their commitment to gaining 'respect' and Ps, no matter how temporary or perilous the lifestyle. The Trident Operational Command Unit then expanded in 2004 with the formation of 'Operation Trafalgar', which investigates all other non-fatal shootings in London.

The vast majority of incidences of black-on-black gang-related activities now go unreported, it's no longer considered horrifying or newsworthy enough to feature. However, when it affects 'outsiders' (non-blacks, especially whites), it slips back into the mainstream.

Something akin to this was the recent murder and decapitation of a white English soldier in the broad daylight of a sunny Wednesday afternoon on May 22nd in Greenwich, southeast London. My first reaction on hearing the news was disbelief, revulsion and incomprehension. Then, when I'd had the chance to assimilate the event, I thought:

'Welcome to south London!'

I still don't truly understand what happened there. I struggle to accept it as a 'race hate crime' or 'terrorist atrocity' committed by two young, black, fundamentalist Muslims. Their actions were certainly, in my view, symptomatic of something that's gone seriously wrong, but quite what that 'something' is I don't know.

Can I empathise with their anger and frustration at a system that relentlessly militates against them? Yes I can.

Can I condone their actions? No I can't.

Such actions can never be supported or condoned in a (so-called) civilised democracy. So, even ultimate-atheist I believe that to claim the murder on the behalf of Islam, is to insult, offend and discredit the faith and those who follow it. However, this tawdry episode leads me to consider another change.

Religion.

Logically, for me, the past twenty or thirty years in the UK has seen a massive decline in religious practice in the established, mainstream religions or, put another way, a steep rise in secularisation. Where there has been significantly comparable change to match the decline in the influence of religion, is the increasing popularity and uptake of Islam, which is now the fastest growing religion in the UK. Not that I'm equating Islam with increasing levels of terrorism per se, but it is becoming increasingly associated with and linked to major atrocities like the 9/11 suicide attacks on the Twin Towers in New York City and The Pentagon in Washington DC, or the 7/7 suicide attacks in London. Large- and small-scale ideological wars, if not to say crusades, are *still* being fought in the name of religion.

However, it still remains the case that, universally, religion appears to be at the heart of the overwhelming majority of social disruption, disharmony, chaos, and different levels of war, conflict and confrontation; all of which leads to increased misery and despair, disease, famine and asylum-seeking 'refugee-ism' for those most blighted.

So little or no change there then!

There has, however, been massive change with regards to the sheer number of 'mixed-race' people in the UK since the 1950s, especially those aged under 16. Apparently, mixed-race people are the fastest-growing ethnic group in the UK and numbered over 1 million in the 2011 Census. 'Mixed' appeared for the first time in the 1991 Census as an ethnic category, and consists of a wide variety of subgroups. Colloquially it refers to British citizens whose parents are of two or more different races or ethnic minority backgrounds.

No doubt white liberal, left-wing multi-culturalist Britain is giddily performing triumphal cartwheels in celebration of the (assumed?)

successful integration, assimilation and increasing levels of 'tolerance' in the UK as it strives towards becoming a true 'rainbow' nation, where skin colour is deemed irrelevant and doesn't matter. Especially when we consider the success of the likes of Jessica Ennis, Lewis Hamilton, Alesha Dixon (to name but a few), who have become the 'poster people' of their respective fields.

But a cautionary note of warning is necessary here. We need to slow down.

Bob Marley achieved worldwide success throughout the 1970s and 80s and was dearly loved in Britain. The illegitimate son of a Scottish father and Jamaican mother, the popularity of his music in Britain catapulted him to super-star status not only in Britain, but around the world.

Olympic gold medal winning athlete Daley Thompson had similar success in the 1980s and became the UK's national poster-boy; yet the racist National Front (NF), the British National Party (BNP), the English Defence League (EDL), and the United Kingdom Independence Party (UKIP), have all developed and flourished since the 'dark' days of the 70s.

A similar situation exists in France where, after having won the 1998 FIFA Football World Cup with a multiracial team of players composed of black, white, mixed-race and Arabic origin, the French wallowed in back-patting, self-congratulatory hubris with regards its new and developing status as a rainbow nation. Yet, fast forward a mere 15 years and we see France as a nation wracked with race-riots, with anti-immigration bills at the top of their political agenda, the rising power and influence of Marine le Pen's extreme right wing political party Front National (FN), and even the once-glorified (if not to say deified!), French national football team itself being embroiled in a race row after team manager Laurent Blanc was secretly taped discussing proposals to reduce the number of black and Arabic players in the squad in order to address concerns that the team 'wasn't white enough'!

So let's not get *too* carried away!

I think it's fair to say that the UK *has* 'become more tolerant' of mixed-race relationships and mixed-race people who, as I suggested earlier, may well represent the 'acceptable' and 'prettier, more attractive' face of blackness. But I don't see this as a reason to celebrate; it is not a 'cause celebre'. Such 'qualities' are superficial and fleeting at best and, as such, almost valueless other than for those rare individuals who may just happen to benefit from being mixed-race at any given point in time. For every one 'successful' mixed-race person in the UK, there are many thousands who struggle to exist at the other, polar, extreme of the spectrum. A salutary point here being that, like popularity and fashion, what's in and what's not, trends change over time.

Also, history clearly dictates that, during lean times, majority communities tend to look for scapegoats to blame and, irrespective of the 'shade' of black an individual may be, they are still black, and 'different' in the eyes of the majority. As such, they will remain potential scapegoats. For the ultra-ignorant, the fact that there are far more mixed-race people in the UK may provide the evidence to support their pernicious claims that black men have, indeed, not only taken their houses and jobs, but their women also!

So be warned, my mixed-race brothers and sisters. Don't allow yourselves to be lulled into a false sense of security. Whilst you may be riding high on the wave of popularity and enjoying the benefits of preferential treatment today, that wave may soon run dry. So, as the saying goes:

"Be careful how you treat people on the way up, because you may need them in the future on the way down!"

An interesting change that *has* taken place regarding mixed-race relationships is the increasing numbers of white men marrying black women. This *never* used to be the case in post-war 1940s and 50s Britain. Where mixed-race relationships occurred they tended to be black man-white woman. This was often determined by the practice that the (black) men from the colonies would emigrate first in order to secure employment and accommodation, before 'sending' for their wives and girlfriends. This happened in many cases, but there were also many cases that saw the wife or girlfriend left forgotten or unwanted once her man had arrived and become established in the UK. Left to their own devices, it would appear the men 'assimilated' quite quickly into the host community on this matter!

However, this 'matter' has continued to be the cause of much concern in the black community, particularly the black female community in the UK, many of whom feel betrayed by 'their' black men. I've been privy to many conversations where black women have bemoaned their lot and, in a sense, expressed the notion that they'd 'given up' on finding a 'good' black man:

> "There's no good black man out there!"
> "If he's over 25, single and with no baggage (children), he must have been in prison, unemployed all his life, or gay!"
> "It makes me sick seeing black men with white women"
> "How come they treat white women so well and us so badly?"
> "Cho, dem a wotless!" ("they're worthless!").

These comments are typical examples of many I've heard over the years but, interestingly, they are often mournfully mouthed by black women who have had children with black men! I think it's definitely the case that black women have become far more liberated over the past decade and, whereas before they'd have been more circumspect about dating or being seen in public with a white guy, they're far less likely to care now. Indeed, increasingly, it is black women who are succeeding, and want to find partners who can match or exceed their achievements. Black men are failing to do this, and failing miserably!

It's no longer the case, as it was in my day, that a sure-fire way of 'pulling' a woman was to own or drive a car. Nowadays, black women have entered the professions in their droves (compared to black men at least); they own their own homes and drive their own cars, often past the same black men who are now increasingly still pushing bicycles or trodding!

What Unique Selling Point, what 'game', do black men have to attract black women as a potential life partner today?

What is he bringing to the table?

Very little, if anything, that she hasn't already achieved and obtained under her own steam, it would appear.

Stereotypically, where black men *are* achieving success is in the field of sports and, to a lesser degree, entertainment. Black and mixed-race footballers are probably among the most high-profile and highest-earning group and, as such, possibly the most likely suitors of 'successful' black women. Yet we see a huge anomaly here, because it would appear, in the vast majority of cases, these footballers invariably select big-busted-blonde-bimbo-type (gold-digging?) white wives and girlfriends (WAGs) as their ideal, trophy partners, as opposed to successful black women (much to their chagrin!).

What might this be indicative of?

True love and attraction?

Profound insecurities?

Superiority or inferiority complexes?

A rejection of their blackness?

A statement of personal preference?

Who knows?

Who really cares?

Whilst there certainly has been a huge increase in the numbers of black and ethnic minority officers joining the police service since the 1970s, in terms of police practice, little seems to have changed. Black youths are still seven times more likely to be 'legally harassed' by the racially-profiled stop-and-search drives and policies. Which brings into question the conduct not only of white police officers, but their black and ethnic minority colleagues; for whom upholding, applying and enforcing the law must put them in daily states of compromise? However, their duty to serve their community must dictate that they do so fairly and with integrity, as opposed to perpetuating the current blatantly racist system and practices which successfully serve to demonise, disaffect, disengage and isolate 'their own'. A useful reminder for these officers might be, again, that:

> "It's just not good enough to be black and in the police force; you need to be black and 'say something' to change the system and practices".

How many *can* honestly say that they've tried?

An interesting and significant change that *has* taken place among the police and how they 'serve' the community that pays their wages has recently developed (as of October) 2015:

> Not only are black people (especially young black men between 17-24 years of age) more likely to be stopped, searched, arrested and charged by the boys in blue, they're also *three* times more likely to be *tasered* during part of the process than their white male counterparts and/or group of comparison! *Three* times more likely to be tasered, knocked unconscious and incapable by an electric taser gun! What does this say about the police? Can this statistic be justified? Are young black men or black people in general *really* three times more likely to resist arrest or act in a way that requires such extreme measures at any point during the process than other groups? Let's just hope Britain doesn't follow its leader America by arming the police with *real* guns because, on this evidence, we would reasonably expect to see a huge rise in 'death-by-police-shooting' murders in addition to this new statistic!

Another huge change in the state of affairs since my childhood and youth has evolved in the corridors of political power. Apart from Dadabhai Naoroji (Liberal Party 1892-1905, Finsbury Central) and Mancherjee Bhonagree (Conservative Party 1895-1906, Bethnal Green North East), in the nineteenth century, and Shapurji Saklatvala (Communist Party of Great Britain 1922-1923, 1924-1929, Battersea North), in the early twentieth century, there were no black or ethnic minority MPs elected to parliament until 1983 when Jonathan Sayeed (Conservative Party, Mid-Bedfordshire), who, though of mixed Anglo-Indian ancestry, preferred to be considered as an "MP without prefixes"!

The first 'black' (African Caribbean) MP to be elected to parliament was Diane Abbott (Labour Party, 1987, Hackney North and Stoke Newington). Just like we were to celebrate nearly 20 years later when Barack Obama was elected to become the 44th President of the United States (and first black President) in 2009, we celebrated Abbott's success. Sadly, embarrassingly, forlornly, it didn't take long for her to crush the hopes, dreams and expectations of the entire UK black population, well, the grassroots majority at least.

Diane Abbott was elected to represent the Hackney North and Stoke Newington constituency, one of *the* most impoverished inner-city areas of London, if not the whole country, populated with very high levels of unemployed, under-employed, unemployable, disempowered, isolated and disaffected black and ethnic minority constituents. She just *had* to step up to the plate and represent! And what did she do? How did she exercise her political power, status and influence on behalf of her downtrodden, exploited, marginalised and dispossessed constituents?

Answer: she spouts on about the (hypothetical, philosophical, imaginary?) strengths and benefits of the state education system, yet sent her own son to a £10,000 per year private school because the local comprehensive schools in her constituency community "weren't good enough or up to scratch"!

Despite the fact that she'd previously commented on BBC1's 'This Week' programme that:

"Private schools prop up the class system in society."

She went on to confess:

"It is inconsistent, to put it mildly, for someone who believes in a fairer and more egalitarian society to send their child to a fee-paying school."

Before finally lamenting:

> "I had to choose between my reputation as a politician and my son."

She'd also previously had the gall and temerity to criticise Solicitor General Harriett Harman (Labour Party) for sending her son to a selective grammar school in Orpington, Kent, when she said:

> "She made the Labour Party look as if we do one thing and say another."
>
> How foul?

What a waste of hundreds of thousands of hopes and dreams!

Such a monumentally shameful, hypocritical betrayal of not only black people, but of *all* working class and ethnic minority people!

She got in on 'the black and ethnic minority vote', from the support of people who aren't in her enviable position to make such a choice, yet, once in, she used her position to shamelessly self-serve. Irrespective of her lame attempts to justify her duplicitous actions, it's arguable that she contributed to the perpetuation of a divisive, elitist system, which I find utterly despicable!

Let's just cross our fingers and hope that the likes of David Lammy (Labour, 2000, Tottenham), Chukka Umunna (Labour, 2010, Streatham), and Chinyelu Onwurah (Labour, 2010, Newcastle upon Tyne Central), don't emulate the disgusting precedent Dianne Abbott appears to have set. Let's hope they don't lose sight of who and what they are and stand for, where they started, and the people who've contributed to their political achievements. I'm far less hopeful for the Black and Asian Tory MPs. It's probably more a reflection of my starting point in life, but I just can't imagine what inspired them, what put them on the road to aspire to become Conservative MPs!

I'm now 58 years old, a 'settled' professional member of the 'respectable' middle-class, fortunate enough to have a 'secure' job as

Programme Manager in one of the largest inner-London FE colleges, and white people *still* see my black face. Recently, one morning, as I made the five-minute walk from Kings Cross station to the college, I was confronted by a complete stranger, a 6' 2" white guy in his late 20s:

"You got a spare fag mate?"

"Nah, sorry."

He got in my space:

"Gissa twos on that one then." (Can I smoke the one you're smoking?)

"Nah mate."

"Prick!"

"Who's the prick, *me* with the cigarette or *you* without one and begging for it?"

"Black cunt!"

"Fuck off!"

"Nigger!"

"Fuck off!!!!!"

"Nigger!"

"Fuck off!!!!!!!!!!"

This exchange happened around 10.00am in the morning. I wasn't sure if he was drunk or under the influence of any other form of mind-altering substance but, even if he was (though he seemed very lucid to me), he proved mum's oft-quoted point:

"What's in ye sober comes out when ye're drunk!" Her version of:

"What soberness conceals, drunkenness reveals!"

When he called me Nigger for the last time I stopped in my tracks, turned, and looked at him. I'll be honest, I wanted to kick his stupid head in. It's frightening. The anger and rage still lies deep within me, lurking, churning, waiting to rise to the surface, to be expressed and transformed into unrestrained violent retribution. But, clearly, there's been a massive change in me! I had instant flashbacks to the 'good old bad old days'. I could see myself ripping into this arsehole and decking him with the trusted right hand.

But I just couldn't be bothered.

Just as troubling, though unsurprising these days, was that he was accompanied by a black 'mate'! A *fully* black guy, of similar age, he even had dreadlocks! He stayed out of the fleeting confrontation, but strolled off together with his 'master-mate' when the exchange abated. His actions, like those of Diane Abbott, prove one thing to me that, regardless of background, status and position, there are two main types of poverty: one that is characterised by a lack of financial, materialistic, status and influential clout; the other by a lack of moral fibre, spirit, integrity, soul, empathy and principle. Essentially, that which amounts to a poverty of the mind. The two aren't mutually exclusive, and I can identify and empathise with those who suffer financial poverty.

Though still desperately low comparatively, we've also experienced and seen a significant change in the visibility of black 'role models' including, for example, teachers, nurses, social workers, business owners and actors. Things *must* be better now if black actors actually headline and make it through to the last reel on a regular basis these days, but have also broken through on advertisements, documentaries and soaps! This was *never* the case back in the day. I remember being happily shocked, stunned and excited when I saw the first black face in a TV advert for Cox's Orange Pippin apples, a fully black guy with short dreadlocks, oh joy of joys that a company would risk associating their product with a black face!

There seems to have been little if any change in the popular (street level) youth culture, music, language and fashion scene though. All still tend to be underpinned, influenced and driven by popular black culture. From Ska to reggae, conscious roots, steppers, lovers, dancehall and bashment; calypso and soca; high-life and Afro-beats; from soul to hip-hop, house, garage, old school and R&B, the prevalent youth music scene has been dominated by black creativity and (no change here) bastardised, adulterated, mimicked and produced for the mass mainstream market by shameless and talentless (in comparison), white wannabes!

Fifty-Four

So, where do we go from here?

Or, more specifically, where have I got to and where am I going now?

What, if anything, has this all meant?

Not a lot probably.

There are certain things I still want to do in life, for example, I want to travel to the Far East, Indonesia, China, Thailand, Vietnam, the Philippines and maybe even India.

There's also one thing I'd love to happen before I die, and that is for Biafra to secede from 'Nigeria' and become an independent sovereign state again. After more than forty years of what was a genocidal civil war, sponsored by the British government under the serving Labour Party Prime Minister Harold Wilson, the Eastern Region of Nigeria is still suffering, especially through lack of infrastructure investment compared to other regions.

Human life and times seem to be cyclical because, as was the case prior to the war, today we are again witnessing the systematic persecution and annihilation of Biafrans, Igbos, especially in the north of Nigeria. In the northern Muslim sharia states, Igbos continue to be subjected to regular pogroms within the communities they've settled. It is, again, becoming commonplace to hear and read of sickening accounts of violence and mass murder of Igbo women, children and men in schools and churches.

An independent Biafra would be populated by more than 50 million people! There are only five European countries with larger populations than Biafra: Russia, Germany, United Kingdom, France and Italy. Not only does the Eastern Region have immense human resources, but also oil, minerals, and agriculture, with unlimited technological potential. Surely, rather than persist with the current bleeding and corrupt Federal State of Nigeria, it would make political, economic and human sense for Biafra to be self-governing, self-ruling, and self-determining?

This is not an emotional, blindly patriotic and bigoted 'son of the soil' rant. This is logic speaking. Over the past 20 to 30 years in Europe we have seen countries devolve where racial, ethnic, religious and cultural differences have become too toxic for their continued co-existence. The former USSR fractured into a myriad of new, independent self-governing countries: Russia, Ukraine, Estonia, Armenia, Azerbaijan, Belarus, Georgia, Kazakhstan, Kyrgyzstan, Latvia, Lithuania, Moldova, Tajikistan, Turkmenistan and Uzbekistan. The old Yugoslavia is now made up of: Croatia, Serbia and Montenegro, Serbian Krajina, Boznia and Herzegovinia, Kosovo, Macedonia and Slovenia. The former Czechoslovakian Republic devolved into two distinct independent sovereign states, the Czech Republic and the Slovak Republic, with a combined total population of under 16 million people, which is less than one third of the population of Biafra!

I can't envisage anything sweeter, or more satisfying, than to see the Biafran flag flying once again, and to sing our National Anthem "Land of the Rising Sun" with pride, purpose and meaning.

I also look forward to becoming a grandfather - maybe that will give me a push to motivate me through what's left of my life. I hope I'm a better grandfather than I am a father!

I definitely want my children to continue to enjoy their lives, to progress, prosper, succeed and achieve their potential, and to be healthy and happy. I'd like to see as much of this as possible before I 'turn me toes up'!

On that note, as the only guaranteed event in life, I don't *fear* death, but I don't want a long, slow, agonising one! I don't want to go through that myself, and I also don't want my family, Yvonne and our children, to agonise over me. The thought of me making my exit to the haunting bass-heavy beat of Bob Marley's 'Natural Mystic' fills me with a measure of satisfaction. I'd like for me and Yvonne to be buried next to each other, and I don't want my children crying over me. I've had a good life, I've enjoyed it. I had two fantastic parents who loved me. I've been lucky. I've always enjoyed reasonably good health. I've worked hard, and I've tried to set an example for my own children and (what now must be) thousands of other young people.

I'm certainly fortunate enough to be able to say I wouldn't have wanted things to be much, if any, different. I've never stopped loving my mum and dad (to whom I'm eternally grateful), my brother Obi and sisters Chi-chi, Ijem and Kele, even after the disagreements and fall-outs we've had along the way! We're still family, we stayed together through good and bad times, and we're always there for each other when the need arises.

As for my brother and sisters, and in reverse order of arrival:

Kele still lives and prospers in the capital city of Abuja, Nigeria. She was married, is now divorced, and doesn't have any children. She's happy, getting on with life, and could never live in England again. She just loves Nigeria, home, and to a degree I think I and her brother and sisters sometimes wonder about whether or not we should have made the move ourselves. I know she's affected a lot of peoples' lives in a positive way, and she's loved by many in Nigeria. She inherited the pioneer spirit from our parents which manifested itself by her going home permanently in her late teens. I'm sure she misses being with us at times, especially at family occasions, but she's a really strong person and will always live by her decisions. Either way, she's done well, I love her, I'm proud of her, and I'm happy for her.

Obi was married in a traditional wedding in Nigeria, but recently got divorced. He has four beautiful children, two girls and two boys, all of whom are progressing and doing well for themselves at their respective stage of development, and turning out to be young people to be proud of. After graduating in Town Planning he's worked most of his professional life in the resettlement of offenders and caring for clients in the mental health sector in London. Without doubt his work has had a very positive impact in the lives of many. For me, he's set a fantastic example to his children who love and respect him for the ever-present father he's been to them. Obviously, he's still football-crazy, and it was great having him live with us for a few months when his divorce came through and prior to him buying and moving into his new home with his daughters, who are the eldest of his children. He's still the owner of a stiff upper lip, though that's not to say he isn't emotional. Like the rest of us, he is, he just remains very adept at controlling them. As incredible as it may seem, we've still never had a falling out! He's cool, calm and collected, rational and sensible, loving, family-orientated and essentially a really decent man who I love and respect.

Ijeoma, my kindred spirit, still lives in south London. She never married so, ipso facto, hasn't divorced! She qualified as a nurse before going on to foster and look after many less-fortunate children, providing them with the love, care and attention that was previously lacking in their young lives. So she too has had a positive impact on the lives of many, however, she's done so whilst having to cope with her own battles against various forms of cancer which have blighted her life over the past thirty-odd years. She's *so* strong, always has been and always will be. She still provides her two children with a loving safe haven that is her home, as she does for her grandchildren also. I love, admire and respect her for her tenacity and the way she deals with the negative aspects in her life, and also for the inherently good person she is.

Me – I think you've probably read enough already!

Chi-chi, the one among us who, it feels like at least, has lived in a parallel universe to ours, was married and is now divorced, with a son and daughter, both really good young people. On the surface she was the one who appeared the least aware of and affected by issues of race and racism. Maybe it was this that enabled her to flourish so spectacularly to become an icon in the international world of classical music. Not only has she broken down so many barriers for herself as a black woman of mixed-race heritage, she's done so virtually as the sole 'minority' performer in her field. Just like Mohamed Ali, she "shook up the world!" Stereotypically speaking, classical music *must* remain one of the most elite of art forms throughout the world, seemingly *of* the elite and *for* the elite. Yet Chi-chi, through ability, drive and ambition, not only survived and prospered, she excelled. I also think it fair to say that she was the least outspoken about, and apparently affected by, issues of race and racism. She 'just got on with it', developed her career and fame in probably one of, if not *the* most difficult arenas, and against all odds, the world of classical music. She's affected the lives of thousands, if not hundreds of thousands of people nationally and internationally throughout her 30-year career to-date. Not just with her being the only black face in the orchestra, but *the* best in the orchestra. She really has contributed in a massive way to changing the staid and stolid stereotypical expectations of the established opera-loving elite with her impassioned performances and abundantly obvious love she has for her music. Almost single-handedly she's broken down the invisible barriers that previously choked her profession and thwarted non-traditional (non-white, non-European, non-middle/-upper class) participation and appreciation of her craft.

By no stretch of the imagination am I an opera-lover yet I, like every other member of my family over the years, have dutifully and diligently attended many of her orchestral events and performances to support her whilst feigning interest in the genre. Every time I watched her that was precisely what I did – watch *her.* For the duration of the majority of concerts

I only watched her, my eyes rarely strayed to watch the other performers who, on the occasions that I did cast an uninterested eye on them or via peripheral vision, all seemed boring, dull, lethargic, uninspired and uninspiring, and merely going through the technical motions of their job; they were turgidly soulless, passionless, aloof and unentertaining.

How things have changed!

Chi-chi recently spent 18 months putting together the first-ever European classical orchestra comprising solely of Black and Minority Ethnic (BME) classically-trained musicians. After initially having had her interest ignited on the revelation that several composers and musicians of historical note were actually black or of mixed heritage (particularly that of the little-known 18th Century composer Chevalier de Saint-Georges), almost a decade earlier, she researched this phenomenon to find evidence that this, indeed, was the case (yet another example of unrecognised black achievement and contribution to world culture). To quote her:

"What I discovered blew me away.

Saint-Georges was not just a violinist and composer, he was a phenomenon! The finest fencer on the continent, a champion boxer, music teacher to Marie Antoinette and a close personal friend of the Prince of Wales, he was the colonel of his own legion fighting for the new French Republic. US President John Adams also described him as 'the most accomplished man in Europe'. All in all an impressive resume!

But of particular poignancy to me, and the reason Marshall Marcus had encouraged me to look into Saint-George's life, was that he had achieved all of these things as a free black man living in an age of slavery: the son of a French aristocrat and a Senegalese slave, he was sometimes even referred to as 'The Black Mozart'. This virtuoso violinist, composer, athlete was also a pioneer abolitionist and the most famous black figure of his era.

For me, finding Saint-Georges was a bittersweet moment: the more I learned about him, the more excited I became. Although at the same time, I had a terrible feeling of shame; shame that I had not given even a second thought to the idea that there might be somebody of my ethnicity composing and performing classical music of an extremely high standard in previous centuries. I had simply accepted the canon as the status quo, and it set me thinking about how other musicians from ethnic minority backgrounds perceived themselves."

In typical 'dog with a bone' mode, Chi-chi couldn't, wouldn't let go of the importance of Saint-Georges being internationally recognised, and what better way to do it than to perform a concert partly in his honour? She created the Chineke! Orchestra which delivered its debut performance in front of a packed house at the Queen Elizabeth Hall at the Southbank Centre in London on Sunday 13th September 2015.

The word Chineke! is of Igbo origin and pre-dates Christianity. Its meaning describes the spirit of creation of all good things in the world, and all its diverse aspects. In conversation it is most often used as an exclamation confirming everything is true and good with the world. Chi-chi firmly believes that the word chose her orchestra!

The house wasn't packed with overwhelmingly stodgy middle-class white people, as was normally the case, but excited faces of every colour and description, working people, lords and ladies, MPs, newspaper critics, families, the whole shebang, all eagerly anticipating the privilege to witness an event that would be recorded in classical music history.

The orchestra was comprised of musicians from 31 BME nationalities from around the globe, black, brown, yellow and white eastern European, which was truly a sight to behold.

After an introduction from the chief executive officer of the Southbank Centre, Chi-chi took centre-stage to thank the audience for their support and attendance, describing it as having enabled her to "make her dream become a reality". She received a rapturous applause on her entrance to the stage, and a standing ovation when she finished her brief speech before joining the orchestra back stage prior to the performance. Tears welled in my eyes as my heart ponded with joy at her achievement. I was *so* proud of her!

The performance included Samuel Coleridge-Taylor's 'Ballade for Orchestra Op 33'; Philip Herbert's 'Elegy: In Memoriam – Stephen

Lawrence'; Brahms' 'Variations on a theme by Haydn Op 56' and Beethoven's 'Symphony Number 7 in A Op 92'.

For the first time ever I was conscious of the fact that I wasn't focusing *all* of my attention on Chi-chi, *all* of the time. My eyes were all over the stage, soaking in the impassioned performances of *every* musician, which was something I'd never done before. I actually *listened* to and appreciated every piece! Technically, they were superb and easily comparable to, if not better than, the very many orchestral performers I'd survived in the past. The very clear difference was that for the first time ever I was actually being *entertained* by each and every musician on stage, all of whom expressed their love for their art technically, physically and with intensity.

African American lead violinist Tai Murray "went in!" as her whole body acted on and reacted to her instrument as she led her section; Harry Brown (who incidentally I taught at Kingsdale Comprehensive School three decades ago!) played his trombone with such passion it appeared his cheeks were on the point of exploding; I was half expecting the esteemed black British organist, pianist and conductor Wayne Marshall to break into a James Brown side-slide finished off with a cape being placed reverentially around his shoulders as he conducted every piece with poise, body-elegance and precision timing; and the audience responded with equal intensity and passion in a manner I'd never previously witnessed. They were ecstatic with their applause and demands for an encore at the end and, thankfully, the orchestra obliged, repeating the Elegy in memoriam of Stephen Lawrence (who, coincidentally, would have been celebrating his 41st birthday on the day had he not been murdered when he was 18 years old by white racist thugs in Eltham, southeast London, 23 years earlier).

Needless to say, the national newspaper and industry critiques published the following day were stupendous.

This experience was truly uplifting and inspiring, and I was proud and happy to have been a part of this historical event, and even prouder and happier that Chi-chi, a member of my family, my big sis, made this happen!

Chi-chi - far right) with some members of the Chineke! Orchestra

Me standing in front a poster of Chi-chi in recognition
and commemoration of her services to music outside
the London Southbank Centre - 2007

470

Fifty-Five

Nowadays though, there's little I enjoy more than the get-togethers we have on a regular basis that always turn into fantastic parties at each other's houses, just like those we went to as kids at Aunty Margaret's and Uncle Ben's house in Wembley. I take a lot of joy watching our children enjoy each other's company during these 'get-togethers', because it reminds me so much of my happy childhood days. I hope this generation continues the tradition.

I'd like to think I've had a positive impact on others in my life, and I've always tried to act on the basis of principle, rather than political or religious dogma, neither of which I'd consciously seek to impose on others.

Increasingly, over the last ten years or so, I've become aware of the argument that 'mixed-race' ought to be considered a new distinct social category. Whilst I would have found this notion to be absurd in my youth, more latterly, I have begun to be a bit more receptive to the idea. Human beings as social animals need to live together in communities. However, it seems history dictates we're manifestly incapable of doing so without making distinctions among and between ourselves. Whether it's race, gender, ethnicity, culture, belief, height, weight, eye-colour, we'll always find something, anything, as spurious as it may be, to delineate one from the other.

For mixed-race people (formerly considered unequivocally as 'black' and treated as such in predominantly white societies), it's unreasonable to be expected to reject, deny or ignore our 'white half'. So, rather than bury it away in the needy urge to 'belong', it may be more self-fulfilling to acknowledge, embrace and promote our whiteness, our 'other half', in order to be truly recognised as fully-fledged human beings and members of the human race.

Failing that, in an ideal world, I think we'd all benefit from adopting a 'colour-blind' approach to dealing with our relationships, where genetically-determined differences in colour (and every other aspect of our characteristics), are irrelevant. As a parent I've always encouraged my children to be inclusive of the people they befriend, and have never, at least consciously, 'tarred' or restricted their minds with regards the company they keep. I'd like to think that as a result they've successfully managed to make friends for life from a wide variety of backgrounds, including our Vietnamese family friend Kien and her sons Giang and Nam; our Irish family friends Noel, Anne and their sons Sean and Paddy spring to mind, all of whom are wonderful people.

The question remains, however, are these sentiments idealistically naive? Probably.

Ideal? Definitely!

Achievable? Yes.

If we *really* want it.

About the Author

Gus Nwanokwu, the son of a Biafran-Nigerian father and Irish mother, grew up in London, England, during the 1960s and 70s.

Educated in the British state-school system, Nwanokwu earned a joint honors degree in psychology and sociology and a postgraduate certificate in education. He then taught at an inner-city comprehensive school while studying for a master's degree in education. Nwanokwu has spent most of his career teaching in and managing further education colleges, including an unforgettable year teaching with the League for the Exchange of Commonwealth Teachers program in Kingston, Jamaica.

Nwanokwu married his wife in 1982 and they are still together to this day. They have three children.

Printed in Great Britain
by Amazon